Audi Automotive Repair Manual

by A K Legg   T Eng (CEI), AMIMI
and John H Haynes

Member of the Guild of Motoring Writers

Models covered

Audi 4000 Sedan, four-cylinder 1.6, 1.7 and 1.8 liter
Audi 4000 S and 4000 5 + 5 Sedans, five-cylinder 2.2 liter
Audi Coupe, five-cylinder 2.2 liter

Does not cover Quattro or diesel engine

ISBN 1 85010 242 2

© **Haynes North America, Inc. 1983, 1987**
With permission from J. H. Haynes & Co. Ltd.

ABCDE
FGHIJ
2

Printed in the USA   *(11W3 – 615)*

Haynes Publishing Group
Sparkford Nr Yeovil
Somerset BA22 7JJ England

Haynes North America, Inc
861 Lawrence Drive
Newbury Park
California 91320 USA

Acknowledgements

Thanks are due to Volkswagenwerk AG for the supply of technical information and certain illustrations, to Castrol Limited who supplied lubrication data, and to the Champion Sparking Plug Company who supplied the illustrations showing the various spark plug conditions.

Sykes-Pickavant Limited provided some of the workshop tools. Special thanks are due to all those people at Sparkford who helped in the production of this manual.

About this manual

Its aim

The aim of this manual is to help you get the best value from your vehicle. It can do so in several ways. It can help you decide what work must be done (even should you choose to get it done by a garage), provide information on routine maintenance and servicing, and give a logical course of action and diagnosis when random faults occur. However, it is hoped that you will use the manual by tackling the work yourself. On simpler jobs it may even be quicker than booking the car into a garage and going there twice, to leave and collect it. Perhaps most important, a lot of money can be saved by avoiding the costs a garage must charge to cover its labour and overheads.

The manual has drawings and descriptions to show the function of the various components so that their layout can be understood. Then the tasks are described and photographed in a step-by-step sequence so that even a novice can do the work.

Its arrangement

The manual is divided into twelve Chapters, each covering a logical sub-division of the vehicle. The Chapters are each divided into Sections, numbered with single figures, eg 5; and the Sections into paragraphs (or sub-sections), with decimal numbers following on from the Section they are in, eg 5.1, 5.2, 5.3 etc.

It is freely illustrated, especially in those parts where there is a detailed sequence of operations to be carried out. There are two forms of illustration: figures and photographs. The figures are numbered in sequence with decimal numbers, according to their position in the Chapter – eg Fig. 6.4 is the fourth drawing/illustration in Chapter 6. Photographs carry the same number (either individually or in related groups) as the Section or sub-section to which they relate.

There is an alphabetical index at the back of the manual as well as a contents list at the front. Each Chapter is also preceded by its own individual contents list.

References to the 'left' or 'right' of the vehicle are in the sense of a person in the driver's seat facing forwards.

Unless otherwise stated, nuts and bolts are removed by turning anti-clockwise, and tightened by turning clockwise.

Vehicle manufacturers continually make changes to specifications and recommendations, and these, when notified, are incorporated into our manuals at the earliest opportunity.

Whilst every care is taken to ensure that the information in this manual is correct, no liability can be accepted by the authors or publishers for loss, damage or injury caused by any errors in, or omissions from, the information given.

Introduction to the Audi 80 and 4000

The 'new' Audi 80 was announced in late 1978 and was available in the UK in March 1979. The equivalent North American Audi 4000 became available in 1980. These models are similar to the 'new' 100 range, but differ from the earlier Audi 80 (UK) and Audi Fox (North America) by incorporating a sloping bonnet, an additional side window behind the rear door, and wrap-around plastic bumpers. The Coupe version incorporates front and rear spoilers and side rubbing strips, while the top saloon model, the CD, incorporates a front spoiler and side rubbing strips.

The model range is comprehensive and offers a choice of trim, four or five-cylinder engine, and four or five-speed gearbox or automatic transmission. Full instrumentation is provided together with electric windows, a central locking system and power steering, according to model. UK models are available with a carburettor or fuel injection engine – North American models are only available in fuel injected form.

Contents

Audi 80 Saloon

Audi 80 Coupe

Audi 4000 Sedan

General dimensions, weights and capacities

Dimensions

Overall length
UK models without headlight cleaners .... 4383 mm (172.5 in)
UK models with headlight cleaners .... 4391 mm (172.9 in)
North American models .... 4487 mm (176.7 in)

Overall width .... 1682 mm (66.2 in)

Overall height (unladen) .... 1365 mm (53.7 in)

Ground clearance (laden)
UK models .... 112 mm (4.4 in)
North American models .... 96 mm (3.8 in)

Wheelbase .... 2541 mm (100.0 in)

Turning circle (between kerbs) .... 9.5 m (31.2 ft)

Weights

Kerb weight
Saloon with manual gearbox .... 950 kg (2094 lb)
Saloon with automatic transmission .... 975 kg (2150 lb)
    Deduct 20 kg (44 lb) for Coupe models
    Add 15 kg (33 lb) for sunroof
    Add 40 kg (88 lb) for air conditioner
    Add 23 kg (51 lb) for towing bracket

Gross vehicle weight .... 1410 kg (3109 lb)

Maximum roof rack load .... 75 kg (165 lb)

Maximum towing weight (12% gradient)
Manual gearbox models .... 1100 kg (2425 lb)
Automatic transmission models .... 1200 kg (2646 lb)
Note: *On North American models the weights are given on a Safety Compliance Sticker located on the left-hand side door jamb*

Capacities

Engine oil
Four-cylinder with filter .... 3.0 litre; 5.3 Imp pt; 3.2 US qt
Four-cylinder without filter .... 2.5 litre; 4.4 Imp pt; 2.6 US qt
Five-cylinder 1.9 with filter .... 4.5 litre; 7.9 Imp pt; 4.8 US qt
Five-cylinder 1.9 without filter .... 4.0 litre; 7.0 Imp pt; 4.2 US qt
Five-cylinder 2.2 with filter .... 3.5 litre; 6.2 Imp pt; 3.7 US qt
Five-cylinder 2.2 without filter .... 3.0 litre; 5.3 Imp pt; 3.2 US qt
Difference between engine oil dipstick minimum and maximum
marks .... 1.0 litre; 1.8 Imp pt; 1.1 US qt

Cooling system (including heater)
1.6/1.7 engine without A/C .... 6.2 litre; 10.9 Imp pt; 6.6 US qt
1.6/1.7 engine with A.C .... 7.0 litre; 12.3 Imp pt; 7.4 US qt
1.9/2.2 engine .... 8.0 litre; 14.1 Imp pt; 8.5 US qt

Fuel tank
UK models .... 68.0 litre; 15.0 Imp gal; 71.9 US qt
North American models .... 60.0 litre; 13.2 Imp gal; 63.4 US qt

Manual gearbox
014/1 and 014/11 .... 1.7 litre; 3.0 Imp pt; 1.8 US qt
013 .... 2.0 litre; 3.5 Imp pt; 2.1 US qt
093 .... 2.4 litre; 4.1 Imp pt; 2.5 US qt

Automatic transmission
089 gearbox ATF (total) .... 6.0 litre; 10.6 Imp pt; 6.3 US qt
089 gearbox ATF (service) .... 3.0 litre; 5.3 Imp pt; 3.2 US qt
089 final drive .... 0.75 litre; 1.3 Imp pt; 0.8 US qt
087 gearbox ATF (total) .... 6.0 litre; 10.6 Imp pt; 6.3 US qt
087 gearbox ATF (service) .... 3.0 litre; 5.3 Imp pt; 3.2 US qt
087 final drive .... 0.7 litre; 1.2 Imp pt; 0.7 US qt

Use of English

As this book has been written in England, it uses the appropriate English component names, phrases, and spelling. Some of these differ from those used in America. Normally, these cause no difficulty, but to make sure, a glossary is printed below. In ordering spare parts remember the parts list may use some of these words:

English	American	English	American
Accelerator	Gas pedal	Locks	Latches
Aerial	Antenna	Methylated spirit	Denatured alcohol
Anti-roll bar	Stabiliser or sway bar	Motorway	Freeway, turnpike etc
Big-end bearing	Rod bearing	Number plate	License plate
Bonnet (engine cover)	Hood	Paraffin	Kerosene
Boot (luggage compartment)	Trunk	Petrol	Gasoline (gas)
Bulkhead	Firewall	Petrol tank	Gas tank
Bush	Bushing	'Pinking'	'Pinging'
Cam follower or tappet	Valve lifter or tappet	Prise (force apart)	Pry
Carburettor	Carburetor	Propeller shaft	Driveshaft
Catch	Latch	Quarterlight	Quarter window
Choke/venturi	Barrel	Retread	Recap
Circlip	Snap-ring	Reverse	Back-up
Clearance	Lash	Rocker cover	Valve cover
Crownwheel	Ring gear (of differential)	Saloon	Sedan
Damper	Shock absorber, shock	Seized	Frozen
Disc (brake)	Rotor/disk	Sidelight	Parking light
Distance piece	Spacer	Silencer	Muffler
Drop arm	Pitman arm	Sill panel (beneath doors)	Rocker panel
Drop head coupe	Convertible	Small end, little end	Piston pin or wrist pin
Dynamo	Generator (DC)	Spanner	Wrench
Earth (electrical)	Ground	Split cotter (for valve spring cap)	Lock (for valve spring retainer)
Engineer's blue	Prussian blue	Split pin	Cotter pin
Estate car	Station wagon	Steering arm	Spindle arm
Exhaust manifold	Header	Sump	Oil pan
Fault finding/diagnosis	Troubleshooting	Swarf	Metal chips or debris
Float chamber	Float bowl	Tab washer	Tang or lock
Free-play	Lash	Tappet	Valve lifter
Freewheel	Coast	Thrust bearing	Throw-out bearing
Gearbox	Transmission	Top gear	High
Gearchange	Shift	Torch	Flashlight
Grub screw	Setscrew, Allen screw	Trackrod (of steering)	Tie-rod (or connecting rod)
Gudgeon pin	Piston pin or wrist pin	Trailing shoe (of brake)	Secondary shoe
Halfshaft	Axleshaft	Transmission	Whole drive line
Handbrake	Parking brake	Tyre	Tire
Hood	Soft top	Van	Panel wagon/van
Hot spot	Heat riser	Vice	Vise
Indicator	Turn signal	Wheel nut	Lug nut
Interior light	Dome lamp	Windscreen	Windshield
Layshaft (of gearbox)	Countershaft	Wing/mudguard	Fender
Leading shoe (of brake)	Primary shoe		

Buying spare parts and vehicle identification numbers

Buying spare parts

Replacement parts are available from many sources, which generally fall into one of two categories – authorized dealer parts departments and independent retail auto parts stores. Our advice concerning these parts is as follows:

Retail auto parts stores: Good auto parts stores will stock frequently needed components which wear out relatively fast, such as clutch components, exhaust systems, brake parts, tune-up parts, etc. These stores often supply new or reconditioned parts on an exchange basis, which can save a considerable amount of money. Discount auto parts stores are often very good places to buy materials and parts needed for general vehicle maintenance such as oil, grease, filters, spark plugs, belts, touch-up paint, bulbs, etc. They also usually sell tools and general accessories, have convenient hours, charge lower prices and can often be found not far from home.

Authorized dealer parts department: This is the best source for parts which are unique to the vehicle and not generally available elsewhere (such as major engine parts, transmission parts, trim pieces, etc.).

Warranty information: If the vehicle is still covered under warranty, be sure that any replacement parts purchased – regardless of the source – do not invalidate the warranty!

To be sure of obtaining the correct parts, have engine and chassis numbers available and, if possible, take the old parts along for positive identification.

Vehicle identification numbers

Modifications are a continuing and unpublicised process in vehicle manufacture. Spare parts manuals and lists are compiled on a numerical basis, the individual vehicle numbers being essential to identify correctly the component required.

The vehicle identification plate is located in the engine compartment on the right-hand side of the air intake plenum chamber on UK models (photo), or on the left-hand side windscreen pillar on North American models. Cars exported to certain countries may not have a vehicle identification plate.

The chassis number is stamped on the rear panel of the engine compartment.

The engine number is stamped on the left-hand side of the cylinder block (photo).

The manual gearbox number is stamped on the right-hand side of the gearbox, above the drive flange.

The automatic transmission number is stamped inside the torque converter housing, but the transmission type number is on the top of the gear casing.

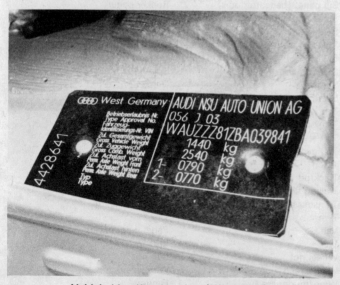

Vehicle identification plate (UK models)

Engine number

Tools and working facilities

Introduction

A selection of good tools is a fundamental requirement for anyone contemplating the maintenance and repair of a motor vehicle. For the owner who does not possess any, their purchase will prove a considerable expense, offsetting some of the savings made by doing-it-yourself. However, provided that the tools purchased meet the relevant national safety standards and are of good quality, they will last for many years and prove an extremely worthwhile investment.

To help the average owner to decide which tools are needed to carry out the various tasks detailed in this manual, we have compiled three lists of tools under the following headings: *Maintenance and minor repair*, *Repair and overhaul*, and *Special*. The newcomer to practical mechanics should start off with the *Maintenance and minor repair* tool kit and confine himself to the simpler jobs around the vehicle. Then, as his confidence and experience grow, he can undertake more difficult tasks, buying extra tools as, and when, they are needed. In this way, a *Maintenance and minor repair* tool kit can be built-up into a *Repair and overhaul* tool kit over a considerable period of time without any major cash outlays. The experienced do-it-yourselfer will have a tool kit good enough for most repair and overhaul procedures and will add tools from the *Special* category when he feels the expense is justified by the amount of use to which these tools will be put.

It is obviously not possible to cover the subject of tools fully here. For those who wish to learn more about tools and their use there is a book entitled *How to Choose and Use Car Tools* available from the publishers of this manual.

Maintenance and minor repair tool kit

The tools given in this list should be considered as a minimum requirement if routine maintenance, servicing and minor repair operations are to be undertaken. We recommend the purchase of combination spanners (ring one end, open-ended the other); although more expensive than open-ended ones, they do give the advantages of both types of spanner.

Combination spanners - 10, 11, 12, 13, 14 & 17 mm
Adjustable spanner - 9 inch
Engine sump/gearbox/rear axle drain plug key
Spark plug spanner (with rubber insert)
Spark plug gap adjustment tool
Set of feeler gauges
Brake adjuster spanner
Brake bleed nipple spanner
Screwdriver - 4 in long x 1/4 in dia (flat blade)
Screwdriver - 4 in long x 1/4 in dia (cross blade)
Combination pliers - 6 inch
Hacksaw (junior)
Tyre pump
Tyre pressure gauge
Grease gun
Oil can
Fine emery cloth (1 sheet)
Wire brush (small)
Funnel (medium size)

Repair and overhaul tool kit

These tools are virtually essential for anyone undertaking any major repairs to a motor vehicle, and are additional to those given in the *Maintenance and minor repair* list. Included in this list is a comprehensive set of sockets. Although these are expensive they will be found invaluable as they are so versatile - particularly if various drives are included in the set. We recommend the ½ in square-drive

type, as this can be used with most proprietary torque wrenches. If you cannot afford a socket set, even bought piecemeal, then inexpensive tubular box spanners are a useful alternative.

The tools in this list will occasionally need to be supplemented by tools from the *Special* list.

Sockets (or box spanners) to cover range in previous list
Reversible ratchet drive (for use with sockets)
Extension piece, 10 inch (for use with sockets)
Universal joint (for use with sockets)
Torque wrench (for use with sockets)
'Mole' wrench - 8 inch
Ball pein hammer
Soft-faced hammer, plastic or rubber
Screwdriver - 6 in long x 5/16 in dia (flat blade)
Screwdriver - 2 in long x 5/16 in square (flat blade)
Screwdriver - 1 1/2 in long x 1/4 in dia (cross blade)
Screwdriver - 3 in long x 1/8 in dia (electricians)
Pliers - electricians side cutters
Pliers - needle nosed
Pliers - circlip (internal and external)
Cold chisel - 1/2 inch
Scriber
Scraper
Centre punch
Pin punch
Hacksaw
Valve grinding tool
Steel rule/straight-edge
Allen keys (inc. splined/Torx type if necessary)
Selection of files
Wire brush (large)
Axle-stands
Jack (strong trolley or hydraulic type)

Special tools

The tools in this list are those which are not used regularly, are expensive to buy, or which need to be used in accordance with their manufacturers' instructions. Unless relatively difficult mechanical jobs are undertaken frequently, it will not be economic to buy many of these tools. Where this is the case, you could consider clubbing together with friends (or joining a motorists' club) to make a joint purchase, or borrowing the tools against a deposit from a local garage or tool hire specialist.

The following list contains only those tools and instruments freely available to the public, and not those special tools produced by the vehicle manufacturer specifically for its dealer network. You will find occasional references to these manufacturers' special tools in the text of this manual. Generally, an alternative method of doing the job without the vehicle manufacturers' special tool is given. However, sometimes, there is no alternative to using them. Where this is the case and the relevant tool cannot be bought or borrowed, you will have to entrust the work to a franchised garage.

Valve spring compressor (where applicable)
Piston ring compressor
Balljoint separator
Universal hub/bearing puller
Impact screwdriver
Micrometer and/or vernier gauge
Dial gauge
Stroboscopic timing light

Dwell angle meter/tachometer
Universal electrical multi-meter
Cylinder compression gauge
Lifting tackle (photo)
Trolley jack
Light with extension lead

Buying tools

For practically all tools, a tool factor is the best source since he will have a very comprehensive range compared with the average garage or accessory shop. Having said that, accessory shops often offer excellent quality tools at discount prices, so it pays to shop around.

There are plenty of good tools around at reasonable prices, but always aim to purchase items which meet the relevant national safety standards. If in doubt, ask the proprietor or manager of the shop for advice before making a purchase.

Care and maintenance of tools

Having purchased a reasonable tool kit, it is necessary to keep the tools in a clean serviceable condition. After use, always wipe off any dirt, grease and metal particles using a clean, dry cloth, before putting the tools away. Never leave them lying around after they have been used. A simple tool rack on the garage or workshop wall, for items such as screwdrivers and pliers is a good idea. Store all normal wrenches and sockets in a metal box. Any measuring instruments, gauges, meters, etc, must be carefully stored where they cannot be damaged or become rusty.

Take a little care when tools are used. Hammer heads inevitably become marked and screwdrivers lose the keen edge on their blades from time to time. A little timely attention with emery cloth or a file will soon restore items like this to a good serviceable finish.

Working facilities

Not to be forgotten when discussing tools, is the workshop itself. If anything more than routine maintenance is to be carried out, some form of suitable working area becomes essential.

It is appreciated that many an owner mechanic is forced by circumstances to remove an engine or similar item, without the benefit of a garage or workshop. Having done this, any repairs should always be done under the cover of a roof.

Wherever possible, any dismantling should be done on a clean, flat workbench or table at a suitable working height.

Any workbench needs a vice: one with a jaw opening of 4 in (100 mm) is suitable for most jobs. As mentioned previously, some clean dry storage space is also required for tools, as well as for lubricants, cleaning fluids, touch-up paints and so on, which become necessary.

Another item which may be required, and which has a much more general usage, is an electric drill with a chuck capacity of at least $\frac{5}{16}$ in (8 mm). This, together with a good range of twist drills, is virtually essential for fitting accessories such as mirrors and reversing lights.

Last, but not least, always keep a supply of old newspapers and clean, lint-free rags available, and try to keep any working area as clean as possible.

Spanner jaw gap comparison table

Jaw gap (in)	Spanner size
0.250	$\frac{1}{4}$ in AF
0.276	7 mm
0.313	$\frac{5}{16}$ in AF
0.315	8 mm
0.344	$\frac{11}{32}$ in AF; $\frac{1}{8}$ in Whitworth
0.354	9 mm
0.375	$\frac{3}{8}$ in AF
0.394	10 mm
0.433	11 mm
0.438	$\frac{7}{16}$ in AF
0.445	$\frac{3}{16}$ in Whitworth; $\frac{1}{4}$ in BSF
0.472	12 mm
0.500	$\frac{1}{2}$ in AF
0.512	13 mm
0.525	$\frac{1}{4}$ in Whitworth; $\frac{5}{16}$ in BSF
0.551	14 mm
0.563	$\frac{9}{16}$ in AF
0.591	15 mm
0.600	$\frac{5}{16}$ in Whitworth; $\frac{3}{8}$ in BSF
0.625	$\frac{5}{8}$ in AF
0.630	16 mm
0.669	17 mm
0.686	$\frac{11}{16}$ in AF
0.709	18 mm
0.710	$\frac{3}{8}$ in Whitworth; $\frac{7}{16}$ in BSF
0.748	19 mm
0.750	$\frac{3}{4}$ in AF
0.813	$\frac{13}{16}$ in AF
0.820	$\frac{7}{16}$ in Whitworth; $\frac{1}{2}$ in BSF
0.866	22 mm
0.875	$\frac{7}{8}$ in AF
0.920	$\frac{1}{2}$ in Whitworth; $\frac{9}{16}$ in BSF
0.938	$\frac{15}{16}$ in AF
0.945	24 mm
1.000	1 in AF
1.010	$\frac{9}{16}$ in Whitworth; $\frac{5}{8}$ in BSF
1.024	26 mm
1.063	$1\frac{1}{16}$ in AF; 27 mm
1.100	$\frac{5}{8}$ in Whitworth; $\frac{11}{16}$ in BSF
1.125	$1\frac{1}{8}$ in AF
1.181	30 mm
1.200	$\frac{11}{16}$ in Whitworth; $\frac{3}{4}$ in BSF
1.250	$1\frac{1}{4}$ in AF
1.260	32 mm
1.300	$\frac{3}{4}$ in Whitworth; $\frac{7}{8}$ in BSF
1.313	$1\frac{5}{16}$ in AF
1.390	$\frac{13}{16}$ in Whitworth; $\frac{15}{16}$ in BSF
1.417	36 mm
1.438	$1\frac{7}{16}$ in AF
1.480	$\frac{7}{8}$ in Whitworth; 1 in BSF
1.500	$1\frac{1}{2}$ in AF
1.575	40 mm; $\frac{15}{16}$ in Whitworth
1.614	41 mm
1.625	$1\frac{5}{8}$ in AF
1.670	1 in Whitworth; $1\frac{1}{8}$ in BSF
1.688	$1\frac{11}{16}$ in AF
1.811	46 mm
1.813	$1\frac{13}{16}$ in AF
1.860	$1\frac{1}{8}$ in Whitworth; $1\frac{1}{4}$ in BSF
1.875	$1\frac{7}{8}$ in AF
1.969	50 mm
2.000	2 in AF
2.050	$1\frac{1}{4}$ in Whitworth; $1\frac{3}{8}$ in BSF
2.165	55 mm
2.362	60 mm

A Haltrac hoist and gantry in use during a typical engine removal sequence

Jacking and towing

To change a roadwheel, first remove the spare wheel and jack from the left-hand side of the luggage compartment and remove the tool kit from the rear panel (photo). With the car on firm level ground apply the handbrake and chock the wheel diagonally opposite the one to be changed. Using the tools provided remove the hub cap where necessary, then loosen the wheel bolts half a turn (photo). Locate the lifting arm of the jack beneath the reinforced seam of the side sill panel (photo) directly beneath the wedge shaped depression nearest to the wheel to be removed. Turn the jack handle until the base of the jack contacts the ground directly beneath the sill (photo) then continue to turn the handle until the wheel is free of the ground. Unscrew the wheel bolts and remove the wheel. On light alloy wheels prise off the centre trim cap and press it into the spare wheel.

Locate the spare wheel on the hub, then insert and tighten the bolts in diagonal sequence. Lower the jack and fully tighten the bolts. Refit the hub cap where necessary, remove the chock and relocate the tool kit, jack and wheel in the luggage compartment.

When jacking up the car with a trolley jack, position the jack beneath the reinforced plate behind the front wheel (see illustration) or beneath the reinforced seam at the rear of the side sill panel. Use the same positions when supporting the car with axle stands. *Never jack up the car beneath the suspension or axle components, the sump, or the gearbox.*

Towing eyes are fitted to the front and the rear of the vehicle (photos) and a tow line should not be attached to any other points. It

Spare wheel location

Loosening the wheel bolts

Locate the jack on the reinforced seam ...

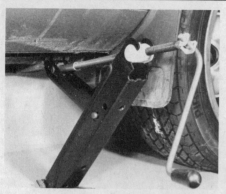

... and turn the handle to raise the car ...

Front towing eye

Rear towing eye

is preferable to use a slightly elastic tow line, to reduce the strain on both vehicles, either by having a tow line manufactured from synthetic fibre, or one which is fitted with an elastic link.

When towing, the following important precautions must be observed:

(a) Turn the ignition key of the vehicle being towed, so that the steering wheel is free (unlocked).

(b) Remember that when the engine is not running the brake servo will not operate, so that additional pressure will be required on the brake pedal after the first few applications

(c) On vehicles with automatic transmission, ensure that the gear selector lever is at 'N'. Do not tow faster than 30 mph (50 kph), or further than 30 miles (50 km) unless the front wheels are lifted clear of the ground.

Tool kit location in the luggage compartment

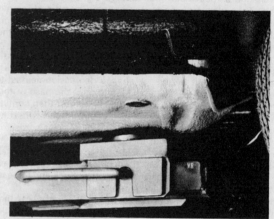

Front jacking point when using a trolley jack

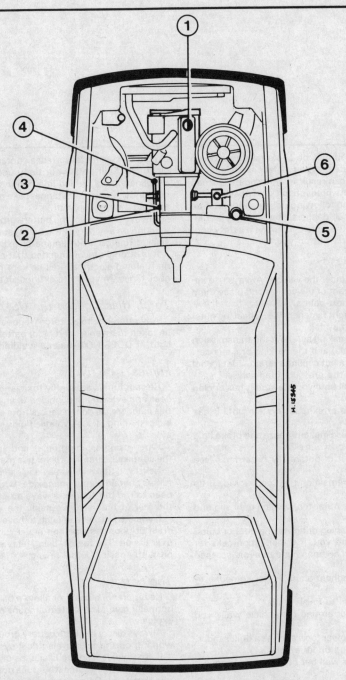

Recommended lubricants and fluids

Component or systems	Lubricant type or specification	Castrol product
Engine (1)	SAE 20W/50 or 15W/50 multigrade engine oil	GTX
Manual gearbox/final drive (2)	SAE 80W or 80W/90 hypoid gear oil	Hypoy Light
Final drive (automatic transmission) (3)	SAE 90 hypoid gear oil	Hypoy B EP 90
Automatic transmission (4) and power steering (5)	Dexron ® type automatic transmission fluid	TQ Dexron ® II
Brake fluid (6)	FMVSS 116 DOT 3 or 116 DOT 4	Universal Brake and Clutch Fluid

Note: *The above are general recommendations only. Lubrication requirements vary from territory to territory and depend on vehicle usage. If in doubt, consult the operator's handbook supplied with the vehicle, or your nearest dealer.*

Safety first!

Regardless of how enthusiastic you may be about getting on with the job at hand, take the time to ensure that your safety is not jeopardized. A moment's lack of attention can result in an accident, as can failure to observe certain simple safety precautions. The possibility of an accident will always exist, and the following points should not be considered a comprehensive list of all dangers. Rather, they are intended to make you aware of the risks and to encourage a safety conscious approach to all work you carry out on your vehicle.

Essential DOs and DON'Ts

DON'T rely on a jack when working under the vehicle. Always use approved jackstands to support the weight of the vehicle and place them under the recommended lift or support points.

DON'T attempt to loosen extremely tight fasteners (i.e. wheel lug nuts) while the vehicle is on a jack — it may fall.

DON'T start the engine without first making sure that the transmission is in Neutral (or Park where applicable) and the parking brake is set.

DON'T remove the radiator cap from a hot cooling system — let it cool or cover it with a cloth and release the pressure gradually.

DON'T attempt to drain the engine oil until you are sure it has cooled to the point that it will not burn you.

DON'T touch any part of the engine or exhaust system until it has cooled sufficiently to avoid burns.

DON'T siphon toxic liquids such as gasoline, antifreeze and brake fluid by mouth, or allow them to remain on your skin.

DON'T inhale brake lining dust — it is potentially hazardous (see *Asbestos* below)

DON'T allow spilled oil or grease to remain on the floor — wipe it up before someone slips on it.

DON'T use loose fitting wrenches or other tools which may slip and cause injury.

DON'T push on wrenches when loosening or tightening nuts or bolts. Always try to pull the wrench toward you. If the situation calls for pushing the wrench away, push with an open hand to avoid scraped knuckles if the wrench should slip.

DON'T attempt to lift a heavy component alone — get someone to help you.

DON'T rush or take unsafe shortcuts to finish a job.

DON'T allow children or animals in or around the vehicle while you are working on it.

DO wear eye protection when using power tools such as a drill, sander, bench grinder, etc. and when working under a vehicle.

DO keep loose clothing and long hair well out of the way of moving parts.

DO make sure that any hoist used has a safe working load rating adequate for the job.

DO get someone to check on you periodically when working alone on a vehicle.

DO carry out work in a logical sequence and make sure that everything is correctly assembled and tightened.

DO keep chemicals and fluids tightly capped and out of the reach of children and pets.

DO remember that your vehicle's safety affects that of yourself and others. If in doubt on any point, get professional advice.

Asbestos

Certain friction, insulating, sealing, and other products — such as brake linings, brake bands, clutch linings, torque converters, gaskets, etc. — contain asbestos. *Extreme care must be taken to avoid inhalation of dust from such products since it is hazardous to health.* If in doubt, assume that they *do* contain asbestos.

Fire

Remember at all times that gasoline is highly flammable. Never smoke or have any kind of open flame around when working on a vehicle. But the risk does not end there. A spark caused by an electrical short circuit, by two metal surfaces contacting each other, or even by static electricity built up in your body under certain conditions, can ignite gasoline vapors, which in a confined space are highly explosive. Do not, under any circumstances, use gasoline for cleaning parts. Use an approved safety solvent.

Always disconnect the battery ground (–) cable *at the battery* before working on any part of the fuel system or electrical system. Never risk spilling fuel on a hot engine or exhaust component.

It is strongly recommended that a fire extinguisher suitable for use on fuel and electrical fires be kept handy in the garage or workshop at all times. Never try to extinguish a fuel or electrical fire with water.

Torch (flashlight in the US)

Any reference to a "torch" appearing in this manual should always be taken to mean a hand-held, battery-operated electric light or flashlight. It DOES NOT mean a welding or propane torch or blowtorch.

Fumes

Certain fumes are highly toxic and can quickly cause unconsciousness and even death if inhaled to any extent. Gasoline vapor falls into this category, as do the vapors from some cleaning solvents. Any draining or pouring of such volatile fluids should be done in a well ventilated area.

When using cleaning fluids and solvents, read the instructions on the container carefully. Never use materials from unmarked containers.

Never run the engine in an enclosed space, such as a garage. Exhaust fumes contain carbon monoxide, which is extremely poisonous. If you need to run the engine, always do so in the open air, or at least have the rear of the vehicle outside the work area.

If you are fortunate enough to have the use of an inspection pit, never drain or pour gasoline and never run the engine while the vehicle is over the pit. The fumes, being heavier than air, will concentrate in the pit with possibly lethal results.

The battery

Never create a spark or allow a bare light bulb near a battery. They normally give off a certain amount of hydrogen gas, which is highly explosive.

Always disconnect the battery ground (–) cable *at the battery* before working on the fuel or electrical systems.

If possible, loosen the filler caps or cover when charging the battery from an external source (this does not apply to sealed or maintenance-free batteries). Do not charge at an excessive rate or the battery may burst.

Take care when adding water to a non maintenance-free battery and when carrying a battery. The electrolyte, even when diluted, is very corrosive and should not be allowed to contact clothing or skin.

Always wear eye protection when cleaning the battery to prevent the caustic deposits from entering your eyes.

Mains electricity (household current in the US)

When using an electric power tool, inspection light, etc., which operates on household current, always make sure that the tool is correctly connected to its plug and that, where necessary, it is properly grounded. Do not use such items in damp conditions and, again, do not create a spark or apply excessive heat in the vicinity of fuel or fuel vapor.

Secondary ignition system voltage

A severe electric shock can result from touching certain parts of the ignition system (such as the spark plug wires) when the engine is running or being cranked, particularly if components are damp or the insulation is defective. In the case of an electronic ignition system, the secondary system voltage is much higher and could prove fatal.

Routine maintenance

Maintenance is essential for ensuring safety and desirable for the purpose of getting the best in terms of performance and economy from your car. Over the years the need for periodic lubrication has been greatly reduced, if not totally eliminated. This has unfortunately tended to lead some owners to think that because no such action is required, the items either no longer exist, or will last for ever. This is certainly not the case; it is essential to carry out regular visual examination as comprehensively as possible in order to spot any possible defects at an early stage, before they develop into major expensive repairs.

Every 250 miles (375 km) or weekly – whichever comes first

Engine

Check the level of engine oil and top up if necessary (photos)
Check the coolant level and top up if necessary (photo)
Check the battery electrolyte level and top up if necessary (photo)

Tyres

Check and adjust the tyre pressures (photo)

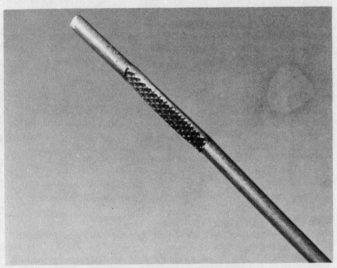

Engine oil level dipstick marking

Topping up the engine oil (four-cylinder engine shown)

Topping up the cooling system

Topping up the battery electrolyte level

Checking the tyre pressures

Windscreen washer fluid reservoir

Headlight washer fluid reservoir

Lights and wipers

Check that all the lights work
Clean the headlamps
Check the washer fluid level(s) and top up if necessary (photos)

Brakes

Check the level of fluid in the brake master cylinder reservoir – the level will drop slightly as the disc pads and rear brake linings wear, but if topping up is necessary the hydraulic circuit should be checked for leaks

---

Every 5000 miles (7500 km) or 6 months – whichever comes first

Engine

Change engine oil (photo)

Brakes

Check front disc pads for wear

Body

Lubricate the bonnet lock and hinges
Grease the door check straps

Every 10 000 miles (15 000 km) or 12 months – whichever comes first

Engine

Check antifreeze strength and add as necessary
Check drivebelts for condition and tension, and adjust if necessary
Renew the spark plugs
Renew the contact breaker points where applicable and adjust the dwell angle

Check and adjust the ignition timing
Check and adjust the engine idling speed and exhaust CO content
Check the engine for oil, coolant and fuel leaks
Change engine oil and renew the oil filter
Check the exhaust system for security and leakage

Transmission

Adjust clutch play, where applicable
Check the driveshaft rubber boots for damage and leaks
Check level of oil/fluid in gearbox/transmission and final drive and top up if necessary (photo)
Check transmission for leaks

Brakes and tyres

Check operation of brake pressure regulator where applicable
Visually check the brake hydraulic circuit lines, hoses and unions for damage, deterioration and leaks
Check front disc pads and rearbrake shoes for wear
Check the tyres for wear and tread depth (photo)

Lights

Check the headlight beam alignment and adjust if necessary

Suspension and steering

Check the steering tie-rod end balljoints for wear, and damage to the dust covers
Check the suspension balljoints for wear, and damage to the dust covers
Check the steering gear bellows for damage and leaks
Check the power-assisted steering fluid level and top up if necessary

Body

Check the body underseal for damage and apply more if necessary

Sump drain plug location

Topping up the gearbox oil

Checking tyre tread depth

General
Road test car and check the operation of all systems, in particular brakes and steering

Every 20 000 miles (30 000 km) or 2 years – whichever comes first

Engine
Renew the fuel filter
Renew the air cleaner element and clean the body
Adjust valve clearances and renew valve cover gasket

Every 2 years

Brakes
Change the brake hydraulic fluid

Every 30 000 miles (45 000 km) or 3 years – whichever comes first

Transmission
Change the automatic transmission fluid

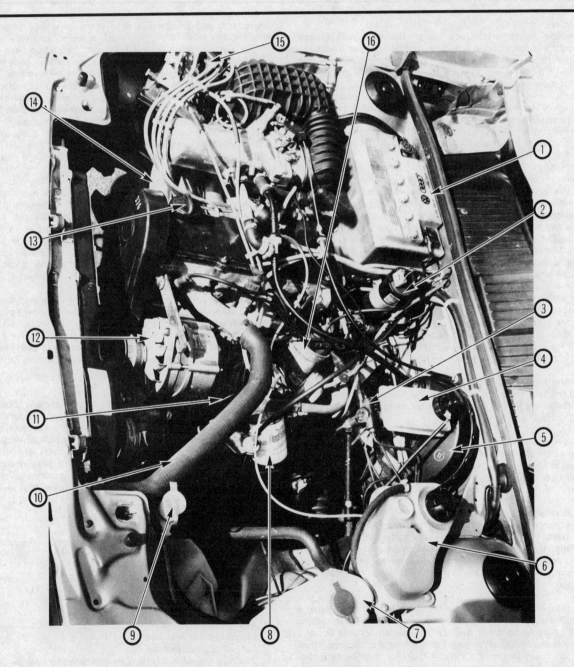

Under-bonnet view – four-cylinder fuel injected UK model

1 Battery	6 Coolant expansion tank	9 Headlamp washer fluid reservoir	13 Oil filler cap
2 Ignition coil	7 Windscreen washer fluid reservoir	10 Radiator top hose	14 Inlet manifold
3 Brake master cylinder	8 Oil filter	11 Engine oil dipstick	15 Fuel distributor
4 Brake fluid reservoir		12 Alternator	16 Ignition distributor
5 Brake servo			

Fault diagnosis

Introduction

The vehicle owner who does his or her own maintenance according to the recommended schedules should not have to use this section of the manual very often. Modern component reliability is such that, provided those items subject to wear or deterioration are inspected or renewed at the specified intervals, sudden failure is comparatively rare. Faults do not usually just happen as a result of sudden failure, but develop over a period of time. Major mechanical failures in particular are usually preceded by characteristic symptoms over hundreds or even thousands of miles. Those components which do occasionally fail without warning are often small and easily carried in the vehicle.

With any fault finding, the first step is to decide where to begin investigations. Sometimes this is obvious, but on other occasions a little detective work will be necessary. The owner who makes half a dozen haphazard adjustments or replacements may be successful in curing a fault (or its symptoms), but he will be none the wiser if the fault recurs and he may well have spent more time and money than was necessary. A calm and logical approach will be found to be more satisfactory in the long run. Always take into account any warning signs or abnormalities that may have been noticed in the period preceding the fault — power loss, high or low gauge readings, unusual noises or smells, etc — and remember that failure of components such as fuses or spark plugs may only be pointers to some underlying fault.

The pages which follow here are intended to help in cases of failure to start or breakdown on the road. There is also a Fault Diagnosis Section at the end of each Chapter which should be consulted if the preliminary checks prove unfruitful. Whatever the fault, certain basic principles apply. These are as follows:

Verify the fault. This is simply a matter of being sure that you know what the symptoms are before starting work. This is particularly important if you are investigating a fault for someone else who may not have described it very accurately.

Don't overlook the obvious. For example, if the vehicle won't start, is there petrol in the tank? (Don't take anyone else's word on this particular point, and don't trust the fuel gauge either!) If an electrical fault is indicated, look for loose or broken wires before digging out the test gear.

Cure the disease, not the symptom. Substituting a flat battery with a fully charged one will get you off the hard shoulder, but if the underlying cause is not attended to, the new battery will go the same way. Similarly, changing oil-fouled spark plugs for a new set will get you moving again, but remember that the reason for the fouling (if it wasn't simply an incorrect grade of plug) will have to be established and corrected.

Don't take anything for granted. Particularly, don't forget that a 'new' component may itself be defective (especially if it's been rattling round in the boot for months), and don't leave components out of a fault diagnosis sequence just because they are new or recently fitted. When you do finally diagnose a difficult fault, you'll probably realise that all the evidence was there from the start.

Electrical faults

Electrical faults can be more puzzling than straightforward mechanical failures, but they are no less susceptible to logical analysis if the basic principles of operation are understood. Vehicle electrical wiring exists in extremely unfavourable conditions — heat, vibration and chemical attack — and the first things to look for are loose or corroded connections and broken or chafed wires, especially where the wires pass through holes in the bodywork or are subject to vibration.

All metal-bodied vehicles in current production have one pole of the battery 'earthed', ie connected to the vehicle bodywork, and in nearly all modern vehicles it is the negative (–) terminal. The various electrical components — motors, bulb holders etc — are also connected to earth, either by means of a lead or directly by their mountings. Electric current flows through the component and then back to the battery via the bodywork. If the component mounting is loose or corroded, or if a good path back to the battery is not available, the circuit will be incomplete and malfunction will result. The engine and/or gearbox are also earthed by means of flexible metal straps to the body or subframe; if these straps are loose or missing, starter motor, generator and ignition trouble may result.

Assuming the earth return to be satisfactory, electrical faults will be due either to component malfunction or to defects in the current supply. Individual components are dealt with in Chapter 10. If supply wires are broken or cracked internally this results in an open-circuit, and the easiest way to check for this is to bypass the suspect wire temporarily with a length of wire having a crocodile clip or suitable connector at each end. Alternatively, a 12V test lamp can be used to verify the presence of supply voltage at various points along the wire and the break can be thus isolated.

If a bare portion of a live wire touches the bodywork or other earthed metal part, the electricity will take the low-resistance path thus formed back to the battery: this is known as a short-circuit. Hopefully a short-circuit will blow a fuse, but otherwise it may cause burning of the insulation (and possibly further short-circuits) or even a fire. This is why it is inadvisable to bypass persistently blowing fuses with silver foil or wire.

Spares and tool kit

Most vehicles are supplied only with sufficient tools for wheel changing; the *Maintenance and minor repair* tool kit detailed in *Tools and working facilities,* with the addition of a hammer, is probably sufficient for those repairs that most motorists would consider attempting at the roadside. In addition a few items which can be fitted without too much trouble in the event of a breakdown should be carried. Experience and available space will modify the list below, but the following may save having to call on professional assistance:

Spark plugs, clean and correctly gapped
HT lead and plug cap — long enough to reach the plug furthest from the distributor
Distributor rotor, condenser and contact breaker points as applicable
Drivebelt(s) — emergency type may suffice
Spare fuses
Set of principal light bulbs
Tin of radiator sealer and hose bandage
Exhaust bandage
Roll of insulating tape
Length of soft iron wire
Length of electrical flex
Torch or inspection lamp (can double as test lamp)
Battery jump leads
Tow-rope
Ignition waterproofing aerosol
Litre of engine oil
Sealed can of hydraulic fluid
Emergency windscreen
Worm drive hose clips
Tube of filler paste

If spare fuel is carried, a can designed for the purpose should be used to minimise risks of leakage and collision damage. A first aid kit and a warning triangle, whilst not at present compulsory in the UK, are obviously sensible items to carry in addition to the above.

When touring abroad it may be advisable to carry additional spares which, even if you cannot fit them yourself, could save having to wait while parts are obtained. The items below may be worth considering:

Clutch and throttle cables
Cylinder head gasket
Alternator brushes
Tyre valve core

One of the motoring organisations will be able to advise on availability of fuel etc in foreign countries.

Engine will not start

Engine fails to turn when starter operated

Flat battery (recharge, use jump leads, or push start – manual gearbox models)
Battery terminals loose or corroded
Battery earth to body defective

Checking for a spark by holding a spark plug against an earthing point (using insulated pliers)

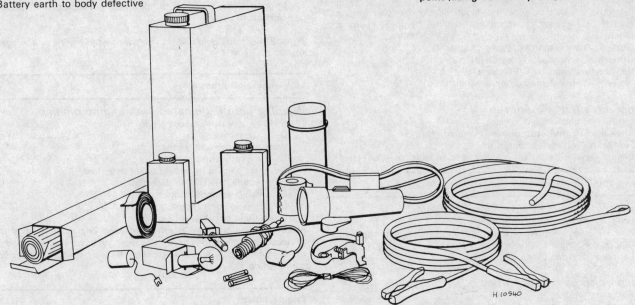

A few spares carried in the car can save you a long walk!

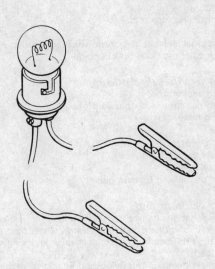

A simple test lamp is useful for tracing electrical faults

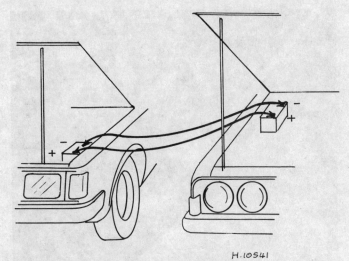

Correct way to connect jump leads – do not allow the car bodies to touch!

Engine earth strap loose or broken
Starter motor (or solenoid) wiring loose or broken
Automatic transmission selector in wrong position, or inhibitor switch faulty
Ignition/starter switch faulty
Major mechanical failure (seizure)
Starter or solenoid internal fault (see Chapter 10)

Starter motor turns engine slowly

Partially discharged battery (recharge, use jump leads, or push start – manual gearbox models)
Battery terminals loose or corroded
Battery earth to body defective
Engine earth strap loose
Starter motor (or solenoid) wiring loose
Starter motor internal fault (see Chapter 10)

Engine turns normally but fails to start

Damp or dirty HT leads and distributor cap (crank engine and check for spark) (photo)
Dirty or incorrectly gapped distributor points (if applicable)
No fuel in tank (check for delivery at carburettor or fuel distributor) (photo)
Excessive choke (hot engine) or insufficient choke (cold engine)
Fouled or incorrectly gapped spark plugs (remove, clean and regap)
Other ignition system fault (see Chapter 4)
Other fuel system fault (see Chapter 3)
Poor compression (see Chapter 1)
Major mechanical failure (eg camshaft drive)

Engine fires but will not run

Insufficient choke (cold engine)
Air leaks at carburettor or inlet manifold
Fuel starvation (see Chapter 3)
Ballast resistor defective, or other ignition fault (see Chapter 4)

Engine cuts out and will not restart

Engine cuts out suddenly – ignition fault

Loose or disconnected LT wires
Wet HT leads or distributor cap (after traversing water splash)
Coil or condenser failure (check for spark)
Other ignition fault (see Chapter 4)

Engine misfires before cutting out – fuel fault

Fuel tank empty
Fuel pump defective or filter blocked (check for delivery)
Fuel tank filler vent blocked (suction will be evident on releasing cap)

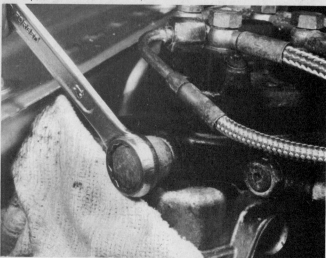

Checking for fuel delivery to the fuel distributor on fuel injection engines (refer to Chapter 3)

Carburettor needle valve sticking
Carburettor jets blocked (fuel contaminated)
Other fuel system fault (see Chapter 4)

Engine cuts out – other causes

Serious overheating
Major mechanical failure (eg camshaft drive)

Engine overheats

Ignition (no-charge) warning light illuminated (four-cylinder engine only)

Slack or broken drivebelt – retension or renew (Chapter 10)

Ignition warning light not illuminated

Coolant loss due to internal or external leakage (see Chapter 2)
Thermostat defective
Low oil level
Brakes binding
Radiator clogged externally or internally
Electric cooling fan not operating correctly
Engine waterways clogged
Ignition timing incorrect or automatic advance malfunctioning
Mixture too weak

Note: *Do not add cold water to an overheated engine or damage may result*

Low engine oil pressure

Warning light illuminated with engine running

Oil level low or incorrect grade
Defective sender unit
Wire to sender unit earthed
Engine overheating
Oil filter clogged or bypass valve defective
Oil pressure relief valve defective
Oil pick-up strainer clogged
Oil pump worn or mountings loose
Worn main or big-end bearings

Note: *Low oil pressure in a high-mileage engine at tickover is not necessarily a cause for concern. Sudden pressure loss at speed is far more significant. In any event, check the warning light sender before condemning the engine.*

Engine noises

Pre-ignition (pinking) on acceleration

Incorrect grade of fuel
Ignition timing incorrect
Distributor faulty or worn
Worn or maladjusted carburettor or fuel injection equipment
Excessive carbon build-up in engine

Whistling or wheezing noises

Leaking vacuum hose
Leaking carburettor or manifold gasket
Blowing head gasket

Tapping or rattling

Incorrect valve clearances
Worn valve gear
Broken piston ring (ticking noise)

Knocking or thumping

Unintentional mechanical contact (eg incorrect exhaust mounting)
Peripheral component fault (generator, water pump etc)
Worn big-end bearings (regular heavy knocking, perhaps less under load)
Worn main bearings (rumbling and knocking, perhaps worsening under load)
Piston slap (most noticeable when cold)

Chapter 1 Engine

Refer to Chapter 13 for Specifications applicable to 1984 through 1987 models

Contents

Specifications

Part A – four-cylinder engines

General

	1.6	1.7
Code letters	WP, YG, YK, YN, YP, YU, YZ, YH	WT
Capacity	1588 cc (96.9 cu in)	1715 cc (104.7 cu in)
Bore	79.5 mm (3.13 in)	79.5 mm (3.13 in)
Stroke	80.0 mm (3.15 in)	86.4 mm (3.40 in)
Compression ratio	WP, YU – 7.0:1 YG, YK, YN, YP, YH – 8.2:1 YZ – 9.5:1	8.2:1
Cylinder compression:		
Compression pressure	9 to 13 bar (131 to 189 lbf/in^2)	9 to 12 bar (131 to 174 lbf/in^2)
Minimum pressure	7 bar (102 lbf/in^2)	7 bar (102 lbf/in^2)
Maximum pressure difference between cylinders	2 bar (29 lbf/in^2)	3 bar (44 lbf/in^2)
Firing order	1-3-4-2 (No 1 at timing belt end)	

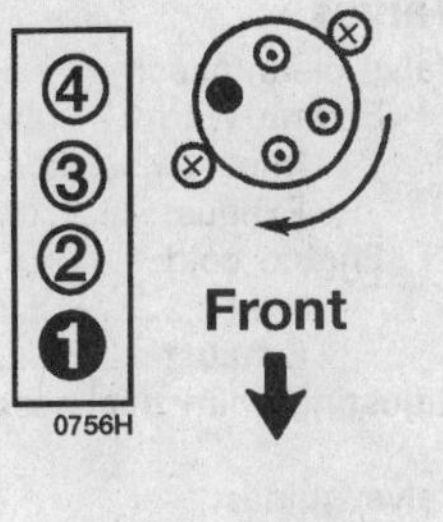

Cylinder location and distributor rotation

Lubrication system

Oil capacity:	
Including filter	3.0 litre; 5.3 Imp pt; 3.2 US qt
Excluding filter	2.5 litre; 4.4 Imp pt; 2.6 US qt

Difference between dipstick minimum and maximum marks .... 1.0 litre; 1.8 Imp pt; 1.1 US qt
Oil pressure (minimum) .... 2 bar (29 lbf/in²)

Intermediate shaft
Endplay .... 0.25 mm (0.010 in)

Crankshaft
Needle bearing depth .... 1.5 mm (0.059 in)
End play:
   New .... 0.07 to 0.17 mm (0.003 to 0.007 in)
   Wear limit .... 0.25 mm (0.010 in)
Maximum main bearing running clearance .... 0.17 mm (0.007 in)
Main bearing journal diameter:
   Standard size .... 53.96 to 53.98 mm (2.1244 to 2.1252 in)
   1st undersize .... 53.71 to 53.73 mm (2.1146 to 2.1154 in)
   2nd undersize .... 53.46 to 53.48 mm (2.1047 to 2.1055 in)
   3rd undersize .... 53.21 to 53.23 mm (2.0949 to 2.0957 in)
Big-end bearing journal diameter:
   Standard size .... 45.96 to 45.98 mm (1.8094 to 1.8102 in)
   1st undersize .... 45.71 to 45.73 mm (1.7996 to 1.8004 in)
   2nd undersize .... 45.46 to 45.48 mm (1.7898 to 1.7906 in)
   3rd undersize .... 45.21 to 45.23 mm (1.7799 to 1.7807 in)
Maximum journal out-of-round .... 0.03 mm (0.0012 in)

Pistons and rings
Piston-to-bore clearance:
   New .... 0.03 mm (0.0012 in)
   Wear limit .... 0.07 mm (0.0028 in)
Groove-to-ring clearance:
   New .... 0.02 to 0.05 mm (0.0008 to 0.0020 in)
   Wear limit .... 0.15 mm (0.0059 in)
Piston size:

	Piston diameter	Bore diameter
Standard size	79.48 mm (3.1291 in)	79.51 mm (3.1307 in)
	79.49 mm (3.1295 in)	79.52 mm (3.1307 in)
	79.50 mm (3.1299 in)	79.53 mm (3.1311 in)
1st oversize	79.73 mm (3.1390 in)	79.76 mm (3.1402 in)
	79.74 mm (3.1394 in)	79.77 mm (3.1406 in)
	79.75 mm (3.1398 in)	79.78 mm (3.1410 in)
2nd oversize	79.98 mm (3.1488 in)	80.01 mm (3.1500 in)
	79.99 mm (3.1492 in)	80.02 mm (3.1504 in)
	80.00 mm (3.1496 in)	80.03 mm (3.1508 in)
3rd oversize	80.48 mm (3.1685 in)	80.51 mm (3.1697 in)
	80.49 mm (3.1689 in)	80.52 mm (3.1701 in)
	80.50 mm (3.1693 in)	80.53 mm (3.1705 in)

Cylinder bore:
   Maximum out-of-round .... 0.04 mm (0.0016 in)
Piston ring endgap clearance (ring 15 mm/0.6 in from bottom of bore):
   New .... 0.30 to 0.45 mm (0.012 to 0.018 in)
   Wear limit .... 1.0 mm (0.040 in)

Connecting rods
Maximum endplay .... 0.37 mm (0.015 in)
Big-end bearing running clearance:
   New .... 0.028 to 0.088 mm (0.0011 to 0.0035 in)
   Wear limit .... 0.12 mm (0.0047 in)

Camshaft
Maximum endplay .... 0.15 mm (0.006 in)

Valves
Valve clearances:
   Engine warm:
      Inlet .... 0.20 to 0.30 mm (0.008 to 0.012 in)
      Exhaust .... 0.40 to 0.50 mm (0.016 to 0.020 in)
   Engine cold:
      Inlet .... 0.15 to 0.25 mm (0.006 to 0.010 in)
      Exhaust .... 0.35 to 0.45 mm (0.014 to 0.018 in)
Adjusting shim thicknesses .... 3.00 to 4.25 mm (0.118 to 0.167 in) in increments of 0.05 mm (0.002 in)
Valve guides:
   Maximum valve rock (measured at head):
      Inlet .... 1.0 mm (0.039 in)
      Exhaust .... 1.3 mm (0.051 in)

Valve timing at 1 mm lift/0 mm clearance):	1.6 except YZ from Aug'79	1.6 YZ from Aug '79	1.7
Inlet opens BTDC	4°	6°	1°
Inlet closes ABDC	46°	49°	37°
Exhaust opens BBDC	44°	45°	42°
Exhaust closes ATDC	6°	8°	2°

Cylinder head
Minimum height (between faces) .... 132.55 mm (5.2185 in)
Maximum gasket face distortion .... 0.1 mm (0.004 in)
Valve seat angle .... 45°

Oil pump
Gear backlash .... 0.05 to 0.20 mm (0.002 to 0.008 in)
Gear endplay (maximum) .... 0.15 mm (0.006 in)

Part B – five-cylinder engines
General

	1.9	2.2
Code letters	WN	WE
Capacity	1921 cc (117.2 cu in)	2144 cc (130.8 cu in)
Bore	79.5 mm (3.13 in)	79.5 mm (3.13 in)
Stroke	77.4 mm (3.05 in)	86.4 mm (3.40 in)
Compression ratio	10.0:1	8.0:1
Cylinder compression:		
Compression pressure	10.0 to 14.0 bar (145 to 203 lbf/in²)	8.5 to 12.0 bar (123 to 174 lbf/in²)
Minimum pressure	8 bar (116 lbf/in²)	7 bar (102 lbf/in²)
Maximum pressure difference between cylinders	3 bar (44 lbf/in²)	
Firing order	1-2-4-5-3 (No 1 at timing belt end)	

Lubrication system

	1.9	2.2
Oil capacity:		
Including filter	4.5 litre; 7.9 Imp pt; 4.8 US qt	3.5 litre; 6.2 Imp pt; 3.7 US qt
Excluding filter	4.0 litre; 7.0 Imp pt; 4.2 US qt	3.0 litre; 5.3 Imp pt; 3.2 US qt
Difference between dipstick minimum and maximum marks	1.0 litre; 1.76 Imp pt; 1.1 US qt	
Oil pressure (minimum)	1 bar (14.5 lbf/in²)	

Crankshaft
Needle bearing depth .... 5.5 mm (0.217 in)
Endplay:
    New .... 0.07 to 0.18 mm (0.003 to 0.007 in)
    Wear limit .... 0.25 mm (0.010 in)
Maximum main bearing running clearance .... 0.16 mm (0.006 in)
Main bearing journal diameter:
    Standard size .... 57.96 to 57.98 mm (2.2819 to 2.2827 in)
    1st undersize .... 57.71 to 57.73 mm (2.2721 to 2.2728 in)
    2nd undersize .... 57.46 to 57.48 mm (2.2622 to 2.2630 in)
    3rd undersize .... 57.21 to 57.23 mm (2.2524 to 2.2532 in)
Big-end bearing journal diameter:
    Standard size .... 45.96 to 45.98 mm (1.8094 to 1.8102 in)
    1st undersize .... 45.71 to 45.73 mm (1.7996 to 1.8004 in)
    2nd undersize .... 45.46 to 45.48 mm (1.7898 to 1.7906 in)
    3rd undersize .... 45.21 to 45.23 mm (1.7799 to 1.7807 in)
Maximum journal out-of-round .... 0.03 mm (0.0012 in)

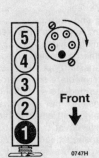

Cylinder location and distributor rotation

Pistons and rings
Piston-to-bore clearance:
    New .... 0.025 mm (0.001 in)
    Wear limit:
        1.9 .... 0.07 mm (0.0028 in)
        2.2 .... 0.08 mm (0.0032 in)
Groove-to-ring clearance:
    New .... 0.02 to 0.08 mm (0.0008 to 0.0032 in)
    Wear limit .... 0.1 mm (0.004 in)
Piston size .... As 1.6 and 1.7 four-cylinder engines
Cylinder bore:
    Maximum out-of-round .... 0.04 mm (0.0016 in)
Piston rings endgap clearance (ring 15 mm/0.6 in from bottom of bore):
    New .... 0.25 to 0.50 mm (0.010 to 0.020 in)
    Wear limit .... 1.0 mm (0.040 in)

Connecting rods
Maximum endplay .... 0.4 mm (0.016 in)
Big-end bearing running clearance:
   New .... 0.015 to 0.062 mm (0.0006 to 0.0024 in)
   Wear limit .... 0.12 mm (0.0047 in)

Camshaft
Maximum endplay .... 0.15 mm (0.006 in)

Valves
Valve clearances .... As 1.6 and 1.7 four-cylinder engines
Valve guides .... As 1.6 and 1.7 four-cylinder engines

Valve timing (at 1 mm lift/0 mm clearance):	**1.9**	**2.2**
Inlet opens BTDC	10°	6°
Inlet closes ABDC	36°	40°
Exhaust opens BBDC	45°	47°
Exhaust closes ATDC	3°	1°

Cylinder head
Minimum height (between faces) .... 132.75 mm (5.2264 in)
Maximum gasket face distortion .... 0.1 mm (0.004 in)
Valve seat angle .... 45°

Torque wrench settings
Part A – 1.6 and 1.7 litre

	lbf ft	Nm
Cylinder head bolts:		
Stage 1	29	40
Stage 2	43	60
Stage 3	54	75
Stage 4	Tighten a further quarter turn (90°)	
Note: *Do not retighten the socket head bolts during servicing*		
Engine to transmission	40	55
Engine mountings	25	35
Engine stop to body	18	25
Main bearing caps	47	65
Crankshaft front oil seal housing	7	10
Intermediate shaft flange	18	25
Crankshaft rear oil seal housing	7	10
Flywheel	54	75
Big-end nuts	33	45
Camshaft gear sprocket	58	80
Timing cover	7	10
Crankshaft pulley to sprocket	14	20
Crankshaft sprocket	58	80
Intermediate shaft sprocket	58	80
Intermediate shaft flange	18	25
Tensioner nut	33	45
Timing belt cover to block	14	20
Valve cover	7	10
Camshaft bearing cap	14	20
Oil pressure switch	7	10
Oil filter head	18	25
Oil pump to block	14	20
Oil pump cover	7	10
Sump bolt – steel	7	10
Sump bolt – aluminium	6	8
Sump drain plug	22	30
Sump side covers – aluminium	11	15

Part B – 1.9 and 2.2 litre

	lbf ft	Nm
Cylinder head bolts:		
Stage 1	29	40
Stage 2	43	60
Stage 3	54	75
Stage 4	Tighten a further quarter turn (90°)	
Note: *Do not retighten the socket head bolts during servicing*		
Engine to transmission:		
M8	14	20
M10	32	45
M12	43	60
Subframe to body	51	70
Engine mountings	32	45
Engine stop to body	32	45
Main bearing caps	47	65

Oil pump to block:		
Bolt	14	20
Stud	7	10
Oil pick-up	7	10
Flywheel	54	75
Crankshaft rear oil seal housing	7	10
Big-end nuts	36	50
Valve cover	7	10
Timing cover	7	10
Camshaft bearing cap	14	20
Camshaft gear/sprocket	58	80
Oil pump pressure relief valve	29	40
Crankshaft pulley (using tool 2079 – see text)	252	350
Sump bolt	7	10
Sump drain plug	29	40

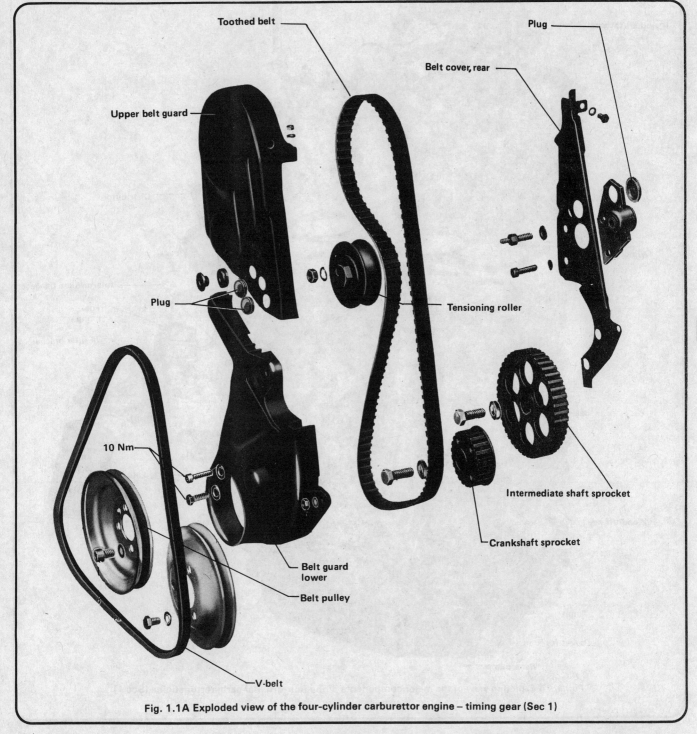

Fig. 1.1A Exploded view of the four-cylinder carburettor engine – timing gear (Sec 1)

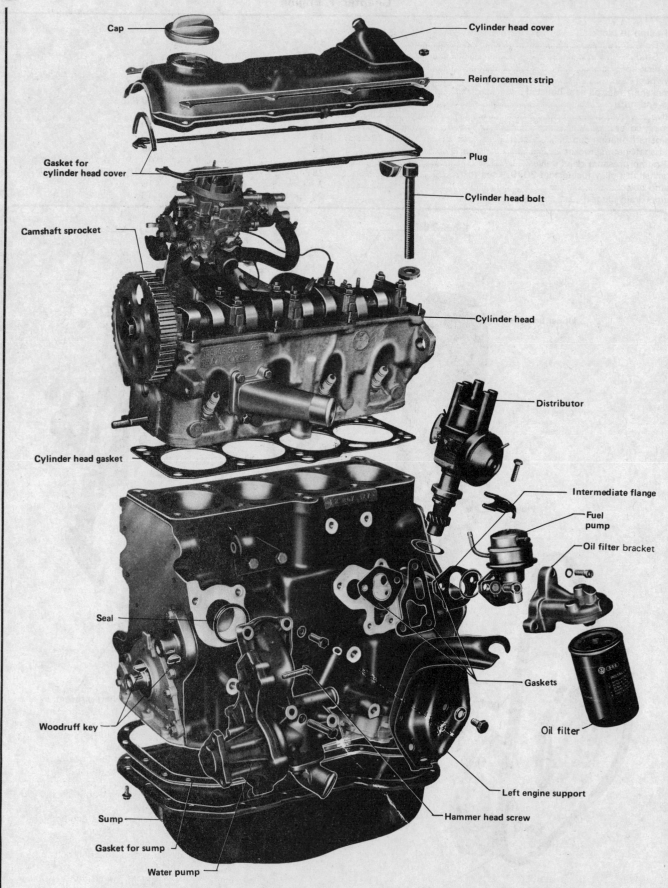

Cap

Cylinder head cover

Reinforcement strip

Gasket for cylinder head cover

Plug

Cylinder head bolt

Camshaft sprocket

Cylinder head

Cylinder head gasket

Distributor

Intermediate flange

Fuel pump

Oil filter bracket

Seal

Gaskets

Woodruff key

Oil filter

Left engine support

Hammer head screw

Sump

Gasket for sump

Water pump

Fig. 1.1B Exploded view of the major components of the four-cylinder carburettor engine (Sec 1)

1.2 The oil pressure switch is located on the rear of the cylinder head on UK models

PART A – FOUR-CYLINDER ENGINE

1 General description

The engine is of four-cylinder, in-line overhead camshaft type mounted conventionally at the front of the car. The crankshaft is of five-bearing type and the centre main bearing shells incorporate flanged or separate thrust washers to control crankshaft endfloat. The camshaft is driven by a toothed belt from the crankshaft sprocket, and the belt also drives the intermediate shaft which is used to drive the distributor, oil pump and on carburettor engines, the fuel pump. The valves are operated from the camshaft through bucket type tappets, and valve clearances are adjusted by the use of shims located in the top of the tappets.

The engine has a full-flow lubrication system from a gear type oil pump mounted in the sump, and driven by an extension of the distributor which is itself geared to the intermediate shaft. The oil filter is of the cartridge type, mounted on the left-hand side of the cylinder block. The oil pressure switch is located on the rear of the cylinder head on UK models (photo) and on the oil filter housing on North American models.

2 Major operations possible with the engine in the car

The following operations can be carried out without having to remove the engine from the car:

(a) Removal and servicing of the cylinder head and camshaft
(b) Removal of the timing belt and gears
(c) Removal of the flywheel or driveplate (after first removing the transmission)
(d) Removal of the sump (after first lowering the subframe)
(e) Removal of the oil pump, pistons and connecting rods

3 Major operations only possible after removal of the engine from the car

The following operations can only be carried out after removal of the engine from the car:

(a) Removal of the intermediate shaft
(b) Removal of the crankshaft and main bearings

4 Method of engine removal

The engine can be lifted from the car either separately or together with the manual gearbox. On automatic transmission models it is recommended that the engine is removed separately because of the extra weight involved.

5 Engine – removal and refitting

1 Remove the bonnet, as described in Chapter 12, and stand it on cardboard or rags in a safe place.
2 Disconnect the battery negative lead.
3 Remove the radiator, as described in Chapter 2.
4 Disconnect the wiring from the rear of the alternator – where a cooling duct is fitted it will be necessary to disconnect the bypass hose from the cylinder head outlet and remove the duct first.
5 On carburettor models remove the air cleaner, as described in Chapter 3.
6 On fuel injection models remove the air cleaner and air flow meter, as described in Chapter 3.
7 Identify all fuel and vacuum hoses using marking tape then disconnect those affecting engine removal. These will include, where applicable:

Fuel hoses to the fuel pump and filter, or warm-up regulator
Vacuum hoses to the inlet manifold, carburettor, distributor, and emission control components (see Chapter 3)

8 Identify all wiring for location using marking tape, then disconnect those affecting engine removal. These will include, where applicable:

Fuel injection wiring to cold start valve, thermo-time switch, auxiliary air valve and warm-up regulator
Wiring to oil pressure switch, temperature sender, distributor, coil and inlet manifold preheater

9 On manual gearbox models disconnect the clutch cable from the release lever and cable bracket.
10 Disconnect the throttle cable, as described in Chapter 3.
11 Disconnect the hose from the inlet manifold (where applicable) and the heater hoses from the bulkhead. Also disconnect the hose from the cylinder head outlet.
12 On models with air conditioning, remove the compressor as described in Chapter 12, leaving the refrigerant hoses connected. Wire the compressor to the front towing eye without straining the hoses.
13 Unscrew the left-hand side engine mounting nut from the top and the right-hand side engine mounting from the bottom.
14 Unscrew the nuts and separate the exhaust downpipe from the exhaust manifold.
15 Unbolt the support arm from the front of the engine – on models with air conditioning remove the compressor drivebelt.
16 Disconnect the wiring from the starter, with reference to Chapter 10.
17 On models with power steering remove the power steering pump and tie it to one side, with reference to Chapter 11.

Removing engine without transmission

18 On fuel injection models remove the inlet duct assembly, with reference to Chapter 3.
19 Remove the starter motor, as described in Chapter 10.
20 On automatic transmission models unscrew the three torque converter-to-driveplate bolts while holding the starter ring gear stationary with a screwdriver. It will be necessary to rotate the engine to position the bolts in the starter aperture, using a socket on the crankshaft pulley bolt.
21 Unbolt the cover plate from the front of the transmission.
22 Detach the exhaust downpipe from the front mounting and tie the pipe to one side. Where applicable on fuel injection models unbolt the downpipe from the front of the catalytic converter or silencer and remove the pipe.
23 Connect a hoist and take the weight of the engine – the hoist should be positioned centrally over the engine (photo).
24 Support the weight of the transmission with a trolley jack.
25 Unscrew and remove the engine-to-transmission bolts noting the location of the brackets and earth strap.
26 Lift the engine from the mountings and reposition the trolley jack beneath the transmission.
27 Pull the engine from the transmission – make sure on automatic transmission models that the torque converter remains fully engaged with the transmission splines.

1

5.23 Hoist position for removing the engine without transmission

5.28 Removing the rear engine plate

5.37 Removing the engine with manual transmission attached

28 Turn the engine slightly and lift it from the engine compartment, then lower it to the floor. Remove the rear engine plate, if necessary (photo).

Removing engine with manual transmission attached
29 Detach the exhaust downpipe from the front mounting and tie the pipe to one side. On fuel injection models unbolt and remove the downpipe complete.
30 Disconnect the wiring to the reversing light switch and release the cable clip. Remove the earth strap.
31 Unscrew the nut and disconnect the speedometer cable from the differential cover or gearbox casing (as applicable).
32 Disconnect the driveshafts from the drive flanges, with reference to Chapter 8, and tie them to one side.
33 Unscrew the lockbolt securing the selector adaptor to the selector rod on the rear of the gearbox after first removing the locking wire. Press the support rod from the balljoint and withdraw the adaptor from the selector lever.
34 Support the transmission with a trolley jack.
35 Loosen the bolt securing the gearbox stay to the underbody. Unscrew and remove the stay inner bolt and pivot the stay from the gearbox.
36 Unbolt the bonded rubber mounting from the gearbox and also unbolt the front gearbox support bracket.

37 Connect a hoist and take the weight of the engine – the hoist should be positioned near the front of the engine so that the engine and gearbox will hang at a steep angle (photo).
38 Lift the engine from the mountings and move it forwards, then lower the trolley jack and lift the engine and gearbox from the engine compartment while turning it, as necessary, to clear the body. Lower the engine and gearbox to the floor.
39 If necessary, separate the gearbox from the engine by removing the starter (Chapter 10), gearbox front cover, and engine-to-gearbox bolts. Remove the rear engine plate.

Refitting
40 Refitting is a reversal of the removal procedure, but before starting the engine check that it has been filled with oil and also that the cooling system is full. Delay tightening the engine and gearbox mountings until the engine is idling – this will ensure that the engine is correctly aligned, as shown in Figs. 1.2 to 1.7 inclusive. Make sure that the starter cable is not touching the engine or mounting bracket.

6 Engine dismantling – general

1 If possible position the engine on a bench or strong table for the dismantling procedure. Two or three blocks of wood will be necessary to support the engine in an upright position.
2 Cleanliness is most important, and if the engine is dirty, it should be cleaned with paraffin before commencing work.
3 Avoid working with the engine directly on a concrete floor, as grit presents a real source of trouble.
4 As parts are removed, clean them in a paraffin bath. However, do not immerse parts with internal oilways in paraffin as it is difficult to remove, usually requiring a high pressure hose. Clean oilways with nylon pipe cleaners.
5 It is advisable to have suitable containers to hold small items according to their use, as this will help when reassembling the engine and also prevent possible losses.
6 Always obtain complete sets of gaskets when the engine is being dismantled, but retain the old gaskets with a view to using them as a pattern to make a replacement if a new one is not available.
7 When possible, refit nuts, bolts, and washers in their location after being removed, as this helps to protect the threads and will also be helpful when reassembling the engine.
8 Retain unserviceable components in order to compare them with the new parts supplied.

7 Ancillary components – removal and refitting

With the engine removed from the car, the externally mounted

Fig. 1.2 Engine and manual gearbox alignment dimension (Sec 5)

a = 99.5 to 101.5 mm (3.917 to 3.996 in)

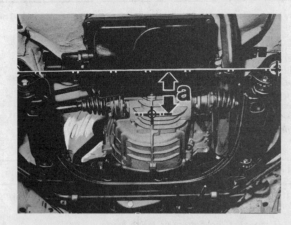

Fig. 1.3 Engine and automatic transmission alignment dimension (Sec 5)

a = 152.5 to 154.5 mm (6.004 to 6.083 in)

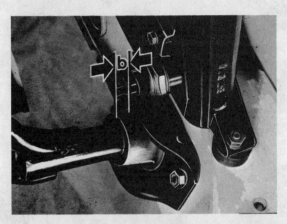

Fig. 1.4 Engine front support alignment dimension (Sec 5)

b = 2.5 to 10.5 mm (0.098 to 0.413 in)

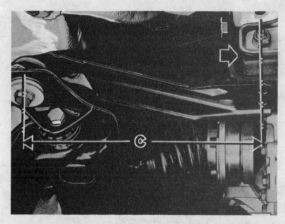

Fig. 1.5 Manual gearbox mounting alignment dimension (Sec 5)

c = 251.5 to 255.5 mm (9.902 to 10.059 in)

Fig. 1.6 The manual gearbox mounting rubber must be central (Sec 5)

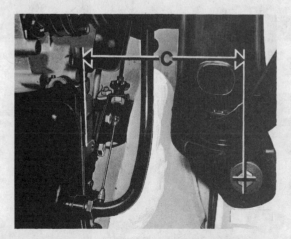

Fig. 1.7 Automatic transmission alignment dimension (Sec 5)

c = 221.0 to 223.0 mm (8.701 to 8.780 in)

1

ancillary components in the following list can be removed. The removal sequence need not necessarily follow the order given:

Inlet and exhaust manifolds (Chapter 3)
Fuel pump or warm-up regulator, as applicable (Chapter 3)
HT leads and spark plugs (Chapter 4)
Oil filter cartridge (Section 27 of this Chapter)
Distributor (Chapter 4)
Dipstick
Alternator (Chapter 10)
Engine mountings (Section 28 of this Chapter)

8 Cylinder head and camshaft – removal

Note: *If the engine is still in the car, first carry out the following operations:*

(a) *Disconnect the battery negative lead*
(b) *Drain the cooling system*
(c) *Remove the alternator*
(d) *Remove the inlet and exhaust manifolds*
(e) *Remove the HT leads and spark plugs*
(f) *Disconnect all wiring, cables and hoses*
(g) *Disconnect the exhaust downpipe from the exhaust manifold*

1   Unscrew the nuts and lift off the upper timing cover, using an Allen key where necessary (photos).
2   Unscrew the nuts and lift off the valve cover, together with the reinforcement strips and gaskets (photos).
3   Unbolt the outlet elbows and remove the gaskets, if necessary (photos).
4   Using a socket on the crankshaft pulley bolt, turn the engine so that the piston in No 1 cylinder is at TDC (top dead centre) on its compression stroke. The notch in the crankshaft pulley must be in line with the arrow on the lower timing cover (photo), and both No 1 cylinder valves must be closed (ie cam peaks away from the tappets). The notch on the rear of the camshaft gear will also be in line with the top of the timing belt rear cover.
5   Loosen the nut on the timing belt tensioner, and using an open-

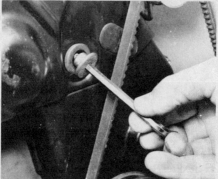

8.1A Upper timing cover top nuts

8.1B Upper timing cover bottom nut

8.2A Removing the reinforcement strips ...

8.2B ... and valve cover

8.2C Removing the valve cover front gasket ...

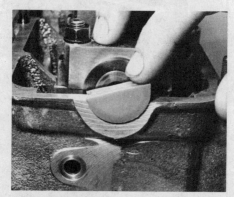

8.2D ... and rear plug

8.3A Removing the cylinder head side outlet ...

8.3B ... and rear outlet

8.4 Crankshaft pulley notch aligned with the TDC arrow on the lower timing cover

ended spanner, rotate the eccentric hub anti-clockwise to release the belt tension.

6   Remove the timing belt from the camshaft gear and tensioner and move it to one side while keeping it in firm contact with the intermediate and crankshaft gears. *The intermediate gear must not be moved, otherwise the ignition timing will be lost and the lower timing cover will have to be removed.*

7   Unscrew the nut and remove the timing belt tensioner.

8   Unscrew the bolt securing the timing belt rear cover to the cylinder head.

9   Using a splined socket unscrew the cylinder head bolts a turn at a time in reverse order to that shown in Fig. 1.11.

10 With all the bolts removed lift the cylinder head from the block. If it is stuck, tap it free with a wooden mallet. *Do not insert a lever into the gasket joint.*

11 Remove the cylinder head gasket.

9   Camshaft and tappets – removal

Note: *If the engine is still in the car, first carry out the following operations:*

(a) *Disconnect the battery negative lead*
(b) *Disconnect the wiring, cables and hoses which cross the engine valve cover – remove the air cleaner on carburettor models*
(c) *Remove the alternator/water pump drivebelt*

1   Follow paragraphs 1 to 6 of Section 8, excluding paragraph 3.

2   Unscrew the centre bolt from the camshaft gear while holding the gear stationary with a bar through one of the holes.

3   Withdraw the gear from the camshaft and extract the Woodruff key (photos).

4   Unscrew the nuts from bearing caps 1, 3 and 5. Identify all the caps for position then remove caps 1, 3 and 5 (photos).

5   Loosen the nuts on bearing caps 2 and 4 evenly until all valve spring tension has been released, then remove the caps.

6   Lift out the camshaft and discard the oil seal (photo).

7   Have ready a board with eight pegs on it, or alternatively use a box with internal compartments, marked to identify cylinder number and whether inlet or exhaust or position in the head, numbering from the front of the engine. As each tappet is removed (photo), place it on the appropriate peg, or mark the actual tappet to indicate its position. *Note that each tappet has a shim (disc) fitted into a recess in its top. This shim must be kept with its particular tappet.*

10 Valves – removal and renovation

1   With the cylinder head removed as previously described, the valve gear can be dismantled as follows. Because the valves are recessed deeply into the top of the cylinder head, their removal requires a valve spring compressor with long claws or the use of some ingenuity in adapting other types of compressor. One method which can be employed is to use a piece of tubing of roughly the same diameter as the valve spring cover and long enough to reach above the top of the

9.3A Removing the camshaft gear

9.3B Showing the camshaft gear Woodruff key

9.4A Removing No 3 camshaft bearing cap

9.4B Removing No 1 camshaft bearing cap

9.6 Removing the camshaft

9.7 Removing a tappet together with its shim

cylinder head. To be able to remove the valve collets, either cut a window in the tube on each side, or cut a complete section away, so that the tube is about three quarters of a circle.

2   Have ready a board with holes in it, into which each valve can be fitted as it is removed, or have a set of labelled containers so that each valve and its associated parts can be identified and kept separate. Inlet valves are Nos. 2-4-5-7, Exhaust valves are Nos 1-3-6-8, numbered from the timing belt end of the engine.

3   Compress each valve spring until the collets can be removed (photo). Take out the collets, release the spring compressor and remove it.

4   Remove the valve spring cover, the outer and inner spring and the valve (photos). Thread the springs over the valve stem to keep them with the valve, and put on the valve spring cover. It is good practice, but not essential, to keep the valve springs the same way up, so that parts are refitted exactly as they were before removal.

5   Prise off the valve stem seals, or pull them off with pliers and discard them, then lift off the valve spring seat and plate it with its valve (photos).

6   Examine the heads of the valves for pitting and burning, paying particular attention to the heads of the exhaust valves. The valve seats should be examined at the same time. If the pitting on the valve and seat is only slight, the marks can be removed by grinding the seats and valves together with coarse and then fine grinding paste. Where bad pitting has occurred, it will be necessary to have the valve seat re-cut and either use a new valve, or have the valve re-faced.

10.3 Compressing a valve spring and removing the collets

10.4A Removing the valve spring cover and springs ...

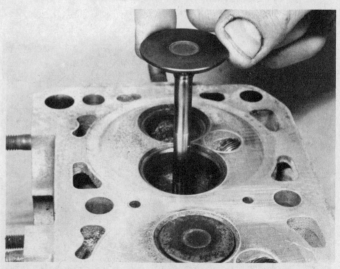

10.4B ... and valve

10.5A Remove the valve stem seal ...

10.5B ... and spring seat

7   The refacing of valves and cutting of valve seats is not expensive and gives a far better result than grinding in valves which are badly pitted. Exhaust valves, if too worn for grinding in, must be discarded. Re-machining of exhaust valves is not permissible.

8   Valve grinding is carried out as follows: Smear a small quantity of coarse carborundum paste around the contact surface of the valve or seat and insert the valve into its guide. Apply a suction grinder tool to the valve head and grind in the valve by semi-rotary motion. This is produced by rolling the valve grinding tool between the palms of the hands. When grinding action is felt to be at an end, extract the valve, turn it and repeat the operation as many times as is necessary to produce a uniform matt grey surface over the whole seating area of the valve head and valve seat. Repeat the process using fine grinding paste.

9   Scrape away all carbon from the valve head and valve stem. Carefully clean away every trace of grinding paste, taking care to leave none in the ports, or in the valve guides. Wipe the valves and valve seats with a paraffin soaked rag and then with a clean dry rag.

11 Cylinder head – examination and renovation

1   Check the cylinder head for distortion, by placing a straight edge across it at a number of points, lengthwise, crosswise and diagonally, and measuring the gap beneath it with feeler gauges. If the gap exceeds the limit given in the Specifications, the head must be re-faced by a workshop which is equipped for this work. Re-facing must not reduce the cylinder head height below the minimum dimension given in the Specifications.

2   Examine the cylinder head for cracks. If there are minor cracks of not more than 0.5 mm (0.020 in) width between the valve seats, or at the bottom of the spark plug holes, the head can be re-used, but a cylinder head cannot be repaired or new valve seat inserts fitted.

3   Check the valve guides for wear. First clean out the guide and then insert the stem of a new valve into the guide. Because the stem diameters are different, ensure that only an inlet valve is used to check the inlet valve guides, and an exhaust valve for the exhaust valve guides. With the end of the valve stem flush with the top of the valve guide, measure the total amount by which the rim of the valve head can be moved sideways. If the movement exceeds the maximum amount given in the Specifications, new guides should be fitted, but this is a job for an Audi dealer or specialist workshop.

12 Camshaft and bearings – examination and renovation

1   Examine the camshaft for signs of damage or excessive wear. If either the cam lobes or any of the journals have wear grooves, a new camshaft must be fitted.

2   With the camshaft fitted in its bearings, but with the bucket

Fig. 1.8 Checking the cylinder head for distortion using a straight edge and feeler blade (Sec 11)

Fig. 1.9 Checking valve guide wear by measuring valve movement using a dial gauge (Sec 11)

tappets removed so that there is no pressure on the crankshaft. measure the endfloat of the camshaft, which should not exceed the limit given in the Specifications.

3   The camshaft bearings are part of the cylinder head and cannot be renewed. The bearing clearance is very small and the clearances can only be checked with a dial gauge. *If there is excessive looseness in the camshaft bearings, do not attempt to decrease it by grinding or filing the bottoms of the bearing caps.*

13 Valves – refitting

1   Locate the valve spring seats over the guides, then press a new seal on to the top of each valve guide. A plastic sleeve should be provided with the valve stem seals, so that the seals are not damaged when the valves are fitted.

2   Apply oil to the valve stem and the stem seal. Fit the plastic sleeve over the top of the valve stem and insert the valve carefully. Remove the sleeve after inserting the valve. If there is no plastic sleeve, wrap a piece of thin adhesive tape round the top of the valve stem, so that it covers the recess for the collets and prevents the sharp edges of the recess damaging the seal. Remove the tape after fitting the valve.

3   Fit the inner and outer valve springs, then the valve spring cover. If renewing springs, they must only be renewed as a pair on any valve.

4   Fit the spring compressor and compress the spring just enough to allow the collets to be fitted. If the spring is pressed right down there is a danger of damaging the stem seal.

5   Fit the collets, release the spring compressor slightly and check that the collets seat properly, then remove the compressor.

6   Tap the top of the valve stem with a soft-headed hammer to ensure that the collets are seated.

7   Repeat the procedure for all the valves.

14 Camshaft and tappets – refitting

1   Fit the bucket tappets to their original positions; the adjustment shims on the top of the tappets must be fitted so that the lettering on them is downwards. Lubricate the tappets and the camshaft journals.

2   Lay the camshaft into the lower half of its bearings so that the lowest point of the cams of No 1 cylinder are towards the tappets, and fit the bearing caps in their original positions, making sure that they are the right way round before fitting them over the studs.

3   Fit the nuts to bearing cap Nos 2 and 4 and tighten them in diagonal sequence until the camshaft fully enters its bearings.

4   Fit the nuts to bearing caps Nos 1, 3 and 5, then tighten all the nuts to the specified torque in diagonal sequence (photo).

5   Smear a little oil onto the sealing lip and outer edge of the camshaft oil seal, then locate it open end first in the cylinder head No 1 camshaft bearing cap (photo).

6   Using a metal tube, drive the seal squarely into the cylinder head

until flush with the front of the cylinder head – *if the seal is driven in further, it will block the oil return hole.*

7   Fit the Woodruff key in its groove and locate the gear on the end of the camshaft.

8   Fit the centre bolt and spacer and tighten the bolt to the specified torque while holding the gear stationary with a bar through one of the holes (photo).

9   Turn the camshaft gear and align the rear notch with the top of the timing belt rear cover.

10 Without disturbing the intermediate gear setting, and keeping the timing belt in firm contact with the intermediate gear and crankshaft gear, locate the timing belt on the camshaft gear and tensioner. The crankshaft must be positioned with No 1 cylinder at TDC. If the position of the intermediate gear is in doubt, it must be checked with reference to Section 17.

11 Turn the timing belt tensioner clockwise and tension the timing belt until it can just be twisted 90° with the thumb and index finger midway between the camshaft and intermediate gears. Tighten the nut to secure the tensioner.

12 Check and, if necessary, adjust the valve clearances, as described in Section 16.

13 Refit the valve cover and reinforcement strips, together with new gaskets and seals, and tighten the nuts.

14 Refit the upper timing belt cover and tighten the nuts.

15 If the engine is in the car, reverse the preliminary procedures given in Section 9.

14.4 Tightening the camshaft bearing cap nuts

14.5 Installing the camshaft oil seal

14.8 Tightening the camshaft gear centre bolt

Fig. 1.10 Camshaft gear TDC mark aligned with the top of the timing belt rear cover (Sec 14)

15.1A Locate the new cylinder head gasket on the block ...

15 Cylinder head and camshaft – refitting

1   Check that the top of the block is perfectly clean, then locate a new gasket on it with the words OBEN – TOP facing upward (photos).
2   Check that the cylinder head face is perfectly clean. Place two long rods or pieces of dowel in two cylinder head bolt holes at opposite ends of the block, to position the gasket and give a location for fitting the cylinder head. Lower the head on to the block (photo), remove the guides and insert the bolts and washers. Do not use jointing compound on the cylinder head joint.
3   Tighten the bolts using the sequence shown in Fig. 1.11 in the four stages given in the Specifications to the specified torque (photo).
4   Insert and tighten the bolt securing the timing belt rear cover to the cylinder head.
5   Refit the timing belt tensioner and fit the nut finger tight.
6   Follow paragraphs 9 to 14 inclusive of Section 14.
7   Refit the outlet elbow together with a new gasket and tighten the bolts.
8   If the engine is in the car, reverse the preliminary procedures given in Section 8.

16 Valve clearances – checking and adjustment

1   Valve clearances are adjusted by inserting the appropriate thickness shim to the top of the tappet. Shims are available in

15.1B ... with the OBEN – TOP words uppermost

1

15.2 Lowering the cylinder head onto the block

15.3 Tightening the cylinder head bolts

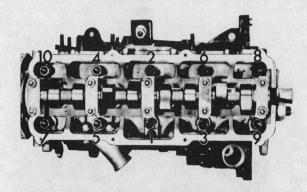

Fig. 1.11 Cylinder head bolt tightening sequence (Sec 15)

thicknesses from 3.00 to 4.25 mm (0.118 to 0.167 in) in increments of 0.05 mm (0.002 in).

2   Adjust the valve clearances for the initial setting-up after fitting a new camshaft, or grinding in the valves with the engine cold. The valve clearances should be re-checked after 620 miles (1000 km), with the engine warm, and the coolant over 35°C (95°F).

3   Remove the valve cover after removing the upper timing cover.
4   Fit a spanner to the crankshaft pulley bolt and turn the crankshaft until the highest points of the cams for one cylinder are pointing upwards and outwards at similar angles. Use feeler gauges to check the gap between the cam and the tappet and record the dimension (photo).
5   Repeat the operation for all four cylinders and complete the list of clearances. Valves are numbered from the timing belt end of the engine. Inlet valves are Nos 2-4-5-7, exhaust valves are Nos 1-3-6-8.
6   Where any tolerances exceed those given in the Specifications, remove the existing shim by placing a cranked dowel rod with a suitably shaped end between two tappets with the rod resting on the edge of the tappets (photo). With the piston for the relevant cylinder at TDC compression, lever against the camshaft to depress the tappets sufficiently to remove the shim(s) from the top of the tappet(s). Do not overdepress the tappets so that the valves touch the pistons. Note that each tappet incorporates a notch in its upper rim so that a small screwdriver or similar tool can be used to remove the shim (photos).
7   Note the thickness of the shim (engraved on its underside), and calculate the shim thickness required to correct the clearance (photo). For example, if the measured clearance on an inlet valve (warm engine) is 0.35 mm (0.014 in) this is outside the tolerance specified for inlet valves which is 0.20 and 0.30 mm (0.008 to 0.012 in). The best adjustment is the mid-point of the range i.e. 0.25 mm (0.010 in) and the measured gap of 0.35 mm (0.014 in) is 0.1 mm (0.004 in) too

16.4 Checking the valve clearances

16.6A Using a cranked dowel rod to depress the tappets

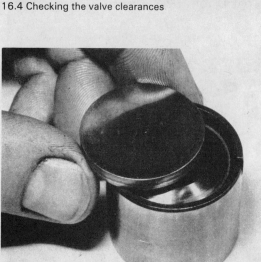

16.6B Removing a shim from a tappet (tappet removed)

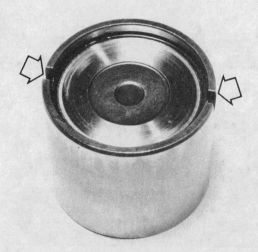

16.6C Showing notches (arrowed) in the tappet for removing the shim

16.7 Showing the engraved thickness in mm on the underside of the tappet shim

great. If the shim which is taken out is 3.05 mm (0.120 in), it should be replaced by one of 3.15 mm (0.124 in).

8   Provided they are not worn or damaged, shims which have been removed can be re-used in other positions if they are of the correct thickness.

9   Refit the valve cover and upper timing cover, together with new gaskets, after checking and adjusting the valve clearances.

17 Timing belt and gears – removal and refitting

1   If the engine is still in the car, disconnect the battery negative lead.

2   Remove the alternator drivebelt, with reference to Chapter 10.

3   Unscrew the nuts and lift off the upper timing cover, using an Allen key where necessary.

4   Unbolt and remove the pulley from the water pump (photo).

5   Using a socket on the crankshaft pulley bolt, turn the engine so that the piston in No 1 cylinder is at TDC (top dead centre) on its compression stroke. The notch in the crankshaft pulley must be in line with the arrow on the lower timing cover, and both No 1 cylinder valves must be closed (ie cam peaks away from the tappets).

6   If it is required to remove the crankshaft gear, loosen the centre bolt now. Hold the crankshaft stationary with a wide-bladed screwdriver in the starter ring gear (starter motor removed) or engage top gear and apply the handbrake if the engine is still in the car.

7   With the TDC marks aligned unbolt the crankshaft pulley from the gear (photo).

8   Unbolt and remove the lower timing cover (photo).

9   Loosen the nut on the timing belt tensioner, and using an open-ended spanner rotate the eccentric hub anti-clockwise to release the belt tension (photo).

10 Remove the timing belt from the crankshaft, camshaft and intermediate gears, and from the tensioner.

11 Unscrew the nut and remove the timing belt tensioner (photo).

12 Unscrew the centre bolt and withdraw the intermediate gear (photo). Remove the Woodruff key. When loosening the centre bolt, hold the gear stationary with a socket and bar on the rear timing cover bolt.

13 Remove the centre bolt and withdraw the crankshaft gear (photos). Remove the Woodruff key.

14 Unscrew the centre bolt from the camshaft gear while holding the gear stationary with a bar through one of the holes. Withdraw the gear and remove the Woodruff key.

15 Unbolt and remove the rear timing cover together with the alternator mounting bracket from the block and cylinder head (photos).

16 Commence refitting by locating the alternator mounting bracket and rear timing cover on the engine and tightening the bolts.

17 Locate the Woodruff key and camshaft gear on the camshaft, insert the centre bolt and washer, and tighten the bolt.

18 Locate the Woodruff key and crankshaft gear on the crankshaft,

17.4 Removing the water pump pulley

17.7 Removing the crankshaft pulley

17.8 Removing the lower timing cover

17.9 Turn the timing belt tensioner anti-clockwise to release the belt tension

17.11 Removing the timing belt tensioner

17.12 Removing the gear from the intermediate shaft

17.13A Unscrew the centre bolt ...

17.13B ... and withdraw the crankshaft gear

17.15A Removing the rear timing cover ...

17.15B ... and alternator mounting bracket

17.18 Tightening the crankshaft gear centre bolt

coat the threads of the centre bolt with a liquid locking agent, then insert the bolt with its washer and tighten it while holding the crankshaft stationary (photo).

19 Locate the Woodruff key and intermediate gear on the intermediate shaft, then insert the centre bolt and washer, and tighten the bolt (photo).

20 Refit the timing belt tensioner and fit the nut finger tight.

21 Make sure that the notch on the rear of the camshaft gear is aligned with the top of the timing belt rear cover.

22 Temporarily fit the crankshaft pulley to the gear then, with No 1 piston at TDC, turn the intermediate gear so that the indentation is aligned with the notch in the pulley (photo). If the distributor has not been disturbed the rotor arm will point in the direction of No 1 distributor cap segment.

23 Locate the timing belt on the gears and tensioner, turn the tensioner clockwise to pretension the timing belt, and check that the TDC marks are still correctly aligned.

24 Turn the tensioner clockwise until the timing belt can just be twisted 90° with the thumb and index finger midway between the camshaft and intermediate gears. Tighten the nut to secure the tensioner.

25 Remove the crankshaft pulley, fit the lower timing cover, and tighten the bolts.

26 Refit the crankshaft pulley and tighten the bolts.

27 Locate the pulley on the water pump and tighten the bolts.

17.19 Tightening the intermediate shaft gear centre bolt

17.22 Crankshaft pulley TDC notch aligned with the indentation in the intermediate gear (arrowed)

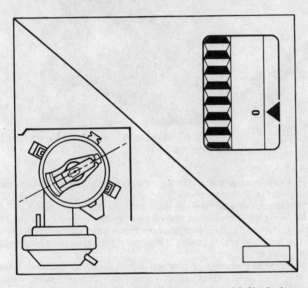

Fig. 1.12 Position of the distributor rotor arm with No 1 piston at TDC on its compression stroke (Sec 17)

18.1A Removing the flywheel bolts

1

28 Refit the upper timing cover and tighten the nuts.
29 Refit the alternator drivebelt, with reference to Chapter 10.
30 Reconnect the battery negative lead, where necessary.

18 Flywheel/driveplate – removal and refitting

Note: *If the engine is still in the car, first carry out the following operations:*

(a)   On manual gearbox models, remove the gearbox (Chapter 6), and clutch (Chapter 5)

(b)   On automatic transmission models, remove the automatic transmission (Chapter 7)

1 The flywheel/driveplate bolts are offset to ensure correct refitting. Unscrew the bolts while holding the flywheel/driveplate stationary (photos).
2 Lift the flywheel/driveplate from the crankshaft (photo). If removing a driveplate note the location of the shim and spacer.
3 Refitting is a reversal of removal, but coat the threads of the bolts with a liquid locking agent before inserting them and tightening them to the specified torque. If a replacement driveplate is to be fitted, its position must be checked and adjusted if necessary. The distance from

18.1B Using a bar and angle iron to hold the flywheel stationary

18.2 Removing the flywheel

19.3A Removing the intermediate shaft sealing flange ...

19.3B ... and O-ring

19.4A Removing the intermediate shaft

19.4B The intermediate shaft

19.4C Showing the intermediate shaft front bearing

the rear face of the block to the torque converter *mounting face* on the driveplate (Fig. 1.14) must be between 30.5 and 32.1 mm (1.20 and 1.26 in). If necessary, remove the driveplate and fit a spacer behind it to achieve the correct dimension.

19 Intermediate shaft – removal and refitting

1   Remove the distributor (Chapter 4), and on carburettor models the fuel pump (Chapter 3).
2   Remove the timing belt and intermediate gear as described in Section 17.

3   Remove the two bolts from the sealing flange, take off the sealing flange and the O-ring (photos).
4   Withdraw the intermediate shaft from the block (photos).
5   With the flange removed, the oil seal can be removed (photo). Fit a new seal with its open face towards the engine and use a block of wood to drive the seal in flush. Oil the lips of the seal before fitting the sealing flange.
6   Refitting is a reversal of removal, but fit a new O-ring and check that the shaft endfloat does not exceed the amount given in the Specifications. Refer to Section 17 when refitting the timing belt and intermediate gear, and to Chapters 3 and 4 when refitting the fuel pump and distributor.

Fig. 1.13 Driveplate (automatic transmission) showing location of spacer (1) and shim (2) (Sec 18)

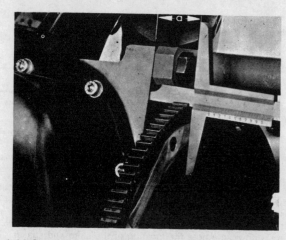

Fig. 1.14 Checking the driveplate-to-block dimension 'a' (Sec 18)

19.5 Levering out the intermediate shaft oil seal from the flange

20 Sump – removal and refitting

Note: *If the engine is still in the car, first carry out the following operations:*

   (a) Jack up the front of the car and support it on axle stands
   (b) Support the weight of the engine with a hoist
   (c) Unbolt and remove the transmission front cover
   (d) Drain the engine oil
   (e) Unscrew the subframe front bolts and lower the subframe

1 Unbolt and remove the sump, using an Allen key where necessary (photo). Remove the dipstick (photo).
2 Remove the gasket.
3 Refitting is a reversal of removal, but use a new gasket without adhesive (photo), and tighten the bolts evenly to the specified torque.

21 Crankshaft oil seals – renewal

Front oil seal
1 Remove the timing belt and crankshaft gear, as described in Section 17.
2 If an extractor tool is available the seal may be renewed without removing the housing, otherwise unbolt and remove the housing

20.1A Removing the sump

20.1B Oil level dipstick location

20.3 Locating a new sump gasket on the block

21.2 Removing the crankshaft front oil seal housing

1

(including the relevant sump bolts) and remove the gasket (photo). If the sump gasket is damaged while removing the housing it will be necessary to remove the sump and fit a new gasket. However, refit the sump *after* fitting the housing.

3   Drive the old seal out of the housing then dip the new seal in engine oil and drive it into the housing with a block of wood or a socket until flush (photos). Make sure that the closed end of the seal is facing outwards.

4   Fit the housing together with a new gasket and tighten the bolts evenly in diagonal sequence.

5   Refit the crankshaft gear and timing belt, as described in Section 17.

Rear oil seal

6   Remove the flywheel or driveplate, as described in Section 18.
7   Follow paragraphs 2 to 4 inclusive (photos).
8   Refit the flywheel or driveplate, as described in Section 18.

22 Oil pump – removal, examination and refitting

1   Remove the sump, as described in Section 20.
2   Using an Allen key unscrew the socket-headed bolts and withdraw the oil pump and strainer from the cylinder block (photo).
3   Remove the two hexagon-headed bolts from the pump cover and lift off the cover (photo).
4   Bend up the metal rim of the filter plate so that it can be removed and take the filter screen out (photo). Clean the screen thoroughly with paraffin and a brush.
5   Clean the pump casing, cover and gears.
6   Check the backlash of the gears with a feeler gauge (photo) and with a straight edge across the end face of the pump, measure the end-play of the gears (photo). Examine the pump cover grooves worn by the ends of the gears, which will effectively increase the endplay of the gears. If the wear on the pump is beyond the specified limits a new pump should be fitted.

21.3A Using a socket to fit a new crankshaft front oil seal

21.3B Crankshaft front oil seal correctly fitted in the housing

21.7A Removing the crankshaft rear oil seal housing

21.7B Locate the new crankshaft rear oil seal housing gasket on the dowels

22.2 Removing the oil pump and strainer

22.3 Removing the oil pump cover

22.4 Oil pump filter screen

22.6A Checking the oil pump gear backlash ...

22.6B ... and endplay

7 Fill the pump housing with engine oil then reassemble and refit it using a reversal of the removal and dismantling procedure. Refer to Section 20 when refitting the sump.

23 Pistons and connecting rods – removal and dismantling

1 Remove the cylinder head (Section 8), timing belt (Section 17) and oil pump (Section 22).
2 Mark each connecting rod and cap in relation to its cylinder and position.
3 Turn the crankshaft so that No 1 piston is at the bottom of its bore, then unscrew the nuts/bolts and remove the big-end bearing cap (photo).
4 Using the handle of a hammer, push the piston and connecting rod out of the top of the cylinder. Put the bearing cap with its connecting rod and make sure that they both have the cylinder number marked on them. If any of the bearing shells become detached while removing the connecting rod and bearing cap, ensure that they are placed with their matching cap or rod (photo).
5 Repeat the procedure given in paragraphs 3 and 4 to remove the remaining pistons and connecting rods.
6 Before removing the pistons from the connecting rods, if necessary mark the connecting rods to show which side of them is

towards the front of the engine. The casting marks on the rod and cap face towards the front of the engine (photo).
7 Remove the circlips from the grooves in the gudgeon pin holes and push the pin out enough for the connecting rod to be removed (photo). Do not remove the pins completely unless new ones are to be fitted, to ensure that the pin is not turned end for end when the piston is refitted. If the pin is difficult to push out, heat the piston by immersing it in hot water.
8 New bushes can be fitted to the connecting rods, but as they need to be reamed to size after fitting, the job is best left to an Audi agent.
9 Using old feeler gauges, or pieces of rigid plastic inserted behind the piston rings, carefully ease each ring in turn off the piston. Lay the rings out so that they are kept the right way up and so that the top ring can be identified. Carefully scrape the rings free of carbon and clean out the ring grooves on the pistons, using a piece of wood or a piece of broken piston ring.

24 Pistons and cylinder bores – examination

1 Examine the pistons and the bores for obvious signs of damage and excessive wear. If they appear to be satisfactory, make the following checks.
2 Measure the piston diameter at a position 15 mm (0.60 in) from

23.3 Removing a big-end bearing cap

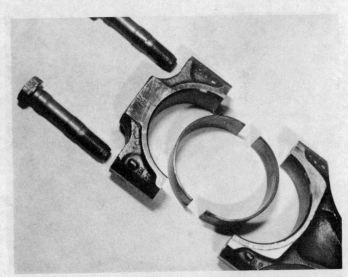
23.4 Big-end bearing components

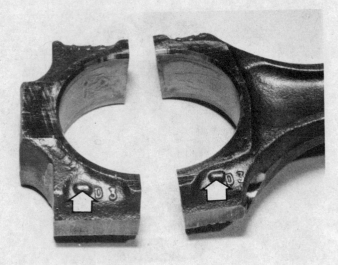
23.6 The casting marks (arrowed) which must face the front of the engine

23.7 Location of a gudgeon pin circlip (arrowed) in the piston

1

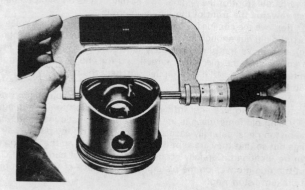

Fig. 1.15 Checking the piston diameter (Sec 24)

the lower edge of the skirt and at 90° to the axis of the piston (Fig. 1.15) and compare this with the information in the Specifications.

3 Push a piston ring into the cylinder bore and use a piston to push the ring down the bore so that it is square in the bore and about 15 mm (0.6 in) from the bottom of the cylinder. Measure the ring gap

24.3 Checking the piston ring gap

using a feeler gauge (photo). If the gap is above the top limit, look for obvious signs of bore wear, or if a new piston ring is available, measure the gap when a new piston ring is fitted to the bore.

4 To measure the bore diameter directly a dial gauge with an internal measuring attachment is required. If one is available, measure each bore in six places and compare the readings with the wear limit given. Bore diameter should be measured 10 mm (0.4 in) from the top of the bore, 10 mm (0.4 in) from the bottom and at the mid-point. At each of the three stations, measure in-line with the crankshaft and at right angles to it. If the bores are worn beyond the limit, they will need to be rebored and new pistons fitted.

5 If one bore is oversize, all four must be rebored and a new set of pistons fitted, otherwise the engine will not be balanced. Connecting rods must only be fitted as complete sets and not be replaced individually.

6 Fit the rings to the pistons and use a feeler gauge to measure the gap between the piston ring and the side of its groove (photo). If the gap is beyond the wear limit, it is more likely that it is the piston groove rather than the ring which has worn, and either a new piston or a proprietary oversize ring will be required. If new piston rings are fitted the wear ridge at the top of the cylinder bore must be removed, or a stepped top ring used.

25 Piston and connecting rods – reassembly and refitting

1 Heat each piston in hot water, then insert the connecting rod and push in the pin until central. Make sure that the casting marks on the connecting rod and the arrow on the piston crown (photo) are facing the same way, then refit the circlips.

2 Before refitting the piston rings, or fitting new rings, check the gap of each ring in turn in its correct cylinder bore using a piston to push the ring down the bore, as described in the previous Section. Measure the gap between the ends of the piston ring, using feeler gauges. The gap must be within the limits given in the Specifications.

3 If the piston ring gap is too small, carefully file the piston ring end until the gap is sufficient. Piston rings are very brittle, so handle them carefully.

4 When fitting piston rings, look for the word TOP etched on one side of the ring and fit this side so that it is towards the piston crown. The outer recessed edge on the centre ring must face the gudgeon pin (photo).

5 Unless the big-end bearing shells are known to be almost new, it is worth fitting a new set when reassembling the engine. Clean the connecting rods and bearing caps thoroughly and fit the bearing shells so that the tang on the bearing engages in the recess in the connecting rod, or cap, and the ends of the bearing are flush with the joint face.

6 To refit the pistons, first space the joints in the piston rings so that

24.6 Checking the piston ring clearance in its groove

25.1 The arrow on the piston crown (arrowed) must face the front of the engine

25.4 Piston with rings fitted

25.7 Inserting a piston into its bore using a ring compressor

25.9 Tightening the big-end bearing cap bolts

they are at 120° intervals. Oil the rings and grooves generously and fit a piston ring compressor over the piston. To fit the pistons without using a piston ring compressor is difficult and there is a high risk of breaking a piston ring.

7   Oil the cylinder bores and insert the pistons (photo) with the arrow on the piston crown pointing towards the front of the engine. Make sure that the relevant crankpin is at its furthest point from the cylinder.

8   When the piston is pushed in flush with the top of the bore, oil the two bearing halves and the crankshaft journal and guide the connecting rod half-bearing on to the crankpin.

9   Fit the big-end bearing cap complete with shell and tighten the nuts/bolts to the specified torque wrench setting (photo).

10 Rotate the crankshaft to ensure that everything is free, before fitting the next piston and connecting rod.

11 Using feeler gauges between the machined face of each big-end bearing, and the machined face of the crankshaft web, check the endplay, which should not exceed the maximum amount given in the Specifications.

12 Refit the oil pump (Section 22), timing belt (Section 17), and cylinder head (Section 15).

26 Crankshaft – removal, examination and refitting

1   With the engine removed from the car, remove the pistons and connecting rods, as described in Section 23.

2   Reassemble the big-end bearings to their matching connecting rods to ensure correct refitting.

3   Remove the crankshaft oil seals complete with housings, as described in Section 21.

4   Check that each main bearing cap is numbered for position.

5   Remove the bolts from each bearing cap in turn, then remove the caps and lift out the crankshaft (photos).

6   If the bearings are not being renewed, ensure that each half-bearing shell is identified so that it is put back in the same place from which it was removed. This also applies to the thrust washers if fitted – see paragraph 7. If the engine has done a high mileage and it is suspected that the crankshaft requires attention, it is best to seek the opinion of an Audi dealer or crankshaft re-finishing specialist for advice on the need for regrinding. Unless the bearing shells (and thrust washers if applicable) are known to be almost new, it is worth fitting a new set when the crankshaft is refitted. If available, Plastigage may be used to check the running clearance of the existing bearings – a strip of the perfect circle plastic is placed across the crankshaft journal and then the bearing is assembled and tightened to the specified torque. After dismantling the bearing the width of the strip is measured with a gauge supplied with the strip, and the running clearance read off (photo).

7   Clean the crankcase recesses and bearing caps thoroughly and fit the bearing shells so that the tang on the bearing engages in the recess in the crankcase or bearing cap. Make sure that the shells fitted to the crankcase have oil holes, and that these line up with the drillings in the bearing housings. The shells fitted to the bearing caps do not have oil holes. Note that the bearing shells of the centre bearing (No 3) may either be flanged to act as thrust washers, or may have separate thrust washers. These should be fitted oil groove outwards as shown. Fit the bearing shells so that the ends of the bearing are flush with the joint face (photos).

8   Oil the bearings and journals (photo) then locate the crankshaft in the crankcase.

1

26.5A Removing a crankshaft main bearing cap

26.5B Removing the crankshaft

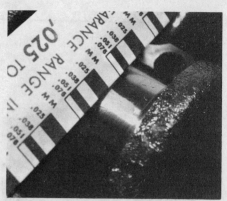

26.6 Using Plastigage to check a crankshaft journal running clearance

26.7A Fitting the flanged type centre main bearing to the cap

26.7B Fitting the centre main bearing and separate thrust washers to the cap

26.7C Fitting the flanged type centre main bearing to the crankcase ...

26.7D .. making sure that the ends of the bearing are flush with the joint face

26.7E Fitting the alternative type centre main bearing to the crankcase ...

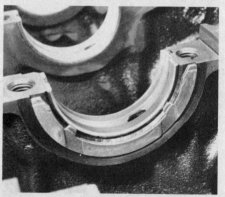

26.7F ... together with the thrust washers

26.8 Lubricating the main bearing shells

26.10 Tightening the main bearing cap bolts

26.12 Checking the crankshaft endfloat

26.13A Location of the spigot needle roller bearing in the end of the crankshaft

26.13B Checking the position of the spigot needle roller bearing

9 Fit the main bearing caps (with centre main bearing thrust washers if applicable) in their correct positions.

10 Fit the bolts to the bearing caps and tighten the bolts of the centre cap to the specified torque (photo), then check that the crankshaft rotates freely. If it is difficult to rotate the crankshaft, check that the bearing shells are seated properly and that the bearing cap is the correct way round. Rotation will only be difficult if something is incorrect, and the fault must be found. Dirt on the back of a bearing shell is sometimes the cause of a tight main bearing.

11 Working out from the centre, tighten the remaining bearing caps in turn, checking that the crankshaft rotates freely after each bearing has been tightened.

12 Check that the endfloat of the crankshaft is within specification, by inserting feeler gauges between the crankshaft and the centre bearing thrust face/washer while levering the crankshaft first in one direction and then in the other (photo).

13 The rear end of the crankshaft carries a needle roller bearing (photo) which supports the front end of the gearbox input shaft. Inspect the bearing for obvious signs of wear and damage. If the gearbox has been removed and dismantled, fit the input shaft into the bearing to see if there is excessive clearance. If the bearing requires renewing, insert a hook behind the bearing and pull it out of the end of the crankshaft. Install the new bearing with the lettering on the end of the bearing outwards. Press it in until the end of the bearing is 1.5 mm (0.059 in) below the face of the flywheel flange (photo).

14 Fit new crankshaft oil seals (Section 21) then refit the pistons and connecting rods, as described in Section 25.

27 Oil filter and housing – removal and refitting

1 Place a suitable container beneath the left-hand side of the engine.

2 Unscrew the filter cartridge and discard it – it will be necessary to use a filter strap or special spanner, although if neither of these items is available drive a long screwdriver through the cartridge.

3 If it is required to remove the housing, use an Allen key to unscrew the bolts, then withdraw the housing and gasket (photos). On North American models it will first be necessary to disconnect the wiring from the oil pressure switch.

4 Clean the mating faces of the housing and block then refit the housing, together with a new gasket, and tighten the bolts. Reconnect the oil pressure switch wiring, where applicable.

5 Clean the mating faces of the new oil filter cartridge and housing, and smear a little engine oil on the filter seal.

6 Screw the cartridge onto the housing and tighten it by hand only (photo).

28 Engine mountings – removal and refitting

1 The engine front support bar (photo) can be unbolted from the block and removed. When refitting the bar check the engine alignment, as described in Section 5.

2 To remove the left and right engine mountings (photos) first remove the front support bar, then unbolt the mountings using a hoist

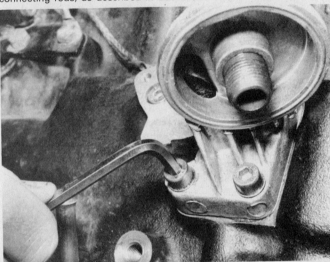

27.3A Unscrew the socket-headed bolts ...

27.3B ... and remove the oil filter housing

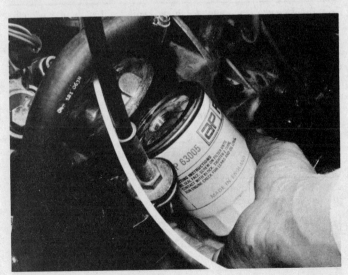

27.6 Fitting a new oil filter cartridge

28.1 Engine front support bar

28.2A Left-hand side engine mounting

28.2B Left-hand side engine mounting bracket

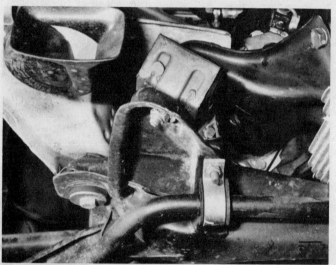

28.2C Right-hand side engine mounting

to support the weight of the engine. When refitting the mountings, check the engine alignment, as described in Section 5.

PART B – FIVE-CYLINDER ENGINE

29 General desciption

The engine is of five-cylinder, in-line, overhead camshaft type, mounted conventionally at the front of the car. The crankshaft is of six-bearing type and the No 4 (from front) main bearing shells incorporate flanged thrust washers to control crankshaft endfloat. The camshaft is driven by a toothed belt from the crankshaft sprocket, and the belt also drives the water pump mounted on the left-hand side of the block. A gear on the rear of the camshaft drives the distributor, and on carburettor models the camshaft also drives the fuel pump.

The valves are operated from the camshaft through bucket type tappets, and valve clearances are adjusted by the use of shims located in the top of the tappets.

The engine has a full-flow lubrication system. A gear and crescent type oil pump is mounted on the front of the crankshaft. The oil filter is of the cartridge type, mounted on the right-hand side of the cylinder block.

30 Major operations possible with the engine in the car

The following operations can be carried out without having to remove the engine from the car:

    (a) *Removal and servicing of the cylinder head and camshaft*
    (b) *Removal of the timing belt and gears*
    (c) *Removal of the flywheel or driveplate (after first removing the transmission)*
    (d) *Removal of the sump (after first lowering the subframe)*
    (e) *Removal of the oil pump*
    (f) *Removal of the pistons and connecting rods*

31 Major operation only possible after removal of the engine from the car

The following operation can only be carried out after removal of the engine from the car:

Removal of the crankshaft and main bearings

32 Method of engine removal

The engine must be disconnected from the transmission then lifted from the car.

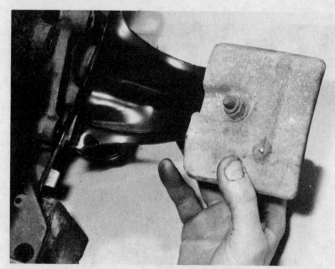

28.2D Right-hand side engine mounting bracket

33 Engine – removal and refitting

1   Remove the bonnet, as described in Chapter 12, and stand it on cardboard or rags in a safe place.

2   Disconnect the battery negative lead.

3   Drain the cooling system, as described in Chapter 2.

4   Unscrew the bolt securing the coolant pipe to the left-hand side of the engine, then disconnect the pipe from the front hose. On some models the coolant pipe is attached to a transmission bellhousing bolt.

5   Remove the screws and withdraw the upper radiator cover.

6   Disconnect the top hose from the cylinder head.

7   Prise the one-way valve and hose from the brake vacuum servo unit.

8   Remove the power steering pump (where applicable), with reference to Chapter 11, but leaving the hoses connected. Tie the pump to the bulkhead (photo).

9   Disconnect the bottom hose from the thermostat housing on the block.

10 Disconnect the wiring from the oil pressure switch on the left-hand side of the engine (photo), and on fuel injection models from the warm-up regulator (photo). Unclip the wiring and place it on one side.

11 On carburettor models remove the air cleaner, as described in Chapter 3.

12 On fuel injection models remove the air cleaner and air flow meter, as described in Chapter 3.

13 Identify all fuel and vacuum hoses using masking tape, then disconnect those affecting engine removal. These will include, where applicable:

Fuel hoses to the fuel pump, non-return valve or warm-up regulator
Vacuum hoses to the vacuum reservoir, distributor, cruise control unit, and emission control components (see Chapter 3)

14 Identify all wiring for location using masking tape, then disconnect those affecting engine removal. These will include, where applicable:

Fuel injection wiring to cold start valve, thermo-time switch, auxiliary air valve, and throttle switch
Wiring to temperature sender, distributor, coil, oil temperature switch, inlet manifold preheater and bypass air cut-off valve

15 On manual gearbox models disconnect the clutch cable from the release lever and cable bracket.

16 Disconnect the throttle cable or pushrod, as described in Chapter 3.

17 Disconnect the heater hoses.

18 Remove the alternator, as described in Chapter 10, and where necessary unbolt the alternator bracket from the block.

19 Unscrew and remove the upper transmission-to-engine bolts noting the location of any brackets.

20 Remove the lower radiator grille.

21 Unbolt and remove the engine front support from the front panel.

22 On manual gearbox models, unbolt and remove the engine upper and lower timing covers, using an Allen key where necessary.

33.8 Power steering pump tied to one side

33.10A Oil pressure switch

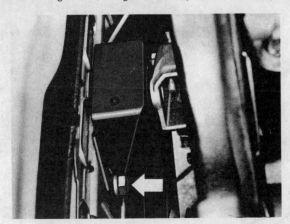

Fig. 1.16 Engine front support mounting bolts (Sec 33)

33.10B Warm-up regulator and wiring

1

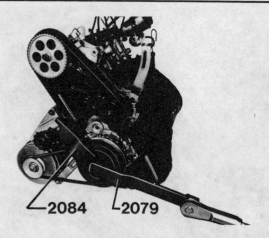

Fig. 1.17 Using tools 2084 and 2079 to unscrew the crankshaft
pulley centre bolt (Sec 33)

Fig. 1.18 Showing the vibration damper location hole in the
crankshaft gear (Sec 33)

23 On North American models disconnect the OXS oxygen sensor
plug.
24 On automatic transmission models, where applicable, disconnect
the coolant hoses from the oil cooler, and remove the flange.
25 For additional room when removing the engine, it is recommended
that the vibration damper on the front of the crankshaft is removed.
First, where applicable, remove the air conditioning compressor
drivebelt. To remove the damper the crankshaft must be held
stationary using Audi tool 2084 and the centre bolt loosened with
Audi tool 2079. The bolt is tightened to a high torque and it is
therefore better to use the correct tools. However, it may be possible
to loosen the bolt while an assistant engages top gear and applies the
brakes (manual gearbox) or by holding the starter ring gear stationary
using a wide-bladed screwdriver.
26 With the centre bolt removed, loosen two diagonally opposite
bolts using an Allen key and remove the remaining two bolts. Release
the vibration damper from the crankshaft gear by tapping the bolts and
removing them – do not pull off the gear.
27 Unscrew the nuts from the left and right-hand side engine
mountings.
28 Unbolt the earth strap from the mounting bracket.
29 On models with air conditioning remove the compressor, as
described in Chapter 12, leaving the refrigerant hoses connected. Tie
the compressor to one side.
30 Remove the starter, as described in Chapter 10.
31 Jack up the front of the car until the front wheels are just free of
the floor then support it with axle stands positioned beneath the
underbody.

32 Connect a hoist and take the weight of the engine – the hoist
should be positioned centrally over the engine.
33 Unscrew and remove the subframe front mounting bolts.
34 Detach the exhaust downpipe from the manifold (Chapter 3) and
unbolt the mounting bracket (photo). Tie the exhaust pipe to one side.
35 On automatic transmission models unscrew the three torque
converter-to-driveplate bolts while holding the starter ring gear stationary with a screwdriver. It will be necessary to rotate the engine to
position the bolts in the starter aperture.
36 Support the weight of the transmission with a trolley jack.
37 Unscrew and remove the lower transmission-to-engine bolts.
38 Where necessary unbolt and remove the left-hand side engine
mounting bracket – on some models it will first be necessary to
remove the radiator panel.
39 Lift the engine from the mounting(s) and reposition the trolley jack
beneath the transmission.
40 Pull the engine from the transmission – make sure on automatic
transmission models that the torque converter remains fully engaged
with the transmission splines.
41 Turn the engine slightly and lift it from the engine compartment
(photo) then lower it to the floor.
42 Refitting is a reversal of the removal procedure, but before starting
the engine check that it has been filled with oil, and that the cooling
system is full. Make sure that the starter cable is not touching the
engine or mounting bracket. Delay tightening the engine mountings

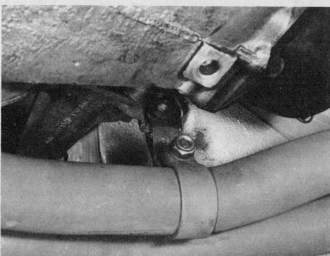

33.34 Exhaust pipe mounting bracket

33.41 Removing the engine

Fig. 1.19 Engine and manual gearbox alignment dimension (Sec 33)

a = 21.2 to 23.2 mm (0.835 to 0.913 in)

Fig. 1.20 Engine and automatic transmission alignment dimension (Sec 33)

a = 123.7 to 125.7 mm (4.870 to 4.949 in)

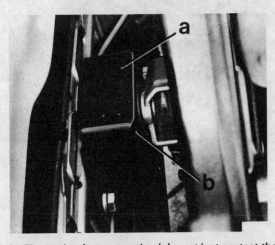

Fig. 1.21 The engine front mounting (a) must just contact the top of rubber (b), and rubber (b) must be central between the sides of the mounting (Sec 33)

until the engine is idling – this will ensure that the engine is correctly aligned, as shown in Figs. 1.19 to 1.23. If necessary loosen the transmission mounting bolts before tightening all of the mountings.
43 Coat the threads of the crankshaft damper centre bolt with a liquid locking agent before inserting it and tightening to the specified torque. Note that the torque wrench setting given for this bolt is only applicable when using Audi tool 2079; if you are not using this tool,

Fig. 1.22 Manual gearbox mounting alignment dimension (Sec 33)

c = 393.4 to 395.4 mm (15.488 to 15.567 in)

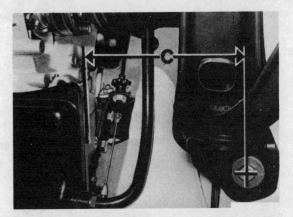

Fig. 1.23 Automatic transmission alignment dimension (Sec 33)

c = 222.6 to 224.6 mm (8.764 to 8.843 in)

tighten the bolt to at least the specified torque and have your Audi dealer check its tightness on completion. (The special tool increases the leverage of the standard torque wrench).

34 Engine dismantling – general

Refer to Part A, Section 6 of this Chapter.

35 Ancillary components – removal and refitting

Refer to Part A, Section 7 of this Chapter, with the following exceptions:

Oil filter cartridge (Section 54 of this Chapter)
Engine mountings (Section 55 of this Chapter)

36 Camshaft and tappets – removal

Note: *If the engine is still in the car, first carry out the following operations:*

(a) *Disconnect the battery negative lead*
(b) *Remove the air cleaner and fuel pump on carburettor models (Chapter 3)*
(c) *Disconnect all relevant wiring, cables and hoses*
(d) *Remove the distributor (Chapter 4)*
(e) *Remove the upper radiator cowl*
(f) *Disconnect the drivebelts from the crankshaft pulley*
(g) *Where fitted, remove the power steering pump leaving the hoses connected (Chapter 11)*

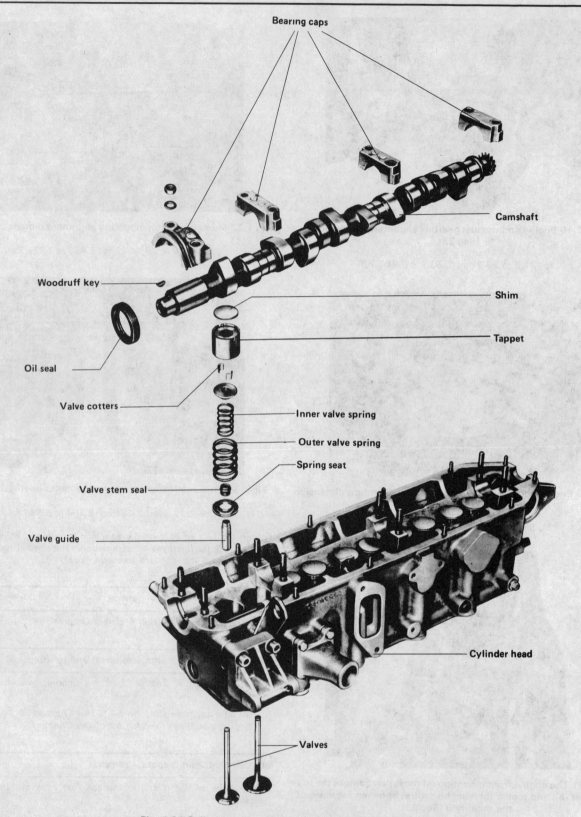

Fig. 1.24 Cylinder head and camshaft components (Sec 36)

1   Unscrew the nuts and lift off the valve cover, together with the reinforcement strips and gaskets. Note the location of the HT lead holder.

2   Unscrew the nuts and bolts and remove the timing belt cover(s). The 1.9 engine has two covers, and an Allen key is required – the lower cover need not be removed.

3   Using a socket on the crankshaft pulley bolt (temporarily refit the bolt and damper if removed during engine removal), turn the engine so that the piston in No 1 cylinder is at TDC (top dead centre) on its compression stroke. The notch in the crankshaft pulley must be in line with the pointer on the oil pump housing – alternatively the 'O' mark (TDC) on the flywheel/driveplate must be aligned with the pointer in

the bellhousing aperture. Both No 1 cylinder valves must be closed (ie cam peaks away from the tappets) and the indentation on the rear of the camshaft gear in line with the upper surface of the valve cover gasket (temporarily refit the gasket and valve cover, if necessary).

4   Loosen the water pump mounting and adjustment bolts, using an Allen key where necessary, and rotate the pump clockwise to release the tension on the timing belt.

5   Remove the timing belt from the camshaft gear and move it to one side.

6   Unscrew the centre bolt from the camshaft gear while holding the gear stationary with a bar through one of the holes or using a wide-bladed screwdriver, as shown in Fig. 1.27.

7   Withdraw the gear from the camshaft and extract the Woodruff key.

8   Check that each bearing cap has its number stamped on it; if not, make an identifying mark to ensure that each cap is put back where it was originally. Note that the caps are offset and can only be fitted one way round.

9   *It is important that the camshaft is removed exactly as described so that there is no danger of it becoming distorted.* Loosen one of the nuts on bearing cap No 2 about two turns and then loosen the diagonally opposite nut on bearing cap No 4 about two turns. Repeat the operations on the other nut of bearing cap No 2 and bearing cap No 4. Continue the sequence until the nuts are free, then remove them. Loosen and remove the nuts of bearing caps Nos 1 and 3 using a similar diagonal sequence.

10 Lift the bearing caps off (photo) and lift the camshaft out (photo). Discard the oil seal.

Fig. 1.27 Using a wide-bladed screwdriver to hold the camshaft gear stationary (Sec 36)

36.10A Removing a camshaft bearing cap

Fig. 1.25 Alignment of the TDC marks on the crankshaft pulley and oil pump housing (Sec 26)

Fig. 1.26 The TDC indentation on the rear of the camshaft gear aligned with the upper surface of the valve cover gasket (Sec 36)

36.10B Removing the camshaft (2.2 engine)

1

36.11A Removing a tappet (cam follower)

36.11B Board for keeping tappets in correct order

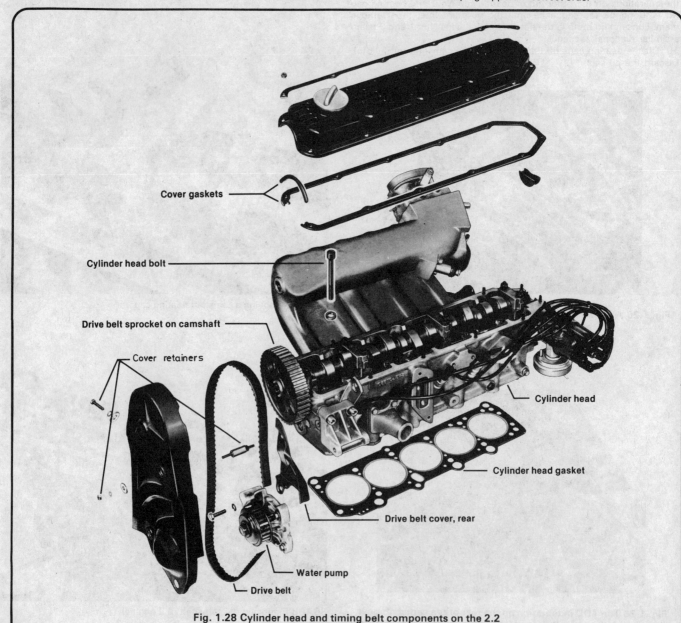

Cover gaskets

Cylinder head bolt

Drive belt sprocket on camshaft

Cover retainers

Cylinder head

Cylinder head gasket

Drive belt cover, rear

Water pump

Drive belt

Fig. 1.28 Cylinder head and timing belt components on the 2.2 engine (Sec 37)

11 Withdraw each tappet (cam follower) in turn (photo) and mark its position (1 to 10 numbering from the timing belt end of the engine) using adhesive tape or a box with divisions (photo). Take care to keep the adjustment shims with their respective tappets.

37 Cylinder head – removal

Note: *If the engine is still in the car, first carry out the following operations:*

    (a) Disconnect the battery negative lead
    (b) Drain the cooling system (Chapter 2)
    (c) Remove the inlet and exhaust manifolds (Chapter 3)
    (d) Remove the distributor, HT leads and spark plugs (Chapter 4)
    (e) Disconnect the drivebelts from the crankshaft pulley
    (f) Disconnect all relevant wiring, cables and hoses
    (g) Remove the upper radiator cowl
    (h) Where fitted, remove the power steering pump, leaving the hoses connected (Chapter 11)

1 Follow paragraphs 1 to 7 inclusive of Section 36.
2 Unbolt and remove the timing belt rear cover – note that the water pump pivot bolt must be removed and, on 1.9 engines three of the oil pump bolts. Note the location of the spacers on 1.9 engines.
3 Using a splined socket unscrew the cylinder head bolts a turn at a time in reverse order to that shown in Fig. 1.30.
4 With all the bolts removed, lift the cylinder head from the block (photo). If it is stuck, tap it free with a wooden mallet. *Do not insert a lever into the gasket joint.*
5 Remove the cylinder head gasket.

38 Valves – removal and renovation

1 Remove the camshaft and tappets, as described in Section 36, and the cylinder head, as described in Section 37.
2 Follow the procedure given in Part A, Section 10 – inlet valves are 2-4-5-7-9 and exhaust valves are 1-3-6-8-10, numbered from the timing belt end of the engine.

39 Cylinder head – examination and renovation

    Refer to Part A, Section 11 of this Chapter.

40 Camshaft and bearings – examination and renovation

1 Refer to Part A, Section 12, of this Chapter.
2 Check that the oil spray jets located in the top of the cylinder head direct the spray at 90° to the camshaft.

37.4 Removing the cylinder head (2.2 engine)

41 Valves – refitting

    Refer to Part A, Section 13, of this Chapter.

42 Cylinder head – refitting

1 Check that the top of the block is perfectly clean, then locate a new gasket on it with the part number or TOP marking facing upward.
2 Check that the cylinder head face is perfectly clean. Insert two long rods, or pieces of dowel into the cylinder head bolt holes at opposite ends of the block, to position the gasket and to give a location for fitting the cylinder head (photo). Lower the head on to the block, remove the guide dowels and insert the bolts and washers. Do not **use** jointing compound on the cylinder head joint.
3 Tighten the bolts using the sequence shown in Fig. 1.30 in **the** four stages given in the Specifications to the specified torque.
4 Locate the timing belt rear cover on the front of the cylinder **head** and block and tighten the retaining bolts and studs, as applicable. **On** the 1.9 engine refit the spacers. Leave the water pump pivot bolt loose.
5 Fit the Woodruff key in its groove and locate the gear on the end of the camshaft.
6 Fit the centre bolt and spacer and tighten the bolt to the specified

Fig. 1.29 Correct position of the oil spray jets in the cylinder head (Sec 40)

42.2 Guide rod positions when fitting the cylinder head

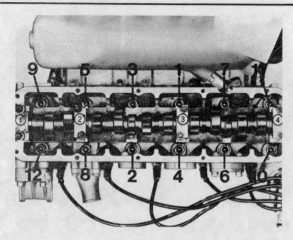

Fig. 1.30 Cylinder head bolt tightening sequence (Sec 42)

Fig. 1.31 Using a screwdriver to turn the water pump when tensioning the timing bolt (Sec 42)

torque while holding the gear stationary with a bar through one of the holes, or using a wide-bladed screwdriver as shown in Fig. 1.27.

7   Turn the camshaft gear and align the rear indentation with the upper surface of the valve cover gasket (temporarily locate the gasket on the head), or on 2.2 engines, the upper edge of the timing belt rear cover.

8   Check that No 1 piston is at TDC with the 'O' mark on the flywheel aligned with the pointer in the bellhousing aperture. The notch in the crankshaft pulley will also be in line with the pointer on the oil pump housing.

9   Locate the timing belt on the crankshaft, camshaft and water pump gears, turn the water pump anti-clockwise to pre-tension the belt, then check that the TDC timing marks are still aligned.

10 With the upper radiator cowl removed (if engine is in the car) use a screwdriver, as shown in Fig. 1.31, to turn the water pump anti-clockwise and tension the timing belt until it can just be twisted 90° with the thumb and index finger midway between the camshaft and water pump gears. Tighten the water pump mounting and adjustment bolts when the adjustment is correct.

11 Refit the timing belt cover(s) and tighten the nuts and bolts.

12 Refit the valve cover and reinforcement strips, together with the HT lead holder, new gaskets and seals, and tighten the nuts.

13 If the engine is in the car, reverse the preliminary procedures given in Section 37.

43 Camshaft and tappets – refitting

1   Fit the bucket tappets in their original positions – the adjustment shims on the top of the tappets must be fitted so that the lettering on

them is downwards. Lubricate the tappets and the camshaft journals.

2   Lay the camshaft into the lower half of its bearings so that the lowest point of the cams of No 1 cylinder are towards the tappets, then fit the bearing caps in their original positions, making sure that they are the right way round before fitting them over the studs.

3   Fit the nuts to bearing caps Nos 2 and 4 and tighten them in diagonal sequence until the camshaft fully enters its bearings.

4   Fit the nuts to bearing caps 1 and 3, then tighten all the nuts to the specified torque in diagonal sequence.

5   Smear a little oil onto the sealing lip and outer edge of the camshaft oil seal, then locate it open end first in the cylinder head and No 1 camshaft bearing cap.

6   Using a metal tube drive the seal squarely into the cylinder head until flush with the front of the cylinder head – *do not drive it in further otherwise it will block the oil return hole.*

7   Follow paragraph 5 to 11 inclusive of Section 42.

8   Check and, if necessary, adjust the valve clearances, as described in Section 44 with the engine cold.

9   Refit the valve cover and reinforcement strips, together with the HT lead holder, new gaskets and seals, and tighten the nuts.

10 If the engine is in the car, reverse the preliminary procedures given in Section 36.

44 Valve clearances – checking and adjustment

Refer to Part A, Section 16 of this Chapter. The procedure is identical to that for the four-cylinder engine with the following exceptions:

(a) It is not necessary to remove the timing cover
(b) From the timing belt end of the engine inlet valves are numbered 2-4-5-7-9, and exhaust valves 1-3-6-8-10

45 Timing belt and gears – removal and refitting

Note: *If the engine is still in the car, first carry out the following operations:*

(a) *Disconnect the battery negative lead*
(b) *Where fitted, remove the power steering pump bearing and the hoses connected (Chapter 11)*
(c) *Remove the alternator drivebelt (Chapter 10) and, if fitted, the air conditioning compressor drivebelt (Chapter 12)*
(d) *Remove the lower radiator grille*

1   Using Audi tool 2084 lock the vibration damper on the front of the crankshaft stationary, then using Audi tool 2079 loosen the centre bolt. The bolt is tightened to a high torque and it is recommended that these tools are used if at all possible. However, it may be possible to loosen the bolt while holding the starter ring gear stationary using a wide-bladed screwdriver or the method shown (photo).

45.1 One method of locking the starter ring gear

2 Follow paragraphs 2 to 7 inclusive of Section 36 (remove both timing covers on the 1.9 engine).

3 Unscrew the centre bolt and withdraw the vibration damper, together with the crankshaft gear and timing belt.

4 Separate the vibration damper from the crankshaft gear by removing the bolts using an Allen key, then reinserting two diagonally opposite bolts on a few threads and tapping them through the damper.

5 **Do not** *turn the crankshaft with the timing belt removed.*

6 If necessary, unbolt and remove the timing belt rear cover – note that the water pump pivot bolt must be removed and, on 1.9 engines, three of the oil pump bolts. Note the location of the spacers on 1.9 engines.

7 Commence refitting by locating the timing belt rear cover on the front of the cylinder head and block and tighten the retaining bolts and studs, as applicable. On the 1.9 engine refit the spacers. Leave the water pump pivot bolt loose.

8 Reassemble the vibration damper to the crankshaft gear, then insert and tighten the bolts.

9 Align the key on the crankshaft gear with the slot in the crankshaft, then locate the timing belt on the crankshaft gear and fit the gear to the crankshaft (photo). Take care not to trap the belt between the gear and the oil pump housing.

10 Coat the threads of the centre bolt with a liquid locking agent (photo), then insert the bolt and tighten it while holding the crankshaft

stationary – refer to the note in Section 33 paragraph 43.

11 Follow paragraphs 3 to 11 inclusive of Section 42.

12 If the engine is in the car, reverse the preliminary procedures at the beginning of this Section.

46 Flywheel/driveplate – removal and refitting

1 The procedure is as given in Part A, Section 18 of this Chapter. However the retaining bolts may not be offset so the flywheel/driveplate and crankshaft should be marked in relation to each other before separation (photo).

2 When refitting a driveplate note that the raised pip must face the torque converter. If a replacement driveplate is to be fitted, its position must be checked and adjusted if necessary. The distance from the rear face of the block to the torque converter *mounting face* on the driveplate (Fig. 1.33) must be between 17.2 and 18.8 mm (0.667 and 0.740 in). If necessary, remove the driveplate and fit a spacer behind it to achieve the correct dimension.

47 Sump – removal and refitting

Refer to Part A, Section 20 of this Chapter.

45.9 Fitting the crankshaft gear and vibration damper to the crankshaft – note the location key (arrowed) which is an integral part of the gear

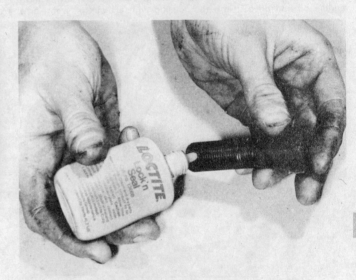

45.10 Applying liquid locking agent to the crankshaft centre bolt

46.1 Centre punch alignment marks (arrowed) on the crankshaft and flywheel

Fig. 1.32 Torque converter-to-cylinder block dimension checking faces – check in two places for average (Sec 46)

48 Crankshaft oil seals – renewal

Front oil seal

1   Remove the timing belt and crankshaft gear, as described in Section 45.
2   If an extractor tool is available the seal may be renewed without removing the oil pump, otherwise refer to Section 49. It is also recommended that Audi tool 2080 together with a guide sleeve be used to install the new seal. Dip the seal in engine oil before fitting, and if the old seal has scored the crankshaft, position the new seal on the unworn surface.
3   Refit the crankshaft gear and timing belt, as described in Section 45.

Rear oil seal

4   Remove the flywheel or driveplate, as described in Section 46.
5   If an extractor tool is available the seal may be renewed without removing the housing, otherwise unbolt and remove the housing (including the two sump bolts) and remove the gasket (photo). If the sump gasket is damaged while removing the housing it will be necessary to remove the sump and fit a new gasket. However, refit the sump *after* fitting the housing.
6   Drive the old seal out of the housing, then dip the new seal in engine oil and drive it into the housing with a block of wood or a socket, until flush. Make sure that the closed end of the seal is facing outwards.
7   Fit the housing together with a new gasket and tighten the bolts evenly in diagonal sequence.
8   Refit the flywheel or driveplate, as described in Section 46.

49 Oil pump – removal, examination and refitting

1   Remove the timing belt and crankshaft gear, as described in Section 45.
2   Remove the sump, with reference to Section 47.
3   Remove the dipstick.
4   Remove the two bolts securing the oil intake pipe stay to the crankcase (photo). Knock back the tabs of the lockplate on the intake pipe flange (photo), remove the bolts and the intake pipe.
5   Remove the bolts securing the oil pump (photo) and take off the oil pump and gasket (photo).
6   Remove the countersunk screws securing the pump backplate and lift the backplate off, exposing the gears (photo).
7   Check that there is a mark on the exposed face of the gears and if not, make a mark to show which side of the gears is towards the engine before removing them.
8   Unscrew the pressure relief valve and remove the plug, sealing ring, spring and plunger (photo).

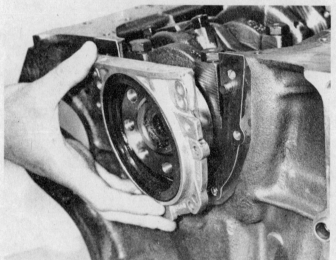

48.5 Removing the crankshaft rear oil seal and housing

49.4A Oil pump intake pipe

49.4B Oil pump intake pipe flange

49.5A Fitted oil pump

49.5B Removing the oil pump

49.6 Oil pump with backplate removed

49.8 Removing the oil pressure relief valve

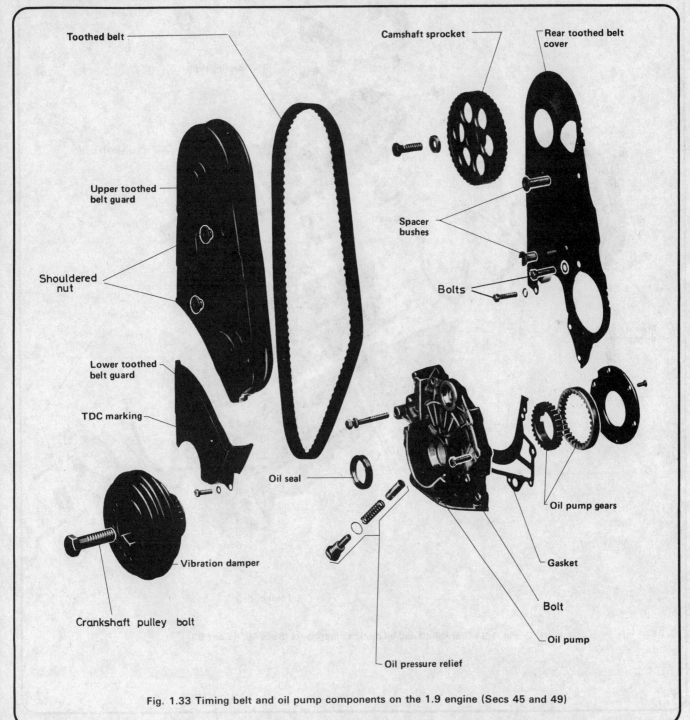

Fig. 1.33 Timing belt and oil pump components on the 1.9 engine (Secs 45 and 49)

1

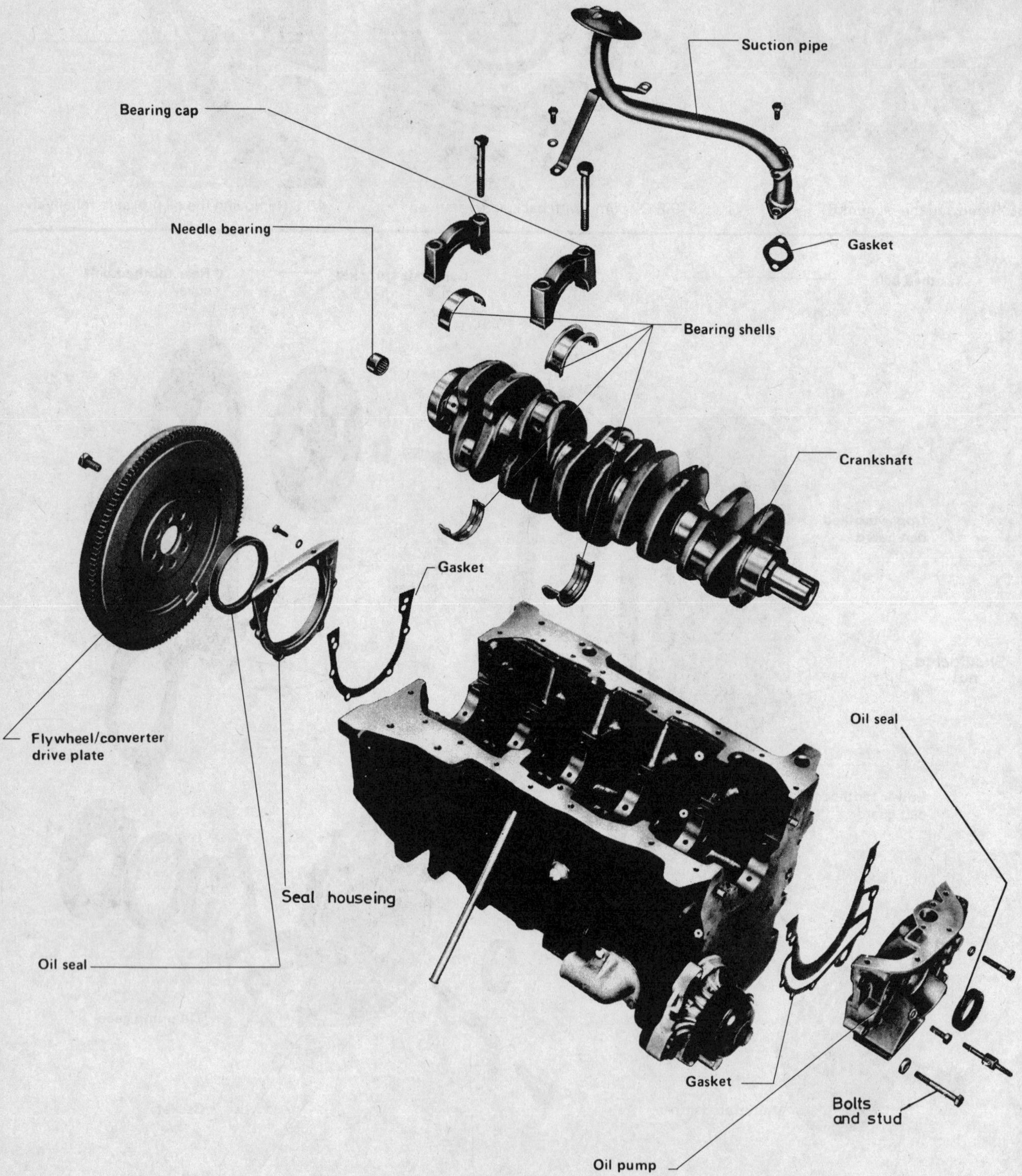

Suction pipe

Bearing cap

Needle bearing

Gasket

Bearing shells

Crankshaft

Gasket

Oil seal

Flywheel/converter
drive plate

Seal houseing

Oil seal

Gasket

Bolts
and stud

Oil pump

Fig. 1.34 Crankshaft and oil pump components (Secs 48, 49 and 53)

9   Clean all the parts thoroughly and examine the pump casing and backplate for signs of wear or scoring. Examine the pressure relief valve plunger and its seating for damage and wear and check that the spring is not damaged or distorted. Check the gears for damage and wear. New gears may be fitted, but they must be fitted as a pair.
10   Prise out the oil seal from the front of the pump. Oil the lip of the new seal, enter the seal with its closed face outwards and use a block of wood to tap the seal in flush. If there is any scoring on the crankshaft in the area on which the lip of the seal bears, the seal may be pushed to the bottom of its recess so that the lip bears on an undamaged part of the crankshaft.
11   Reassemble the pump by fitting the gears and the backplate. The inner gear has its slotted end towards the crankshaft and although the outer gear can be fitted either way round, it should be fitted the same way round as it was before removal. Some gears have a triangle stamped on them and this mark should be towards the front.
12   Refit the oil pump, together with a new gasket, making sure that the slot on the inner gear engages the dog on the crankshaft.
13   Insert the bolts and tighten them in diagonal sequence to the specified torque.
14   Fit the oil intake pipe, together with a new gasket, tighten the bolts, and bend the lockplate tabs onto the flange bolts.
15   Refit the dipstick, sump (Section 47), and timing belt and crankshaft gear (Section 45).

53.3A Removing No 4 main bearing cap

50 Pistons and connecting rods – removal and dismantling

Refer to Part A, Section 23 of this Chapter. Removal of the cylinder head is described in Section 37, and the timing belt in Section 45. Instead of removing the oil pump, remove the sump, as described in Section 47, then unbolt the oil intake pipe, as described in Section 49.

51 Pistons and cylinder bores – examination

Refer to Part A, Section 24 of this Chapter.

52 Pistons and connecting rods – reassembly and refitting

Refer to Part A, Section 25 of this Chapter. With the pistons fitted, refit the oil intake pipe, together with a new gasket, tighten the bolts, and bend the lockplate tabs onto the flange bolts. Refitting of the sump is described in Section 47, the timing belt in Section 45, and the cylinder head in Section 42.

53.3B Removing the crankshaft

53 Crankshaft – removal, examination and refitting

1   With the engine removed from the car, remove the pistons and connecting rods, as described in Section 50. Keep the big-end bearings with their matching connecting rods to ensure correct refitting.
2   Remove the oil pump (Section 49) and rear oil seal complete with housing (Section 48).
3   Follow the procedure in Part A, Section 26, of this Chapter, paragraphs 4 to 13 inclusive (photos) but note the following exceptions:

   (a)   *The flanged main bearing shells are fitted to main bearing No 4 (from the front of the engine)*
   (b)   *The needle roller bearing in the rear of the crankshaft must be pressed in to a depth of 5.5 mm (0.217 in) below the face of the flange*

4   Fit the oil pump and rear oil seal housing complete with new seals, as described in Sections 49 and 48 respectively.
5   Refit the pistons and connecting rods, as described in Section 52.

54 Oil filter – removal and refitting

1   Place a suitable container beneath the right-hand side of the engine.
2   Unscrew the filter cartridge and discard it – it will be necessary to use a filter strap, although if this is not available drive a long screwdriver through the cartridge.
3   Clean the mating faces of the new oil filter and block, and smear a little engine oil on the filter seal.
4   Screw on the cartridge and seal, and tighten it by hand only.

55 Engine mountings – removal and refitting

Refer to Part A, Section 28 of this Chapter. When refitting the mountings, check the engine alignment as described in Section 33.

Part C

56 Fault diagnosis – engine

Symptom   Reason(s)

Engine fails to start

Discharged battery
Loose battery connection
Loose or broken ignition leads
Moisture on spark plugs, distributor cap, or HT leads
Incorrect spark plug or contact points gap (as applicable)
Cracked distributor cap or rotor
Dirt or water in carburettor (as applicable)
Empty fuel tank
Faulty fuel pump
Faulty starter motor
Low cylinder compression

Engine idles erratically

Intake manifold air leak
Leaking cylinder head gasket
Worn camshaft lobes
Faulty fuel pump
Incorrect valve clearances
Loose crankcase ventilation hoses
Idling adjustments incorrect
Uneven cylinder compressions

Engine misfires

Spark plugs or contact points gap incorrect (as applicable)
Faulty coil, condenser or transistorised ignition component (as applicable)
Dirt or water in carburettor (as applicable)
Burnt out valve
Leaking cylinder head gasket
Distributor cap cracked
Incorrect valve clearances
Uneven cylinder compressions
Idling adjustments incorrect

Engine stalls

Idling adjustments incorrect
Intake manifold air leak
Ignition timing incorrect

Excessive oil consumption

Worn pistons and cylinder bores
Valve guides and valve stem seals worn
Oil leaking from crankshaft oil seals, valve cover gasket etc

Engine backfires

Idling adjustments incorrect
Ignition timing incorrect
Incorrect valve clearances
Intake manifold air leak
Sticking valve

Engine lacks power

Incorrect ignition timing
Incorrect spark plug or contact points gap (as applicable)
Low cylinder compression
Excessive carbon build up in engine
Air filter choked

Chapter 2 Cooling system

Contents

Specifications

System type ....

Pressurized radiator and expansion tank (integral on some models), belt driven water pump, thermostatically controlled electric cooling fan

Filler cap opening pressure ....

17 to 19 lbf/in^2 (1.2 to 1.35 bar)

Thermostat

Starts to open:
Four-cylinder (carburettor)	85°C (185°F)
Four-cylinder (fuel injection)	90°C (194°F)
Five-cylinder	87°C (188°F)

Fully open:
Four-cylinder (carburettor)	105°C (221°F)
All engines except four-cylinder carburettor	102°C (216°F)

Stroke (minimum):
Four-cylinder	7.0 mm (0.276 in)
Five-cylinder	8.0 mm (0.315 in)

Electric cooling fan thermo-switch operating temperatures

Switches on:
All engines except 2.2 litre	93° to 98°C (199° to 208°F)
2.2 litre engine	90° to 95°C (194° to 203°F)

Switches off:
All engines except 2.2 litre	88° to 93°C (190° to 199°F)
2.2 litre engine	85° to 90°C (185° to 194°F)

Antifreeze

Type .... Ethylene glycol, with corrosion inhibitor

Concentration for protection down to: **Percent antifreeze by volume**
–25°C (–14°F)	40
–30°C (–22°F)	45
–35°C (–31°F)	50

System capacity (including heater)

1.6 and 1.7 litre engine without air conditioning	6.2 litre; 10.9 Imp pt; 6.6 US qt
1.6 and 1.7 litre engine with air conditioning	7.0 litre; 12.3 Imp pt; 7.4 US qt
1.9 and 2.2 litre engine	8.0 litre; 14.1 Imp pt; 8.5 US qt

2

Torque wrench settings

	lbf ft	Nm
Radiator mountings (except five-cyl centre)	7	10
Radiator mounting (five-cyl centre)	14	20
Electric cooling fan mounting	7	10
Thermo-switch	18	25
Temperature sender unit	7	10
Water pump to block	14	20
Water pump to housing (four-cyl)	7	10
Water pump pulley (four-cyl)	14	20
Thermostat cover (four-cyl)	14	20
Thermostat cover (five-cyl)	7	10
Cylinder head rear outlet (four-cyl)	7	10

1 General description

The cooling system is of pressurized type and includes a front (four-cylinder) or side (five-cylinder) mounted radiator, a water pump driven by an external V-belt on four-cylinder engines or by the timing belt on five-cylinder engines, and an electric cooling fan. On models with air conditioning a condenser is fitted in front of the radiator. A remote expansion tank is fitted to all models, except the 1.6 litre carburettor version without air conditioning, where the expansion tank is incorporated within the radiator. The cooling system thermostat is located in the water pump housing on four-cylinder models, and in the inlet on the left-hand side of the cylinder block on five-cylinder models.

The system functions as follows. With the engine cold, the thermostat is shut and the water pump forces the water through the internal passages then via the bypass hose (and heater circuit if turned on) over the thermostat capsule and to the water pump inlet again. This circulation of water cools the cylinder bores, combustion surfaces and valve seats. However, when the coolant reaches the predetermined temperature, the thermostat begins to open. The coolant now circulates through the top hose to the top of the radiator. As it passes through the radiator matrix it is cooled by the inrush of air when the car is in forward motion, supplemented by the action of the electric cooling fan when necessary. Finally the coolant is returned to the water pump via the bottom hose and through the open thermostat.

The electric cooling fan is controlled by a thermo-switch located in the bottom of the radiator. Water temperature is monitored by a sender unit in the cylinder head.

Note: *the electric cooling fan will operate when the temperature of the coolant in the radiator reaches the predetermined level even if the ignition is switched off. Therefore extreme caution should be exercised when working in the vicinity of the fan blades.*

2 Cooling system – draining

1   It is preferable to drain the cooling system when the engine is

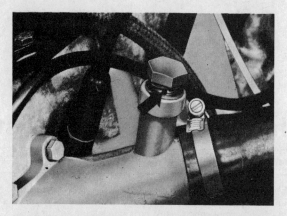

Fig. 2.1 Cooling system vent screw on the four-cylinder carburettor engine, showing the vent hole (arrowed) (Sec 2)

cold. If this is not possible, place a cloth over the filler cap and turn it slowly in an anti-clockwise direction until the pressure starts to escape – leave it in this position until all pressure has dissipated.

2   Remove the filler cap (photo).

3   Set the heater controls on the facia to WARM.

4   Place a suitable container beneath the water pump and radiator.

5   Where the radiator incorporates a drain plug (photo), unscrew it and drain the coolant, otherwise follow the procedure in paragraphs 6 or 7.

6   On four-cylinder engines loosen the clips and disconnect the bottom hose and heater/inlet manifold return hoses from the water pump housing. Drain the coolant into the container.

7   On five-cylinder engines unscrew the bolt retaining the heater return pipe to the cylinder block, then loosen the clip and pull the pipe

2.2 Cooling system expansion tank and filler cap

2.5 Drain plug incorporated into the radiator

from the hose. Also loosen the clip and disconnect the expansion tank hose from the bottom of the radiator. Drain the coolant into the container.

8   On four-cylinder engines loosen the vent screw (carburettor engines) or thermo-time switch (fuel injection engines) located on the cylinder head outlet housing.

3   Cooling system – flushing

1   After some time the radiator and engine waterways may become restricted or even blocked with scale or sediment. When this occurs the coolant will appear rusty and dark in colour and the system should then be flushed. In severe cases, reverse flushing may also be required.
2   Drain the cooling system, as described in Section 2.
3   Disconnect the top hose from the radiator, insert a hose in the radiator and allow water to circulate through the matrix and out of the bottom of the radiator until it runs clear.
4   Insert the hose in the expansion tank (where fitted) and allow the water to run through the supply hose.
5   In severe cases of contamination remove the radiator, invert it, and flush it with water until it runs clear.
6   To flush the engine and heater, insert a hose in the top hose and allow the water to circulate through the system until it runs clear from the return hose.
7   The use of chemical cleaners should only be necessary as a last resort, and the regular renewal of antifreeze should prevent the contamination of the system.

4   Cooling system – filling

1   Reconnect all hoses and check that the heater controls are set to WARM. Refit the radiator plug, if applicable.
2   Pour coolant into the radiator or expansion tank until full.
3   On four-cylinder engines tighten the vent screw (carburettor engines) or thermo-time switch (fuel injection engines) when the emerging water is free of air bubbles (photo), then top up the system until full.
4   Screw on the filler cap and run the engine at a fast idling speed for a few minutes.
5   Stop the engine and check the coolant level. Top up if necessary, and refit the filler cap.
6   Run the engine to normal operating temperature then allow it to cool. On models with an expansion tank the coolant level must reach the tip of the arrow with the engine cold or be a little higher when the engine is warm. On models without an expansion tank, remove the radiator cap with the engine cold and check that the coolant reaches the upper level mark; top up if necessary, and refit the cap.

4.3 Purging air from the cooling system by loosening the thermo-time switch (fuel injection engines)

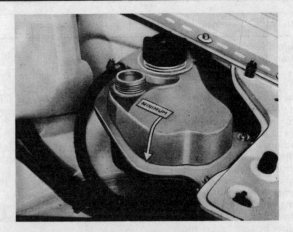

Fig. 2.2 Expansion tank showing the minimum coolant level (Sec 4)

Fig. 2.3 Maximum coolant level mark on the radiator for models without an expansion tank (Sec 4)

2

5   Antifreeze mixture

1   The cooling system is filled at the factory with an antifreeze mixture which contains a corrosion inhibitor. The antifreeze mixture prevents freezing, raises the boiling point of the coolant and so delays the tendency of the coolant to boil, while the corrosion inhibitor reduces corrosion and the formation of scale. For these reasons the cooling system should be filled with antifreeze all the year round.
2   Any good quality antifreeze is suitable, if it is of the ethylene glycol type and also contains a corrosion inhibitor. Do not use an antifreeze preparation based on methanol, because these mixtures have a shorter life and methanol has the disadvantage of being inflammable and evaporates quickly.
3   The concentration of antifreeze should be adjusted to give the required level of protection selected from the table given in the Specifications.
4   When topping-up the cooling system always use the same mixture of water and antifreeze which the system contains. Topping-up using water only will gradually reduce the antifreeze concentration and lower the level of protection against both freezing and boiling.
5   At the beginning of the winter season, check the coolant for antifreeze concentration and add pure antifreeze if necessary.
6   Antifreeze mixture should not be left in the system for longer than its manufacturers' recommendation, which does not usually exceed three years. At the end of this time drain the system and refill with fresh mixture.

6 Radiator – removal, inspection, cleaning and refitting

1   Disconnect the battery negative lead.
2   Drain the cooling system, as described in Section 2.

Four-cylinder engines

3   On models equipped with air conditioning, remove the front grille with reference to Chapter 12, then detach the condenser from the radiator by removing the screws.
4   On all models loosen the clips and disconnect the top and bottom hoses from the radiator (photo).
5   Where fitted, disconnect the expansion tank vent pipe and supply hose from the radiator.
6   Disconnect the wiring from the electric cooling fan and the thermo-switch (photo).
7   Unscrew and remove the mounting nuts and washers (photos).
8   Move the top of the radiator to the rear, then unscrew and remove the upper bonded rubber mountings.
9   Lift the radiator from the lower mountings then move it to one side and lift it from the engine compartment, complete with the electric cooling fan and cowling (photo).
10 If necessary, unbolt the cooling fan and cowling from the radiator, then unscrew the nuts and separate the fan and motor from the cowling.

6.4 Top and bottom hose connections on the radiator

6.6 Electric cooling fan thermo-switch location in the radiator (four-cylinder engine)

6.7A A radiator upper mounting (four-cylinder engine)

6.7B A radiator lower mounting (four-cylinder engine)

6.9 Removing the radiator (four-cylinder engine)

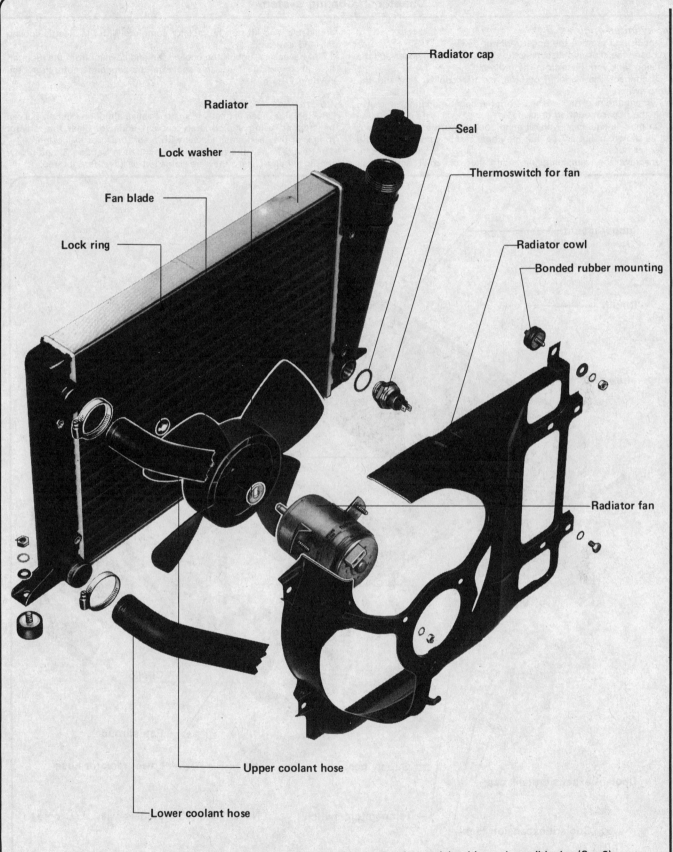

Fig. 2.4 Radiator and cooling fan components on 1.6 carburettor engine models without air conditioning (Sec 6)

2

Five-cylinder engines

11 Unbolt and remove the upper radiator cowl.

12 Loosen the clips and disconnect the top and bottom hoses and the expansion tank vent hose from the radiator.

13 Disconnect the wiring from the electric cooling fan and the thermo-switch.

14 Remove the nuts and washers from the upper mountings and also unbolt the upper mounting bracket.

15 On models equipped with air conditioning, cut the lower radiator cowl as shown in Fig. 2.7 so that the panel can be threaded over the condenser hose.

16 Unscrew the remaining mounting nut or cowl screws, as applicable, and lift out the radiator complete with the electric cooling fan and cowling.

17 If necessary, unbolt the cooling fan and cowling from the radiator, then unscrew the nuts and separate the fan and motor from the cowling.

All models

18 Radiator repair is best left to a specialist, although minor leaks can be stopped using a proprietary coolant additive. Clear the radiator matrix of flies and small leaves with a soft brush or by hosing.

19 Reverse flush the radiator, as described in Section 3, and renew the hoses and clips if they are damaged or have deteriorated.

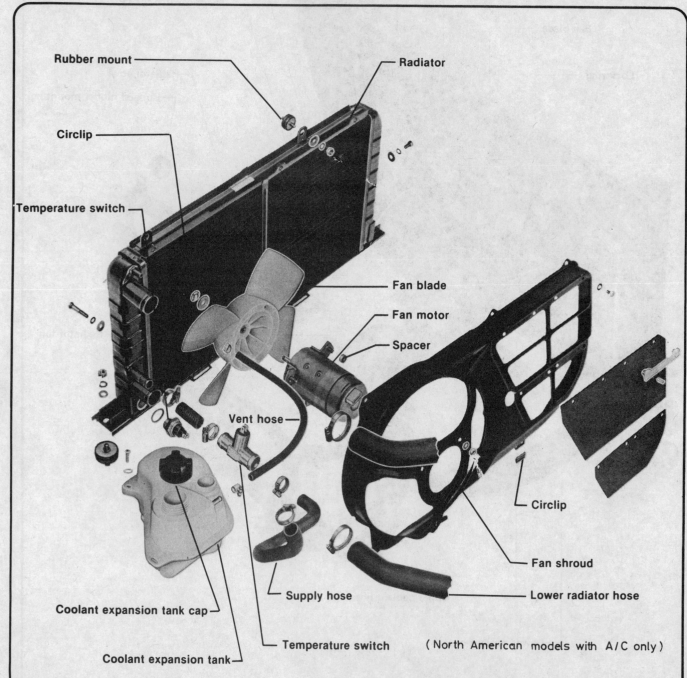

Rubber mount

Radiator

Circlip

Temperature switch

Fan blade

Fan motor

Spacer

Vent hose

Circlip

Fan shroud

Supply hose

Lower radiator hose

Coolant expansion tank cap

Temperature switch

(North American models with A/C only)

Coolant expansion tank

Fig. 2.5 Radiator and cooling fan components on four-cylinder models, except 1.6 carburettor engine models without air conditioning (Sec 6)

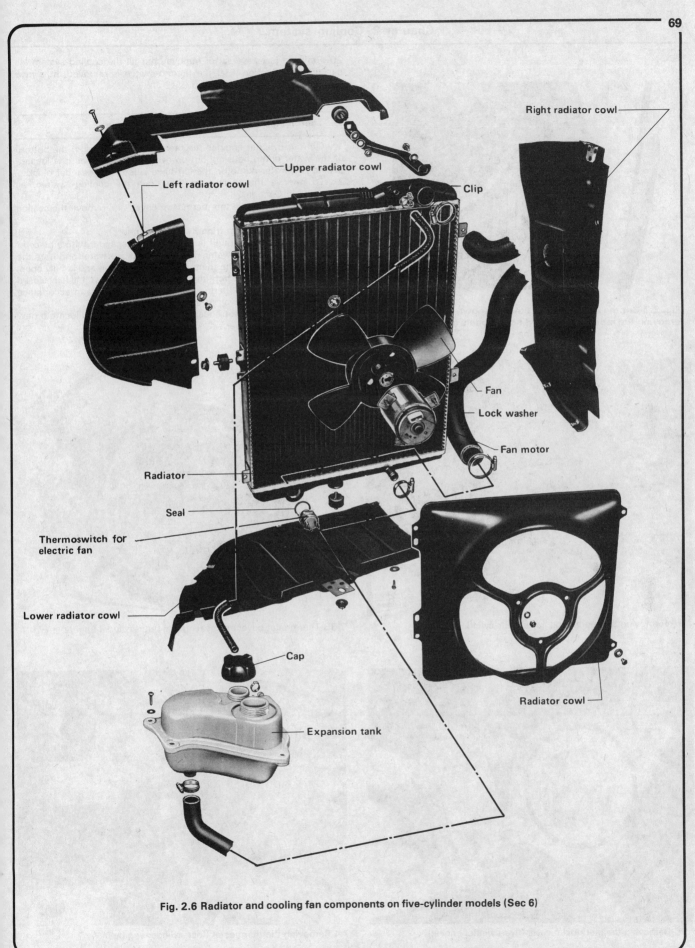

Fig. 2.6 Radiator and cooling fan components on five-cylinder models (Sec 6)

2

Fig. 2.7 Cut the lower radiator cowl as shown (arrowed) when removing the radiator on five-cylinder models equipped with air conditioning (Sec 6)

20   Refitting is a reversal of removal, but fill the cooling system, as described in Section 4. If the thermo-switch is removed, fit a new sealing washer when refitting it.

7   Thermostat – removal, testing and refitting

1   On four-cylinder engines the thermostat is located in the bottom of the water pump housing, but on five-cylinder engines it is located behind the water pump on the left-hand side of the cylinder block.
2   To remove the thermostat first drain the cooling system, as described in Section 2.
3   Unbolt and remove the thermostat cover, and remove the sealing ring (photos).
4   Prise the thermostat from its housing (photo).
5   To test whether the unit is serviceable, suspend it with a piece of string in a container of water. Gradually heat the water and note the temperatures at which the thermostat starts to open and is fully open. Remove the thermostat from the water and check that it is fully closed when cold. Renew the thermostat if it fails to operate in accordance with the information given in the Specifications.
6   Clean the thermostat housing and cover faces, and locate a new sealing ring on the cover.

7.3A Removing the thermostat cover (four-cylinder engine)

7.3B Thermostat cover and sealing ring (four-cylinder engine)

7.3C Removing the thermostat cover (five-cylinder engine)

7.4 Removing the thermostat (four-cylinder engine)

Fig. 2.8 Correct fitted position of the thermostat on five-cylinder engines (Sec 7)

7   Locate the thermostat in the housing — on four-cylinder engines the arrow on the crosspiece must point away from the engine, but on five-cylinder engines the arrow must point downwards.
8   Fit the thermostat cover and tighten the bolts evenly.
9   Fill the cooling system, as described in Section 4.

8   Water pump – removal and refitting

1   Drain the cooling system, as described in Section 2.

Four-cylinder engines
2   Remove the alternator and drivebelt, as described in Chapter 10.
3   Unbolt the pulley from the water pump drive flange.

4   Loosen the clips and disconnect the hoses from the rear of the water pump housing (photo).
5   Unscrew the nut and remove the special bolt retaining the lower timing cover to the water pump assembly.
6   Unbolt the water pump assembly from the cylinder block and remove the sealing ring (photos).
7   Unscrew the bolts and remove the water pump from its housing using a mallet to break the seal. Remove the gasket.

Five-cylinder engines
8   On models equipped with power steering, remove the pump leaving the hoses connected and place it to one side, with reference to Chapter 11.
9   Using an Allen key where necessary, unscrew the nuts and withdraw the timing cover.
10 Set the engine on TDC compression No 1 cylinder, and unbolt the timing belt rear cover, with reference to Chapter 1.
11 Loosen the water pump mounting and adjustment bolts, again using an Allen key where necessary, and rotate the pump to release the tension on the timing belt.
12 Unscrew and remove the bolts noting the location of the stay, where applicable (photo).
13 Withdraw the water pump from the cylinder block and remove the sealing ring (photo). *Do not move the crankshaft or camshaft with the timing belt slack.*

All models
14 If the water pump is faulty, renew it, as individual components are not available. Clean the mating faces of the water pump, cylinder block, and pump housing (four-cylinder engines).
15 Refitting is a reversal of removal, but use a new sealing ring and gasket as applicable. On five-cylinder engines remove the upper radiator cowl and tension the timing belt, as described in Chapter 1. At the same time check that the crankshaft and camshaft are still on TDC No 1 cylinder. Fill the cooling system, as described in Section 4. Tension the alternator/power-assisted steering pump/air conditioning compressor drivebelts, as applicable, with reference to Chapters 10, 11 and 12 respectively.

2

8.4 Hose connections to the rear of the water pump housing (four-cylinder engine)

8.6A Removing the water pump assembly (four-cylinder engine)

8.6B Water pump housing sealing ring (four-cylinder engine)

8.12 Water pump and mounting bolts (five-cylinder engine)

8.13 Removing the water pump (five-cylinder engine)

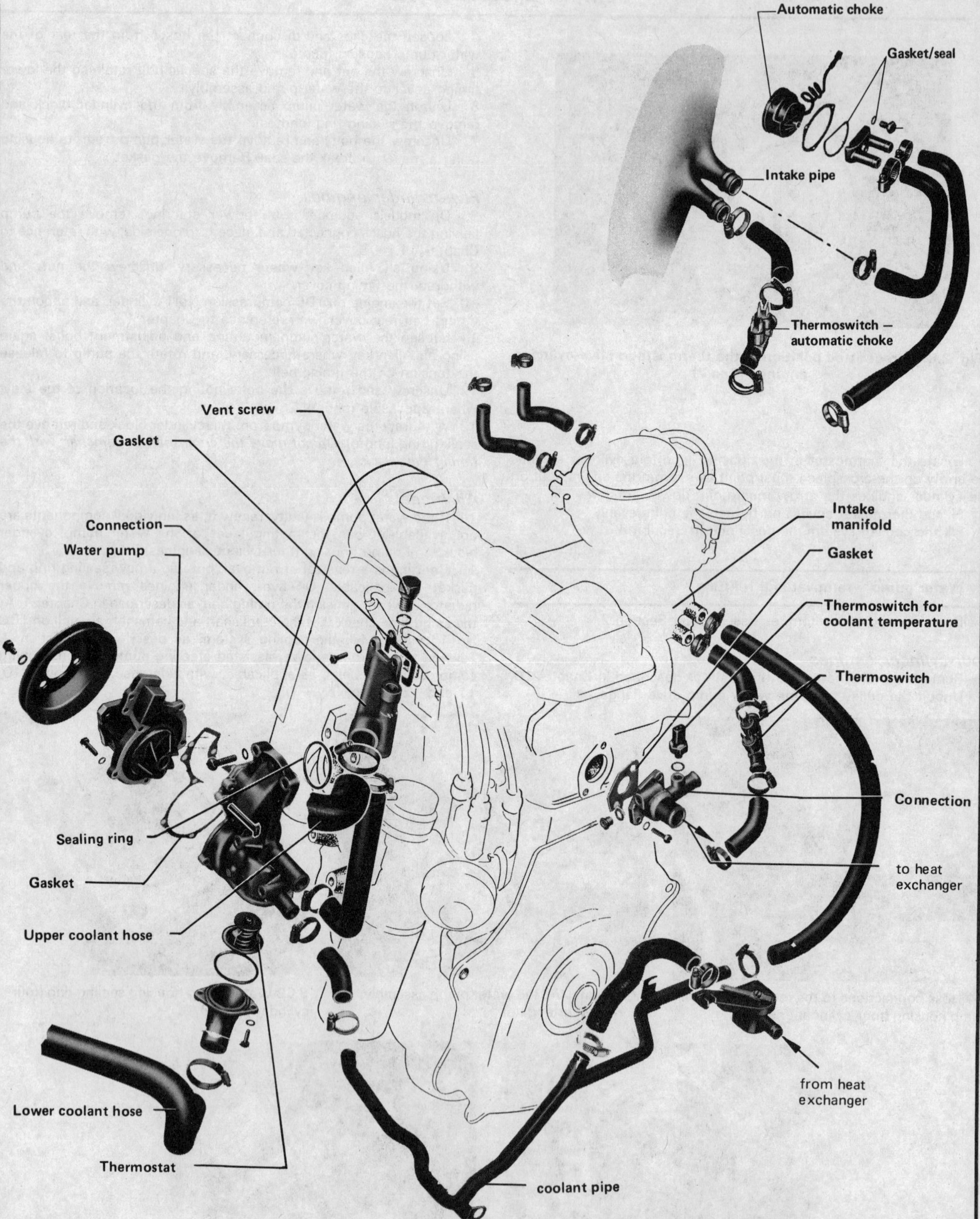

Automatic choke

Gasket/seal

Intake pipe

Thermoswitch —
automatic choke

Vent screw

Gasket

Connection

Water pump

Intake
manifold

Gasket

Thermoswitch for
coolant temperature

Thermoswitch

Connection

Sealing ring

Gasket

to heat
exchanger

Upper coolant hose

Lower coolant hose

Thermostat

from heat
exchanger

coolant pipe

Fig. 2.9 Water pump and cooling system hoses on 1.6 litre carburettor engines (Sec 8)

Inset applicable to early models

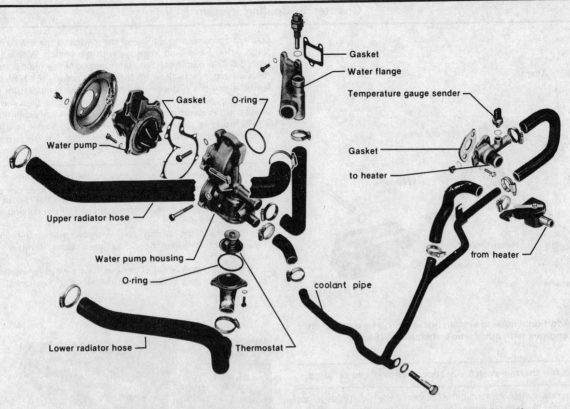

Fig. 2.10 Water pump and cooling system hoses on 1.6 and 1.7 litre fuel injection engines (Sec 8)

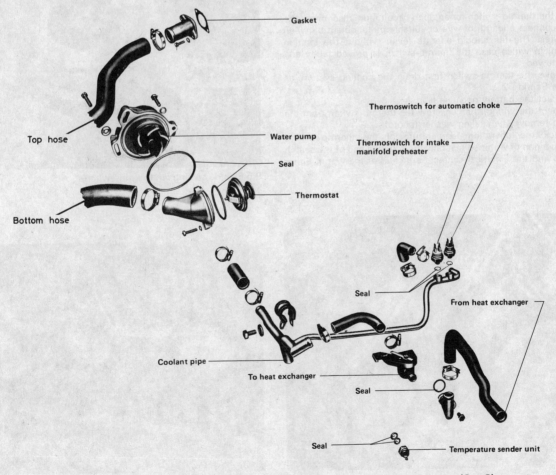

Fig. 2.11 Water pump and cooling system hoses on 1.9 litre carburettor engines (Sec 8)

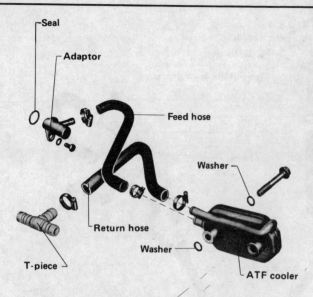

Fig. 2.12 Additional cooling system hoses for 1.9 litre carburettor engines with automatic transmission (Sec 8)

9 Cooling fan thermo-switch – testing, removal and refitting

1   If the thermo-switch located in the bottom of the radiator develops a fault, it is most likely to fail open circuit. This will cause the fan motor to remain stationary even though the coolant reaches the operating temperature.

2   To test the thermo-switch for an open circuit fault, disconnect the wiring and connect a length of wire or suitable metal object between the two wires. The fan should operate (even without the ignition switched on) in which case the thermo-switch is proved faulty and must be renewed.

3   To remove the thermo-switch first drain the cooling system, as described in Section 2.

4   Disconnect the battery negative lead.

5   Disconnect the wiring, then unscrew the thermo-switch from the radiator and remove the sealing washer (photo).

6   To check the operating temperature of the thermo-switch, suspend it in a pan of water so that only the screwed end of the switch is immersed and the electrical contacts are clear of the water. Either

connect an ohmmeter between the switch terminals, or connect up a torch battery and bulb in series with the switch. With a thermometer placed in the pan, heat the water and note the temperature at which the switch contacts close, so that the ohmmeter reads zero, or the bulb lights. Allow the water to cool and note the temperature at which the switch contacts open. Discard the switch and fit a new one if the operating temperatures are not within the specified limits.

7   Refitting is a reversal of removal, but always fit a new sealing washer. Fill the cooling system, as described in Section 4.

10 Coolant temperature sender unit – removal and refitting

1   The temperature sender unit is located on the rear of the cylinder head (photo). To remove it, first drain half of the cooling system, with reference to Section 2.

2   Disconnect the wiring and unscrew the sender unit from the connector or cylinder head, as applicable. Remove the sealing washer(s).

3   Refitting is a reversal of removal, but always renew the washer(s). Top up the cooling system, with reference to Section 4.

9.5 Electric cooling fan thermo-switch

10.1 Coolant temperature sender unit location (arrowed) on the rear of the cylinder head (four-cylinder engine)

11.1 Showing core plugs in the cylinder block (four-cylinder engine)

11 Fault diagnosis – cooling system

Symptom	Reason(s)
Overheating	Low coolant level
	Faulty pressure cap
	Thermostat sticking shut
	Drivebelt broken (four-cyl)
	Open circuit thermo-switch
	Faulty cooling fan motor
	Clogged radiator matrix
	Retarded ignition timing
Slow warm-up	Thermostat sticking open
	Short circuit thermo-switch
Coolant loss	Deteriorated hose
	Leaking water pump or cooling system joints
	Blown cylinder head gasket
	Leaking radiator
	Leaking core plugs (photo)

Chapter 3
Fuel, exhaust and emission control systems

Refer to Chapter 13 for information applicable to 1984 through 1987 models

Contents

Specifications

Air cleaner type .... Renewable paper element; automatic air temperature control on some models

Fuel pump
Type:
  Carburettor engine .... Mechanical, diaphragm, operated by eccentric on intermediate shaft
  Fuel injection engine .... Electrically operated roller cell
Operating pressure:
  1.6 Carburettor engine .... 0.2 to 0.25 bar (2.9 to 3.6 lbf/in²)
  1.9 Carburettor engine .... 0.35 to 0.40 bar (5.1 to 5.8 lbf/in²)
  Fuel injection engine .... 4.5 to 5.4 bar (65 to 78 lbf/in²)

Carburettor 1.6 litre – 35 PDSIT

Type .... Single choke downdraught, automatic choke

Jets and settings:	Manual gearbox	Automatic transmission
Venturi	27 mm	27 mm
Main jet	x140	x140
Air correction jet with emulsion tube	110	110
Idle fuel jet	55	55
Idle air jet	150	150
Auxiliary air jet	1.04	1.04
Auxiliary fuel jet	50	50
Enrichment jet with cone	90	90
Injection capacity	0.85 to 1.15 cc/stroke	0.35 to 0.65 cc/stroke
Float needle valve	1.5	1.5
Float needle valve washer	1.0 mm	1.0 mm
Throttle valve gap	0.75 to 0.85 mm	0.85 to 0.95 mm
Choke valve gap	4.25 to 4.55 mm	3.85 to 4.15 mm
Idle speed	900 to 1000 rpm	900 to 1000 rpm
CO content	1 to 2%	1 to 2%

Carburettor 1.6 litre – 1 B3

Type: Single choke downdraught, automatic choke

Jets and settings	Manual gearbox	Automatic transmission
Venturi	26 mm	26 mm
Main jet	x125	x122.5
Air correction jet with emulsion tube	100	100
Idle fuel/air jet	50/130	50/130
Auxiliary fuel/air jet	37.5/130	37.5/130
Float needle valve	2.0	2.0
Float setting	27.5 to 28.5 mm	27.5 to 28.5 mm
Enrichment valve	to April 1980 – 110 / from May 1980 – 95	110
Pump injection tube	0.40	0.55
Injection capacity	0.75 to 1.05 cc/stroke	0.75 to 1.05 cc/stroke
Choke valve gap	4.15 to 4.45 mm	4.15 to 4.45 mm
Fast idle speed	3700 to 4100 rpm	3500 to 3900 rpm
Idle speed	900 to 1000 rpm	900 to 1000 rpm
CO content	0.5 to 1.5%	0.5 to 1.5%

Carburettor 1.6 litre – 2B2 and 2B5

Type: Twin progressive choke downdraught, automatic choke

Jets and settings	Manual gearbox		Automatic transmission	
	Stage 1	Stage 2	Stage 1	Stage 2
Venturi	24 mm	28 mm	24 mm	28 mm
Main jet	x117.5	x125	x117.5	x125
Air correction jet with emulsion tube	135	92.5	135	92.5
Idle fuel/air jet	52.5/135	40/125	52.5/135	40/125
Auxiliary fuel/air jet	42.5/130	–	42.5/130	–
Idle air jet for progression reserve	–	180	–	180
Idle fuel jet for progression reserve	–	130	–	100
Float needle valve	2.0	2.0	2.0	2.0
Float setting	27.0 to 29.0 mm	29.0 to 31.0 mm	27.0 to 29.0 mm	29.0 to 31.0 mm
Enrichment valve	65	–	65	–
Pump injection tube (vertical/horizontal)	0.4/0.4 mm	–	0.4/0.4 mm	–
Injection capacity	0.85 to 1.15 cc/stroke	–	0.75 to 1.05 cc/stroke	–
Choke valve gap: 2B2	3.00 to 3.30 mm	–	4.15 to 4.45 mm	–
Choke valve gap: 2B5	3.75 to 4.05 mm	–	3.55 to 3.85 mm	–
Fast idle speed	3350 to 3450 rpm		3550 to 3650 rpm	
Idle speed	900 to 1000 rpm		900 to 1000 rpm	
CO content	0.5 to 1.0%		0.5 to 1.0%	

Carburettor 1.9 litre – 2B5

Type: Twin progressive choke downdraught, automatic choke

Jets and settings	Manual gearbox		Automatic transmission	
	Stage 1	Stage 2	Stage 1	Stage 2
Venturi	24 mm	28 mm	24 mm	28 mm
Main jet	x115	x122.5	x115	x122.5
Air correction jet with emulsion tube	135	115	135	115
Idle fuel/air jet	42.5/125	40/125	42.5/125	40/125
Auxiliary fuel/air jet	45/125	–	45/125	–
Idle air jet for progression reserve	–	205	–	205
Idle fuel jet for progression reserve	–	95	–	95
Float needle valve	2.0	2.0	2.0	2.0
Float setting	27.0 to 29.0 mm	29.0 to 31.0 mm	27.0 to 29.0 mm	29.0 to 31.0 mm
Enrichment valve	100	–	100	–
Pump injection tube (vertical/horizontal)	0.4/0.55 mm	–	0.4/0.55 mm	–
Injection capacity	1.35 to 1.65 cc/stroke	–	1.35 to 1.65 cc/stroke	–
Choke valve gap	3.45 to 3.75 mm	–	3.25 to 3.55 mm	–
Fast idle speed	3500 to 3700 rpm		3600 to 3800 rpm	
Idle speed	750 to 800 rpm		750 to 800 rpm	
CO content	0.8 to 1.2%		0.8 to 1.2%	

Continuous fuel injection system (CIS)

System pressure:
UK models	4.5 to 5.2 bar (65 to 75 lbf/in^2)
North American models	4.7 to 5.4 bar (68 to 78 lbf/in^2)

Warm-up regulator heater coil resistance .... 16 to 22 ohm
Idle speed:
    UK models ....
    North American models (excluding California) ....
    Californian models ....

900 to 1000 rpm
850 to 1000 rpm
880 to 1000 rpm

CO content:
    UK models ....
    1980 North American models (excluding California) ....
    1980 Californian models ....
    1981/1982 North American models ....

1.0 to 2.0%
0.9% maximum
0.4 to 1.2%
0.3 to 1.2%

Fuel tank capacity
UK models .... 68.0 litre; 15.0 Imp gal; 71.9 US qt
North American models .... 60.0 litre; 13.2 Imp gal; 63.4 US qt

Torque wrench settings

	lbf ft	Nm
Fuel tank mounting	18	25
Fuel pump (carburettor engines)	15	20
Non-return valve (carburettor engines)	15	20
Carburettor	7	10
Inlet manifold	18	25
35 PDSIT carburettor:		
Cover	4	5
Automatic choke centre bolt	7	10
Accelerator pump	4	5
Throttle valve housing	7	10
Cut-off valve solenoid	4	5
Air cleaner	7	10
1B3 carburettor:		
Manifold preheater	7	10
Cover	4	5
Automatic choke centre bolt	7	10
Cut-off valve solenoid	4	5
Air cleaner	7	10
2B carburettor:		
Manifold preheater	7	10
Cover	4	5
Automatic choke centre bolt	7	10
Throttle valve housing	7	10
Cut-off valve solenoid	4	5
Air cleaner	7	10
CIS system:		
Fuel line to metering unit	7	10
Non-return valve to filter	29	40
Fuel line to pump	14	20
Fuel pump	7	10
Metering unit	25	35
Fuel line to injector	18	25
Air flow meter	3	4
Thermo-time switch	22	30
Cold start valve	7	10
Warm-up regulator	14	20
Throttle valve housing	14	20
Exhaust manifold to head	18	25
Downpipe to manifold	22	30
Exhaust system joints	18	25

1 General description

The fuel system comprises a fuel tank mounted behind the rear seat, and either a mechanical fuel pump and downdraught carburettor, or a Bosch K-Jetronic fuel injection system.

The air cleaner incorporates a renewable paper element, and on some models an automatic temperature control.

The exhaust system is in four sections on all models, except USA models where a catalytic converter is fitted in addition.

All models are fitted with a crankcase ventilation system and North American models are fitted with additional emission control systems.

2 Air cleaner element – renewal and cleaning

1   A dirty air cleaner element will cause a loss of performance and an increase in fuel consumption. A new element should be fitted every 20 000 miles (30 000 km) and the element should be cleaned every twelve months, or more frequently under dusty conditions.

Carburettor models

2   Release the spring clips securing the air cleaner lid and remove the lid.

3   Cover the carburettor entry port to prevent any dirt entering it when the element is lifted out, and remove the element. Wipe the inside of the air cleaner with a moist rag to remove all dust and dirt and then remove the covering from the entry port.

4   If cleaning the element, place well away from the vehicle, then tap the air cleaner element to remove dust and dirt. If necessary use a soft brush to clean the outside or blow air at very low pressure from the inside surface towards the outside

5   Refit the element, clean the cover and put it in place, then clip the cover down, ensuring that the two arrows are aligned.

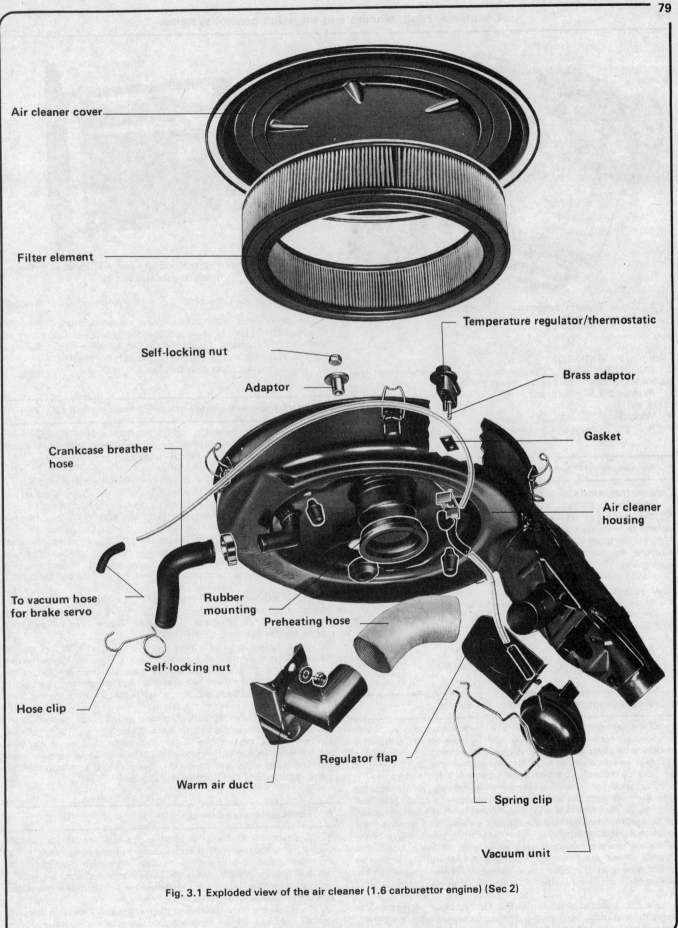

Air cleaner cover

Filter element

Self-locking nut

Adaptor

Temperature regulator/thermostatic

Brass adaptor

Gasket

Crankcase breather hose

Air cleaner housing

To vacuum hose for brake servo

Rubber mounting

Preheating hose

Self-locking nut

Hose clip

Regulator flap

Warm air duct

Spring clip

Vacuum unit

3

Fig. 3.1 Exploded view of the air cleaner (1.6 carburettor engine) (Sec 2)

2.6 Air cleaner element location on fuel injection models

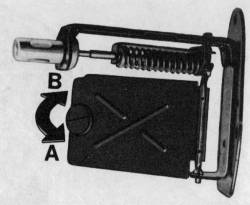

Fig. 3.2 Automatic air temperature control flap fitted to fuel injection models (Sec 4)

A – warm air open direction   *B – warm air closed direction*

Fuel injection models

6   Release the spring clips securing the air cleaner cover and separate the cover from the air flow meter (photo).
7   Remove the element, and if applicable clean it as described in paragraph 4.
8   Wipe clean the inside of the cover.
9   Refit the element and secure the cover by pressing the clips.

3   Air cleaner – removal and refitting

Carburettor models

1   Remove the element, as described in Section 2.
2   Unscrew the nut(s) securing the air cleaner body and remove the adaptor or retaining ring.
3   Note the location of all hoses and tubes, then disconnect them and withdraw the air cleaner body from the carburettor. Remove the sealing ring.

Fuel injection models

4   Remove the element, as described in Section 2.
5   Disconnect the air inlet hose, then unclip the air cleaner body from the body panel.

All models

6   Refitting is a reversal of removal.

4   Automatic air temperature control – general

1   On some models the air intake incorporates an automatic temperature control which is operated by vacuum on carburettor models or by a wax type canister on fuel injection models. A flap in the air intake directs warm air from the exhaust manifold, or cold air from the front of the car, according to the temperature of the air.
2   *To check the control on carburettor engines,* disconnect the regulator hose from the adaptor in the brake servo vacuum hose, and plug the adaptor. Start the engine (cold) and run it at a fast idle speed for several minutes. Remove the air cleaner cover and reconnect the regulator hose to the adaptor – the control flap should move to the fully open position to admit warm air only. If the flap remains shut connect a hose direct from the adaptor to the vacuum unit – the flap should now open. If it does, the temperature control valve within the air cleaner has proved faulty, but if it stays shut the vacuum unit is faulty.
3   *On fuel injection engines* the flap control must be removed to check its operation. Remove the cross-head screws from the control and withdraw the unit from the air cleaner body. Dip the thermostat in water at a temperature below 30°C (86°F) and check that the flap

moves to the warm air position. Increase the temperature of the water to above 38°C (100°F) and check that the flap moves to close off the warm air. If necessary, the thermostat can be removed by unhooking the flap and pushing the thermostat through the bracket.
4   On both types check that the flap moves freely.

5   Mechanical fuel pump – removal, servicing and refitting

1   The fuel pump is located on the left-hand side of the engine and is operated by an eccentric on the intermediate shaft (four-cylinder engines) or camshaft (five-cylinder engines).
2   Disconnect the battery negative lead.
3   *Ensure that the car is in a well ventilated place and that there is no danger of ignition from sparks or naked flames. Never work on any part of a fuel system when the car is over an inspection pit.*
4   Unclamp and disconnect the fuel lines from the pump. Remove the two securing bolts and lift the pump, flange and gasket off.
5   The pump is not repairable and the only servicing operation possible is cleaning the filter. To do this, remove the screw from the centre of the pump and take off the cover, sealing ring and filter.
6   Clean the pump cover with a lint-free cloth and wash the filter in fuel.
7   Refit the filter, then a new sealing ring and finally the cover. When fitting the cover, the notch on its rim must engage in the corresponding recess in the pump body. Tighten the centre screw firmly, but do not distort the pump cover.
8   Refit the pump using a new gasket in contact with the cylinder block, followed by the flange, sealing ring, and pump. When offering up the pump to the engine, ensure that its lever, or plunger fits correctly against the cam, not under it. Bolt the pump in place and attach the suction (fuel inlet) pipe, which is the pipe from the fuel filter, to the pipe on the cover of the pump.
9   Place a container beneath the pump delivery pipe, reconnect the battery leads and disconnect *and earth* the high tension cable from the ignition coil to prevent the engine firing and to prevent electrical sparks. With an assistant operating the starter for a few seconds check that the pump is delivering regular spurts of fuel. If satisfactory, fit the pump delivery hose and tighten the clamps.

6   Fuel line filter – renewal

1   A disposable fuel filter is fitted in the fuel line. On carburettor engines it is located near the fuel pump in the supply line. On fuel injection engines it is located in the supply line from the fuel tank to the fuel pump (photo) – in addition fuel injection engines have a canister type filter, located in the supply line to the metering unit and positioned on the bulkhead.
2   To renew the filter, disconnect the fuel lines and, where necessary, remove the nut from the mounting clip. It will be necessary to jack up the rear of the car to renew the filter near the fuel tank on fuel injection engines.

6.1 Fuel filter location on fuel injection models

7.2 Fuel tank filler cap

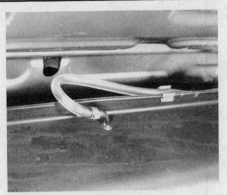

7.10 Fuel tank vent line

3   Fit the new filter making sure that the arrow points in the direction of flow of the fuel (ie towards the engine). Fit new clips and washers, as applicable; *do not allow any dirt or foreign matter to enter the fuel lines.*

7   Fuel tank – removal, servicing and refitting

Note: *For safety reasons the fuel tank must always be removed in a well ventilated area.*
1   Disconnect the battery negative lead.
2   Remove the fuel tank filler cap (photo).

3   Prise the clamping ring from the filler neck rubber, and pull the rubber from the panel.
4   Open the boot lid and remove the floor covering.
5   Pull the vent lines from the filler neck rubber and on North American models from the gravity/vent valve.
6   Jack up the rear of the car and support it on axle stands. Check the front wheels.
7   Position a suitable container beneath the fuel tank outlet, identify the supply and return lines, then disconnect them and drain the fuel.
8   Prise the sealing cap from the underbody.
9   Disconnect the overflow line from the righthand side of the luggage compartment.
10 Disconnect and unclip the vent line from the top of the fuel tank (photo).

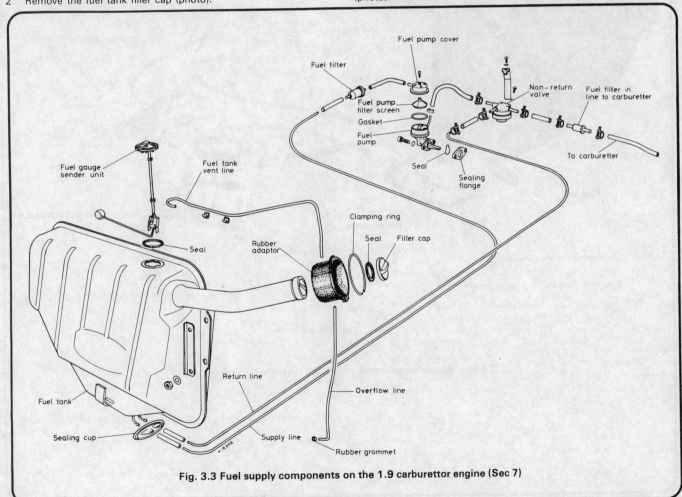

Fig. 3.3 Fuel supply components on the 1.9 carburettor engine (Sec 7)

3

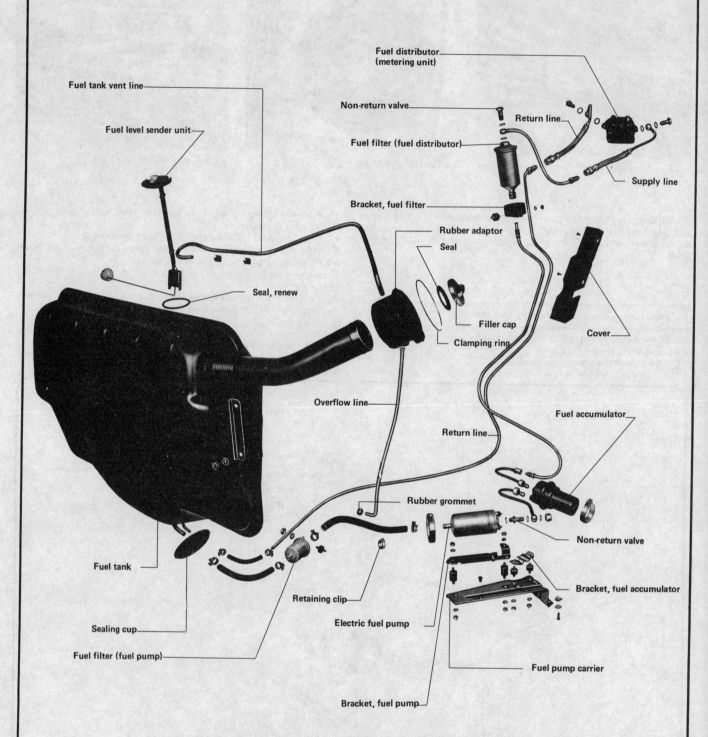

Fuel distributor (metering unit)

Non-return valve

Return line

Fuel filter (fuel distributor)

Supply line

Bracket, fuel filter

Rubber adaptor

Seal

Filler cap

Clamping ring

Cover

Fuel tank vent line

Fuel level sender unit

Seal, renew

Overflow line

Fuel accumulator

Return line

Rubber grommet

Non-return valve

Fuel tank

Retaining clip

Bracket, fuel accumulator

Electric fuel pump

Sealing cup

Fuel pump carrier

Fuel filter (fuel pump)

Bracket, fuel pump

Fig. 3.4 Fuel supply components on the 1.6 fuel injection engine (Sec 7)

11 Disconnect the wiring from the fuel gauge sender unit (photo).
12 Unscrew the mounting nuts and bolts and remove the clamping plates. Lift the fuel tank from the luggage compartment.
13 If the tank is contaminated with sediment or water, remove the gauge sender unit, as described in Section 8, and swill the tank out with clean fuel. If the tank is damaged or leaks, it should be repaired by specialists, or alternatively renewed. **Note:** *Do not, under any circumstances, solder or weld a fuel tank, for safety reasons.*
14 Refitting is a reversal of removal.

8 Fuel gauge sender unit – removal and refitting

Note: *For safety reasons the fuel gauge sender unit must always be removed in a well ventilated area.*
1 Disconnect the battery negative lead.
2 Open the boot lid and remove the floor covering.
3 Disconnect the wiring from the fuel gauge sender unit.
4 Using two crossed screwdrivers, turn the locking ring anti-clockwise, then withdraw the sender unit and float. Remove the sealing ring.
5 Refitting is a reversal of removal, but use a new sealing ring and smear it with a little glycerine. The electrical connection of the sender unit must face forward.

9 Accelerator cable – removal, refitting and adjustment

1 On automatic transmission models refer to Chapter 7 where necessary.
2 On carburettor engines remove the air cleaner, as described in Section 3.
3 Disconnect the cable from the engine.
4 Disconnect the cable from the top of the accelerator pedal or the automatic transmission, as applicable and withdraw the cable (photo).
5 Refitting is a reversal of removal, but make sure that the cable is not kinked.

Fig. 3.5 Accelerator cable adjustment clip location (Sec 9)

6 Adjustment of the cable on automatic transmission models is described in Chapter 7. On manual gearbox models, first disconnect the cable from the throttle lever on the carburettor or throttle housing (photos).
7 Set the accelerator pedal to the idle position so that the distance from the stop on the floor to the pedal is 60.0 mm (2.36 in).
8 With the throttle lever in its idling position, reconnect the cable and take up the slack in the cable. Insert the clip in the nearest groove to the bracket on carburettor models, or tighten the clamp screw or nuts on fuel injection models (photo).
9 To check the adjustment, fully depress the accelerator pedal and check that the distance between the throttle lever and stop is no more than 1.0 mm (0.04 in).
10 Refit the air cleaner on carburettor engines.

7.11 Fuel gauge sender unit

9.4 Accelerator cable location on bulkhead

9.6A On fuel injection engines remove the clip ...

9.6B ... and unhook the accelerator cable

9.8 Accelerator cable adjuster on fuel injection engines

3

10 Carburettor – removal and refitting

1 Disconnect the battery negative lead.
2 Remove the air cleaner, as described in Section 3.
3 Drain half of the coolant from the cooling system, with reference to Chapter 2.

4 Disconnect the coolant hoses from the automatic choke.
5 As applicable, disconnect the wiring from the automatic choke and fuel cut-off solenoid.
6 Disconnect the accelerator cable.
7 Disconnect the fuel and vacuum hoses.
8 Unscrew the through-bolts or nuts, and lift the carburettor from the inlet manifold. Remove the insulating flange gasket.

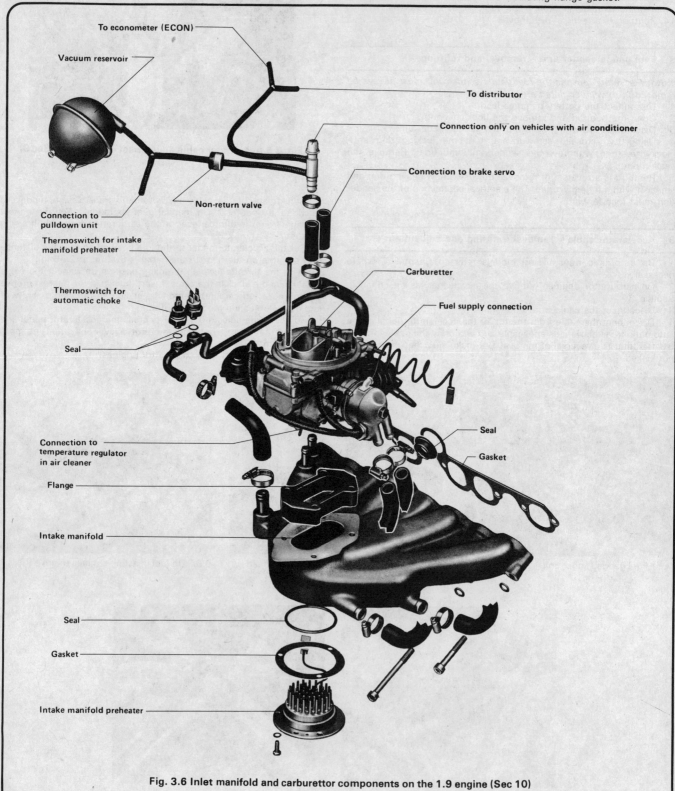

Fig. 3.6 Inlet manifold and carburettor components on the 1.9 engine (Sec 10)

9   Refitting is a reversal of removal, but clean the mating faces of the carburettor and inlet manifold and always fit a new gasket. Tighten the mounting bolts evenly to the specified torque.

11 Carburettor – dismantling, servicing and reassembly

1   Wash the exterior of the carburettor with a suitable solvent and allow to dry.

2   Dismantle and reassemble the carburettor, with reference to Figs. 3.7, 3.8, and 3.9, having first obtained a repair set of gaskets. Before dismantling the automatic choke, note the position of the cover in relation to the carburettor cover.

3   To check the fuel cut-off valve, apply 12 volts to the terminal and earth the body. With the valve pin depressed approximately 3 to 4 mm (0.12 to 0.16 in), the core must be pulled in.

4   When inserting the accelerator pump piston seal in the 1B3 carburettor, press it towards the opposite side of the vent drilling. The

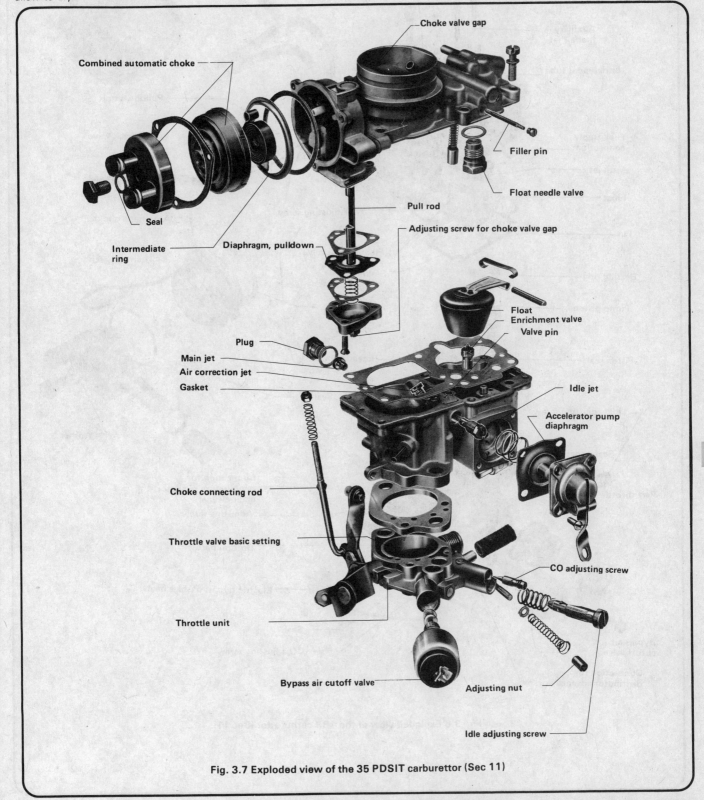

Fig. 3.7 Exploded view of the 35 PDSIT carburettor (Sec 11)

3

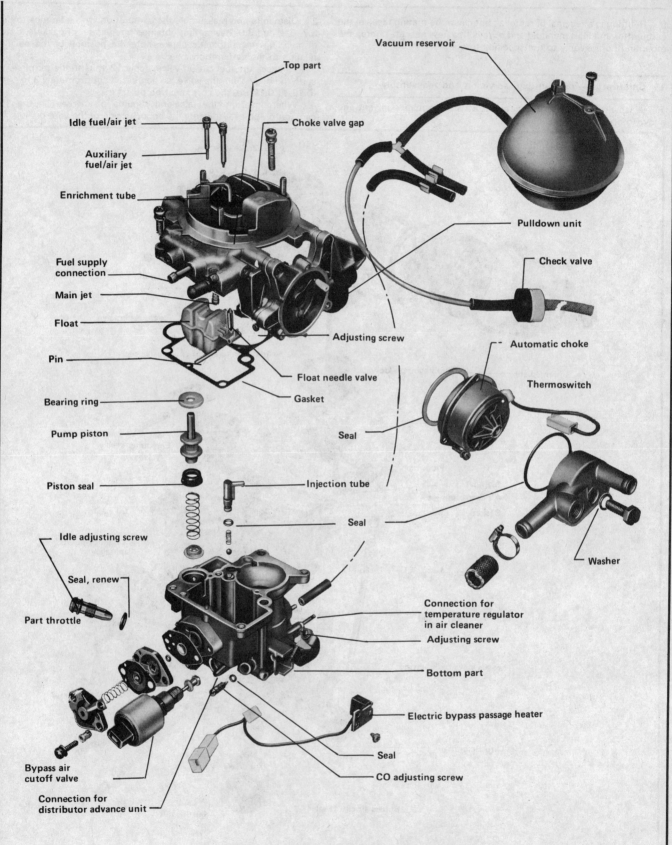

Vacuum reservoir

Top part

Choke valve gap

Idle fuel/air jet

Auxiliary fuel/air jet

Enrichment tube

Pulldown unit

Fuel supply connection

Check valve

Main jet

Float

Pin

Adjusting screw

Float needle valve

Automatic choke

Thermoswitch

Gasket

Bearing ring

Seal

Pump piston

Piston seal

Injection tube

Seal

Idle adjusting screw

Washer

Seal, renew

Part throttle

Connection for temperature regulator in air cleaner

Adjusting screw

Bottom part

Electric bypass passage heater

Bypass air cutoff valve

Seal

CO adjusting screw

Connection for distributor advance unit

Fig. 3.8 Exploded view of the 1B3 carburettor (Sec 11)

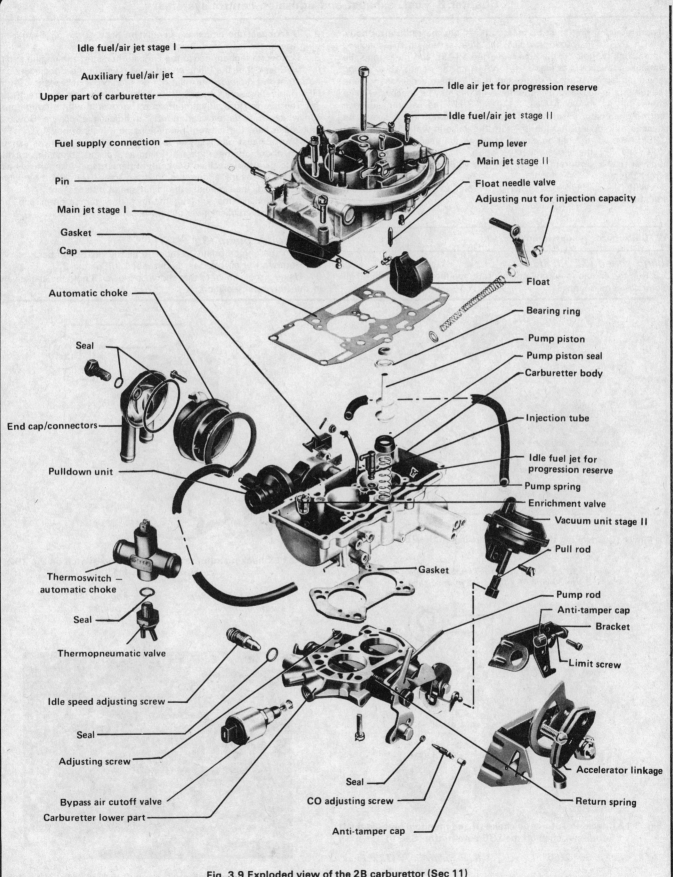

Idle fuel/air jet stage I

Auxiliary fuel/air jet

Upper part of carburetter

Fuel supply connection

Pin

Main jet stage I

Gasket

Cap

Automatic choke

Seal

End cap/connectors

Pulldown unit

Thermoswitch — automatic choke

Seal

Thermopneumatic valve

Idle speed adjusting screw

Seal

Adjusting screw

Bypass air cutoff valve

Carburetter lower part

Idle air jet for progression reserve

Idle fuel/air jet stage II

Pump lever

Main jet stage II

Float needle valve

Adjusting nut for injection capacity

Float

Bearing ring

Pump piston

Pump piston seal

Carburetter body

Injection tube

Idle fuel jet for progression reserve

Pump spring

Enrichment valve

Vacuum unit stage II

Pull rod

Gasket

Pump rod

Anti-tamper cap

Bracket

Limit screw

Accelerator linkage

Return spring

Seal

CO adjusting screw

Anti-tamper cap

Fig. 3.9 Exploded view of the 2B carburettor (Sec 11)

piston retaining ring must be pressed flush into the carburettor body.

5   On the 2B carburettor, adjust the float setting to the specified dimensions by holding the cover inverted at 45° and measuring the dimension 'a' shown in Fig. 3.10 – note that the needle valve spring tensioned pin must not be depressed. If adjustment is necessary, bend the tab on the float arm. The thermo-switches may be checked with an ohmmeter, as shown in Figs. 3.11 and 3.12. The vacuum advance thermo-pneumatic valve on automatic transmission models may be checked by blowing through it – with the valve in water below 58°C (136°F) the valve must be closed, but with the valve in water above 62°C (143°F) the valve must be open. When fitting the throttle housing to the carburettor body, apply a liquid locking agent to the screw threads.

6   With the carburettor reassembled, refer to Section 12 for the adjustment procedure.

12 Carburettor – adjustments

Idling speed (35 PDSIT)

1   Run the engine to normal operating temperature and switch off all electrical components.

2   Disconnect the crankcase ventilation hose at the air cleaner and plug the hose.

3   Connect a tachometer to the engine, then start the engine and let it idle. Check that the idling speed is as given in the Specifications – note that the radiator fan must not be running. If necessary, turn the idling adjusting screw in or out until the idling speed is correct.

4   The idle mixture adjustment screw is covered with a tamperproof cap which must be removed in order to adjust the mixture. However, first make sure that current regulations permit its removal.

5   If an exhaust gas analyser is available, connect it to the exhaust system, then run the engine at idling speed and adjust the mixture screw to give the specified CO content percentage. Alternatively as a temporary measure adjust the mixture screw to give the highest engine speed, then readjust the idling speed if necessary.

6   After making the adjustment, fit a new tamperproof cap, and reconnect the crankcase ventilation hose.

Accelerator pump (35 PDSIT)

7   Run the engine briefly in order to fill the float chamber.

8   Remove the air cleaner, as described in Section 3.

9   Using a tool similar to that shown in Fig. 3.13 hold the choke valve in the fully open position.

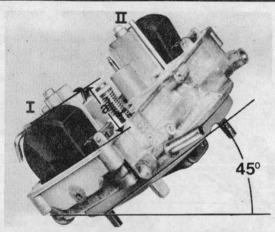

Fig. 3.10 Checking the float level setting on the 2B carburettor (Sec 11)

a = 27 to 29 mm (1.06 to 1.14 in) for Stage 1
a = 29 to 31 mm (1.14 to 1.22 in) for Stage 2

Fig. 3.11 Checking automatic choke thermo-switch on the 2B2 carburettor (Sec 11)

Below 31°C (88°F)   *Above 31°C (88°F)*
– zero ohm   *– infinity*

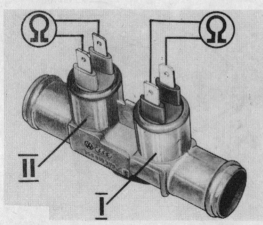

Fig. 3.12 Checking automatic choke (I) and manifold preheater (II) thermo-switches on the 2B5 carburettor (Sec 11)

I   Below 30°C (86°F)   *II   Below 50°C (122°F)*
– zero ohm   *– zero ohm*
*   Above 40°C (104°F)*   *   Above 55°C (131°F)*
– infinity   *– infinity*
Note: Where the thermo-switches are individual the automatic choke thermo-switch is coloured red

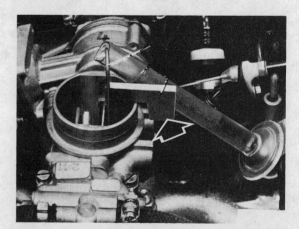

Fig. 3.13 Using a special tool (arrowed) to hold the choke valve open on the 35 PDSIT carburettor (Sec 12)

10 Connect some plastic tubing to the injection pipe in the carburettor venturi, and operate the throttle until fuel comes out of the tube.

11 With the end of the tubing in a measuring glass, fully open the throttle ten times allowing at least three seconds per stroke. Divide the total quantity by ten and check that the resultant injection capacity is as given in the Specifications. If not, turn the adjustment nut as necessary to increase or decrease the injection pump stroke, and recheck. After making the adjustment, seal the nut with a spot of paint.

Throttle valve basic setting (35 PDSIT)

12 This setting is made during manufacture and will not normally require adjustment. However, if the setting has been disturbed proceed as follows. First run the engine to normal operating temperature.

13 Remove the air cleaner, as described in Section 3.

14 Disconnect the vacuum advance hose at the carburettor and connect a vacuum gauge.

15 Run the engine at idling speed, then turn the idle limiting screw on the lever until vacuum is indicated on the gauge. Turn the screw out until the vacuum drops to zero, then turn it out a further quarter turn.

16 After making the adjustment, adjust the idling speed as described in paragraphs 1 to 6.

Throttle valve gap (35 PDSIT)

17 With the carburettor removed and the choke closed, half open the throttle valve and release it again.

18 Using the shank of a twist drill, check that the distance between the throttle lever valve and carburettor wall is as given in the Specifications. If not, adjust the nut on the end of the choke connecting rod as necessary.

Choke pull-down system (35 PDSIT)

19 Remove the air cleaner cover, as described in Section 2.

20 Half open the throttle valve then completely close the choke valve.

21 Without touching the accelerator pedal, start the engine.

22 Close the choke valve by hand and check that resistance is felt over the final 4 mm (0.16 in) of travel. If no resistance is felt there may be a leak in the vacuum connections or the pull-down diaphragm may be broken.

Choke valve gap (35 PDSIT)

23 Remove the automatic choke cover together with the bi-metallic spring.

24 Close the choke valve, then using a screwdriver, press in the pullrod to the stop.

25 Half open the throttle valve, then close the choke valve so that the operating lever is against the upper stop on the pullrod.

26 Using the shank of a twist drill, check that the distance from the choke valve to the carburettor wall is as given in the Specifications. If not, adjust the screw on the end of the pullrod as necessary. Seal the screw with paint after making the adjustment.

Intake manifold preheater (1B3)

27 Using an ohmmeter as shown in Fig. 3.14 check that the resistance of the preheater is between 0.25 and 0.50 ohms. If not, renew the unit.

Enrichment tube (1B3)

28 With the choke valve closed, the bottom of the enrichment tube should be level with the upper surface of the valve, as shown in Fig. 3.15.

Automatic choke (1B3)

29 The line on the cover must be in alignment with the dot on the automatic choke body.

Idling speed (1B3)

30 The procedure is identical to that described in paragraphs 1 to 6 inclusive. However, make sure that the automatic choke is fully open, otherwise the throttle valve linkage may still be on the fast idle cam.

Fast idling speed (1B3)

31 With the engine at normal operating temperature and switched off, connect a tachometer and remove the air cleaner.

32 Fully open the throttle valve, then turn the fast idle cam and release the throttle valve so that the adjustment screw is positioned on the highest part of the cam.

33 Without touching the accelerator pedal, start the engine and check that the fast idling speed is as given in the Specifications. If not, turn the adjustment screw on the linkage as necessary. If a tamperproof cap is fitted renew it after making the adjustment.

Choke pull-down system (1B3)

34 The procedure is identical to that described in paragraphs 19 to 22 inclusive.

Choke valve gap (1B3)

35 Fully open the throttle valve, then turn the fast idle cam and release the throttle valve so that the adjustment screw is positioned on the highest part of the cam.

36 Press the choke operating rod as far as possible towards the pull-down unit.

37 Using the shank of a twist drill, check that the distance from the choke valve to the carburettor wall is as given in the Specifications. If

3

Fig. 3.14 Checking the inlet manifold preheater resistance (Sec 12)

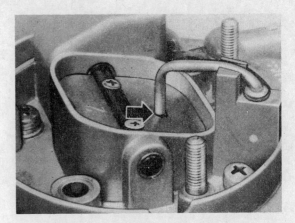

Fig 3.15 Correct position of the enrichment tube on the 1B3 carburettor (Sec 12)

not, adjust the screw behind the automatic choke – note that on carburettor 049 129 015 R/S adjustment is made by turning the hexagon flats (not the adjustment screw).

Throttle valve basic setting (1B3)
38 The procedure is as described in paragraphs 12 to 16 inclusive, but make sure that the automatic choke is fully open, otherwise the throttle valve linkage may still be on the fast idle cam.

Electric bypass air heating element (1B3)
39 Disconnect the wiring from the fuel cut-off solenoid and thermo-switch, and connect a test lamp to the heating element wire and the battery positive terminal.
40 If the lamp lights up, the heater element is in good working order.

Accelerator pump (1B3)
41 Hold the carburettor over a funnel and measuring glass.
42 Turn the fast idle cam so that the adjusting screw is off the cam. Hold the cam in this position during the following procedure.
43 Fully open the throttle ten times, allowing at least three seconds per stroke. Divide the total quantity by ten and check that the resultant injection capacity is as given in the Specifications. If not, refer to Fig. 3.17 and loosen the cross-head screw, turn the cam plate as required, and tighten the screw.
44 If difficulty is experienced in making the adjustment, check the pump seal and make sure that the return check valve and injection tube are clear.

Automatic choke (2B2 and 2B5)
45 The line on then cover must be in alignment with the dot on the automatic choke body.

Idling speed (2B2 and 2B5)
46 The procedure is identical to that described in paragraphs 1 to 6 inclusive. However, make sure that the automatic choke is fully open, otherwise the throttle valve linkage may still be on the fast idle cam.

Fast idling speed (2B2 and 2B5)
47 The procedure is as given in paragraphs 31 to 33 inclusive. However, access to the adjustment screw is difficult when it is on the highest part of the cam, so it is necessary to move the cam in order to turn the screw.
48 After making the adjustment, seal the screw with a spot of paint or fit a new tamperproof cap, as necessary.

Choke pull-down system (2B2)
49 The procedure is identical to that described in paragraphs 19 to 22 inclusive.

Choke pull-down system (2B5)
50 The system can only be accurately checked using a vacuum pump and gauge; therefore this work should be entrusted to an Audi dealer.

Choke valve gap (2B2 and 2B5)
51 Remove the air cleaner, as described in Section 3.
52 Remove the automatic choke cover.
53 Fully open the throttle valve, then turn the fast idle cam and release the throttle valve so that the adjustment screw is positioned on the highest part of the cam.
54 Using a rubber band, hold the bottom of the choke operating lever against the stop.
55 Using a screwdriver, press the pullrod at the top of the automatic choke against the stop.
56 Check that the distance from the choke valve to the carburettor wall is as given in the Specifications. If not, turn the adjusting screw on the end of the pull-down rod, as necessary. On the 2B2 carburettor seal the screw with a spot of paint.

Accelerator pump (2B2 and 2B5)
57 Hold the carburettor over a funnel and measuring glass.
58 Fully open the throttle ten times allowing at least three seconds per stroke. Divide the total quantity by ten and check that the resultant injection capacity is as given in the Specifications. If not, turn the adjusting nut as necessary.
59 If difficulty is experienced in making the adjustment, check the pump seal and make sure that the return check valve and injection tube are clear.
60 After making the adjustment, seal the nut with a spot of paint.

Stage 1 throttle valve basic setting (2B2 and 2B5)
61 This setting is made during manufacture and will not normally require adjustment. However, if the setting has been disturbed proceed as follows. First run the engine to normal operating temperature.
62 Remove the air cleaner, as described in Section 3.
63 Make sure that the fast idle adjusting screw is not contacting the fast idle linkage.
64 Unscrew the basic throttle setting screw until it no longer contacts the linkage.
65 Open and close the throttle quickly, then turn the setting screw until it just contacts the linkage. From this position screw it in a further quarter turn.
66 Fit a tamperproof cap if necessary, then adjust the idling speed, as described in paragraph 46.

Stage 2 throttle valve basic setting (2B2 and 2B5)
67 This setting is made during manufacture and will not normally

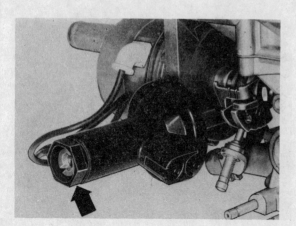

Fig. 3.16 Choke valve gap adjustment hexagon flats on the 1B3 carburettor number 049 129 015 R/S (Sec 12)

Fig. 3.17 Accelerator pump adjustment on the 1B3 carburettor (Sec 12)

a   Locking screw   *b   Cam plate*

Fig. 3.18 Stage 2 vacuum pullrod adjustment dimension on 2B2 and 2B5 carburettors (Sec 12)

a = 1 to 2 mm (0.04 to 0.08 in)

require adjustment. However, if the setting has been disturbed proceed as follows. First remove the carburettor.

68 With the Stage 1 throttle valve in the idling position, unscrew the Stage 2 basic throttle setting screw until it no longer contacts the stop.

69 Disconnect the vacuum unit pullrod then turn the setting screw until it just contacts the stop while lightly pressing the throttle lever shut. From this position screw it in a further quarter turn.

70 Fit a new tamperproof cap if necessary, then reconnect the vacuum unit pullrod.

71 Adjust the idling speed, as described in paragraph 46.

Stage 2 vacuum pullrod (2B2 and 2B5)

72 This adjustment applies only to metal vacuum units. First disconnect the pullrod and slacken the locknut beneath the vacuum unit.

73 Adjust the pullrod to give dimension 'a' (Fig. 3.18) then reconnect the pullrod and tighten the locknut.

13 Fuel injection system – general description

Although the fuel injection system is known as the 'K-Jetronic', it is not an electronically controlled system. The principle of the system is very simple and there are no specialised electronic components.

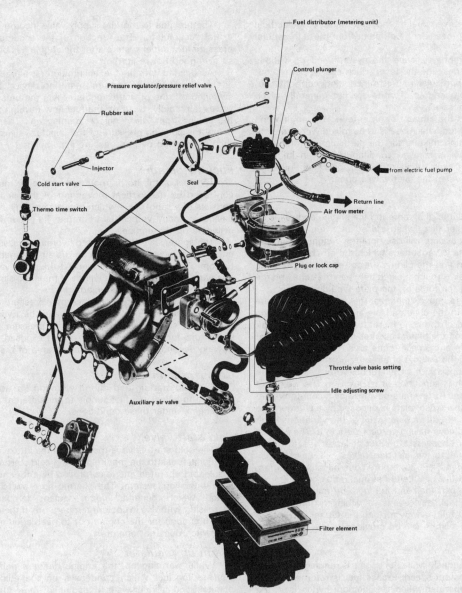

Fig. 3.19 K-Jetronic fuel injection components on the 1.6 engine (Sec 13)

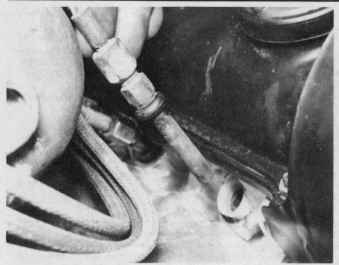

13.3A Removing an injector on fuel injection engines

13.3B Showing the fuel injectors and pipes

There is an electrically driven fuel pump and there are electrical sensors and switches, but these are no different from those in general use on cars.

The following paragraphs describe the system and its various elements. Later Sections describe the tests which can be carried out to ascertain whether a particular unit is functioning correctly, but dismantling and repair procedures of units are not generally given because repairs are not possible.

The system measures the amount of air entering the engine and determines the amount of fuel which needs to be mixed with the air to give the correct combustion mixture for the particular conditions of engine operation. The fuel is sprayed continuously by an injection nozzle to the inlet port of each cylinder (photos). This fuel and air is drawn into the cylinders when the inlet valves open.

Airflow meter

This measures the volume of air entering the engine and relies on the principle that a circular disc, when placed in a funnel through which a current of air is passing, will rise until the weight of the disc is equal to the force on its lower surface which the air creates. If the volume of air is increased and the plate were to remain in the same place, the rate of flow of air through the gap between the cone and the plate would increase and the force on the plate would increase.

If the plate is free to move, then as the force on the plate increases, the plate rises in the cone and the area between the edge of the plate and the edge of the cone increases, until the rate of air flow and hence the force on the plate, becomes the same as it was at the former lower flow rate and smaller cone area. Thus the height of the plate is a measure of the volume of air entering the engine.

The air flow meter consists of an air funnel with a sensor plate mounted on a lever which is supported at its fulcrum. The weight of the air flow sensor plate and its lever are balanced by a counterweight and the upward force on the sensor plate is opposed by a plunger. The plunger, which moves up and down as a result of the variations in air flow, is surrounded by a sleeve having vertical slots in it. The vertical movement of the plunger uncovers a greater or lesser length of the slots, which meters the fuel to the injection valves.

The sides of the air funnel are not a pure cone because optimum operation of the engine requires a different air/fuel ratio under different conditions such as idling, part load and full load. By making parts of the funnel steeper than the basic shape, a richer mixture can be provided for, at idling and full load. By making the funnel flatter than the basic shape, a leaner mixture can be provided.

Fuel supply

Fuel is pumped continuously while the engine is running by a roller cell pump running at constant speed; excess fuel is returned to the tank. The fuel pump is operated when the ignition switch is in the *START* position, but once the starter is released a switch connected to the air plate prevents the pump from operating unless the engine is running.

The fuel line to the fuel supply valve incorporates a filter and also a fuel accumulator. The function of the accumulator is to maintain pressure in the fuel system after the engine has been switched off and so give good hot re-starting.

Associated with the fuel accumulator is a pressure regulator which is an integral part of the fuel metering device. When the engine is switched off, the pressure regulator lets the pressure to the injection valves fall rapidly to cut off the fuel flow through them and so prevent the engine from 'dieseling' or 'running on'. The valve closes at just below the opening pressure of the injector valves and this pressure is then maintained by the pressure accumulator.

Fuel distributor

The fuel distributor is mounted on the air metering device and is controlled by the vertical movement of the air flow sensor plate. It consists of a spool valve which moves vertically in a sleeve, the sleeve having as many vertical slots around its circumference as there are cylinders on the engine.

The spool valve is adjusted to hydraulic pressure on the upper end and this balances the pressure on the air plate which is applied to the bottom of the valve by a plunger. As the spool valve rises and falls, it uncovers a greater or lesser length of metering slot and so controls the volume of fuel fed to each injector.

Each metering slot has a differential pressure valve, which ensures that the difference in pressure between the two sides of the slot is always the same. Because the drop in pressure across the metering slot is unaffected by the length of slot exposed, the amount of fuel flowing depends only on the exposed area of the slots.

Compensation units

For cold starting and during warming up, additional devices are required to adjust the fuel supply to the different fuel requirements of the engine under these conditions.

Cold start valve

The cold start valve is mounted in the intake manifold and sprays additional fuel into the manifold during cold starting (photo). The valve is solenoid operated and is controlled by a thermo-time switch in the engine cooling system. The thermo-time switch is actuated for a period which depends upon coolant temperature, the period decreasing with rise in coolant temperature. If the coolant temperature is high enough for the engine not to need additional fuel for starting, the switch does not operate.

Warm-up regulator

While warming up, the engine needs a richer mixture to compensate for fuel which condenses on the cold walls of the inlet manifold and cylinder walls. It also needs more fuel to compensate for power lost because of increased friction losses and increased oil drag in a cold engine. The mixture is made richer during warming up by the warm-up regulator (photo). This is a pressure regulator which lowers

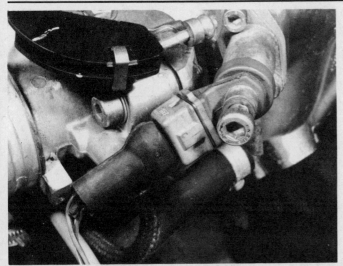

13.15 Cold start valve location (fuel pipe removed)

13.16 Removing the warm-up regulator

the pressure applied to the control plunger of the fuel regulator during warm-up. This reduced pressure causes the air flow plate to rise higher than it would do otherwise, thus uncovering a greater length of metering slot and making the mixture richer.

The valve is operated by a bi-metallic strip which is heated by an electric heater. When the engine is cold the bi-metallic strip presses against the delivery valve spring to reduce the pressure on the diaphragm and enlarge the discharge cross-section. This increase in cross-section results in a lowering of the pressure fed to the control plunger.

When the engine is started, the electrical heater of the bi-metallic strip is switched *ON*. As the strip warms it rises gradually until it ultimately rises free of the control spring plate and the valve spring becomes fully effective to give normal control pressure.

Auxiliary air device

Compensation for power lost by greater friction is compensated for by feeding a larger volume of fuel/air mixture to the engine than is supplied by the normal opening of the throttle. The auxiliary air device bypasses the throttle with a channel having a variable aperture valve in it. The aperture is varied by a pivoted plate controlled by a spring and a bi-metallic strip.

During cold starting the channel is open and increases the volume of air passing to the engine, but as the bi-metallic strip bends it allows a control spring to pull the plate over the aperture until at normal operating temperature the aperture is closed. The heating of the bi-metallic strip is similar to that of the warm-up regulator described above.

14 Fuel metering distributor – removal and refitting

1   Disconnect the battery terminals.

2   *Ensure that the vehicle is in a well ventilated space and that there are no naked flames or other possible sources of ignition.*

3   While holding a rag over the joint to prevent fuel from being sprayed out, loosen the control pressure line from the warm-up valve. The control pressure line is the one connected to the large union of the valve.

4   Mark each fuel line, and its port on the fuel distributor. Carefully clean all dirt from around the fuel unions and distributor ports and then disconnect the fuel lines (photo).

5   Unscrew and remove the connection of the pressure control line to the fuel metering distributor.

6   Remove the locking plug from the CO adjusting screw, then remove the screws securing the fuel metering distributor.

7   Lift off the fuel metering distributor, taking care that the metering plunger does not fall out. If the plunger does fall out accidentally, clean it in fuel and then re-insert it with its chamfered end downwards.

8   Before refitting the metering distributor, ensure that the plunger moves up and down freely. If the plunger sticks, the distributor must be renewed, because the plunger cannot be repaired or replaced separately.

9   Refit the distributor, using a new sealing ring, and after tightening the screws, lock them with paint.

10 Refit the fuel lines and the cap of the CO adjusting screw and tighten the union on the warm-up valve.

15 Air flow meter – removal and refitting

1   Remove the fuel lines from the distributor, as described in paragraphs 1 to 5 of the previous Section.

2   Loosen the clamps at the air cleaner and throttle assembly ends of the air scoop and take off the air scoop (photo).

3   Remove the bolts securing the air flow meter to the air cleaner and

14.4 Fuel feed pipe to the metering distributor

15.2 Crankcase ventilation hose connection to the air scoop on fuel injection engines

15.3 Air flow meter and fuel distributor

lift off the air flow meter and fuel metering distributor (photo).

4   The fuel metering plunger should be prevented from falling out when the fuel metering distributor is removed from the air flow meter (see previous Section).

5   Refitting is the reverse of removing, but it is necessary to use a new gasket between the air flow meter and the air cleaner.

16 Pressure relief valve – removal, servicing and refitting

1   Release the pressure in the fuel system, as described in paragraphs 1 to 3 of Section 14.

2   Unscrew the non-return valve plug and remove the plug and its sealing washer.

3   Take out the O-ring, shims, plunger and O-ring in that order.

4   When refitting the assembly, use new O-rings and ensure that all the shims which were removed are refitted.

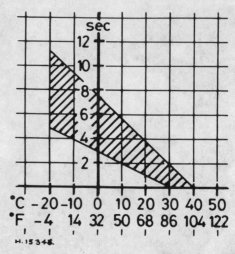

Fig. 3.21 K-Jetronic thermo-time switch operation graph (Sec 17)

4   Operate the starter for 10 seconds and note the interval before the test lamp lights and the period for which it remains alight. Reference to the graph will show that at a coolant temperature of 30°C (86°F) the lamp should light immediately and stay on for two seconds.

5   The check should not be carried out if the coolant temperature is above 30°C (86°F).

6   Refit the high tension lead onto the distributor, and reconnect the lead to the cold start valve.

18 Cold start valve – checking

1   Ensure that the coolant temperature is below 30°C (86°F) and that the car battery is fully charged.

2   Pull the high tension lead off the centre of the distributor and connect the lead to earth.

3   Pull the connectors off the warm-up valve and the auxiliary air unit.

4   Remove the two bolts securing the cold start valve to the inlet manifold and remove the valve, taking care not to damage the gasket (photo).

5   With fuel line and electrical connections connected to the valve, hold the valve over a glass jar and operate the starter for 10 seconds. The cold start valve should produce an even cone of spray during the time the thermo-time switch is ON.

6   After completing the checks refit the valve and reconnect the leads that were disturbed.

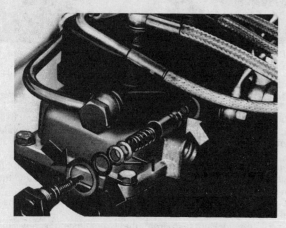

Fig. 3.20 K-Jetronic pressure relief valve components (Sec 16)

Do not change shims (1). Note seals (arrowed)

17 Thermo-time switch – checking

1   The thermo-time switch energises the cold start valve for a short time on starting and the time for which the valve is switched on depends upon the engine temperature (photo).

2   Pull the connector off the cold start valve and connect a test lamp across the contacts of the connector.

3   Pull the high tension lead off the centre of the distributor and connect the lead to earth.

17.1 Thermotime switch location

18.4 Cold start valve location

19 Warm-up regulator – checking

1   With the engine cold, pull the connectors off the warm-up valve and the auxiliary air unit (photo).
2   Connect a voltmeter across the terminals of the warm-up valve connector and operate the starter. The voltage across the terminals should be a minimum of 11.5 volts.
3   Switch the ignition *OFF* and connect an ohmmeter across the terminals of the warm-up valve. If the meter does not indicate a resistance of about 20 ohms, the heater coil is defective and a new valve must be fitted.

20 Air flow sensor lever and control plunger – checking

1   For the correct mixture to be supplied to the engine it is essential that the sensor plate is central in the venturi and that its height is correct.
2   Loosen the hose clips at each end of the air scoop and remove the scoop. If the sensor plate appears to be off-centre, loosen its centre screw and carefully run a 0.10 mm (0.004 in) feeler gauge round the edge of the plate to centralise it, then re-tighten the bolt (photo).
3   Raise the air flow sensor plate and then quickly move it to its rest position. No resistance should be felt on the downward movement; if there is resistance the air flow meter is defective and a new one must be fitted.
4   If the sensor plate can be moved downwards easily, but has a strong resistance to upward movement, the control plunger is sticking. Remove the fuel distributor (Section 14) and clean the control plunger in fuel. If this does not cure the problem, a new fuel distributor must be fitted.
5   Release the pressure on the fuel distributor, as described in Section 14 and then check the rest position of the air flow sensor plate. The upper edge of the plate should be flush with the bottom edge of the air cone. It is permissible for the plate to be lower than the edge by not more that 0.5 mm (0.020 in), but if higher, or lower than the permissible limit, the plate must be adjusted.
6   Adjust the height of the plate by lifting it and bending the wire clips attaching the plate to the balance arm but take care not to scratch or damage the surface of the air cone (photo).
7   After making the adjustment, tighten the warm-up valve union and check the idle speed and CO content.

21 Idle speed (fuel injection) – adjustment

1   Run the engine until the oil temperature is at least 60°C (140°F).
2   Check the ignition timing (Chapter 4), adjusting it if necessary. Leave the wiring disconnected from the idle stabilizer, where applicable.
3   If the car is fitted with an air conditioner, this must be turned *OFF* but the main headlights should be turned *ON*. Disconnect and plug the crankcase breather hose from the valve cover.
4   Remove the locking cap from the adjustment screw on the throttle assembly and turn the screw to achieve the idle speed given in the Specifications. The adjustment should be made only when the electric radiator fan is stationary.
5   After making the adjustment, refit the locking cap over the adjustment screw, and reconnect the wiring to the idle stabilizer, where applicable.

22 Idle mixture (fuel injection) – adjustment

1   The idle CO adjustment screw alters the height of the fuel metering distributor plunger relative to the air control plate of the air flow meter.
2   The screw is accessible by removing the locking plug from between the air duct scoop and the fuel metering distributor on the air flow meter casing.
3   Although a special tool is recommended for this adjustment, it can be made using a long, thin screwdriver.
4   Ensure that the engine is running under the same conditions as those necessary for adjusting the idling speed (see previous Section) and that the idling speed is correct.

19.1 Warm-up regulator and wiring connector

20.2 Showing the air flow sensor plate

3

20.6 Air flow sensor plate adjustment clip (arrowed)

5   Connect an exhaust gas analyser to the tailpipe as directed by the equipment manufacturer, and read the CO level.

6   Turn the adjusting screw clockwise to raise the percentage of CO and anti-clockwise to lower it. It is important that the adjustment is made without pressing down on the adjusting screw, because this will move the air flow sensor plate and affect the adjustment.

7   Remove the tool, accelerate the engine briefly and re-check. If the tool is not removed before the engine is accelerated there is a danger of the tool becoming jammed and getting bent.

23 Electric fuel pump – removal, testing and refitting

1   The electric fuel pump is located beneath the right-hand side of the car (photo). It is a sealed unit and the brushes and commutator are not accessible for servicing. The only replacement part available is the check valve on the fuel outlet.

2   Before removing the pump, *first ensure that the car is in a well ventilated place and that there is no danger of ignition from sparks or naked flames. Never work on any part of a fuel system when the car is over an inspection pit.*

3   Disconnect the battery leads and then disconnect the wires from the pump, noting which wire is connected to which terminal (Fig 3.22).

Fig. 3.22 Disconnecting the wires from the electric fuel pump (Sec 23)

4   Thoroughly clean all dirt away from the fuel pipe unions on the pump. Disconnect the fuel pipe from the fuel tank to the pump and seal the end of the pipe to prevent fuel leakage. Disconnect the fuel pipe from the outlet check valve on the pump and cover the pipe end to keep out the dirt.

5   Remove the bolt securing the fuel pump clamp and remove the clamp.

6   The outlet check valve may be unscrewed if necessary, but the pump body must not be held in a vice. Either grip the hexagon of the valve in the vice and turn the pump by hand, or use a spanner on the valve and a strap wrench on the pump body.

7   The pump is designed to work with all its moving parts immersed in petrol and it will be damaged irreparably if it is run without being connected to the fuel system.

8   The capacity of the pump is much greater than the fuel requirement of the engine and it is unlikely that pump output will fall to a point where it is inadequate. If the pump is suspect, test it while on the vehicle as follows.

9   Disconnect the two wires and connect a voltmeter across them. Operate the starter and check that a minimum of 11.5 volts is registered. If the voltage is less than 11.5 volts, check the condition of the battery and the cleanliness and tightness of the pump connections.

10 Connect an ammeter into the pump circuit, again run the pump and check that it is taking a current of about 8.5 amps. If the current exceeds this figure a new pump must be fitted.

11 If the pump gives satisfactory voltage and current readings but its output is still suspect, check that the fuel filter is connected so that the arrow on it points in the direction of flow and that a new filter was fitted at the correct maintenance interval.

12 Refitting is a reversal of removal.

24 Fuel tank gravity/vent valve – removal, checking and refitting

1   This valve is fitted to North American models only. To remove the valve, disconnect the hoses and unclip the valve from its bracket.

2   To test the valve, plug the centre connection of the valve and attach a piece of tubing to the top connection. Put the open end of the tubing in a glass of water and while holding the valve vertically blow into the bottom connection of the valve.

3   When the valve is vertical there should be some resistance to blowing and air bubbles should emerge from the immersed end of the tube.

4   While still blowing into the bottom connection, tilt the valve to an angle of 45°. Bubbles may continue to be seen, but the flow of air should be reduced.

5   If the valve is satisfactory refit it to its bracket and attach the hoses.

25 Inlet manifold – removal and refitting

1   Remove the carburettor or throttle valve assembly, as applicable (photo).

2   On carburettor models disconnect and plug the coolant and vacuum hoses, and disconnect the wiring from the preheater.

3   On fuel injection models remove the auxiliary air valve and cold start valve.

4   On all models unbolt the manifold from the cylinder head and exhaust manifold and remove the gasket (photos).

5   Refitting is a reversal of removal, but make sure that the mating faces are clean, and always fit new gaskets. Top up the cooling system, if necessary.

23.1 Electric fuel pump location on fuel injection models

25.1 Removing the throttle valve assembly on fuel injection models

25.4A Inlet and exhaust manifold link plate

25.4B Removing the inlet manifold (fuel injection models)

25.4C Inlet manifold gasket in position

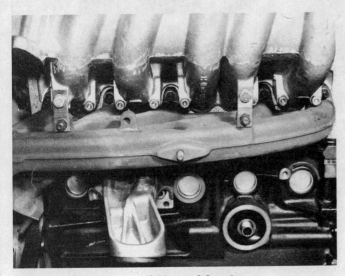

25.4D Inlet and exhaust manifolds on a 2.2 engine

26 Emission control systems – general

Although careful attention to the correct ignition and mixture settings minimises the amount of harmful gases released by the exhaust system, the increasingly stringent legislation in some countries has made the introduction of additional systems necessary.

Crankcase ventilation system

Some of the products of combustion blow past the piston rings and enter the crankcase, from whence they would escape to the atmosphere if special precautions were not taken.

To prevent these gases from escaping to the atmosphere the crankcase breather is connected by a hose to the air cleaner so that the crankcase gases mix with the air/fuel mixture in the manifold and are consumed by the engine.

Exhaust gas recirculation (EGR)

The principle of the system is that some of the hot exhaust gas is ducted from the exhaust manifold to the inlet manifold where it mixes with the fuel/air mixture and again enters the cylinders. This lowers the temperature of combustion in the cylinders and reduces the oxides of nitrogen content of the exhaust.

The system is controlled by a thermostatic valve and by a vacuum valve, controlled by inlet manifold pressure, and system operation must be checked annually as a maintenance item.

Check the physical condition of the hoses of the system, looking for cracks and splits.

Run the engine and check that there are no leaks in the line from the EGR valve to the exhaust manifold.

Disconnect the yellow coloured hose from the straight connection of the temperature control valve and connect it to the T-piece on the hose to the inlet manifold. If the idling speed of the engine falls, or the engine stalls, the EGR valve is working properly. If the idle speed does not change, check that none of the hoses is blocked. If the hoses are clear the EGR valve is faulty and must be renewed.

Catalytic converter

This is only fitted to cars intended for California and it consists of an additional component in the exhaust pipe and silencer system.

The converter contains a catalyst which induces a chemical reaction to turn the carbon monoxide and hydrocarbons in the exhaust gas into carbon dioxide and water.

The converter does not require any maintenance, but should be examined periodically for signs of physical damage.

The catalyst in the converter can be rendered ineffective by lead and other fuel additives, so it is important that only unleaded fuel is used, and that the fuel contains no harmful additives.

The catalytic converter contains a ceramic insert which is fragile and is liable to fracture if the converter is hit, or dropped.

Evaporative fuel control

To prevent fuel vapour escaping to the atmosphere, the fuel tank is vented to a carbon canister. The fuel tank has an expansion chamber and vent lines which are arranged so that no fuel or vapour can escape even though the car may be at a very high temperature, or may be driven or parked on a very steep incline.

The vent lines are connected to a canister containing carbon which absorbs the hydrocarbon vapours. When the engine is not running, fuel vapour collects in the carbon canister. When the engine is running, fresh air is sucked through the canister and the vapours are drawn from the canister through the air cleaner and into the engine, where they are burnt.

Oxygen sensor system

This system consists of a sensor located in the exhaust manifold, on electronic control unit located behind the glove compartment, a thermo-switch relay, and frequency valve. An elapsed mileage odometer also illuminates a warning light on the instrument panel after 30 000 miles to indicate a maintenance check is required on the system.

The system controls the fuel/air mixture according to engine temperature and exhaust gas content, but will only be accurate if the basic mixture adjustments have been made, as described in Section 22.

3

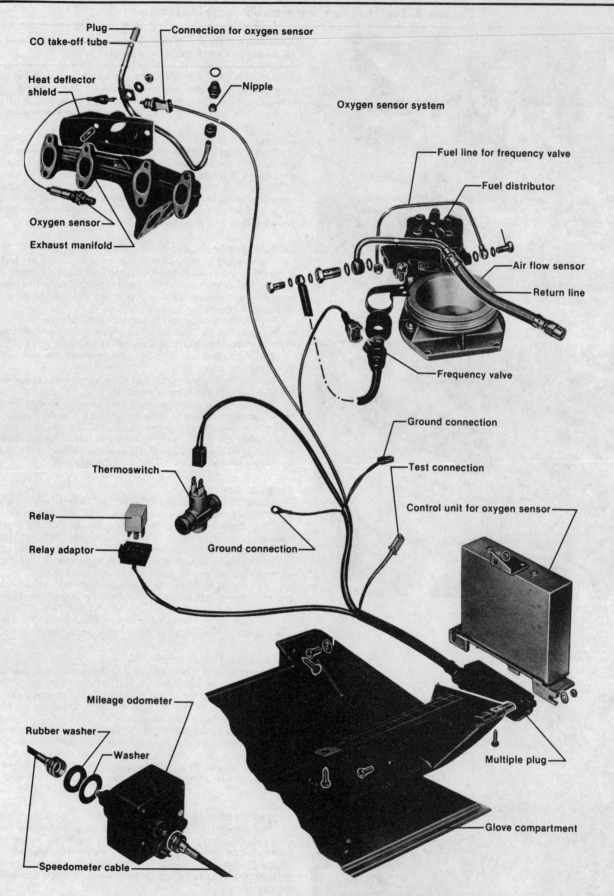

Fig. 3.23 Oxygen sensor system components (Sec 26)

27 Emission control systems – operating precautions

1 The efficiency and reliability of the emission control system is dependent upon a number of operating factors, and the following precautions must be observed.

2 Ensure that the fuel and ignition systems are serviced regularly and that only unleaded fuel, free from harmful additives, is used.

3 Do not alter or remove any parts of the emission control system, or any controls which have been fitted to the vehicle to protect the environment.

4 Do not continue to use the car if it is misfiring, or showing any other symptoms of faulty operation of the engine.

5 Do not leave the car unattended when the engine is running, because any indications of improper operation will not be noticed and prolonged idling can cause the engine to overheat and be damaged.

6 If a catalytic converter is fitted, take care not to park the car on areas of dry grass or leaves, because the external temperature of the converter may be sufficient to ignite them.

7 Do not apply any additional undersealing or rustproofing material to the exhaust system, or anywhere very near to it, because this may lead to a fire.

8 If a catalytic converter is fitted, the car must never be pushed or towed to start it and the engine must not be turned off if the car is moving. To do so would allow unburnt fuel to enter the converter and damage it.

28 Exhaust system – removal and refitting

1 The exhaust systems are shown in Figs. 3.24 to 3.27 (photos).

2 Before doing any dismantling work on the exhaust system, wait until the system has cooled down and then saturate the fixing bolts and joints with a proprietary anti-corrosion fluid.

3 When refitting the system new nuts and bolts should be used, and it may be found easier to cut through the old bolts with a hacksaw, rather than unscrew them.

28.1A Removing the exhaust manifold on a 1.6 engine

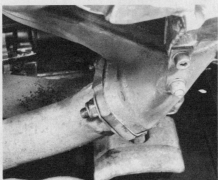

28.1B Exhaust manifold flange joint

28.1C Exhaust system front mounting bracket

28.1D Exhaust system front joint

28.1E Exhaust system central connecting clamp

28.1F Exhaust system central mounting

28.1G Exhaust system rear joint

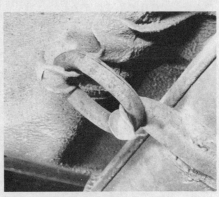

28.1H Exhaust system rear mounting

3

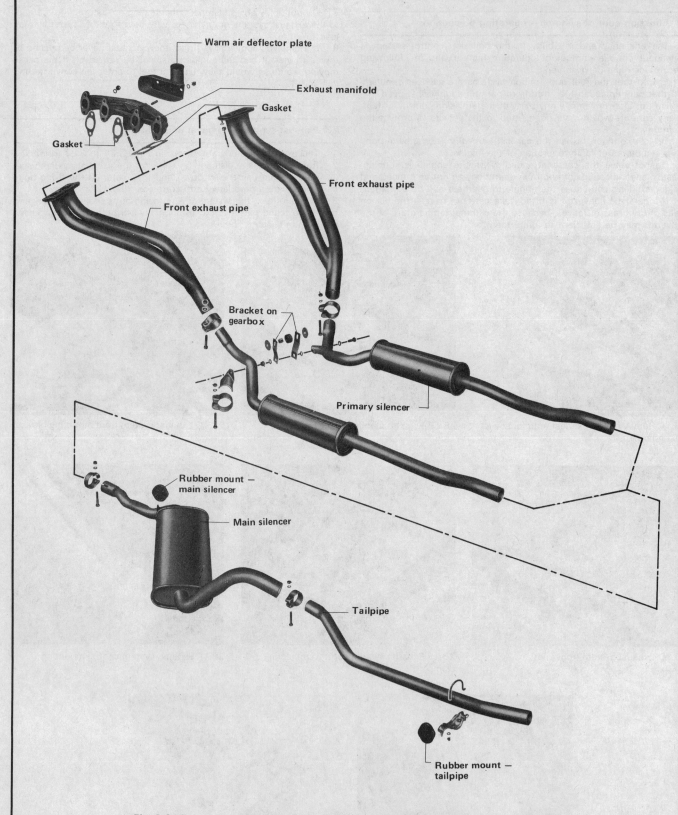

Warm air deflector plate

Exhaust manifold

Gasket

Gasket

Front exhaust pipe

Front exhaust pipe

Bracket on gearbox

Primary silencer

Rubber mount — main silencer

Main silencer

Tailpipe

Rubber mount — tailpipe

Fig. 3.24 Exhaust system components for UK four-cylinder carburettor engines (Sec 28)

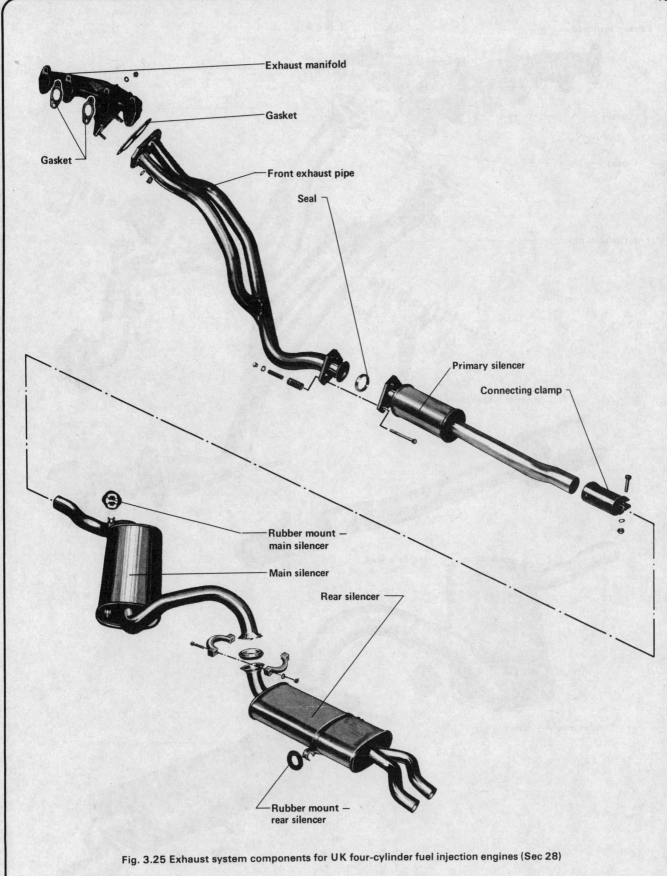

Fig. 3.25 Exhaust system components for UK four-cylinder fuel injection engines (Sec 28)

3

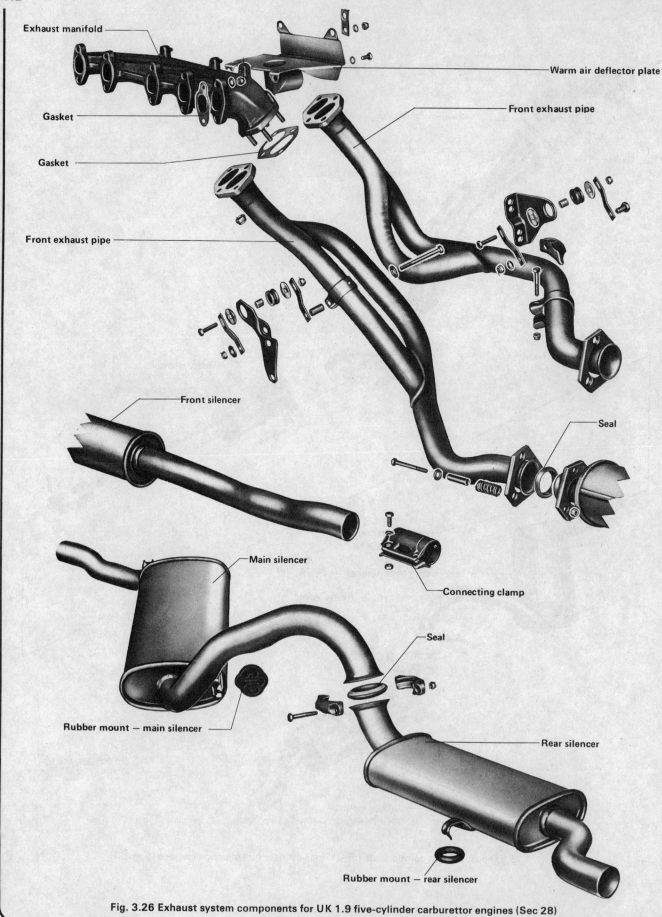

Exhaust manifold

Gasket

Gasket

Front exhaust pipe

Front silencer

Main silencer

Rubber mount — main silencer

Warm air deflector plate

Front exhaust pipe

Seal

Connecting clamp

Seal

Rear silencer

Rubber mount — rear silencer

Fig. 3.26 Exhaust system components for UK 1.9 five-cylinder carburettor engines (Sec 28)

4   When renewing any part of the exhaust system, it is usually easier to undo the manifold-to-front pipe joint and remove the complete system from the car, then separate the various pieces of the system, or cut out the defective part, using a hacksaw.

5   Refit the system a piece at a time, starting with the front pipe. Use a new joint gasket and note that if it has a flanged side, the flanged side should face towards the exhaust pipe.

6   Smear all the joints with a proprietary exhaust sealing compound before assembly. This makes it easier to slide the pieces to align them and ensures that the joints will be gas tight. Leave all bolts loose.

7   Run the engine until the exhaust system is at normal temperature and then, with the engine running at idling speed, tighten all the mounting bolts and clips, starting at the manifold and working towards the rear silencer. *Take care to avoid touching any part of the system with bare hands because of the danger of painful burns.* The catalytic converter, if fitted, requires particular care because of its very high temperature.

8   When the bolts and clips are tightened, it is important to ensure that there is no strain on any part of the system.

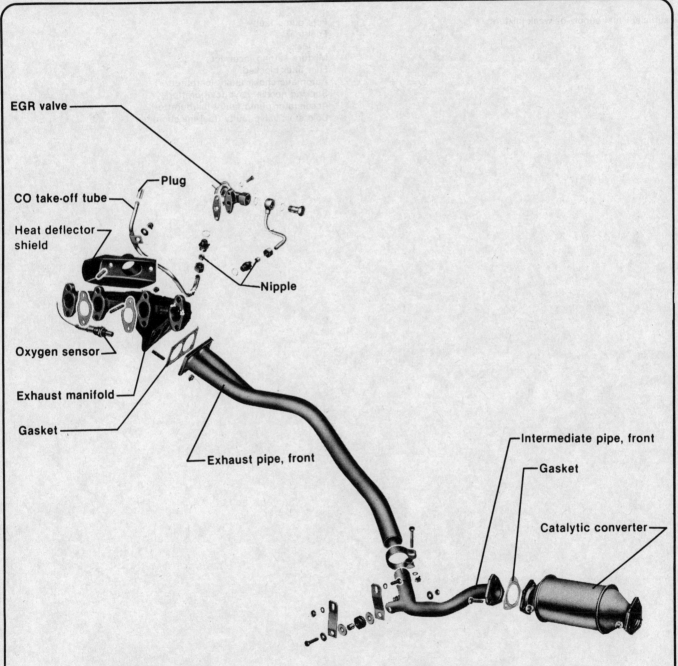

EGR valve

Plug

CO take-off tube

Heat deflector shield

Nipple

Oxygen sensor

Exhaust manifold

Gasket

Exhaust pipe, front

Intermediate pipe, front

Gasket

Catalytic converter

Fig. 3.27 Exhaust system components for North American four-cylinder fuel injection system (Sec 28)

3

29 Fault diagnosis – fuel, exhaust and emission control systems

Symptom	Reason(s)
Excessive fuel consumption	Mixture setting incorrect Air cleaner blocked Fuel leak Incorrect float level (carburettor) Warm-up regulator or fuel metering unit faulty (fuel injection)
Insufficient fuel supply or weak mixture	Fuel pump faulty Fuel leak Air leak Mixture setting incorrect Fuel filter blocked Automatic choke faulty (carburettor) Sticking needle valve (carburettor) Accelerator pump faulty (carburettor) Cold start valve faulty (fuel injection)

Chapter 4 Ignition system

Refer to Chapter 13 for information applicable to 1983 through 1987 models

Contents

Specifications

System type .... 12 volt battery with conventional coil and contact breaker points on early models, or transistorised coil ignition (TCI) on later models

Distributor
Rotor rotation .... Clockwise
Rotor cut-out speed (as applicable) .... 6900 rpm (engine)
Firing order:
    Four-cylinder .... 1-3-4-2 (No 1 at timing belt end)
    Five-cylinder .... 1-2-4-5-3 (No 1 at timing belt end)
Dwell angle (conventional system only) .... 44° to 50°

Coil

	Contact breaker ignition	Transistorised ignition
Primary resistance	1.7 to 2.1 ohm	0.52 to 0.76 ohm
Secondary resistance	7000 to 12 000 ohm	2400 to 3500 ohm

Ignition timing
Note: *On double vacuum unit distributors, the vacuum hoses remain connected, but on single vacuum unit distributors the vacuum hose must be disconnected and plugged*

UK models:
    1.6 litre, engine code YP, YU, YZ, and YN (to 1979 model) .... 0° at 950 rpm
    1.6 litre, engine code YN (from 1980 model) and WP .... 9° BTDC at 950 rpm
    1.9 litre, engine code WN .... 0° at 800 to 850 rpm
North American models:
    1.6 litre, engine code YG (except California) .... 3° ATDC at 850 to 1000 rpm
    1.6 litre, engine code YG and YK (California only) .... 3° ATDC at 940 rpm
    1.7 litre, engine code WT (except California) .... 3° ATDC at 925 rpm
    1.7 litre, engine code WT (California only) .... 3° ATDC at 940 rpm
    2.2 litre, engine code WE with distributor 035 905 205 J (California only) .... 3° ATDC at 940 rpm
    2.2 litre, engine code WE with distributor 035 905 205 J (except California) .... 3° ATDC at 925 rpm
    2.2 litre, engine code WE with distributor 035 905 206 R (1982 manual gearbox) .... 6° BTDC at 850 rpm

4

Spark plugs

Type – UK models

1.6 litre, engine code YN, YP, YU and WP	Bosch W-7D or W-7DC
	Beru 14-7D or RS-35
	Champion N8Y
	NGK BP6E (except on engine code YP)
1.6 litre, engine code YZ	Bosch W-5D or W-5DC
	Beru 14-5D or RS-39
	Champion N6Y
1.9 litre, engine code WN	Bosch W-6D
	Beru 14-6D
	Champion N7Y
Type – North American models:	
1.6 litre, engine code YG (except California)	Bosch W175T30 or W7D
	Beru 175/14/3A or 14-7D
	Champion N8Y
1.6 litre, engine code YG and YK (California only)	Bosch WR7DS
	Beru RS-35
	Champion N8GY
1.7 litre, engine code WT (except California)	Bosch W7D
	Beru 14-7D
	Champion N8Y
1.7 litre, engine code WT (California only)	Bosch WR7DS
	Beru RS-35
	Champion N8GY
2.2 litre, engine code WE	Bosch WR7DS or W7D
	Beru 14-7D or RS-35
	Champion N8Y or N8GY
Gap	0.6 to 0.8 mm (0.024 to 0.032 in)

Torque wrench settings

	lbf ft	NM
Spark plugs	22	30
Distributor clamp bolt	11	15

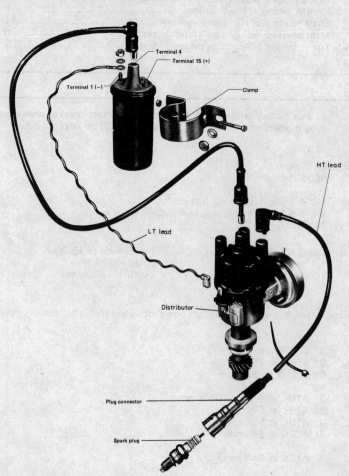

Fig. 4.1 Contact breaker ignition components (Sec 1)

Labels: Terminal 4; Terminal 15 (+); Terminal 1 (−); Clamp; HT lead; LT lead; Distributor; Plug connector; Spark plug

1 General description

The ignition system comprises the battery, coil, distributor, and spark plugs. On early models the system is of conventional type incorporating contact breaker points and a condenser, but later models are fitted with a transistorised system incorporating a magnetic sensor and control unit.

The conventional system functions as follows. Low tension voltage is fed to the coil primary windings and then to the contact breaker points. When the contact points open, the electromagnetic field in the coil induces high tension voltage in the coil secondary windings. The high tension (HT) voltage is then fed via the carbon brush in the centre of the distributor cap to the rotor arm, and then via the metal segments in the cap to each spark plug in turn. The condenser prevents arcing across the contact points and helps collapse the electromagnetic field in the coil, thus ensuring the correct high tension voltage.

The transistorised system functions in a similar manner to the conventional system, but the contact points and condenser are replaced by a magnetic sensor in the distributor and a control unit mounted separately. As the distributor driveshaft rotates, the magnetic impulses are fed to the control unit which switches the primary circuit on and off. No condenser is necessary as the circuit is switched electronically with semiconductor components. *To prevent damage to the system, or personal injury, observe the precautions given in Section 6.*

The ignition advance on both systems is controlled mechanically by centrifugal weights and by a vacuum capsule mounted on the side of the distributor. On some models the ignition is also retarded by an additional section in the vacuum capsule.

2 Contact breaker points – removal, refitting and adjustment

1 Release the two clips securing the distributor cap and remove the cap. Where a radio static shield is fitted also release the earth lead.

2 Pull the rotor arm off the cam spindle and remove the dust cover beneath the rotor arm.

3 Disconnect the contact breaker wire from the terminal inside the distributor. Remove the clamp screw and washer from the contact breaker assembly and remove the assembly.

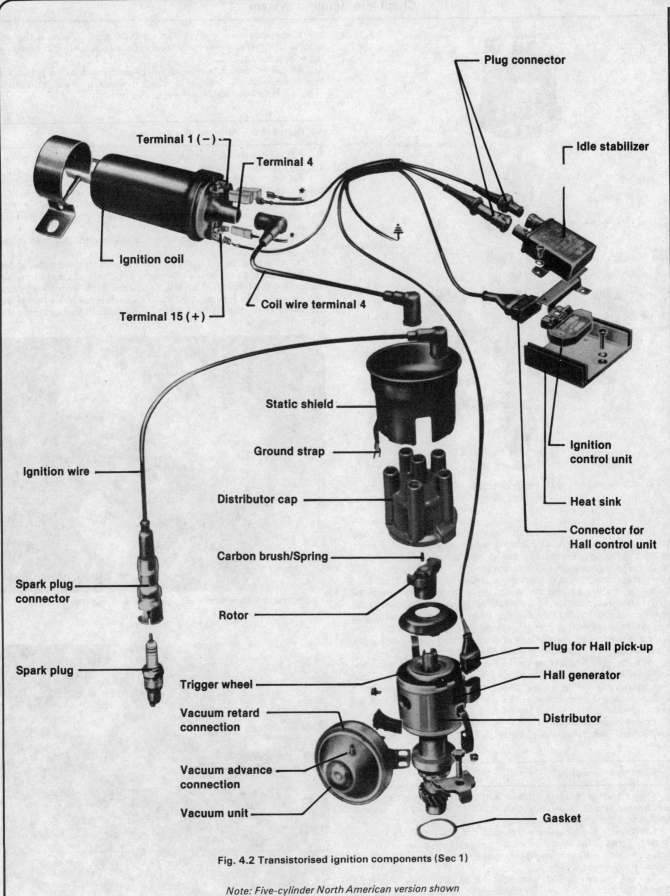

Plug connector

Idle stabilizer

Terminal 1 (−)

Terminal 4

Ignition coil

Terminal 15 (+)

Coil wire terminal 4

Static shield

Ground strap

**Ignition
control unit**

Distributor cap

Heat sink

Ignition wire

**Connector for
Hall control unit**

Carbon brush/Spring

**Spark plug
connector**

Rotor

Plug for Hall pick-up

Hall generator

Spark plug

Trigger wheel

Distributor

**Vacuum retard
connection**

**Vacuum advance
connection**

Vacuum unit

Gasket

4

Fig. 4.2 Transistorised ignition components (Sec 1)

Note: Five-cylinder North American version shown

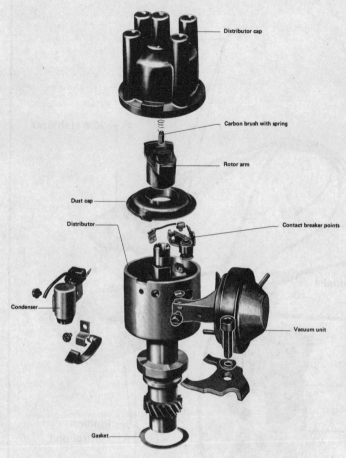

Fig. 4.3 Exploded view of the contact breaker type distributor (Sec 2)

Labels: Distributor cap — Carbon brush with spring — Rotor arm — Dust cap — Distributor — Contact breaker points — Condenser — Vacuum unit — Gasket

points are separated, the test lamp should not be alight. If the test lamp is alight when the contact breaker points are open, the condenser is short-circuited.

4   An open-circuited condenser will cause burning of the points and the engine will be difficult to start. If either of these troubles is experienced a new condenser should be fitted.

4   Distributor – removal and refitting

1   Pull the high tension connection from the centre of the ignition coil and remove the caps from the spark plugs.

2   Release the two spring clips securing the distributor cap, then remove the distributor cap with the ignition harness attached. On models with metal screening round the top of the distributor, it is necessary to remove the screw from the bonding strap before the cap can be taken off (photo).

3   Disconnect the low tension lead or the control unit lead multi-plug, as applicable.

4   Note the exact position of the rotor arm, so that the distributor can be fitted with the rotor arm in the same position, and also put mating marks on the distributor mounting flange and base. By marking these positions and also ensuring that the crankshaft is not moved while the distributor is off, the distributor can be refitted without upsetting the ignition timing.

4.2 Distributor cap screen bonding strap – arrowed (five-cylinder engine)

4   Before fitting the new points, smear the distributor cam with grease and grease the pivot pin of the moving contact breaker contact, but do so sparingly. Excessive greasing may cause contamination of the points, thus leading to ignition malfunction.

5   Fit the contact breaker assembly and tighten the clamp screw so that the fixed contact is just clamped to the baseplate. Either rotate the crankshaft until the plastic cam follower is on the highest point of the cam, or release the distributor clamp plate and turn the distributor body until the contacts are at their maximum separation. If the latter method is used, mark the position of the distributor before moving it, so that it can be re-clamped in its original position.

6   With the cam follower on the highest point of the cam, lever the fixed contact plate until the contacts are 0.40 mm (0.016 in) apart then tighten the clamp screw. This should only be regarded as a nominal setting. For optimum engine performance the setting of the contact breaker points should be checked with a dwell meter.

7   Ensure that the contact breaker lead is securely attached to the side terminal then refit the distributor cap and shield, as applicable.

3   Condenser – testing

1   A high voltage insulation tester is required to test a condenser satisfactorily and it is usually simpler to try substituting another condenser if the original is suspect.

2   Condensers used in mechanical contact breaker type distributors are more liable to fail by short-circuiting than by going open circuit. A short-circuited condenser will result in there being no spark and the engine will not fire.

3   Remove the low tension wire from the distributor and connect a 12 volt test lamp between the distributor terminal and the battery positive terminal. Open the contact breaker points, either by removing the distributor cap and prising the points apart with a screwdriver, or turn the engine so that the distributor cam opens the points. When the

4.6A Distributor clamp and bolt (four-cylinder engine)

4.6B Removing the distributor (four-cylinder engine)

4.7 Distributor gasket (four-cylinder engine)

5   Pull the vacuum pipe(s) from the vacuum control unit, marking the position of the pipes if there is more than one.
6   Remove the bolt and washer from the distributor clamp plate and take the clamp plate off. Remove the distributor and gasket (photos).
7   When refitting the distributor always renew the gasket (photo). Provided the crankshaft has not been moved, turn the rotor arm to such a position that when the distributor is fully installed and the gears mesh, the rotor will turn and take up the position which it held before removal. On the four-cylinder engine if the distributor will not seat fully, withdraw the unit and use pliers to turn the oil pump driveshaft slightly, then try again.
8   Fit the clamp plate and washer, then fit the bolt and tighten it.
9   Fit the distributor cap and clip it in place, then reconnect the high and low tension wires.
10 If the engine has been the subject of overhaul, the crankshaft has been rotated or a new distributor is being fitted, then the procedure for installing the distributor will differ according to engine capacity; refer to Section 8 of this Chapter.

5   Distributor – dismantling, inspection and reassembly

Note: *Before commencing work check if spare parts are individually available for the distributor.*

Contact breaker type
1   Wipe clean the exterior of the distributor.
2   Pull the rotor arm off the cam spindle and then lift off the dust cover beneath it.
3   Disconnect the contact breaker lead from the terminal on the side of the distributor. Remove the clamp screw and washer from the contact breaker and lift the breaker assembly off the baseplate.
4   Remove the screw and withdraw the condenser from the side of the distributor.
5   Remove the small spring clip which secures the operating rod of the vacuum unit to the pin on the contact breaker baseplate. Remove the screw securing the vacuum unit to the distributor case and take off the vacuum unit. This is the limit of dismantling which should be attempted, because none of the parts beneath the contact breaker plate, nor the drivegear, can be renewed individually.
6   Inspect the inside of the distributor cap for signs of burning, or tracking. Make sure that the small carbon brush in the centre of the distributor cap is in good condition and can move up and down freely under the influence of its spring.
7   Check that the rotor arm is not damaged. Use an ohmmeter to measure the resistance between the brass contact in the centre of the rotor arm and the brass contact at the edge of the arm. The measured value of resistance should be between 4000 and 6000 ohms.

8   Suck on the pipe connection to the vacuum diaphragm and check that the operating rod of the diaphragm unit moves. Retain the diaphragm under vacuum to check that the diaphragm is not perforated.
9   The contact breaker and condenser are relatively inexpensive items and it is recommended that the old ones are discarded and new ones fitted on reassembly.
10 Before reassembling, make sure that all the parts are clean and take great care not to get any oil, grease or dirt on the contacts. Smear the cam sparingly with grease, and after fitting the vacuum unit, apply a single spot of oil to the junction of the operating rod and the pin on the contact breaker plate. Also lubricate the felt in the cam recess with two or three drops of engine oil.
11 Fit and adjust the contact breaker points, as described in Section 2.

Transistorised ignition type
12 Wipe clean the exterior of the distributor.
13 Pull the rotor arm off the driveshaft, then lift off the dust cap (photo). Do not allow the cap retaining clips to touch the trigger wheel.
14 Mark the trigger wheel in relation to the driveshaft, then prise out the retainer and withdraw the wheel, together with the locating pin (photo).

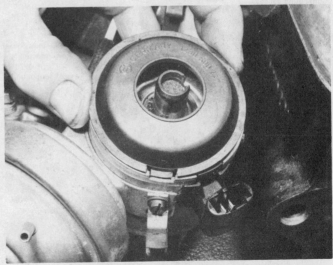

5.13 Removing the dust cap from the distributor (four-cylinder engine with transistorised ignition)

4

5.14 Distributor driveshaft and trigger wheel (four-cylinder engine with transistorised ignition)

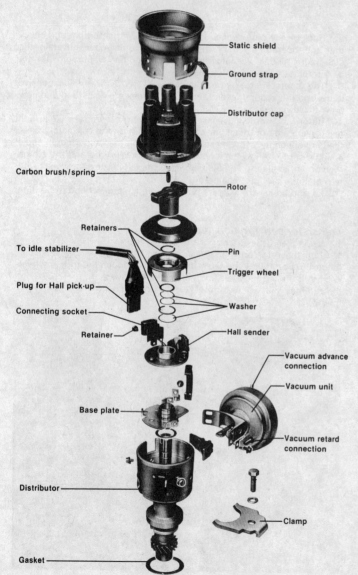

- Static shield
- Ground strap
- Distributor cap
- Carbon brush/spring
- Rotor
- Retainers
- Pin
- To idle stabilizer
- Trigger wheel
- Plug for Hall pick-up
- Washer
- Connecting socket
- Retainer
- Hall sender
- Vacuum advance connection
- Vacuum unit
- Base plate
- Vacuum retard connection
- Distributor
- Clamp
- Gasket

Fig. 4.4 Exploded view of the transistorised ignition type distributor (Sec 5)

15 Remove the retainer and washers, noting their location.

16 Remove the screws and withdraw the vacuum unit and packing after disconnecting the operating arm.

17 Remove the retainer and washer from the baseplate and also remove the screw securing the socket to the side of the distributor. Withdraw the magnetic pick-up and socket together.

18 Remove the screws and lift out the baseplate followed by the washer.

19 Clean all the components and examine them for wear and damage.

20 Check the distributor cap, rotor arm, and vacuum unit, as described in paragraphs 6, 7, and 8. However, note that the rotor arm resistance is 1000 ohms.

21 Reassemble the distributor in reverse order of dismantling, but smear a little grease on the bearing surface of the baseplate.

6 Transistorised coil ignition system – precautions

1 To prevent personal injury and damage to the ignition system, the following precautions must be observed when working on the ignition system.

2 Do not attempt to disconnect any plug lead or touch any of the high tension cables when the engine is running, or being turned by the starter motor.

3 Ensure that the ignition is turned *OFF* before disconnecting any of the ignition wiring.

4 Ensure that the ignition is switched *OFF* before connecting or disconnecting any ignition testing equipment such as a timing light.

5 Do not connect a suppression condenser or test lamp to the coil negative terminal (1).

6 Do not connect any test appliance or stroboscopic lamp requiring a 12 volt supply to the coil positive terminal (15).

7 If the HT cable is disconnected from the distributor (terminal 4), the cable must immediately be connected to earth and remain earthed if the engine is to be rotated by the starter motor, for example if a compression test is to be done.

8 If a high current boost charger is used, the charger output voltage must not exceed 16.5 volts and the time must not exceed one minute.

9 The ignition coil of a transistorised system must never be replaced by the ignition coil from a contact breaker type ignition system.

10 If an electric arc welder is to be used on any part of the vehicle, the car battery must be disconnected while welding is being done.

11 If a stationary engine is heated to above 80°C (176°F) such as may happen after paint drying, or steam cleaning, the engine must not be started until it has cooled.

12 Ensure that the ignition is switched *OFF* when the car is washed.

7 Transistorised coil ignition system – testing

Digital Idle Stabilizer (DIS)

1 The DIS is fitted in the circuit between the Hall generator in the

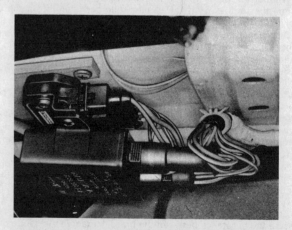

Fig. 4.5 Hall TCI control unit and DIS control unit location in the glove compartment for 1982-on models (Sec 7)

distributor and the control unit. It operates at engine speeds between 600 and 840 rpm and effectively advances the ignition in order to increase the engine speed to the correct idling speed. Not all models are fitted with the DIS.

2   To check the DIS, Audi garages use an electronic tester connected to the flywheel TDC sender unit. However, a timing light may be used just as effectively. Connect the timing light then start the engine and allow it to idle. Note the ignition timing.

3   Switch on all the electrical equipment including the heated rear window and main headlights, then check that the ignition timing has advanced. If not, the DIS unit is faulty.

Control unit

4   First check that the ignition coil and DIS are in order.

5   Disconnect the multi-plug from the control unit and measure the voltage between contacts 4 and 2 with the ignition switched on (Fig. 4.6). Note that on early models the control unit is located on the bulkhead, but on later models it is behind the glove compartment. If the voltage is not approximately the same as battery voltage, check the wiring for possible breakage.

6   Switch off the ignition and reconnect the multi-plug.

7   Disconnect the multi-plug from the distributor and connect a voltmeter across the coil primary terminals. With the ignition switched on at least 2 volts must register, falling to zero after approximately 1 to 2 seconds. If this does not occur, renew the control unit and coil.

8   Connect a wire briefly between the centre terminal of the distributor multi-plug and earth. The voltage should rise to between 5 and 6 volts, otherwise the control unit should be renewed.

9   Switch off the ignition and connect a voltmeter across the outer terminals of the distributor multi-plug. Switch on the ignition and check that 5 volts is registered. If not, check the wiring for possible breakage.

Hall Generator

10 First check the ignition coil, DIS, and control unit. The following test should be made within ambient temperature extremes of 0° and 40°C (32° and 104°F).

11 Disconnect the central HT lead from the distributor cap and earth it with a bridging wire.

12 Pull back the rubber grommet on the control unit and connect a voltmeter across terminals 6 and 3 (Fig. 4.8).

13 Switch on the ignition, then turn the engine slowly in the normal direction using a spanner on the crankshaft pulley bolt. The voltage should alternate between 0 to 0.7 volts, and 1.8 volts to battery voltage; if required, the distributor cap can be removed – with a full air gap 0 to 0.7 volts should register, but when the trigger wheel covers the air gap 1.8 volts to battery voltage should register.

14 If the results are not as given in paragraph 13 the Hall generator is faulty.

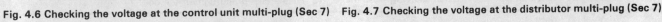

8   Ignition timing – basic setting

1   If the distributor has been removed and the ignition timing disturbed, it will be necessary to reset the timing using the following static method before setting it dynamically, as described in Section 9.

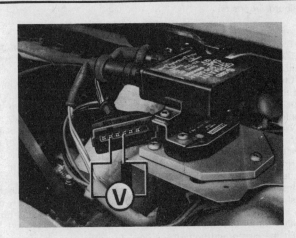

Fig. 4.6 Checking the voltage at the control unit multi-plug (Sec 7)

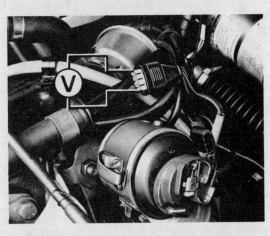

Fig. 4.7 Checking the voltage at the distributor multi-plug (Sec 7)

Fig. 4.8 Checking the voltage at the control unit multi-plug terminals 6 and 3 (Sec 7)

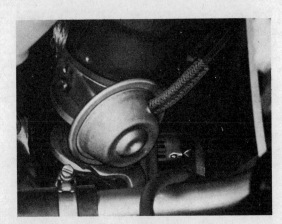

Fig. 4.9 TDC (top dead centre) timing marks on four-cylinder engines (Sec 8)

4

8.2 Showing the flywheel TDC mark and pointer (four-cylinder engine)

8.5 Aligning the rotor arm metal contact with the TDC mark (arrowed) on the rim of the distributor body (four-cylinder engine)

Four-cylinder engines

2   Turn the engine using a spanner on the crankshaft pulley bolt until the TDC mark (O) on the flywheel or driveplate is aligned with the pointer in the timing aperture (photo), which is located next to the distributor.

3   Check that the mark on the rear of the camshaft gear is aligned with the cylinder head cover, as shown in Fig. 4.10. If the mark is on the opposite side of the cylinder head, turn the crankshaft forward one complete revolution, and again align the TDC mark.

4   Turn the oil pump shaft so that its lug is parallel with the crankshaft.

5   With the distributor cap removed turn the rotor arm so that the centre of the metal contact is aligned with the mark on the rim of the distributor body (photo).

6   Hold the distributor over its recess in the cylinder block with the vacuum unit slightly clockwise of the position shown in Fig. 4.12 or 4.13.

7   Insert the distributor fully. As the drivegear meshes with the intermediate shaft, the rotor will turn slightly anti-clockwise and the body can be realigned with the rotor arm to take up the final positions shown in Fig. 4.12 or 4.13. A certain amount of trial and error may be required for this. If the distributor cannot be fully inserted into its mounting hole, slightly reposition the oil pump driveshaft lug. Turn the

distributor body until the original body-to-cylinder head marks are in alignment, or if a new distributor is being fitted, until the contact points, where applicable, are just about to open. Then clamp the distributor in position.

Five-cylinder engines

8   Turn the engine using a spanner on the crankshaft pulley bolt until the TDC mark (O) is aligned with the lug in the timing aperture in the flywheel or driveplate housing.

9   Check that the mark on the rear of the camshaft gear is aligned with the upper edge of the valve cover gasket. If the mark is on the opposite side of the cylinder head, turn the crankshaft forward one complete revolution and again align the TDC mark.

10 With the distributor cap removed, turn the rotor arm so that the centre of the metal contact is aligned with the mark on the rim of the distributor body.

11 Hold the distributor over the location aperture in the rear of the cylinder head with the vacuum unit facing downward.

12 Insert the distributor fully. As the drivegear meshes with the camshaft, the rotor will turn slightly anti-clockwise, and the body can then be realigned with the rotor arm so that the vacuum unit faces slightly to the right.

13 Fit the clamp and tighten the bolt.

Fig. 4.10 TDC timing mark location on the rear of the camshaft gear on four-cylinder engines (Sec 8)

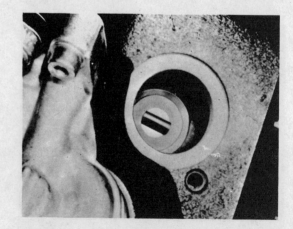

Fig. 4.11 Oil pump shaft lug position, prior to inserting distributor (Sec 8)

Fig. 4.12 Distributor fitted position with rotor arm at TDC on No 1 cylinder – four-cylinder carburettor engines (Sec 8)

Fig. 4.13 Distributor fitted position with rotor arm at TDC on No 1 cylinder – four-cylinder fuel injection engines (Sec 8)

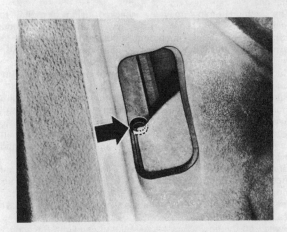

Fig. 4.14 TDC (top dead centre) timing marks on five-cylinder engines (Sec 8)

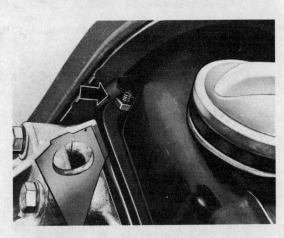

Fig. 4.15 TDC timing mark location on the rear of the camshaft gear on five-cylinder engines (Sec 8)

Fig. 4.16 Distributor fitted position with rotor arm at TDC on No 1 cylinder – five-cylinder engines (Sec 8)

9 Dwell angle and ignition timing – dynamic setting

Dwell angle

1   On models with the conventional contact breaker ignition, the dwell angle should always be checked and, if necessary, adjusted before setting the ignition timing. On models with transistorised ignition, the 'dwell angle' is controlled electronically and cannot be adjusted.

2   The dwell angle is the angle through which the distributor cam turns with the contact points closed between cam peaks.

3   The dwell angle not only provides a more accurate setting of the contact breaker points gap, but the method also evens out any variations in gap caused by wear in the distributor shaft or bushes, or differences in the heights of the cam peaks.

4   To check the dwell angle, connect a dwell meter to the engine in accordance with the manufacturer's instructions, and either run the engine or turn it on the starter, according to the dwell meter used. If the dwell angle is greater than that specified, increase the points gap – if less than specified, reduce the points gap.

Ignition timing

5   Check and, if necessary, adjust the idling speed, as described in

Chapter 3. Note that where a digital idle stabilizer (DIS) is fitted, both plugs must be disconnected from the unit and the plugs connected together. The idling mixture must also be checked at the same time.

6   Switch off the engine. On single vacuum unit distributors disconnect and plug the vacuum hose. However, on double vacuum unit distributors the hoses must remain connected.

7   Check that the air conditioner (where fitted) is switched off. When

Fig. 4.19 Impedance transformer fitted to late North American models – do not confuse this with the idle stabilizer (Sec 9)

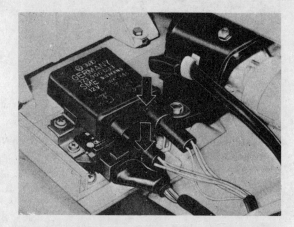

Fig. 4.17 Plug connections to the digital idle stabilizer (DIS) (Sec 9)

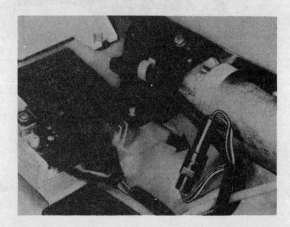

Fig. 4.18 Connect the DIS plugs together (arrow) when checking the ignition timing (Sec 9)

checking the ignition timing, the engine must be at normal operating temperature with the choke fully open, but with the radiator cooling fan stationary.

8   The ignition timing may be checked using a digital tester connected to the TDC sensor in the flywheel or driveplate housing (photo). However, as this equipment is not normally available to the home mechanic, the following method describes the use of a timing light.

9   Connect the timing light to the engine in accordance with the manufacturer's instructions.

10 Run the engine at idling speed and direct the timing light through the timing aperture in the flywheel or driveplate housing. The mark on the flywheel or driveplate should appear in line with the pointer or reference edge on the housing. If adjustment is necessary, loosen the clamp bolt and turn the distributor body until the correct position is achieved, then tighten the bolt.

11 Gradually increase the engine speed and check that the ignition advances – the centrifugal advance can be checked by pinching the vacuum hoses, and an indication of the vacuum advance can be obtained by releasing the hoses and noting that a different advance occurs.

12 Switch off the engine and remove the timing light. Reconnect the vacuum hose and digital idle stabilizer plugs, as applicable.

10 Ignition coil – testing

1   It is rare for an ignition coil (photo) to fail, but if there is reason to

9.8 Hole in bellhousing for fitting a digital tester for checking the ignition timing

10.1 Coil location on the bulkhead

Common spark plug conditions

NORMAL

Symptoms: Brown to grayish-tan color and slight electrode wear. Correct heat range for engine and operating conditions.

Recommendation: When new spark plugs are installed, replace with plugs of the same heat range.

WORN

Symptoms: Rounded electrodes with a small amount of deposits on the firing end. Normal color. Causes hard starting in damp or cold weather and poor fuel economy.

Recommendation: Plugs have been left in the engine too long. Replace with new plugs of the same heat range. Follow the recommended maintenance schedule.

CARBON DEPOSITS

Symptoms: Dry sooty deposits indicate a rich mixture or weak ignition. Causes misfiring, hard starting and hesitation.

Recommendation: Make sure the plug has the correct heat range. Check for a clogged air filter or problem in the fuel system or engine management system. Also check for ignition system problems.

ASH DEPOSITS

Symptoms: Light brown deposits encrusted on the side or center electrodes or both. Derived from oil and/or fuel additives. Excessive amounts may mask the spark, causing misfiring and hesitation during acceleration.

Recommendation: If excessive deposits accumulate over a short time or low mileage, install new valve guide seals to prevent seepage of oil into the combustion chambers. Also try changing gasoline brands.

OIL DEPOSITS

Symptoms: Oily coating caused by poor oil control. Oil is leaking past worn valve guides or piston rings into the combustion chamber. Causes hard starting, misfiring and hesitation.

Recommendation: Correct the mechanical condition with necessary repairs and install new plugs.

GAP BRIDGING

Symptoms: Combustion deposits lodge between the electrodes. Heavy deposits accumulate and bridge the electrode gap. The plug ceases to fire, resulting in a dead cylinder.

Recommendation: Locate the faulty plug and remove the deposits from between the electrodes.

TOO HOT

Symptoms: Blistered, white insulator, eroded electrode and absence of deposits. Results in shortened plug life.

Recommendation: Check for the correct plug heat range, over-advanced ignition timing, lean fuel mixture, intake manifold vacuum leaks, sticking valves and insufficient engine cooling.

PREIGNITION

Symptoms: Melted electrodes. Insulators are white, but may be dirty due to misfiring or flying debris in the combustion chamber. Can lead to engine damage.

Recommendation: Check for the correct plug heat range, over-advanced ignition timing, lean fuel mixture, insufficient engine cooling and lack of lubrication.

HIGH SPEED GLAZING

Symptoms: Insulator has yellowish, glazed appearance. Indicates that combustion chamber temperatures have risen suddenly during hard acceleration. Normal deposits melt to form a conductive coating. Causes misfiring at high speeds.

Recommendation: Install new plugs. Consider using a colder plug if driving habits warrant.

DETONATION

Symptoms: Insulators may be cracked or chipped. Improper gap setting techniques can also result in a fractured insulator tip. Can lead to piston damage.

Recommendation: Make sure the fuel anti-knock values meet engine requirements. Use care when setting the gaps on new plugs. Avoid lugging the engine.

MECHANICAL DAMAGE

Symptoms: May be caused by a foreign object in the combustion chamber or the piston striking an incorrect reach (too long) plug. Causes a dead cylinder and could result in piston damage.

Recommendation: Repair the mechanical damage. Remove the foreign object from the engine and/or install the correct reach plug.

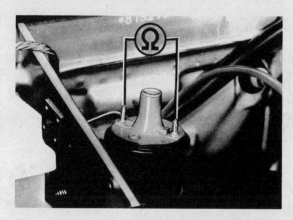

Fig. 4.20 Coil terminals for checking the primary resistance (Sec 10)

Fig. 4.21 Coil terminals for checking the secondary resistance (Sec 10)

suspect it, use an ohmmeter to measure the resistance of the primary and secondary circuits.

2   Measure the primary resistance between the terminals 1 and 15 and the secondary resistance between the centre HT terminal and terminal 1. The correct resistance values are given in the Specifications.

11 Spark plugs and HT leads – general

1   The correct functioning of the spark plugs is vital for the correct running and efficiency of the engine. The spark plugs should be renewed every 10 000 miles (15 000 km). However, if misfiring or bad starting is experienced in the service period, they must be removed, cleaned, and regapped.

2   The condition of the spark plugs will also tell much about the overall condition of the engine.

3   If the insulator nose of the spark plug is clean and white, with no deposits, this is indicative of a weak mixture, or too hot a plug. (A hot plug transfers heat away from the electrode slowly – a cold plug transfers it away quickly).

4   If the tip and insulator nose is covered with hard black-looking deposits, then this is indicative that the mixture is too rich. Should the plug be black and oily, then it is likely that the engine is fairly worn, as well as the mixture being too rich.

5   If the insulator nose is covered with light tan to greyish brown deposits, then the mixture is correct and it is likely that the engine is in good condition.

6   If there are any traces of long brown tapering stains on the outside of the white portion of the plug, then the plug will have to be renewed, as this shows that there is a faulty joint between the plug body and the insulator, and compression is being lost.

7   Plugs should be cleaned by a sand blasting machine, which will free them from carbon more thoroughly than cleaning by hand. The machine will also test the condition of the plugs under compression. Any plug that fails to spark at the recommended pressure should be renewed.

8   The spark plug gap is of considerable importance, as, if it is too large or too small, the size of the spark and its efficiency will be seriously impaired. The spark plug gap should be set to the figure given in the Specifications at the beginning of this Chapter.

9   To set it, measure the gap with a feeler gauge, and then bend open, or close the *outer* plug electrode until the correct gap is achieved. The centre electrode should *never* be bent as this may crack the insulation and cause plug failure, if nothing worse.

10 Always tighten the spark plugs to the specified torque.

11 Periodically the spark plug leads should be wiped clean and checked for security to the spark plugs.

12 Fault diagnosis – ignition system

1   There are two distinct symptoms of ignition faults. Either the engine will not start or fire, or it starts with difficulty and does not run normally.

2   If the starter motor spins the engine satisfactorily, there is adequate fuel and yet the engine will not start, the fault is likely to be on the LT side.

3   If the engine starts, but does not run satisfactorily, it is more likely to be an HT fault.

Engine fails to start

4   If the starter motor spins the engine satisfactorily, but the engine does not start, first check that the fuel supply to the engine is in order, with reference to Chapter 3.

5   Check for broken or disconnected wires to the coil and distributor, and for damp distributor cap and HT leads.

6   For vehicles with electronic ignition follow the procedure detailed in Section 7.

7   For vehicles with contact breaker distributors, remove the LT lead from the distributor and connect a 12 volt test lamp between the end of the lead and the terminal on the side of the distributor. Spin the engine and check that the lamp flashes on and off as the engine turns. If it does, there is no fault in the LT wiring. If it does not flash, but either remains alight, or fails to light, check the contact breaker, condenser and LT wiring.

Engine starts, but misfires

8   Bad starting and intermittent misfiring can be an LT fault, such as an intermittent connection of either the distributor, coil LT leads, or a loose condenser clamping screw (where applicable).

9   If these are satisfactory look for signs of tracking and burning inside the distributor cap, then check the plug leads, plug caps and plug insulators for signs of damage.

10 If the engine misfires regularly, it indicates that the fault is on one particular cylinder. On vehicles with contact breaker type distributors, the following test may be done, *but it should not be done if transistorised ignition is fitted.* While the engine is running, grip each plug cap in turn with a piece of clean dry rag, to avoid getting an electric shock, and pull the cap off the plug. If there is no difference in engine running when a particular plug lead is removed, it indicates a defective plug, or lead. Stop the engine, remove the suspect plug and insert it in a different cylinder. Repeat the test, to see whether the plug performs satisfactorily in the new position and whether a different plug is satisfactory in the position from which the suspect one was removed.

Chapter 5 Clutch

Contents

Specifications

Type .... Single dry plate and diaphragm spring cover, cable actuation

Driven plate
Diameter .... 190 mm (7.48 in), 200 mm (7.87 in), or 215 mm (8.46 in)
Maximum run-out .... 0.4 mm (0.016 in) measured 2.5 mm (0.1 in) from outer rim

Pressure plate
Maximum distortion (inner edge to outer edge) .... 0.3 mm (0.012 in)
Diaphragm spring finger maximum scoring depth .... 0.3 mm (0.012 in

Cable free play (at clutch pedal) .... 15 mm (0.6 in)

Torque wrench settings

	lbf ft	Nm
Pressure plate (clutch cover) bolts	18	25
Clutch release lever pinch bolt	18	25
Release shaft retaining bolt	11	15
Release bearing guide sleeve:		
Four-speed	7	10
Five-speed	11	15

1 General description

The clutch is of single dry plate type with a diaphragm spring cover, and actuation is by cable.

The clutch cover is bolted to the rear face of the flywheel, and the driven plate is located between the cover pressure plate and the flywheel friction surface. The driven plate hub is splined to the gearbox input shaft and is free to slide along the splines. Friction lining material is riveted to each side of the driven plate, and the driven plate hub incorporates cushioning springs to absorb transmission shocks and ensure a smooth take-up of drive.

When the clutch pedal is depressed, the cable moves the release lever, and the release bearing is forced onto the diaphragm spring fingers. As the centre of the spring is pushed in, the outer part of the spring moves out and releases the pressure plate from the driven plate. Drive then ceases to be transmitted to the gearbox.

When the clutch pedal is released, the diaphragm spring forces the pressure plate into contact with the friction linings on the driven plate and at the same time pushes the driven plate along the input shaft splines into engagement with the flywheel. The driven plate is now firmly sandwiched between the pressure plate and the flywheel and so the drive is taken up.

As the friction linings wear, the pressure plate moves closer to the flywheel and the release cable free play is reduced. Periodic adjustment must therefore be carried out, as described in Section 2.

2 Clutch – adjustment

1 The clutch should be checked and, if necessary, adjusted every 10 000 miles (15 000 km).

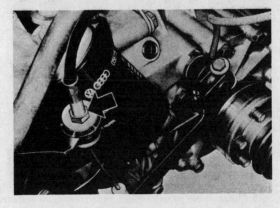

Fig. 5.1 Clutch cable adjuster location (arrowed) on four-cylinder models (Sec 2)

2   To check the adjustment measure the free play at the clutch pedal.
If it is not as given in the Specifications, the cable must be adjusted as
follows.
3   On four-cylinder models, loosen the locknuts on the gearbox end
of the cable, reposition the outer cable to give the required free play,
then tighten the locknuts (photo).
4   On early five-cylinder models, extract the spring clip from the
ferrule on the gearbox end of the cable, reposition the ferrule to give
the required free play, then refit the clip in the groove next to the end
fitting.
5   On later five-cylinder models, an adjuster is located midway along
the outer cable. Loosen the locknut and turn the adjuster in or out to
give the required free play, then tighten the locknut.
6   On all models fully depress the clutch pedal several times, then
recheck the adjustment. Where applicable, lightly grease the adjuster
threads to prevent rusting.

3   Clutch cable – renewal

1   Disconnect the battery negative lead.
2   Slacken off the cable adjustment by loosening the locknut(s) and
turning the ferrule or extracting the spring clip (as applicable).
3   Release the outer cable from the gearbox bracket and unhook the
inner cable from the release arm (photo).
4   Working inside the car, unhook the inner cable from the top of the
clutch pedal.
5   Withdraw the clutch cable through the bulkhead into the engine
compartment.
6   Fit the new cable using a reversal of the removal procedure, and
finally adjust the cable as described in Section 2.

4   Clutch pedal – removal and refitting

1   The clutch and brake pedals share a common bracket assembly
and pivot shaft. On early models the pivot shaft must be removed
completely in order to remove the clutch pedal. However, on later
models the pivot shaft remains in position.
2   Disconnect the battery negative lead.
3   Unhook the inner cable from the top of the clutch pedal, with
reference to Section 3.
4   Where an over-centre return spring is fitted to the top of the pedal,
disconnect it by extracting the spring clip and withdrawing the pivot
pin.
5   Unhook and remove the return spring (where fitted).
6   On early models remove the footbrake pedal with reference to
Chapter 9, then pull out the pivot shaft and withdraw the clutch pedal.

2.3 Clutch cable and release arm (four-cylinder models)

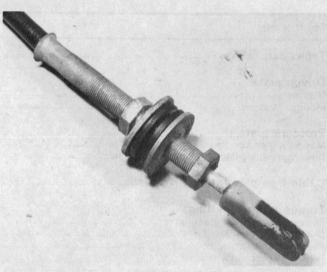

3.3 Clutch cable ferrule end fitting

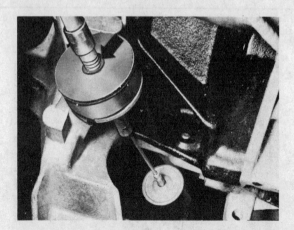

Fig. 5.2 Clutch cable adjuster location (arrowed) on early five-
cylinder models (Sec 2)

Fig. 5.3 Clutch cable adjuster location (arrowed) on later five-
cylinder models (Sec 2)

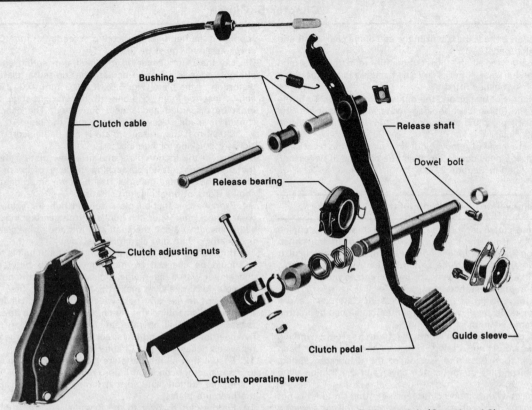

Fig. 5.4 Clutch pedal and release mechanism fitted to early four-cylinder models (Secs 4 and 6)

Labels: Bushing, Clutch cable, Release bearing, Clutch adjusting nuts, Release shaft, Dowel bolt, Clutch pedal, Guide sleeve, Clutch operating lever

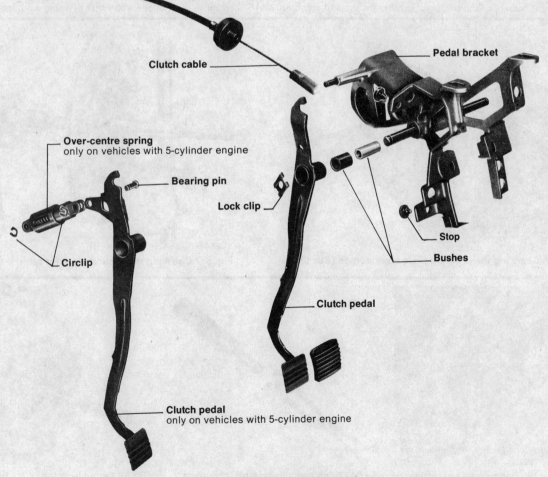

Fig. 5.5 Clutch pedal components on later four-cylinder models and five-cylinder models (Sec 4)

Labels: Clutch cable, Pedal bracket, Over-centre spring only on vehicles with 5-cylinder engine, Bearing pin, Lock clip, Circlip, Stop, Bushes, Clutch pedal, Clutch pedal only on vehicles with 5-cylinder engine

5

7   On later models extract the clip from the end of the pivot shaft and slide off the clutch pedal.

8   Clean the pedal and shaft, then temporarily refit the pedal and check the bushes for wear. If necessary, the bushes can be pressed or driven out and new bushes fitted.

9   The inner bush is of plastic and the outer bush is rubber. To fit the bushes just dip the rubber bush in soapy water and press it into the pedal, then similarly press the plastic bush in from the shouldered side of the pedal until flush.

10 Refitting is a reversal of removal, but first lubricate the pivot shaft with a little grease. Finally check the cable free play and, if necessary, adjust it as described in Section 2.

5   Clutch – removal, inspection and refitting

1   Access to the clutch is obtained either by removing the engine (Chapter 1) or by removing the gearbox (Chapter 6). If the clutch requires attention and the engine is not in need of a major overhaul, it is preferable to gain access to the clutch by removing the gearbox, provided that either a pit is available, or the car can be put on ramps to give a good ground clearance.

2   Put a mark on the rim of the clutch pressure plate cover and a corresponding mark on the flywheel so that the clutch can be refitted in exactly the same position.

3   Slacken the clutch cover retaining bolts a turn at a time, working in diagonal pairs round the casing. When all the bolts have been loosened enough to release the tension of the diaphragm spring, remove the bolts and lift off the clutch cover and the friction plate (photo).

4   Clean the parts with a damp cloth, ensuring that the dust is not inhaled. *Because the dust produced by the wearing of the clutch facing may contain asbestos, which is dangerous to health, parts should not be blown clean or brushed to remove dust.*

5   Examine the fingers of the diaphragm spring for signs of wear, or scoring. If the depth of any scoring exceeds 0.3 mm (0.012 in), a new cover assembly must be fitted.

6   Lay the clutch cover on its diaphragm spring end, place a steel straight edge diagonally across the pressure plate and test for distortion of the plate (Fig. 5.6). If a 0.3 mm (0.012 in) feeler gauge can be inserted in any gap beneath the straight edge, the clutch cover must be discarded and a new one fitted. The check for distortion should be made at several points round the plate.

7   Check that the pressure plate is not badly scored, and shows no signs of cracking, or burning.

8   Inspect the friction plate and fit a new plate if the surface of the friction material left is approaching the level of the rivets. Discard the plate if the friction material has become impregnated with oil, or shows signs of breaking into shreds.

9   Examine the friction plate splined hub for signs of damage, or wear. Check that when the hub is on the gearbox input shaft, the hub slides smoothly along the shaft and that the radial clearance between the gearbox shaft and clutch hub is small.

10 If there is reason to suspect that the clutch hub is not running true, it should be checked by mounting the hub between centres and checking it with a dial gauge. Unless you have the proper equipment, get your local dealer to make this check.

11 Do not re-use any part which is suspect. Having gone to the trouble of dismantling the clutch, it is well worth ensuring that when reassembled it will operate satisfactorily for a long time. Check the flywheel for scoring and tiny cracks caused by overheating; refinish or renew as necessary (see Chapter 1).

12 Ensure that all the parts are clean, free of oil and grease and are in a satisfactory condition before reassembling.

13 Fit the friction plate so that the torsion spring cages are towards the pressure plate.

14 Fit the clutch cover to the flywheel ensuring (where applicable) that the marks made before dismantling are lined up, and insert all bolts finger tight to hold the cover in position.

15 Centralise the friction plate either by using a proprietary tool, or by

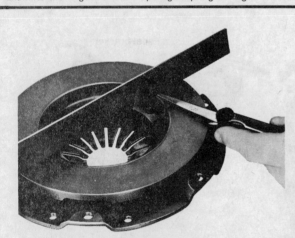

Fig. 5.6 Checking the pressure plate for distortion (Sec 5)

Fig. 5.7 Checking the friction plate for run-out (Sec 5)

5.3 Removing the clutch cover and friction plate

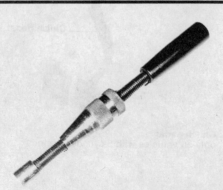

5.15A Clutch centralising tool – the spigot diameter is 15.00 mm (0.590 in)

5.15B Centralising the clutch friction plate

making up a similar tool to hold the friction plate concentric with the hole in the end of the crankshaft (photos). If the clutch cover is tightened without the friction plate being centralised, it will be impossible to refit the gearbox as the input shaft will not pass through the driven plate hub and engage the spigot bearing.

16 With the centraliser holding the clutch friction plate in position, tighten all the clutch cover bolts a turn at a time in diagonal sequence until the specified torque is achieved.

17 Remove the centering tool and smear the hub splines with molybdenum disulphide grease.

18 Check the release bearing in the front of the gearbox for wear and smooth operation, and if necessary renew it, with reference to Section 6.

19 Refit the engine or gearbox with reference to Chapters 1 or 6.

6 Release bearing and mechanism – removal and refitting

1 To remove the release bearing, either lift the release arm to disengage the forks from the spring clips, or extract the clips from each side of the bearing, noting how they are fitted (photos). The bearing can then be withdrawn from the guide sleeve.

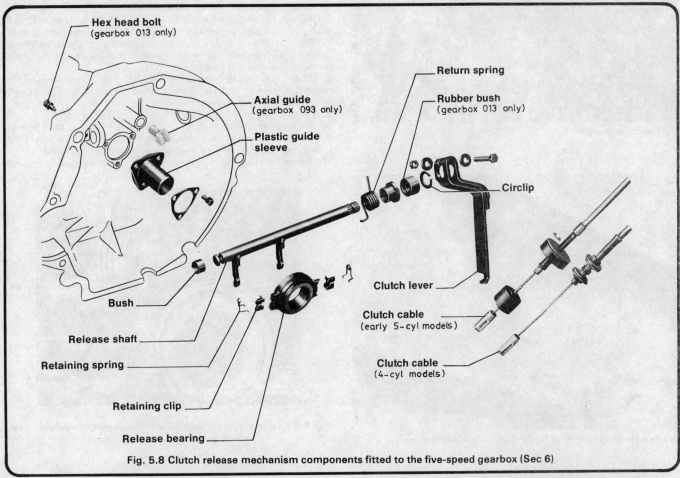

Fig. 5.8 Clutch release mechanism components fitted to the five-speed gearbox (Sec 6)

6.1A Clutch release bearing and release shaft

6.1B Showing the location of the release bearing retaining clips

5

6.2 Clutch release lever

2   Mark the release lever in relation to the shaft then unscrew the clamp bolt and withdraw the lever (photo).

3   On four-cylinder models, remove the dowel bolt from the rear of the bellhousing (photo). The bolt engages a groove in the end of the release shaft.

4   On all models note the position of the return spring – on early four-cylinder models with a return spring fitted to the clutch pedal, the end of the release shaft spring is located in the cast groove. However, later four-cylinder models are fitted with a stronger spring with its end located on the outer side of the cast groove. On five-cylinder models the spring is located in the groove.

5   Unhook the return spring from the release shaft fork (photo).

6   Extract the circlip from the splined end of the release shaft and prise out the rubber bush (where fitted) and the flanged bush (photo).

7   Turn the release shaft so that the forks are free of the guide sleeve, then remove the inner end from the bush and withdraw the shaft from inside the bellhousing (photo).

8   Clean the release bearing with a dry cloth, Do not wash the bearing in solvent, because this will cause its lubricant to be washed out. If the bearing is noisy, or has excessive wear, discard it and obtain a new one.

9   Inspect the release shaft and its bushes for wear. Do not remove the inner bush unless a new one has to be fitted. If a new inner bush is required, the old one will need a special extractor to remove it.

10   Before refitting the release shaft, coat the bearing surfaces with

Fig. 5.9 Return spring location on late four-cylinder models – five-speed gearbox 013 shown (Sec 6)

6.3 Release shaft retaining bolt location on four-cylinder models

6.5 Unhooking the release shaft return spring

6.6 Removing the release shaft flanged bush

molybdenum disulphide grease and ensure that the return spring is fitted to the shaft.

11 Refitting is a reversal of removal. However, on four-cylinder models press in the release shaft until the rubber bush is compressed to approximately 18 mm (0.7 in) (photo) before inserting and tightening the dowel bolt. If a new release lever is being fitted, position it on the splined shaft as shown in Fig. 5.12 (photo). Coat all bearing surfaces with high melting point grease, except for the plastic guide sleeve.

6.7 Removing the release shaft

Fig. 5.10 Return spring location on five-cylinder models – five-speed gearbox 093 shown (Sec 6)

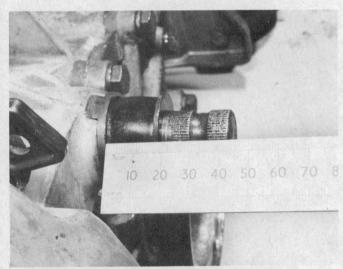

6.11A Checking the release shaft rubber bush dimension

Fig. 5.11 Inserting the dowel bolt (A) on four-cylinder models – press in the release shaft to compress the rubber bush to 18 mm (0.7 in) (Sec 6)

6.11B Checking the release lever fitted dimension

Fig. 5.12 Release lever fitting dimension (Sec 6)

All four-speed gearboxes and five-speed gearbox 013
a = 169 mm (6.65 in)
Five-speed gearbox 093
a = 193 mm (7.6 in)

5

7   Fault diagnosis – clutch

Symptom	Reason(s)
Judder when taking up drive	Oil or grease contamination of friction linings Loose or worn engine/gearbox mountings Worn friction linings Worn driven plate or input shaft splines
Clutch slip	Incorrect adjustment Friction linings worn or contaminated with oil Weak diaphragm spring
Clutch drag (failure to disengage)	Incorrect adjustment Driven plate sticking on input shaft splines Driven plate sticking to flywheel Input shaft spigot bearing seized
Noise evident on depressing clutch pedal	Dry or worn release bearing Input shaft spigot bearing dry or worn

Chapter 6 Manual gearbox and final drive

Contents

Specifications

Type .... Four or five forward speeds, and reverse; synchromesh on all forward speeds; integral final drive

Identification

Gearbox code number:

014/1	Four-speed gearbox fitted to four-cylinder models, except UK GLE
014/11	Four-speed gearbox fitted to UK GLE model
013	Five-speed gearbox fitted to four-cylinder models
093	Five-speed gearbox fitted to five-cylinder models

Ratios

Gearbox 014/1:

	Gearbox code letters			
	WS	**YT/IT**	**XK**	**MY/IM**
Final drive	4.44:1	4.11:1	4.11:1	4.11:1
1st	3.45:1	3.45:1	3.45:1	3.45:1
2nd	1.94:1	1.94:1	1.94:1	1.94:1
3rd	1.29:1	1.29:1	1.29:1	1.29:1
4th	0.969:1	0.909:1	0.882:1	0.909:1
Reverse	3.17:1	3.17:1	3.17:1	3.17:1

Gearbox 014/11:

	YK
Final drive	3.89:1
1st	3.45:1
2nd	1.94:1
3rd	1.29:1
4th	0.909:1
Reverse	3.17:1

Gearbox 013:

	VM/QJ	**MV**	**2M**
Final drive	4.11:1	4.11:1	4.11:1
1st	3.45:1	3.45:1	3.45:1
2nd	1.94:1	1.70:1	1.70:1
3rd	1.29:1	1.10:1	1.06:1
4th	0.909:1	0.75:1	0.778:1
5th	0.684:1	0.60:1	0.60:1
Reverse	3.17:1	3.17:1	3.17:1

6

Gearbox 093:	VW	QF
Final drive	4.90:1	4.45:1
1st	2.85:1	2.85:1
2nd	1.52:1	1.52:1
3rd	0.969:1	0.969:1
4th	0.703:1	0.703:1
5th	0.537:1	0.537:1
Reverse	3.17:1	3.17:1

Oil capacity

Gearbox 014/1 and 014/11	1.7 litre; 3.0 Imp pt; 1.8 US qt
Gearbox 013	2.0 litre; 3.5 Imp pt; 2.1 US qt
Gearbox 093	2.4 litre; 4.1 Imp pt; 2.5 US qt

Synchro ring wear limit

All gearboxes	0.5 mm (0.02 in)

Torque wrench settings

	lbf ft	Nm
Gearbox to engine:		
M10	33	45
M12	41	55
Front support to gearbox (014)	18	25
Rubber mounting to body (014):		
Early (2)	30	40
Late (1)	51	70
Rubber mounting to gearbox (014):		
Early	41	55
Late	80	110
Rubber mounting to body (013 and 093)	80	110
Rubber mounting to gearbox (013 and 093)	30	40
Gear linkage sideplate bolt (014, 013 and 093)	22	30
Gear linkage to gearbox lockbolt (014)	11	15
Gear lever housing and bearing plate (014, 013 and 093)	7	10
Filler and drain plugs (014, 013 and 093)	18	25
Final drive cover (014, 013 and 093)	18	25
Gearshift housing and bearing carrier (014, 013 and 093)	18	25
Ouput (pinion) shaft nut (014, 013 and 093)	74	100
Reverse relay level bolt (014, 013 and 093)	26	35
Reverse light switch (014)	22	30
Gear linkage to gearbox lockbolt (013 and 093)	15	20
Gear linkage support bar (014, 013 and 093)	18	25
Input shaft bolt (013 and 093)	33	45

1 General description

Either a four or five-speed gearbox is fitted according to model, and there are two variations of each gearbox, as listed in the Specifications.

The gearbox is bolted to the rear of the engine in conventional manner, but because of the front wheel drive configuration, drive is transmitted to a differential unit located at the front of the gearbox and then through the driveshafts to the front wheels. All forward gears incorporate synchromesh engagement, and reverse gear is obtained by engaging a spur type idler gear with the 1st/2nd synchro sleeve on the output shaft and a spur gear on the input shaft (photo).

Gearshift is by means of a floor mounted lever, and a single rod and linkage clamped to the selector rod which protrudes from the rear of the gearbox. The selector rod incorporates a finger which engages the other selector rods in the bearing carrier.

When overhauling the gearbox, due consideration should be given to the costs involved, since it is often more economic to obtain a service exchange or good secondhand gearbox rather than fit new parts to the existing gearbox. Repairs to the differential are not covered, as the special instrumentation required is not normally available to the home mechanic.

2 Gearbox – removal and refitting

Note: *If necessary, the engine and gearbox on four-cylinder models can be removed together as described in Chapter 1, and the gearbox then separated on the bench. However, this Section describes the removal of the gearbox leaving the engine in situ.*

1 Position the front of the car over an inspection pit or on car ramps and apply the handbrake firmly.

2 Disconnect the battery negative lead.

3 Unscrew and remove the upper bolts attaching the gearbox to the engine, noting the location of any brackets (photo).

4 Disconnect the wiring to the reversing light switch and release the cable clip.

5 Unscrew the nut and disconnect the speedometer cable from the differential cover or gearbox casing (as applicable).

1.1 Showing the gear positions on the input and output shafts (013 gearbox shown)

2.3 Bracket locations on the upper bellhousing bolts

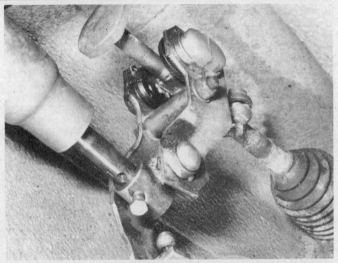

2.15 Disconnecting the selector linkage from the rear of the gearbox (013 gearbox shown)

6   Detach the clutch cable from the gearbox with reference to Chapter 5.

7   Remove the front exhaust downpipe from the manifold and exhaust system with reference to Chapter 3.

8   *On five-cylinder models only*, remove the air cleaner (Chapter 3), and also support the front of the engine with a hoist or bar similar to that shown in Fig. 6.1.

9   Disconnect the driveshafts from the drive flanges with reference to Chapter 8, and tie them to one side.

10 *On four-cylinder models only*, unbolt and remove the centre engine mounting bracket.

11 Unbolt and remove the gearbox front cover.

12 Remove the starter motor, as described in Chapter 10.

13 *On five-cylinder models only*, disconnect the steering tie-rod bracket from the steering gear with reference to Chapter 11.

14 Support the gearbox with a trolley jack or stand.

15 Unscrew the lockbolt securing the selector adaptor to the selector rod on the rear of the gearbox (photo). On four-speed gearboxes it will be necessary to first remove the locking wire.

16 Press the support rod from the balljoint and withdraw the adaptor from the selector lever.

17 Unscrew and remove the lower bolts attaching the gearbox to the engine (photo).

18 Loosen the bolt securing the gearbox stay to the underbody (photo). Unscrew and remove the stay inner bolt and pivot the stay from the gearbox.

19 Unbolt the bonded rubber mounting from the gearbox.

2.17 A lower bellhousing bolt

Fig. 6.1 Support bar required when removing the gearbox on five-cylinder models (Sec 2)

2.18 Gearbox mounting and stay (013 gearbox shown)

6

20 *On four-cylinder models only,* unbolt and remove the front gearbox support bracket.

21 With the help of an assistant withdraw the gearbox from the engine, making sure that the input shaft does not hang on the clutch. Lower the gearbox to the ground (photo).

22 Refitting is a reversal of removal, but lightly lubricate the splines of the input shaft with molybdenum disulphide powder or paste, and make sure that the engine/gearbox mountings are free of strain; if necessary refer to Chapter 1 for the correct alignment procedure. Where applicable secure the selector adaptor lockbolt with new locking wire. Adjust the gear lever and linkage as described in Section 10 or 20. Check and, if necessary, top up the oil level.

3 Gearbox (014) – dismantling into major assemblies

1   Remove the gearbox drain plug, drain out the oil and refit the plug. Clean away external dirt from the gearbox casing.

2   Remove the bolts from the gearshift housing. If necessary give the housing a light tap to separate it from the gear housing and then manoeuvre the gearshift housing off the gear housing. Remove the shim and gasket.

3   Carefully pull the 3rd/4th gear selector rod out of the casing until the small interlock plunger can be removed. Be careful not to pull the shaft out further than is absolutely necessary because the locking keys of the synchro-hub may fall out.

4   Having removed the plunger, push the shaft back in to its neutral position. If the locking keys of the synchro-hub have fallen out it will not be possible to push the rod back in and the alternative method of removing the pinion nut will have to be used after removing the bearing carrier. This involves gripping the 4th gear in a soft-jawed vice, then unscrewing the pinion nut.

2.21 Separating the gearbox from the engine

5   Pull the upper selector rod out to engage reverse gear and the lower one out to engage first gear. By engaging the two gears at once the shafts will be locked and the pinion nut can be undone. Remove the inner race on 014/1 gearboxes.

6   Remove the circlip and thrust washer from the end of the input shaft.

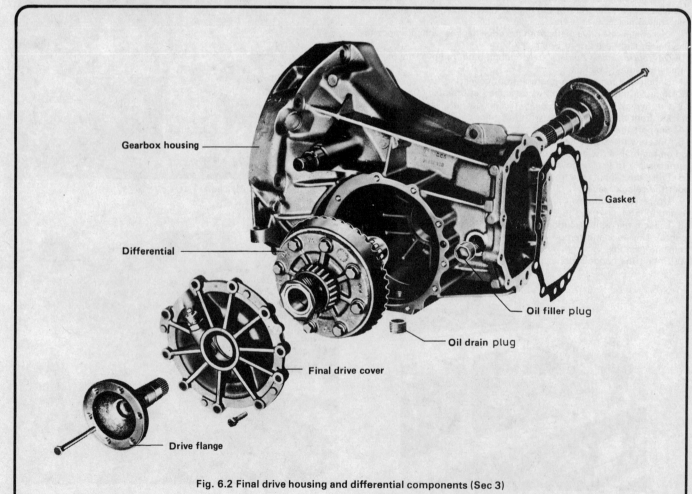

Fig. 6.2 Final drive housing and differential components (Sec 3)

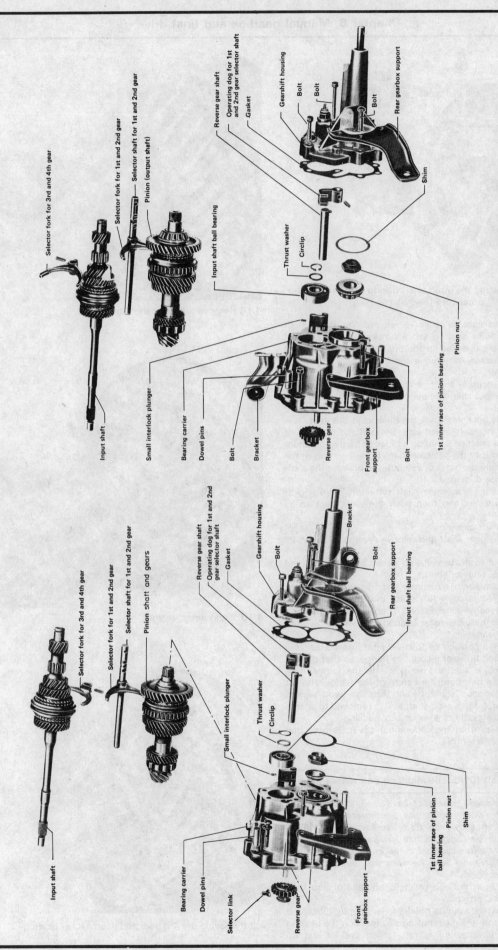

Selector fork for 3rd and 4th gear

Selector fork for 1st and 2nd gear

Selector shaft for 1st and 2nd gear

Pinion (output shaft)

Input shaft

Reverse gear shaft

Operating dog for 1st and 2nd gear selector shaft

Gasket

Gearshift housing

Bolt

Bolt

Bolt

Rear gearbox support

Shim

Thrust washer

Circlip

Input shaft ball bearing

Pinion nut

1st inner race of pinion bearing

Small interlock plunger

Bearing carrier

Dowel pins

Bolt

Bracket

Reverse gear

Front gearbox support

Bolt

Fig. 6.4 Gear components on the 014/11 gearbox (Sec 3)

Selector fork for 3rd and 4th gear

Selector fork for 1st and 2nd gear

Selector shaft for 1st and 2nd gear

Pinion shaft and gears

Input shaft

Reverse gear shaft

Operating dog for 1st and 2nd gear selector shaft

Gasket

Gearshift housing

Bolt

Bracket

Bolt

Rear gearbox support

Input shaft ball bearing

Thrust washer

Circlip

Small interlock plunger

Pinion nut

Shim

1st inner race of pinion ball bearing

Bearing carrier

Dowel pins

Selector link

Reverse gear

Front gearbox support

Fig. 6.3 Gear components on the 014/1 gearbox (Sec 3)

6

Fig. 6.5 Bar for supporting the input shaft during the dismantling procedure (Sec 3)

7   If available, use the special puller to remove the input shaft bearing from the gear carrier housing, while supporting the front end of the input shaft with a bar bolted to the final drive housing. If not available, it will be necessary to remove the input shaft and pinion shaft simultaneously later.

8   Remove the bolts securing the bearing carrier and detach the bearing carrier with the input shaft and pinion shaft from the final drive housing.

9   Drive the dowel pins back until they are flush with the joint face.

10 Clamp the gearbox in a soft-jawed vice. Support the free end of the 3rd/4th gear selector shaft by jamming a block of hardwood under it and drive the roll-pin out of the selector shaft. If the free end of the shaft is not supported while the pin is driven out, the bore for the shaft in the gear carrier may be damaged.

11 Pull out the 3rd/4th gear selector shaft until the 3rd/4th gear selector fork can be removed, and then push the shaft back to its neutral position.

12 Remove the input shaft assembly.

13 Drive out the reverse gear shaft and remove reverse gear and its selector segment (if fitted).

14 Drive out the roll-pin from the 1st/2nd gear operating dog and remove the dog from the selector shaft.

15 Using a soft-faced hammer, or a hammer and drift, drive the pinion shaft out of its bearing. While doing this check that the 1st/2nd gear selector shaft does not become jammed, and if necessary tap the shaft lightly to free it. Recover the taper-roller bearing race when the shaft is removed on 014/11 gearboxes.

16 Dismantle the gearbox housing as follows. First insert a suitable rod through one of the bolt holes of a coupling flange, so that the rod is against one of the cover ribs and so prevents the flange from rotating. Then remove the bolt from the centre of the flange. Repeat the operation on the other coupling flange and then use two levers to prise out the flanged shafts. Mark each shaft as it is removed to ensure that it is fitted to its correct side of the gearbox housing .

17 Remove the ten bolts from the differential cover, remove the cover, and take out the differential.

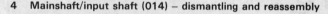

4   Mainshaft/input shaft (014) – dismantling and reassembly

Note: *The four and five-speed gearboxes have many fundamentally similar components. Therefore, whilst the photographic sequence applicable to this Section shows an 013 five-speed unit, for all practical purposes, it can be considered to illustrate the 014 four-speed unit. Any important differences are noted in the relevant photo caption. Other minor differences may be apparent, but should not affect the procedure described.*

1   Remove the circlip from the end of the shaft (photo) and then remove the thrust washer (photo).

2   Lift off the 4th gearwheel with its needle roller bearing (photo). If the bearing is removed from the gear, put a paint mark on the bearing and the gear so that the bearing is not turned end-for-end on reassembling.

4.1A Remove the input shaft circlip ...

4.1B ... and thrust washer

4.2 Removing the 4th gear and needle roller bearing

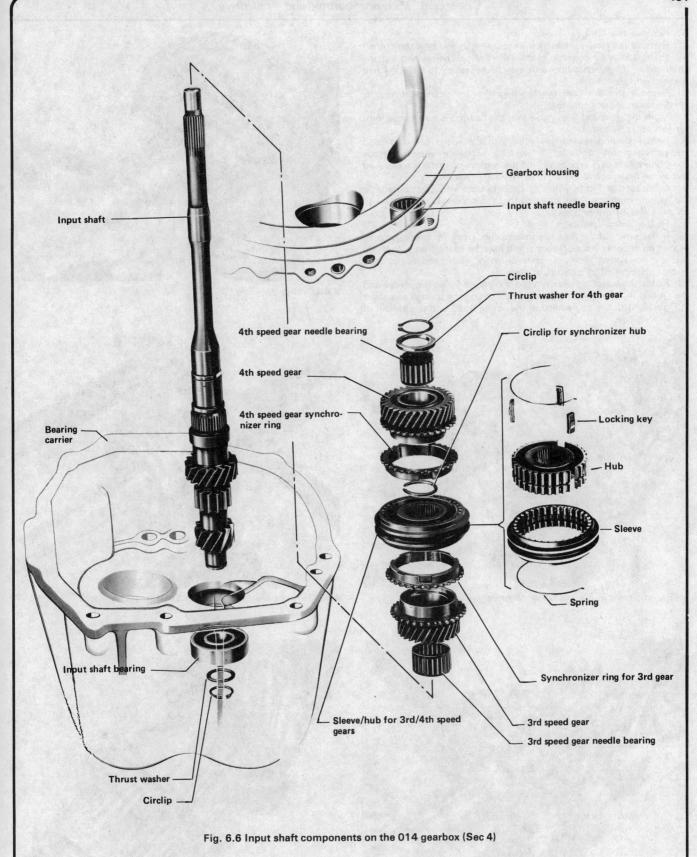

Input shaft

Gearbox housing

Input shaft needle bearing

Bearing carrier

Circlip

Thrust washer for 4th gear

4th speed gear needle bearing

Circlip for synchronizer hub

4th speed gear

4th speed gear synchronizer ring

Locking key

Hub

Sleeve

Input shaft bearing

Spring

Synchronizer ring for 3rd gear

Sleeve/hub for 3rd/4th speed gears

3rd speed gear

3rd speed gear needle bearing

Thrust washer

Circlip

Fig. 6.6 Input shaft components on the 014 gearbox (Sec 4)

6

3   Remove the 4th gear synchro-ring.

4   Remove the circlip retaining the synchro-hub and take the hub off the shaft. It may be possible to hold the 3rd gearwheel and tap the shaft out of the synchro-hub, or it may be necessary to have the hub pressed off (photos).

5   Remove the 3rd gear synchro-ring, the 3rd gearwheel and its needle roller bearing (photos).

6   Mark the gear and bearing so that the bearing is not turned end-for-end on reassembly.

7   Before starting reassembly, ensure that all parts are clean and inspect them for signs of damage or excessive wear. Gearbox components are very expensive, and if any gears or shafts are required it may be more economic to fit an exchange gearbox.

8   Lubricate the 3rd gear needle roller bearing with gear oil and fit the bearing onto the shaft, ensuring that the bearing is the same way up as it was before removal.

9   Fit the 3rd gearwheel.

10   If the synchroniser has been dismantled, look for mating marks etched on the outer edge. If so, the hub must be assembled with these marks in line. Later models do not have mating marks and do not need to be reassembled in a particular position.

11   Fit the three locking keys into the hub before fitting the sleeve and then retain the keys with the springs, positioning the springs as shown in Fig. 6.7, with the angled end of the spring fitted into the hollow of the locking key.

4.4A Extract the circlip ...

4.4B ... and remove the 3rd/4th synchroniser

4.4C Using a puller to remove the 3rd/4th synchroniser

4.5A Removing 3rd gear ...

4.5B ... and the split needle roller bearing

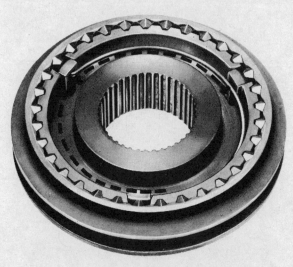

Fig. 6.7 Showing correct fitting of synchro springs

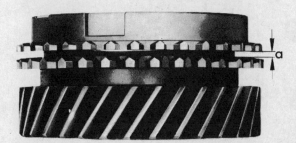

Fig. 6.8 Synchro-ring wear gap (a) (Sec 4)

Fig. 6.9 Synchro-hub groove (white arrow) and chamfer (black arrow) (Sec 4)

12 Fit the 3rd gear synchro-ring onto the cone of the gear and measure the gap (a) in Fig. 6.8, using a feeler gauge. This gap must not exceed the amount given in the Specifications otherwise a new synchro-ring must be fitted.

13 Note that the splines on the bore of the synchro-hub are chamfered at one end. The chamfered end of the hub goes onto the shaft first, facing 3rd gear. The hub also has an additional groove at one end (Fig. 6.9) and this groove faces 4th gear (only on 014/1).

14 Press the synchroniser on to the mainshaft, first turning the 3rd gear synchro-ring so that the grooves on it are aligned with the synchroniser locking keys.

15 Insert the circlip on top of the synchro-hub and then press the synchroniser back against the circlip. This increases the gap between the synchroniser and 3rd gear which ensures better lubrication of the 3rd gear bearing.

16 Fit the 4th gear synchro-ring, aligning the grooves in it with the synchroniser locking keys, then check its clearance, as in paragraph 12.

17 Fit 4th gear and its bearing, first lubricating the bearing with gear oil, fit the thrust washer and finally the circlip.

18 Measure the axial clearance between 4th gear and the thrust washer. This clearance should be at least 0.10 mm (0.004 in), but less than 0.40 mm (0.016 in). If it exceeds the upper limit, a thicker thrust washer must be fitted and these are available in three thicknesses, 3.47 mm (0.136 in), 3.57 mm (0.141 in) and 3.67 mm (0.144 in).

5 Pinion shaft (014) – dismantling and reassembly

Note: *The four and five-speed gearboxes have many fundamentally similar components. Therefore, whilst the photographic sequence applicable to this Section shows an 013 five-speed unit, for all practical purposes, it can be considered to illustrate the 014 four-speed unit. Any important differences are noted in the relevant photo caption. Other minor differences may be apparent, but should not affect the procedure described.*

1 The depth of the pinion's engagement with the crownwheel is adjusted during manufacture to the optimum position for quiet running and long life. When components affecting the pinion engagement are changed, adjustments must be made to regain this optimum position. Before the pinion shaft is dismantled or replacement items fitted, the position of the pinion must be established by measurement. Because this requires the use of specialist measuring equipment the work should be entrusted to your Audi dealer. The components which affect the pinion engagement are the gearbox casing, the bearing carrier, the pinion bearings and the 1st gear needle roller bearing. The crownwheel and pinion must be renewed as a matched pair and the pinion engagement adjusted to the figure etched onto the crownwheel – a job for your Audi dealer.

2 Using a suitable puller, remove the bearing race and 1st gear, then remove the needle roller bearing and sleeve, keeping them identified for position (photos).

3 Lift off the 1st gear synchro-ring.

5.2A From the pinion shaft remove the bearing ...

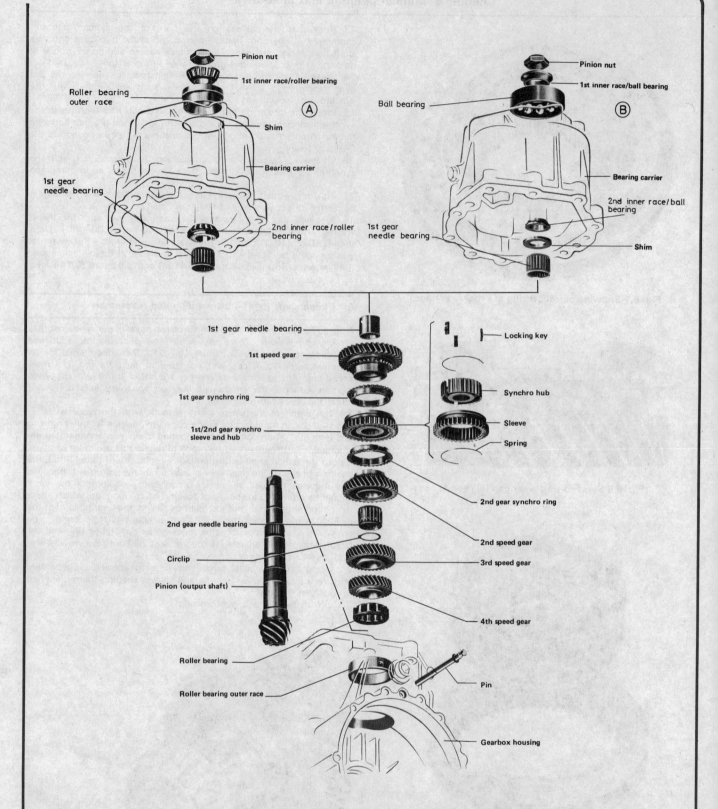

Fig. 6.10 Pinion shaft components on the 014 gearbox (Sec 5)

A   014/11 gearbox   B   014/1 gearbox

5.2B ... 1st gear ...

5.2C ... needler roller bearing ...

5.2D ... and bearing sleeve

5.7A Pinion shaft ready for assembly of ...

5.7B ... roller bearing ...

4   Using a puller with its legs placed beneath the 2nd gearwheel, draw off the gear and the 1st/2nd gear synchroniser assembly. Remove the 2nd gear synchro-ring.

5   Lift off the 2nd gear needle roller bearing and mark it to ensure correct refitting.

6   The 3rd speed and 4th speed gears are pressed and shrunk on to the shaft, and if they need to be removed, the work should be entrusted to an Audi dealer. However, it may be possible to remove them with a suitable puller.

7   Reassembly will commence with the pinion end bearing, 4th gear, 3rd gear and the circlip already on the pinion shaft; complete reassembly of the shaft as follows (photos).

8   Lubricate the 2nd gear needle roller bearing with gear oil and fit it to the shaft.

9   Fit the 2nd gearwheel onto its bearing, then place the syncro-ring on the gear. Measure the gap as in Fig. 6.8. If the gap exceeds the amount given in the Specifications, a new synchro-ring must be fitted (photos).

10 If the synchroniser assembly has been dismantled, it must be reassembled in the following way. The sleeve and the hub may have matching marks, if so they must be assembled with these marks lined up. Fit the three locking keys into their slots and secure the keys with the circlips. The circlips should be spaced 120° apart and the angled end of the circlip should be engaged in the hollow of a locking key. If there are no matching marks on the hub and sleeve the two parts need

5.7C ... and 4th gear

5.7D Using a puller to fit 4th gear

5.7E Fitting 3rd gear ...

5.7F ... checking for size of circlip ...

5.7G ... and fitting circlip

5.9A Fitting 2nd gear ...

5.9B ... and 2nd synchro-ring

5.9C Checking the synchro-ring wear with a feeler gauge

5.9D End view of a synchro-ring

5.11A Fitting the 1st/2nd synchroniser *(Caution – this is shown on the 013 gearbox. Opposite way round on the 014 gearbox)*.

5.11B 1st/2nd synchroniser fully installed (013 gearbox shown)

Fig. 6.11 Identification of 110° synchro-ring for 1st gear on the 014 gearbox (Sec 5)

not be assembled in any particular position, except that the grooves on the hub splines must face the 1st gear.

11 Fit the synchroniser assembly to the shaft, with the end of the sleeve having external teeth towards the pinion. Before pressing the hub down fully, turn the 2nd gear synchro-ring so that the slots in it are aligned with the locking keys in the synchroniser assembly (photos).

12 Fit the 1st gear synchro-ring, lining up its slots with the locking keys in the synchroniser assembly. Later models have a modified synchro-ring with a tooth missing at three points (Fig. 6.11). The tooth

5.13 Fitting 1st synchro-ring and 1st gear needle roller bearing

5.14 Fitting the bearing to the pinion shaft

6.2 Location of input shaft needle roller bearing (A) and pinion shaft roller bearing outer race (B) in the final drive housing

6.3 Removing the pinion shaft bearing outer race retaining pin

angle on these synchro-rings was altered from 120° to 110° to improve the engagement of 1st gear. This type of ring must only be used on 1st gear, and if the 1st gear ring is being renewed, the 120° type having the full number of teeth should be fitted, as the modified ring is not available as a spare part.

13 Fit the 1st gear bearing sleeve, then lubricate the needle roller bearing with gear oil and fit it over the sleeve (photo).

14 Fit the 1st gearwheel and then press on the 2nd inner race of the tapered roller bearing on 014/11 gearboxes, or fit the shim and press on the ball-bearing inner race on 014/1 gearboxes. Use a metal tube to drive on the bearing if necesary (photo).

6   Gearbox/final drive housing (014) – servicing

Note: The four and five-speed gearboxes have many fundamentally similar components. Therefore, whilst the photographic sequence applicable to this Section shows an 013 five-speed unit, for all practical purposes, it can be considered to illustrate the 014 four-speed unit. Any important differences are noted in the relevant photo caption. Other minor differences may be apparent, but should not affect the procedure described.

1   The removal and refitting of the clutch release mechanism fitted in the gearbox housing is described in Chapter 5.

Input shaft needle bearing

2   Using a drift, or piece of hardwood dowel of suitable size, drive the bearing out from the clutch bellhousing end of the casing. Fit the new bearing so that the lettering on the bearing faces the drift used for installation. Enter the bearing into the bore squarely from the gearbox side of the casing, and using a drift, or a piece of hardwood, knock it in until it is flush with the face of the casting (photo).

Pinion bearing

3   The outer track of the pinion bearing is secured by a pin which engages a depression in the outer circumference of the bearing (photo). Grip the grooved end of the pin and pull it out at least $\frac{1}{8}$ in (3.2 mm) so that the other end is clear of the bearing. Using a suitable drift, tap the outer race out of the end of the casing. When fitting a new outer track, line up the depression in the outer track with the pin, and then drive the track in flush with the face of the casting before tapping home the pin (the grooves marking on the end face of the bearing track should face towards the fitting tool). Renewing the roller assembly of the bearing is a job for an Audi agent; the 3rd and 4th gearwheels are shrunk onto the shaft and will require a substantial press tool to remove. On refitting the gears must be heated to 120° (248°F) before being pressed into position (wide shoulder on each gear faces the pinion).

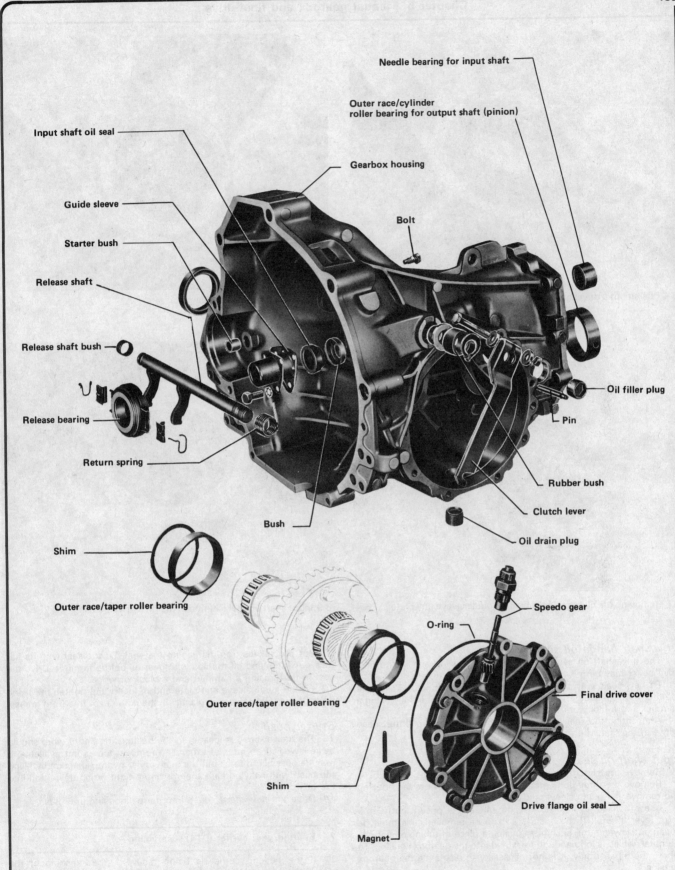

Input shaft oil seal

Guide sleeve

Starter bush

Release shaft

Release shaft bush

Release bearing

Return spring

Bush

Shim

Outer race/taper roller bearing

Needle bearing for input shaft

Outer race/cylinder roller bearing for output shaft (pinion)

Gearbox housing

Bolt

Oil filler plug

Pin

Rubber bush

Clutch lever

Oil drain plug

Outer race/taper roller bearing

Shim

Magnet

Speedo gear

O-ring

Final drive cover

Drive flange oil seal

Fig. 6.12 Final drive housing components on the 014 gearbox (Sec 6)

6

6.4 Prising out a driveshaft flange oil seal

6.5 Installing a driveshaft flange oil seal

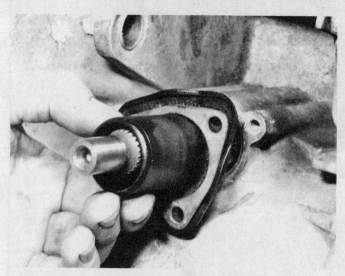

6.8 Removing the clutch release bearing guide sleeve and plate

6.9 Input shaft oil seal location in the final drive housing

Driveshaft flange oil seals

4   The driveshaft oil seals in the gearbox housing and in the final drive cover may be prised out with a large screwdriver (photo).
5   Fit new seals with the lips of the seal inwards (photo). Take care to enter the seal squarely into the housing and drive it in fully using a hammer and a block of wood.
6   After fitting the seal, smear its lip with gear oil and fill the space between the lips with multi-purpose grease.

Input shaft oil seal

7   Remove the clutch release bearing as described in Chapter 5.
8   Remove the three bolts attaching the guide sleeve to the housing and remove the guide sleeve and plate (photo).
9   Use a hooked lever to remove the oil seal, or prise it out with a short lever (photo). If the bush is also to be removed, this must be driven out towards the bellhousing using a piece of tubing of suitable diameter, which is long enough to extend into the gearbox housing. To renew the oil seal only, it is not necessary to dismantle the gearbox housing.
10   Drive the bush into the housing until the flat end of the bush seats against the bottom of the recess.
11   If the oil seal is being fitted with the input shaft in position, slide a piece of plastic sleeving over the splines of the input shaft, or wrap plastic tape round them before sliding the seal over the shaft. This will

prevent the splines from damaging the seal. Fit the seal with its flat face outwards and oil the lips with gear oil before fitting it. Drive the seal in flush, using a hammer and a block of wood.
12   Fit the guide sleeve and plate and re-insert and tighten the fixing bolts. If the guide sleeve is plastic, it should be kept free from grease.

Starter bush

13   The starter bush is located in the bellhousing and if worn should be renewed. If an internal expanding removal tool is not available, it may be possible to force out the bush under hydraulic action by filling the bush with heavy grease then driving a tight fitting dowel rod into the bush.
14   Drive the new starter bush into the bellhousing until flush.

7   Bearing/gear carrier (014) – servicing

1   If the bearing carrier is being renewed, the meshing of the crownwheel and pinion is affected (see Section 5, paragraph 1). To ensure correct meshing, the pinion projection will need to be measured by an Audi dealer before and after the new carrier is fitted. They can then advise on the appropriate thickness of shim and gasket to be fitted between the new gear carrier and the gearbox housing to regain the original pinion projection.

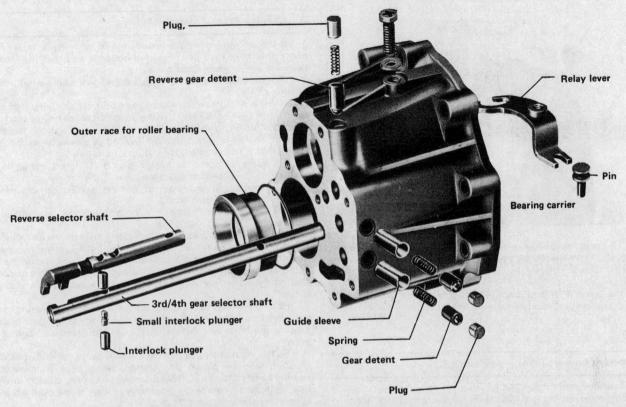

Fig. 6.13 Gear carrier components on the 014/11 gearbox (Sec 7)

Gearbox 014/1 components similar, but ball-bearing fitted

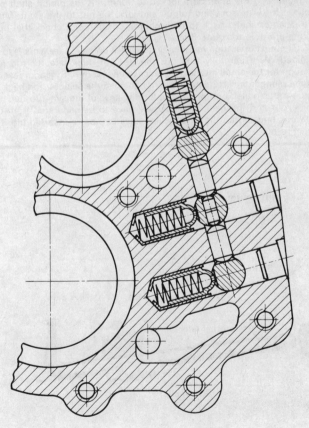

Fig. 6.14 Cross-sectional diagram of the selector rod detents on the 014 gearbox (Sec 7)

Pinion bearing removal

2   The outer track of the bearing can be driven out of the case using a suitable drift, but the fitting of a new bearing and determining the correct thickness of shim needs to be done by an Audi dealer.

Gear detents – removal and refitting

3   Unscrew the pivot bolt and remove the reverse relay lever. Remove the pin from the reverse selector rod and pull the rod from the bearing carrier.

4   Pull the 3rd/4th gear selector rod out of the bearing carrier, taking care to recover the small interlock plunger within the rod.

5   To remove the detent plug at the top of the bearing carrier cut a 6 mm thread in the plug, screw a bolt into the plug and pull the bolt to extract the plug. With the plug removed, the spring and the detent can be removed.

6   The two detents in the side of the box are removed by driving in their plugs until the plugs can be removed from the gear selector rod bores. The detent, spring and sleeves can then be shaken out, together with the large interlock plungers.

7   Refitting is the reverse of removal. The correct position of the detents and interlock plungers is shown in Fig. 6.14.

Relay lever adjustment

8   It is not necessary to remove the selector rods in order to adjust the relay lever.

9   Fit reverse gear and its shaft and then insert the relay lever and selector link.

10   Fit the relay lever bolt and washer. Screw the bolt in until it touches the relay lever, while the relay lever is being pressed in the direction of the arrow (Fig. 6.15).

11   Press the relay lever against the end of the bolt and then screw in the bolt until it just starts to engage the threads in the relay lever.

12   While still holding the relay lever in the same position, screw the bolt in and tighten it to the torque given in the Specifications. The relay lever should now be set at the correct distance from the gearcase.

13   Move the reverse gear selector rod to the reverse gear position several times and check that the relay mechanism moves freely in all positions.

6

Fig. 6.15 Press the reverse relay lever in the direction of the arrow when fitting the pivot bolt (Sec 7)

14 If the relay lever has been adjusted with the selector rods removed, reverse gear must be removed again before the selector rods can be fitted.

8 Gearshift housing (014) – servicing

1   Pull out the selector rod and spring.
2   Before removing the rear bush, lever out the rear oil seal, and then use a long drift to tap out the bush from the front end of the housing.
3   Enter the new bush squarely into the rear of the housing and tap it home flush with the end of the casting, using a block of wood. In order to drive the new bush in fully, rub the outside diameter of the *old* bush with a piece of emery cloth to reduce its diameter enough to make it an easy fit in the casting, then use this bush as a drift.
4   Fit a new oil seal, with the open end of the seal inwards, and using a block of hardwood against the seal, drive it in until its face is flush with the end of the casting.
5   The procedure for removing and fitting the front bush is similar, except that there is no oil seal and it is necessary to note which way round the bush is fitted.
6   Lubricate the bushes and smear the lip of the oil seal with gear oil before refitting the selector rod.

9 Gearbox (014) – reassembly

1   If the selector rods have been removed from the bearing carrier, check that they have been inserted correctly and that the interlock plungers are in their proper places.
2   Fit the pinion assembly and the 1st/2nd gear selector fork into the bearing carrier.
3   Using a suitable piece of tubing as a drift, tap the outer part of the taper-roller bearing (014/11), or the outer part of the ball-bearing inner race (014/1) on to the end of the shaft, but while doing this make frequent checks to ensure that the 1st/2nd gear selector shaft has not jammed. If it has jammed, tap it lightly to free it.
4   Fit the 1st/2nd gear operating dog on the shift rod, line up its hole with the hole in the shift rod, then drive in the roll-pin.
5   Fit reverse gear and segment into the bearing carrier and then drive in the reverse gear shaft.
6   Fit the input shaft assembly loosely into the box without its bearing.
7   Pull back the 3rd/4th gear selector rod until the 3rd/4th gear selector fork can be fitted into the groove in the synchro-hub sleeve. Push the selector rod back to its neutral position and line up the hole in the selector rod with the hole in the fork. Support the free end of the shaft in the same way as when removing the selector fork and drive in the roll-pin.
8   Fit a new gasket to the gearbox housing and fit the bearing carrier, with the input and pinion shaft assemblies, to the gearbox housing. Line up the holes and drive in the dowel pin. Insert and tighten the bolts.
9   Fit the input shaft ball bearing squarely on to the end of its shaft, ensuring that the closed side of the bearing cage is towards the bearing carrier. Using a suitable tube, or a block of hardwood, drive the bearing in, taking care to see that it stays square to the shaft while also supporting the shaft on a block of wood.
10 Fit the thrust washer and circlip on top of the input shaft bearing.
11 Pull back the two selector rods until 1st and reverse gears are both engaged and the shafts are locked together. Fit the pinion shaft nut, tighten it to the specified torque and lock the nut to the shaft. Move the selector shafts back to their neutral position and check that both shafts are able to rotate freely.
12 The next operation requires great care if unnecessary work is to be avoided. Very carefully pull out the 3rd/4th gear selector rod just enough for the small interlock plunger to be inserted. Smear grease on to the plunger, insert it into the hole and push the selector rod back in. If the rod is pulled out too far, the locking keys of the synchro-hub can come out and the gear assembly will have to be separated from the gearbox housing so that the locking keys can be re-inserted into the synchro-hub.

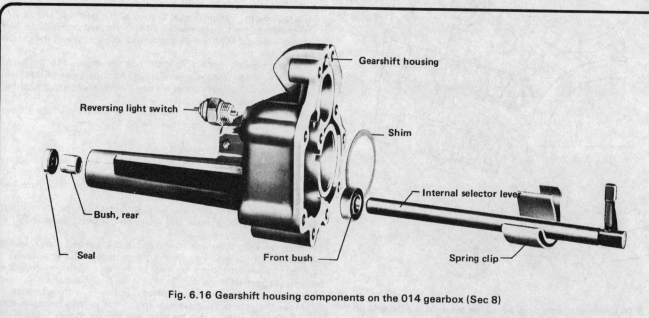

Fig. 6.16 Gearshift housing components on the 014 gearbox (Sec 8)

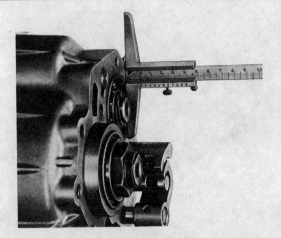

Fig. 6.17 Measuring the input shaft bearing projection on the 014 gearbox (Sec 9)

13 When refitting the gearshift housing to the bearing carrier, use a new gasket; because the thickness of gasket influences the position of the pinion, the correct thickness must be fitted. If no parts of the bearing carrier have been renewed, measure the thickness of the old gasket, which will be either 0.30 or 0.40 mm (0.012 or 0.016 in) and use a new gasket of the same thickness.

14 If a new input shaft bearing has been fitted, measure the amount by which the outer race projects from the end face of the gear assembly (Fig. 6.17). If this is between 0.20 and 0.26 mm (0.008 and 0.010 in) use a 0.30 mm (0.012 in) thick gasket. If the projection is between 0.27 and 0.32 mm (0.011 and 0.013 in), use a 0.40 mm (0.016 in) thick gasket.

15 When refitting the gearshift housing, first ensure that the shim is in place in the housing recess, with the recess in the shim towards the spring.

16 Fit the spring by first putting it over the internal selector lever. Compress the spring and slide it with the internal selector lever into the housing so that the end of the spring rests against the end of the housing and the shim. Move the spring and the selector lever into the housing as far as they will go, and turn the selector lever so that the spring and selector lever are as shown in Fig. 6.18.

17 Insert the finger of the selector lever into the slots in the selector rods and push the gearshift housing into place. Insert the bolts and tighten them to the specified torque.

18 Lower the differential into the final drive housing with the crownwheel teeth facing inward. Fit the O-ring to the cover and locate the cover on the housing. Insert the bolts and tighten them evenly in diagonal sequence to the specified torque.

19 Insert the drive flanges into each side of the differential and tighten the bolts while holding the flanges stationary with a rod through one of the bolt holes.

20 Fill the gearbox with oil.

Fig. 6.18 Fitted position of the selector lever spring in the 014 gearshift housing (Sec 9)

10 Gearshift lever (014) – removal, refitting and adjustment

1 The adjustment of the gearshift linkage requires a special tool, so if the linkage is undone, it is very important to mark the position of the shift rod in the shift finger before separating them.

2 Put a mark to show how far the shift rod is inserted into the clamp, and also mark a horizontal line on both the shift finger and the shift rod so that they can be reconnected without any rotational change.

3 Release the bolt on the clamp and separate the shift rod from the shift finger.

4 From inside the car, remove the four nuts and washers securing the lever housing to the car floor and remove the gear lever assembly and shift rod.

5 To separate the shift rod from the gear lever, undo and remove the shift rod clevis bolt.

6 After refitting the gear lever, by reversing the removal operations, the basic setting of the linkage should be tested by engaging 1st gear and then moving the gear lever as far to the left as it will go. Release the lever and measure the distance which it springs back on its own. This should be between 5 and 10 mm (0.20 and 0.39 in). If this basic adjustment is incorrect, it is unlikely that all the gears can be engaged. The gear lever will either have to be set up using a special Audi gauge, or the adjustment can be made by a lengthy process of trial and error.

11 Gearshift linkage (014) – dismantling and reassembly

1 The gearshift linkage consists of two principal parts, the shift rod coupling assembly and the lever assembly.

Gear lever assembly

2 Remove the gear lever as described in Section 10.

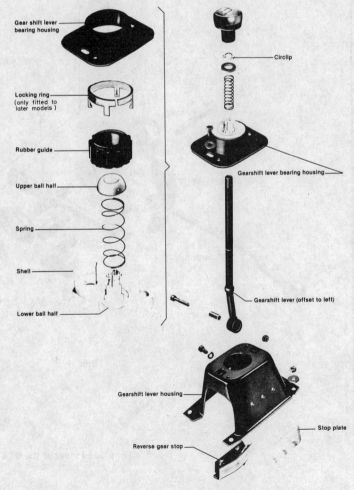

Fig. 6.19 Exploded view of the 014 gearshift lever (Secs 10 and 11)

3   Dismantle the assembly by unscrewing the gear knob, removing the circlip from the gear lever and lifting off the washer and spring. The gear lever can then be pulled down out of the lever bearing assembly.

4   Before separating the lever bearing assembly from the lever housing, mark round the lever bearing plate with a scriber so that it can be returned to exactly the same position, then remove the two screws and washer from the plate.

5   Do not dismantle the bearing unless it is necessary to grease it. Push the rubber guide and locking ring (if fitted) down out of the housing plate, then prise the plastic shells apart and remove the ball halves and spring – the shells can then be removed from the rubber guide.

6   When reassembling have the rubber guide with its shouldered end uppermost and press the two shells into it. Press the lower ball half into the shells, then the spring and finally press in the upper ball half, pushing the shells slightly apart if necessary.

7   After assembling the parts into the rubber guide, push the assembly up into the lever bearing plate together with the locking ring, where fitted.

8   When inserting the lever into the bearing, note that the lever is cranked to the left, and when refitting the lever bearing plate to the housing, take care to line up the plate with the scribed mark made before dismantling.

11.9 Gearshift linkage components

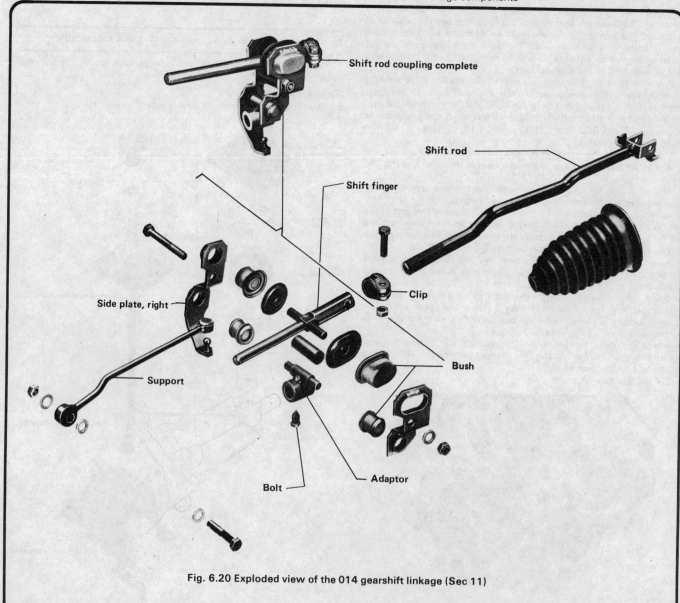

Fig. 6.20 Exploded view of the 014 gearshift linkage (Sec 11)

Shift rod coupling

9   To dismantle the shift rod coupling, remove the bolt from the end of the support rod. Mark the position of the adaptor on the gearbox selector lever, then remove the wire from the bolt (where applicable), loosen the bolt and remove the shift rod coupling assembly (photo).

10 Prise the ball coupling of the support off its mounting on the side plate. Remove the bolt which clamps the two side plates together and extract the shift finger and its bushes.

11 When reassembling the shift rod coupling, note that the adaptor should be fitted so that the hole for the clamp bolt is towards the front and the groove for the clamp bolt on the shift finger is on the left-hand side. Make sure that the holes in the two side plates are exactly in line, so that the coupling is assembled without any strain.

12 All the joints and friction surfaces of the shift rod coupling should be lubricated with multi-purpose grease and after refitting the assembly to the gearbox, the clamp bolt should be tightened and then locked with soft iron wire (where applicable).

12 Gearbox (013 and 093) – dismantling into major assemblies

Note: *Photo sequence shows 013 unit – some components of the 093 unit may differ slightly from those shown.*

1   Remove the drain plug, drain the oil and refit the plug (photos). Clean away external dirt from the gearbox casing.

2   Pierce the cover plate with a screwdriver and prise it out – a new plate must be obtained for the reassembly procedure.

3   Remove the reverse lamp switch wiring and unscrew the switch. Also unscrew the gear indicator switch (photos).

4   Remove the clutch release bearing and shaft, as described in Chapter 5.

5   Unscrew the drive flange centre bolts while holding the flange stationary with a rod inserted through a bolt hole. Mark each flange side for side, then withdraw them from the differential (photo).

6   On the 013 gearbox, unbolt and remove the differential cover and lift out the differential (photos). Although it is possible to remove the

12.1A Location of the drain plug ...

12.1B ... and filler plug

12.3A Gear indicator switch location

12.3B Reverse lamp switch location

12.3C Removing the reverse lamp switch

12.5 Removing a drive flange

12.6A Removing the differential cover (013 gearbox) ...

12.6B ... and differential (013 gearbox)

12.6C Right-hand side view of the differential (013 gearbox)

6

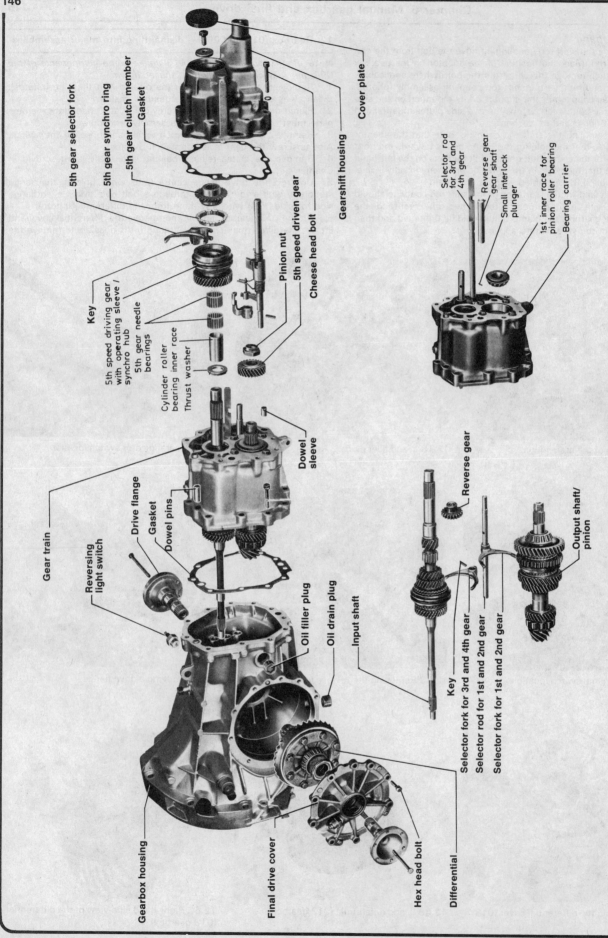

5th gear selector fork

5th gear synchro ring

5th gear clutch member

Gasket

Cover plate

Gearshift housing

Key

5th speed driven gear

Cheese head bolt

Pinion nut

5th speed driving gear with operating sleeve / synchro hub

5th gear needle bearings

Cylinder roller bearing inner race

Thrust washer

Selector rod for 3rd and 4th gear

Reverse gear gear shaft

Small interlock plunger

1st inner race for pinion roller bearing

Bearing carrier

Gear train

Reversing light switch

Drive flange

Gasket

Dowel pins

Dowel sleeve

Oil filler plug

Oil drain plug

Input shaft

Reverse gear

Output shaft/ pinion

Gearbox housing

Final drive cover

Hex head bolt

Differential

Key

Selector fork for 3rd and 4th gear

Selector rod for 1st and 2nd gear

Selector fork for 1st and 2nd gear

Fig. 6.21 Exploded view of the 013 gearbox (Sec.12)

differential from the 093 gearbox at this stage, there is a likelihood of damage to the crownwheel and pinion teeth, and it is therefore recommended that the differential be removed after dismantling the remainder of the gearbox.

7   Unscrew the bolt from the end of the input shaft and remove the thick washer. The input shaft must be held stationary in order to unscrew the bolt – we used a nut splitter and block of wood (photo), but it is possible to make up a tool similar to that shown in Fig. 6.22 using an old clutch driven plate.

8   Using an Allen key, unscrew the bolts from the gearshift housing, noting the location of the brackets (photo).

9   Pull the gearshift housing from the gear carrier and remove the gasket (photo). If the bearing is tight on the end of the input shaft a puller will be required.

10 Using a pin punch drive the roll pin from the 1st/2nd selector dog and turn the dog anti-clockwise (photo).

11 Pull out the notched selector rod to engage 3rd gear, then turn the main selector rod anti-clockwise and extract it from the gear carrier (photo).

12 Remove the 1st/2nd selector dog and move the 3rd/4th selector rod to neutral (photo).

13 Using a pin punch, drive the roll pin from the 5th gear selector fork while supporting the selector rod with a block of wood to prevent damage to the bore in the bearing carrier (photo).

14 Engage 5th gear by moving the synchro sleeve and 1st gear by pulling out the 1st/2nd selector rod. Both the input and output pinion shafts are now locked to enable the nut to be unscrewed from the output/pinion shaft. After removing the nut return the gears to neutral.

15 Unscrew the bolts securing the gear carrier to the final drive housing, noting the location of the mounting and exhaust brackets (photos).

16 Remove the gear carrier and gasket, and if necessary knock out the dowel pins (photo). To prevent unnecessary damage to the oil seal wrap adhesive tape around the input shaft splines before removing the gear carrier.

17 Using a puller beneath the 5th gear, pull off the 5th gear and synchro unit, 5th gear clutch member, and 5th selector fork. It may be possible to lever off these items, but this will depend on how tight the clutch member is on the input shaft.

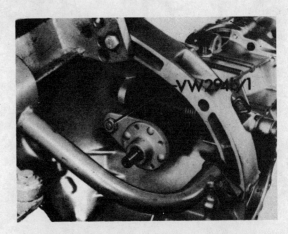

Fig. 6.22 Tool for holding the input shaft stationary on the 013 and 093 gearbox (Sec 12)

18 Separate the clutch member and synchro ring from the 5th gear and synchro unit (photo).

19 Remove the 5th gear needle roller bearings from the input shaft (photo).

20 Using a puller remove the 5th driven gear from the output pinion shaft.

21 Lever off the 5th gear thrust washer and inner race (photo). If the inner race is tight use a puller.

22 Using a pin punch, drive the roll pin from the 3rd/4th selector fork while supporting the selector rod with a block of wood to prevent damage to the bore in the bearing carrier (photo).

23 Pull the 3rd/4th selector rod out of the gear carrier. Remove the small interlock plunger from the rod and put in in a safe place (photo).

24 The output shaft must now be pushed through the tapered roller bearing inner race approximately 6 to 8 mm (0.24 to 0.32 in) to allow

12.6D Left-hand side view of the differential (013 gearbox)

12.7 Using a nut splitter to hold the input shaft stationary

12.8 Mounting bracket location on the gearshift housing

6

12.9 Removing the gearshift housing

12.10 Removing the 1st/2nd selector dog roll pin

12.11 Removing the main selector rod

12.12 Removing the 1st/2nd selector dog

12.13 Removing the 5th gear selector fork roll pin

12.15A Mounting bracket location on the gear carrier

12.15B Exhaust mounting bracket location on the gear carrier

12.16 Removing the gear carrier

12.18 5th gear and synchro unit with the splined clutch member

12.19 Removing the 5th gear needle roller bearings

12.21 Removing the 5th gear thrust washer

12.22 Removing the 3rd/4th selector fork roll pin

12.23A Removing the 3rd/4th selector rod (arrowed)

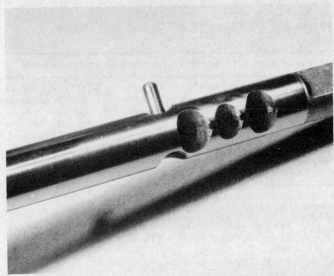

12.23B Interlock plunger location in the 3rd/4th selector rod

12.24 Home-made plate for removing the output/pinion shaft

12.25 Removing the input shaft with 3rd/4th selector fork

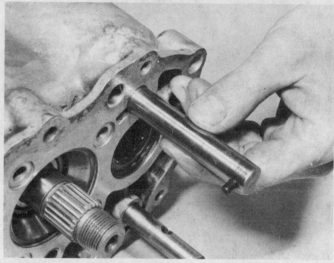

12.27 Removing the reverse gear shaft

12.28 Removing the output/pinion shaft with the 1st/2nd selector rod and fork

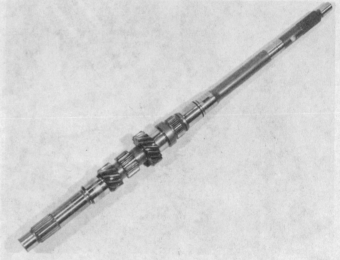

13.1 The input/main shaft

clearance for the input shaft to be removed. To do this support the gear carrier and use a press, or alternatively use a plate (photo) and long bolts inserted into the bearing outer race retaining ring. If the latter method is used remove each bolt and insert the long bolts separately to prevent the ring from dropping.

25 Remove the input shaft together with the 3rd/4th selector fork from the gear carrier (photo).

26 Set the selector rods to neutral.

27 Using a soft metal drift, drive out the reverse gear shaft and remove the reverse gear (photo).

28 Remove the output/pinion shaft together with 1st/2nd selector rod and fork (photo).

29 Recover the interlock plungers from the gear carrier and put them in a safe place.

30 Remove the differential on the 093 gearbox, as necessary (see paragraph 6).

13 Mainshaft/input shaft (013 and 093) – dismantling and re-assembly

Removal of the components from the front of the input shaft is identical to that for the 014 gearbox described in Section 4. The rear end of the input shaft is of course longer to accommodate 5th gear

and incorporates the inner race of the rear roller bearing (photo). To remove the race, insert a clamp beneath it and drive the input shaft through it. A long metal tube may be used to fit the race.

14 Pinion shaft (013 and 093) – dismantling and reassembly

The procedure is identical to that for the 014/11 gearbox as described in Section 5. The rear end of the pinion shaft is of course longer to accommodate 5th gear. *However, note that when refitting the 1st/2nd synchroniser the external teeth must be away from the pinion end of the shaft (ie the opposite way round to the 014 gearbox).*

15 Gearbox/final drive housing (013 and 093) – servicing

The procedure is identical to that for the 014 gearbox with the following exceptions:

(a) *The pinion bearing outer track on the 093 gearbox is secured by a socket-head bolt which must be removed with an Allen key*

(b) *The 093 gearbox does not incorporate an input shaft bush.*

The procedure for the 014 gearbox is described in Section 6.

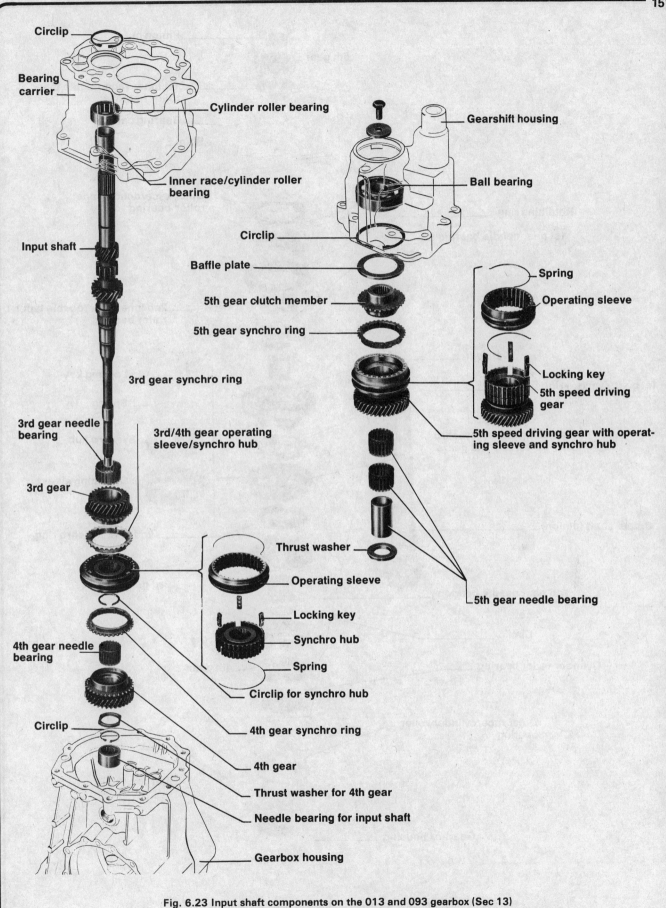

Fig. 6.23 Input shaft components on the 013 and 093 gearbox (Sec 13)

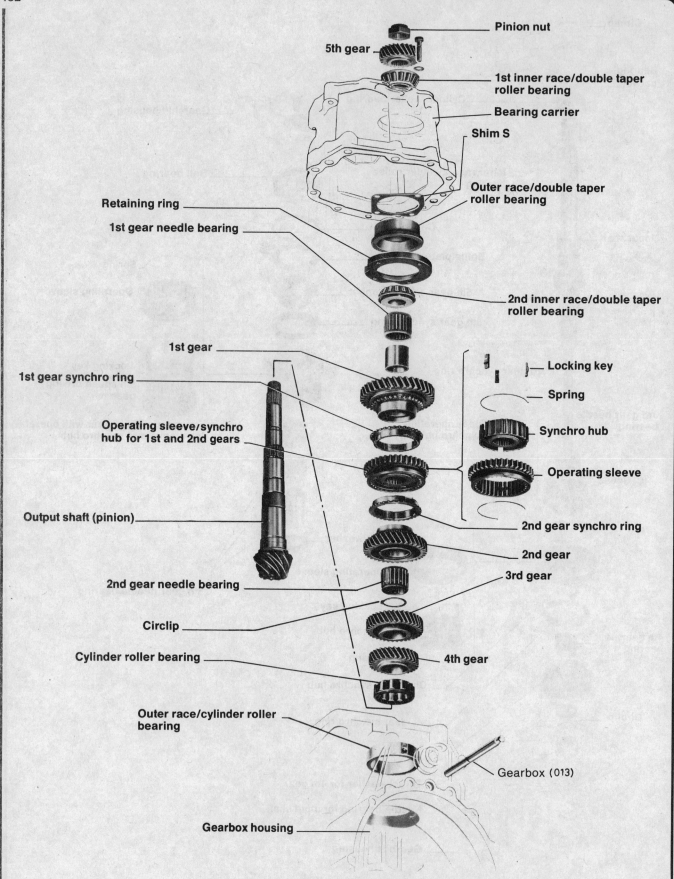

Pinion nut

5th gear

1st inner race/double taper roller bearing

Bearing carrier

Shim S

Retaining ring

1st gear needle bearing

Outer race/double taper roller bearing

2nd inner race/double taper roller bearing

1st gear

1st gear synchro ring

Locking key

Spring

Synchro hub

Operating sleeve/synchro hub for 1st and 2nd gears

Operating sleeve

Output shaft (pinion)

2nd gear synchro ring

2nd gear

3rd gear

2nd gear needle bearing

Circlip

Cylinder roller bearing

4th gear

Outer race/cylinder roller bearing

Gearbox (013)

Gearbox housing

Fig. 6.24 Pinion shaft components on the 013 and 093 gearbox (Sec 14)

16.1A Remove the four bolts ...

16.1B ... and the pinion bearing outer race retaining ring

16.1C Pinion bearing outer race and shim

16 Bearing/gear carrier (013 and 093) – servicing

Note: *Photo sequence shows 013 unit – some components of the 093 unit may differ slightly from those shown.*

The procedure is identical to that for the 014 gearbox given in Section 7 with the following exceptions.

Pinion bearing renewal

1 Unscrew the four bolts and remove the bearing outer race retaining ring, noting the location of the cut-outs (photos).
2 Using a metal tube, drive the outer race from the bearing carrier and remove the shim.
3 Refitting is a reversal of the removal procedure, but it will be necessary for an Audi dealer to determine the correct thickness of shim to fit behind the race.

Gear detents – removal and refitting

4 Before removing the reverse relay lever, unscrew and remove the detent from the side of the bearing carrier. The relay lever is operated by a pin in the 5th/reverse selector rod (photos).
5 All the detents are removed using the 6 mm thread and bolt method (photo).

Main selector rod bush – removal

6 The bush can be removed and refitting using a soft metal drift. Drive the bush in flush when refitting.

Input shaft bearing – renewal

7 Extract the circlip then, using a metal tube, drive the bearing into the bearing carrier.
8 To fit the new bearing, first fit the circlip then, using the metal tube

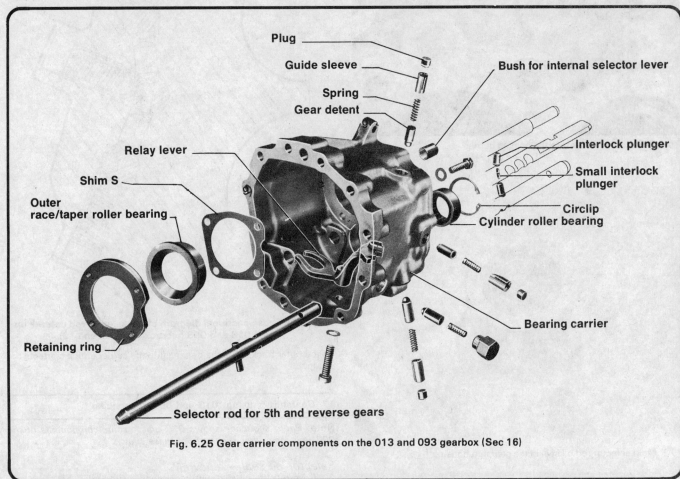

Plug

Guide sleeve

Spring

Gear detent

Bush for internal selector lever

Relay lever

Shim S

Outer race/taper roller bearing

Interlock plunger

Small interlock plunger

Circlip

Cylinder roller bearing

Retaining ring

Bearing carrier

Selector rod for 5th and reverse gears

Fig. 6.25 Gear carrier components on the 013 and 093 gearbox (Sec 16)

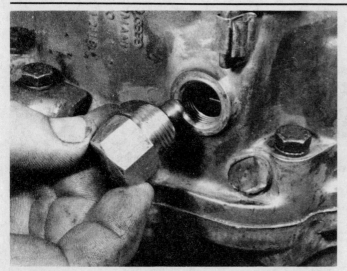

16.4A Removing the reverse detent from the bearing carrier

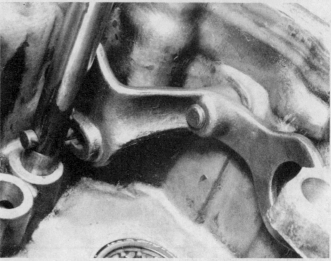

16.4B Location of the reverse relay lever and 5th/reverse selector rod in the bearing carrier

16.5 Selector rod detents in the bearing carrier

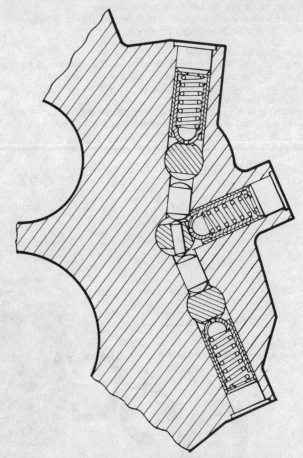

Fig. 6.26 Cross-sectional diagram of the selector rod detents on the 013 and 093 gearbox (Secs 16 and 19)

on the outer track, drive the bearing into the carrier until it contacts the circlip.

---

17 Gearshift housing (013 and 093) – servicing

Note: *Photo sequence shows 013 unit – some components of the 093 unit may differ slightly from those shown.*

Selector oil seal – renewal

1   Prise out the oil seal with a screwdriver (photo).

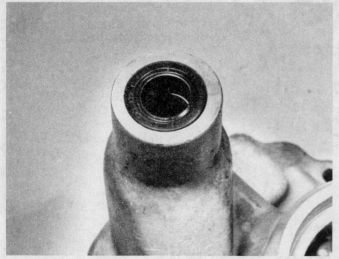

17.1 Main selector rod oil seal in the gearshift housing

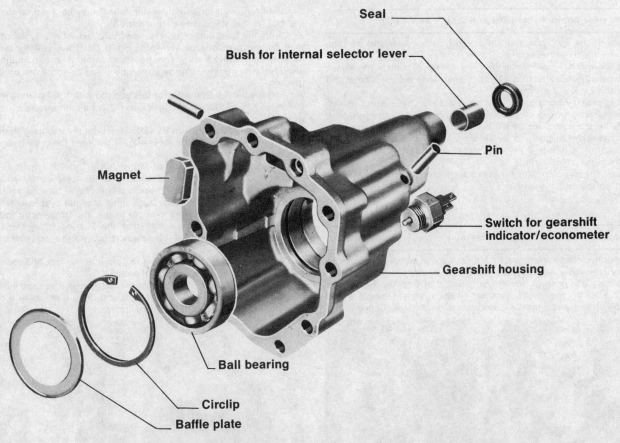

Fig. 6.27 Gearshift housing components on the 013 and 093 gearbox (Sec 17)

2   Insert the new oil seal and drive it in until flush using a block of wood, making sure that it is kept square to the housing.
3   Fill the space between the oil seal lips with multi-purpose grease.

Selector bush – renewal
4   Remove the oil seal and, using a suitable metal tube, drive the bush into the gearshift housing.
5   Drive the new bush into the housing from the same direction, then fit a new oil seal.

Input shaft ball-bearing – removal and refitting
6   Prise out the baffle plate from inside the gearshift housing. As the plate is peened into position it may be necessary to use a round file to remove the peening first.
7   Extract the circlip and, using a soft metal drift on the outer track, drive the bearing into the housing (photo).
8   Drive the bearing fully into the housing using the metal tube on the outer track, then fit the circlip.
9   Press in the baffle plate and peen over the housing shoulder in three places to secure (photo).

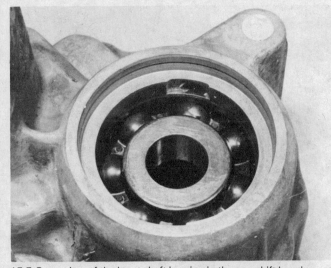

17.7 Outer view of the input shaft bearing in the gearshift housing

17.9 Showing the three peening points securing the input shaft bearing baffle plate

18 Fifth gear components (013 and 093) – servicing

1   Examine the 5th gear and 5th driven gear for wear and damage and renew them, as necessary.

2   If it is required to dismantle the synchroniser, first mark the sleeve and gear hub in relation to each other, then slide off the sleeve and remove the keys and springs.

3   When reassembling the synchroniser observe the mating marks. The selector fork groove on the sleeve must be towards the 5th gear. With the keys inserted, locate the inner spring in one of the keys, then use a screwdriver to position the spring under the other keys. Fit the outer spring in a different key with the free end facing the opposite direction to the inner spring.

4   Check the synchro ring for wear as described in Section 4 by fitting it on the clutch member.

19 Gearbox (013 and 093) – reassembly

Note: *Photo sequence shows 013 unit – some components of the 093 unit may differ slightly from those shown.*

1   On the 093 gearbox lower the differential into the final drive housing and fit the cover together with a new O-ring, where applicable. Insert and tight the cover bolts in diagonal sequence to the specified torque. If required, the differential may be fitted on the 013 gearbox at this stage (see paragraph 28).

2   With the gear carrier on the bench, fit the interlock plungers in their correct positions as shown in Fig. 6.26. If the selector detents have been removed they can be fitted later. If a pen magnet is available the interlock plungers may be fitted as the work proceeds (photo).

3   Engage the 1st/2nd selector fork and rod with the 1st/2nd synchro sleeve on the output shaft, then lower them simultaneously into the gear carrier casing.

4   With the gear carrier on its side, insert the reverse gear shaft and at the same time locate the reverse gear between the relay lever jaws (photo). Drive in the shaft until flush.

5   Engage the 3rd/4th selector fork with the 3rd/4th synchro sleeve on the input shaft, then lower them into the gear carrier and into engagement with the output shaft gears. Take care to keep the synchro sleeves central in their hubs otherwise the keys may fall out.

6   Insert the small interlock plunger in the 3rd/4th selector rod and retain it with grease. Make sure that the interlock plungers are in position then insert the 3rd/4th selector rod into the gear carrier and through the selector fork.

7   Align the holes, then drive the roll pin into the fork end rod while supporting the rod with a block of wood.

8   Support the front ends of the shafts, then fit the tapered roller bearing inner race on the output shaft and drive it on using a metal tube until it contacts the outer race (photos).

19.2 Using a pen magnet to insert an interlock plunger

19.4 Fitting the reverse gear shaft and reverse gear

19.8A Locate the bearing on the output/pinion shaft ...

19.8B ... then drive it on with a metal tube

9   Locate the 5th gear thrust washer on the input shaft, then drive on the 5th gear inner race using a metal tube (photo). The inner race can if necessary be pre-heated to 120°C (248°F) to ease the installation.

10   Locate the 5th driven gear on the output shaft and drive it fully onto the splines using a metal tube (photo). The gear may be pre-heated as the race in paragraph 9 to ease installation.

11   Locate the 5th gear needle roller bearings on the input shaft and lubricate them with gear oil.

12   Engage the 5th selector fork with the synchro sleeve on the 5th gear and synchro unit, then locate the assembly over the input shaft and 5th/reverse selector rod (photo).

13   Fit the 5th synchro-ring to the synchroniser, making sure that the slots are aligned with the keys (photo).

14   Fit the clutch member and drive it fully onto the splines using a metal tube (photo). The member can if necessary be pre-heated to 120°C (248°F) to ease the installation.

15   Locate a new gasket on the final drive housing (photo).

16   To prevent damage to the oil seal, wrap adhesive tape around the input shaft splines (photo). Lower the gear carrier onto the final drive housing and insert the bolts, together with the mounting bracket.

17   Drive in the dowel pins until flush, then tighten the bolts in diagonal sequence to the specified torque. Remove the adhesive tape.

18   Engage 5th gear by moving the synchro sleeve (ie leaving the 5th/reverse selector rod in neutral) and 1st gear by pulling out the 1st/2nd selector rod. Both the input and output shafts are now locked.

19   Fit and tighten the output/pinion shaft nut to the specified torque, and lock by punching the collar onto the shaft flat (photos). After tightening the nut, return the gears to neutral.

20   Align the holes, then drive the roll pin into the 5th gear selector fork and rod while supporting the rod with a block of wood.

21   Locate the 1st/2nd selector dog on its rod near its final position, but do not fit the roll pin at this stage.

22   Pull out the notched selector rod to engage 3rd gear, then insert the main selector rod by engaging the ends of the springs over the

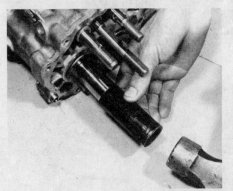

19.9 Installing the 5th gear inner race

19.10 Installing the 5th driven gear

19.12 Installing the 5th gear and synchro unit together with the 5th selector fork

19.13 Fitting the 5th synchro ring

19.14 Installing the 5th gear clutch member

19.15 New gasket located on the final drive housing

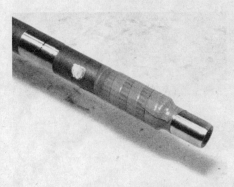

19.16 Wrap adhesive tape around the input shaft splines to prevent damage to the oil seal

19.19A Fit the nut to the output/pinion shaft ...

19.19B ... tighten the nut to the specified torque ...

6

3rd/4th selector rod, locating the finger in the notch, and pushing the main selector rod into the bush. When fitted, push the 3rd/4th selector rod into neutral (photos).

23 Align the holes, then drive the roll pin into the 1st/2nd selector dog and rod while supporting the rod with a block of wood.

24 Locate a new gasket on the gear carrier, then lower the gearshift housing into position. If necessary, gently tap the inner race of the ball-bearing to locate it on the end of the input shaft.

25 Insert the bolts together with the brackets, having first applied sealing compound to the bolt threads. Using an Allen key, tighten the bolts in diagonal sequence.

26 Insert the bolt and thick washer in the end of the input shaft, and tighten to the specified torque while holding the shaft stationary using the method described in Section 12 paragraph 7 (photo).

27 Clean the recess then press in a new cover plate (photo).

28 If not fitted yet, lower the differential into the final drive housing. Clean the cover and housing mating faces and apply a little sealing compound to them. Locate the cover on the housing, then insert and tighten the bolts in diagonal sequence to the specified torque. Note that the magnet on the cover should be positioned at the bottom (photo).

29 Insert the drive flanges into each side of the differential, and tighten the bolts while holding the flanges stationary with a rod through one of the bolt holes (photo).

19.19C ... and punch the collar onto the flat

19.22A Engage 3rd gear and fit the main selector rod ...

19.22B ... then engage neutral

19.26 Tightening the input shaft bolt

19.27 Fitting a new cover plate to the gearshift housing

19.28 The magnet on the differential cover must be at the bottom of the gearbox

19.29 Tightening a drive flange bolt

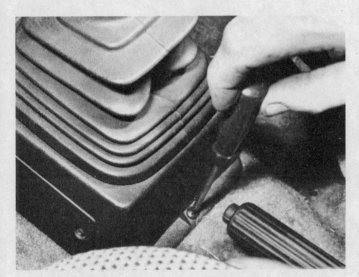

20.1A Removing the gearshift lever surround

20.1B Gearshift lever and housing

30 Refit the clutch release bearing and shaft, as described in Chapter 5.
31 Insert and tighten the reverse lamp switch, and clip the wiring into position.
32 Fill the gearbox with oil.

20 Gearshift lever (013 and 093) – removal, refitting and adjustment

1   The procedure is basically the same as that described for the 014 gearbox in Section 10 (photos). However, after checking the return distance in 1st gear, engage 5th gear and move the gear lever to the right as far as possible. After releasing the gear lever, it should spring back 5 to 10 mm (0.20 to 0.39 in).
2   The return movement from both 1st and 5th gears should be approximately the same, but if not, slight adjustment can be made by moving the gear lever bearing plate sideways within the elongated holes. If this is insufficient, it will be necessary to either use a special Audi gauge, or attempt a lengthy process of trial and error repositioning the shift rod on the shift finger.
3   If the reverse stop in the gear lever housing is disturbed, first set it to the basic position which is fully pressed down. If reverse gear cannot be engaged, move the stop up as required and secure it by tightening the bolts.

21 Gearshift linkage (013 and 093) – dismantling and reassembly

The procedure is identical to that for the 014 gearbox described in Section 11. However, the bottom of the gear lever is not cranked and can therefore be fitted either way round.

6

22 Fault diagnosis – manual gearbox and final drive

Symptom	Reason(s)
Ineffective synchromesh	Worn synchro rings
Jumps out of gear	Weak or broken detent spring
	Worn selector forks or dogs
	Weak synchro springs
	Worn synchro unit or gears
	Worn bearings or gears
Noisy operation	Worn bearings or gears
Difficult engagement of gears	Worn selector components
	Worn synchro units
	Clutch fault
	Gearbox input shaft spigot bearing seized in end of crankshaft
	Incorrect gearshift adjustment

Chapter 7 Automatic transmission and final drive

Contents

Specifications

Type .... Three-speed planetary gearbox with hydrodynamic torque converter, final drive differential located between torque converter and gearbox

Identification
Gearbox code number:
    089 .... Fitted to four-cylinder models
    087 .... Fitted to five-cylinder models

Ratios

	089	**087**
Final drive:		
Audi 80	3.9:1 (43:11)	3.45:1 (38:11)
Audi Coupe	3.25:1 (39:12)	3.45:1 (38:11)
Audi 4000	3.73:1 (41:11)	3.45:1 (38:11)
1st	2.55:1	2.55:1
2nd	1.45:1	1.45:1
3rd	1.00:1	1.00:1
Reverse	2.46:1	2.46:1

Oil capacity

	Total	**Service**
089 gearbox (ATF)	6.0 litre; 10.6 Imp pt; 6.3 US qt	3.0 litre; 5.3 Imp pt; 3.2 US qt
089 final drive	0.75 litre; 1.3 Imp pt; 0.8 US qt	–
087 gearbox (ATF)	6.0 litre; 10.6 Imp pt; 6.3 US qt	3.0 litre; 5.3 Imp pt; 3.2 US qt
087 final drive	0.7 litre; 1.2 Imp pt; 0.7 US qt	–

Torque converter

	089	**087**
Maximum diameter of bush	34.25 mm (1.35 in)	34.12 mm (1.34 in)
Maximum out-of-round of bush	0.03 mm (0.001 in)	0.03 mm (0.001 in)

Torque wrench settings

	lbf ft	**Nm**
Torque converter to driveplate	22	30
Gearbox to engine	41	55
Mounting to body	30	40
Mounting to gearbox	41	55
Gearbox to final drive housing	22	30
Oil pan	15	20
Strainer cover	2	3
Selector cable clamp nut	6	8

7

1 General description

The automatic transmission consists of three main assemblies, these being the torque converter, which is directly coupled to the engine; the final drive unit which incorporates the differential assembly; and the planetary gearbox with its hydraulically operated multi-disc clutches and brake bands. The gearbox also houses a rear mounted oil pump, which is coupled to the torque converter impeller, and this pump supplies automatic transmission fluid to the planetary gears, hydraulic controls and torque converter. The fluid performs a triple function by lubricating the moving parts, cooling the automatic transmission system and providing a torque transfer medium. The final drive lubrication is separate from the transmission lubrication system, unlike the manual gearbox where the final drive shares a common lubrication system.

The torque converter is a sealed unit which cannot be dismantled. It is bolted to the crankshaft driveplate and replaces the clutch found on an engine with manual transmission.

The gearbox is of the planetary type with epicyclic gear trains operated by brakes and clutches through a hydraulic control system. The correct gear is selected by a combination of three control signals; a manual valve operated by the gearshift cable, a manual valve operated by the accelerator pedal, and a governor to control hydraulic pressure. The gearshift cable and selector lever allow the driver to select a specific gear and override the automatic control, if desired. The accelerator control determines the correct gear for the desired rate of acceleration, and the governor determines the correct gear in relation to engine speed.

Because of the need for special test equipment, the complexity of some of the parts and the need for scrupulous cleanliness when servicing automatic transmissions, the amount which the owner can do is limited, but those operations which can reasonably be carried out are detailed in the following Sections. Repairs to the final drive differential are also not recommended.

The automatic transmission has three forward speeds and one reverse, controlled by a six position lever with the following positions:

P	Park
R	Reverse
N	Neutral
D	Drive
2	Low
1	Low

The selector lever has a push button which must be depressed when selecting the following positions:

From	P to R
	R to P
	N to R
	2 to 1

The selector lever can be moved freely between all other positions. If the lever is set to positions D, or 2, the automatic transmission changes gears automatically.

Position D

This position is for normal driving, and once selected the three forward gears engage automatically throughout the speed range from zero to top speed.

Position 2

With the lever in this position, the two lower gears will engage automatically, but the highest gear will not engage. For this reason position 2 should only be selected when the speed of the car is below 70 mph (110 kph). Selecting Position 2 will make use of the engine's braking effect and the actual change can be made without letting up the accelerator pedal.

Position 1

The position is needed rarely, such as on steep inclines or declines. The transmission remains in the lowest gear and Position 1 should only be selected when the car speed is below 40 mph (64 kph).

Reverse

Reverse must only be selected when the car is absolutely stationary and with the engine running at idling speed.

Park

In the park position the transmission is locked mechanically by the engagement of a pawl. This position must only be selected when the car is absolutely stationary, otherwise the transmission will be damaged.

2 Automatic transmission – precautions and maintenance

If the car is being towed, the ignition key must be inserted so that the steering wheel is not locked and the gear selector must be in *Neutral.* Because the lubrication of the transmission is limited when the engine is not running, the car must not be towed for more than 30 miles (48 km), or at a speed greater than 30 mph (48 kph) unless the front wheels of the car are lifted clear of the road.

Routine maintenance consists of checking the final drive oil level and the automatic transmission fluid level every 10 000 miles (15 000 km) or 12 months, whichever occurs first. When checking the final drive oil level, if the level is found to be too high, fluid may be leaking from the gearbox or hydraulic circuit.

Checking the automatic transmission fluid level should be carried out with the engine warm and running at idling speed with the selector lever in *Neutral* and the handbrake applied. Withdraw the dipstick and wipe it with a piece of clean, lint-free rag. It is important that the rag is both clean and lint-free, because even a tiny speck of dirt can damage or cause a malfunction of the transmission. The level of fluid is satisfactory anywhere between the two marks on the dipstick, but either too high, or too low a level must be avoided. The difference between the marks is equivalent to 0.4 litre (0.7 Imp pt; 0.4 US qt). If necessary, top up the level through the dipstick tube using the specified fluid – see *'Recommended lubricants and fluids'* at the beginning of this manual.

3 Automatic transmission fluid – draining and refilling

1   This job should not be attempted unless clean, dust free conditions can be achieved.
2   With the car standing on level ground, place a container of at least six pints capacity beneath the oil pan of the transmission. For working room beneath the car, jack it up and support it with axle stands, or use car ramps.
3   Unscrew the union nut securing the dipstick tube to the oil pan, pull out the tube and allow the fluid to drain out.
4   Remove the retaining screws and withdraw the oil pan. Remove the gasket.

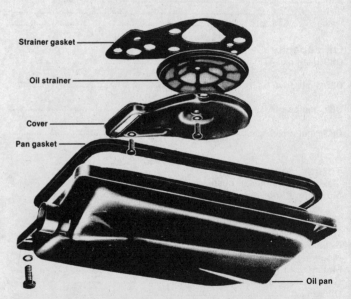

Fig. 7.1 Automatic transmission oil pan and strainer components (Sec 3)

5   Remove the screws and withdraw the cover, strainer, and gasket.
6   Clean the pan and strainer with methylated spirit and allow to dry.
7   Refit the strainer, cover and pan in reverse order using new gaskets and tightening the screws to the specified torque.
8   Insert the dipstick tube and tighten the union nut.
9   Wipe round the top of the dipstick tube, then remove the dipstick.
10 With the car on level ground, fill the transmission with the correct quantity and grade of fluid, using a clean funnel if necessary.
11 Start the engine and with the handbrake applied, select every gear position once. With the engine idling and the transmission in *Neutral*, check the level of the fluid on the dipstick, and if necessary top up to the lower mark.
12 Road test the vehicle until the engine is at normal temperature, then again check the fluid level and top up if necessary. The amount of fluid which must be added to raise the level from the lower mark to the upper mark on the dipstick is about half a pint (0.4 litre). Do not overfill the transmission, because an excess of fluid will upset its operation and any excess fluid will have to be drained.

4   Automatic transmission – removal and refitting

1   Position the car over an inspection pit or on car ramps. Apply the handbrake.
2   Disconnect the battery negative lead.
3   Support the front of the engine using a hoist or support bar. Fig. 7.2 shows the Audi tool specially designed for the job, but it should be relatively easy to make a support bar yourself along similar lines, if you have decided not to use a hoist.

4   Remove the starter, as described in Chapter 10.
5   Unscrew the three torque converter-to-driveplate bolts while holding the starter ring gear stationary with a screwdriver. It will be necessary to rotate the engine to position the bolts in the starter aperture, using a socket on the crankshaft pulley bolt.
6   Unscrew the nut and disconnect the speedometer cable from the transmission. Also release the cable from the clip on the dipstick tube, where applicable.
7   Unscrew and remove the upper engine-to-transmission bolts.
8   Disconnect the driveshafts from the transmission, with reference to Chapter 8. For additional working room it is necessary to remove one or both driveshafts, or alternatively tie them to one side. Where an 087 gearbox is fitted this can be achieved by removing both rear engine subframe bolts and loosening only the front left subframe bolt – the driveshafts can then be swivelled to the rear between the subframe and underbody.
9   Where an oil cooler is bolted to the side of the transmission, drain the cooling system, as described in Chapter 2, then disconnect the hoses from the oil cooler.
10 Unbolt and remove the torque converter cover plate.
11 Unbolt the exhaust pipe bracket from the gearbox. For additional working room, unbolt and remove the front exhaust pipe, with reference to Chapter 3.
12 Unscrew the nuts or bolts and detach the selector lever cable bracket from the transmission. Extract the circlip and disconnect the cable end. Disconnect the return spring, where fitted.
13 Unbolt the accelerator cable bracket and unhook the cable end. Also extract the clip from the pedal cable balljoint, prise off the balljoint and unbolt the bracket (if fitted).

Fig. 7.2 Using a special bar to support the front of the engine (Sec 4)

Fig. 7.4 Location of the coolant hoses on the oil cooler (Sec 4)

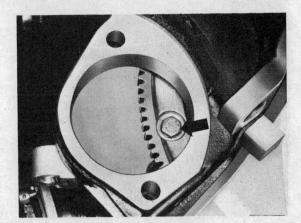

Fig. 7.3 A torque converter-to-driveplate bolt seen through the starter aperture (Sec 4)

14 Support the transmission with a suitable trolley jack, then unscrew and remove the lower engine-to-transmission bolts.
15 Unscrew the centre bolt from the transmission mounting.
16 Where an 089 gearbox is fitted, unbolt the stop bracket at the front of the engine.
17 With the help of an assistant, withdraw the transmission from the engine, making sure that the torque converter remains fully engaged with the transmission splines.
18 Lower the transmission and remove it from under the car.
19 Refitting is a reversal of removal, but make sure that the torque converter is correctly fitted. If the pump shaft is correctly engaged, the boss of the torque converter will be about 10 mm (0.4 in) from the open end of the bellhousing (Fig. 7.5). If the boss of the torque converter is found to be flush with the open end of the bellhousing (Fig. 7.6) it is likely that the pump shaft has pulled out of the pump driveplate splines. *The pump driveplate will be destroyed if the gearbox is bolted to the engine with the pump shaft in this position.* Refill the cooling system with reference to Chapter 2. Reconnect the driveshafts with reference to Chapter 8 and the starter with reference to Chapter 10. If necessary adjust the accelerator and selector cables as described in Sections 9 and 10.

7

5   Torque converter – checking and draining

1   The torque converter is a welded unit and if it is faulty the complete unit must be replaced. Only the bush can be renewed.

2   Examine the bush for signs of scoring and wear. To check for wear requires an internal micrometer or dial gauge; if one is available measure the bore diameter to see if it exceeds the wear limit given in the Specifications.

3   To remove the bush requires a commercial extractor and a slide hammer. After fitting a new bush, its diameter must be between the limits given; if not the bush must be removed and another one fitted. For this reason the job is really one for an Audi agent.

4   Check that the cooling vanes on the converter are secure.

5   Fit the turbine shaft into the converter and check that the turbine turns freely.

6   If the fluid was dirty when drained from the oil pan, drain the fluid from the torque converter before the automatic transmission is refitted.

7   Have ready a container of about half a gallon (2 litres) capacity, a washing-up liquid bottle and a piece of plastic tubing of not more than 8 mm (0.32 in) outside diameter.

8   Put the torque converter on the bench and support it so that it is tipped up slightly.

9   Cut one end of the plastic tube on an angle so that the end of the tube will not be blocked if it comes against a flat surface and push this end into the torque converter hub until it touches the bottom.

10   Connect the spout of the washing up liquid bottle to the other end

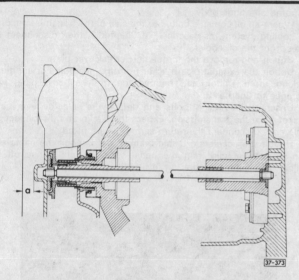

Fig. 7.5 Correct fitting of the transmission oil pump shaft (Sec 4)

a = approx 10 mm (0.4 in)

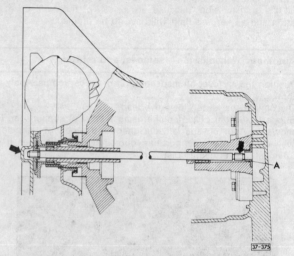

Fig. 7.6 Incorrect fitting of the transmission oil pump shaft (Sec 4)

A – Pump driveplate splines

Fig. 7.7 Checking the torque converter bush internal diameter with a dial gauge (Sec 5)

Fig. 7.8 Syphoning the fluid from the torque converter (Sec 5)

of the tube, hold the bottle below the level of the torque converter and squeeze the bottle. As the bottle expands again, fluid will be sucked into it; as soon as the fluid begins to syphon, pull the tube end off the bottle and rest the tube end in the larger container. Syphon as much fluid as possible from the torque converter. On reassembly and installation, the converter will fill with fluid as soon as the engine is started.

6 Automatic transmission – dismantling and reassembly

1   The gearbox may be separated from the final drive housing and the governor may be removed, but dismantling of the gearbox is not recommended, owing to the number of specialised tools and repair techniques required.
2   With the gearbox on the bench, pull out the torque converter if not already removed.
3   Unscrew and remove the fluid filler pipe if the fluid has been drained.
4   Remove the four nuts and washers which secure the gearbox to the final drive housing and prise away the gearbox. Remove the sealing ring, gasket and the shim.
5   With the gearbox removed, the turbine shaft and pump shaft can be pulled out and examined. When examining the turbine shaft, check that the sealing rings (Fig. 7.10) are seated properly.

Fig. 7.10 Sealing rings (arrowed) correctly seated in the turbine shaft (Sec 6)

6   Both the pump shaft and the turbine shaft are available in various lengths, so it is important to take the old shaft when obtaining a new one.
7   When reassembling be sure to refit the shim to the front of the gearbox and use a new gasket and sealing ring. Make sure that the pump shaft is inserted properly (see Section 4).

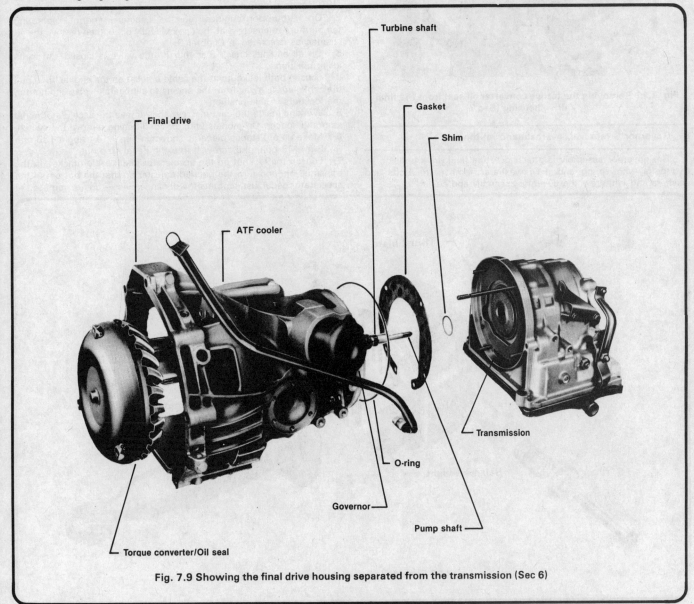

Fig. 7.9 Showing the final drive housing separated from the transmission (Sec 6)

7

7 Final drive housing – servicing

1   The removal and dismantling of the differential and final drive assembly is not recommended, owing to the number of specialised tools and repair techniques required.

2   Removal of the drivshaft flanges and renewal of the oil seals is similar to the procedure for the manual gearbox described in Chapter 6.

3   The torque converter oil seal may be renewed as follows. Using the access holes in the side of the final drive housing, drive off the old seal with a hammer and chisel (Fig. 7.11). Fit a new seal over the boss, taking care to keep the seal square, and then carefully drive it on fully with a hammer and metal tube. Note that the seal is made of very soft material and should *not* be cleaned with liquid solvents.

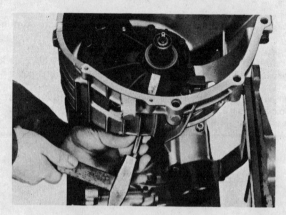

Fig. 7.11 Removing the torque converter oil seal from the final drive housing (Sec 7)

8 Governor – removal, overhaul and refitting

1   The governor assembly is attached to the final drive housing by two bolts with spring and plain washers. Remove the bolts and washers and withdraw the governor assembly and cover.

2   Remove the two bolts which pass through the assembly and remove the governor shaft, the balance weight, transfer plate and filter (if fitted).

3   If the thrust plate is scored, fit a new one.

4   If the governor shaft is worn, a new shaft can be fitted, but the balance weight must not be changed.

5   Remove the circlip from the end of the pin and remove the centrifugal weight, the valve, the spring and the spring cup.

6   Clean all the parts thoroughly and lubricate them with transmission fluid before reassembly.

7   When fitting the transfer plate make sure that it is fitted in the position shown in Fig. 7.12. As the filter is no longer fitted to new units, discard it where applicable.

8   When refitting the governor, ensure that the ring seal inside the cover is in place and in good condition.

9 Accelerator pedal and linkage – adjustment

1   The accelerator linkage must be adjusted so that the operating lever on the gearbox is at its idle position when the throttle is closed. If the adjustment is incorrect the shaft speeds will be too high when the throttle is partially open and the main pressure will be too high when the engine is idling.

089 transmission

2   On carburettor engines run the engine to normal operating temperature to ensure that the choke is fully open, then remove the air cleaner, as described in Chapter 3.

3   On all engines check that the throttle valve is closed and in its idling position.

4   Loosen both locknuts at the cable bracket on the engine, then pull the cable ferrule away from the engine to eliminate all play and tighten the locknuts in this position.

5   Working inside the car, unscrew and remove the accelerator pedal stop and spacer. On models with air conditioning remove the switch.

6   Make up a distance piece as shown in Fig. 7.14 using a 135 mm (5.32 in) M8 bolt, and screw it into the pedal stop nut.

7   Loosen the locknut on the accelerator pedal cable bracket on the transmission, and turn the knurled adjuster so that the bottom of the accelerator pedal just contacts the distance piece – do not confuse the

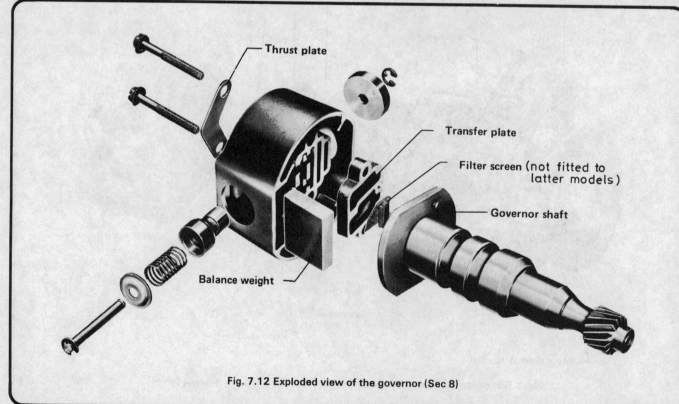

Fig. 7.12 Exploded view of the governor (Sec 8)

Thrust plate

Transfer plate

Filter screen (not fitted to latter models)

Governor shaft

Balance weight

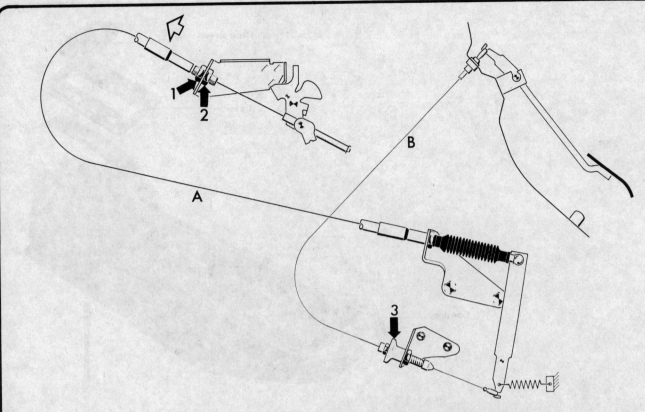

Fig. 7.13 Accelerator pedal and linkage on the 089 transmission (Sec 9)

A Throttle cable
B Accelerator pedal cable

1 and 2 Locknuts
3 Adjuster nut

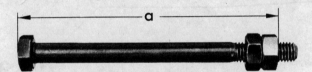

Fig. 7.14 Accelerator pedal and linkage adjustment distance piece (Sec 9)

a = 124 mm (4.88 in)

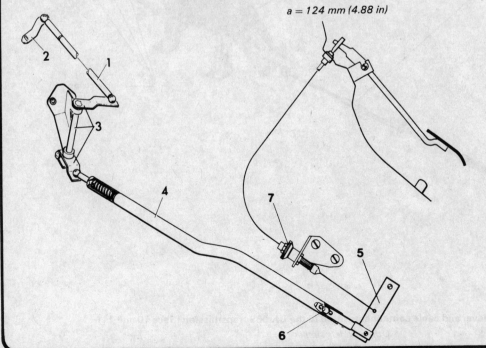

Fig. 7.15 Accelerator pedal and linkage on the 087 transmission (Sec 9)

1 Pullrod
2 Lever
3 Relay lever
4 Pushrod
5 Lever
6 Clamp bolt
7 Knurled nut

7

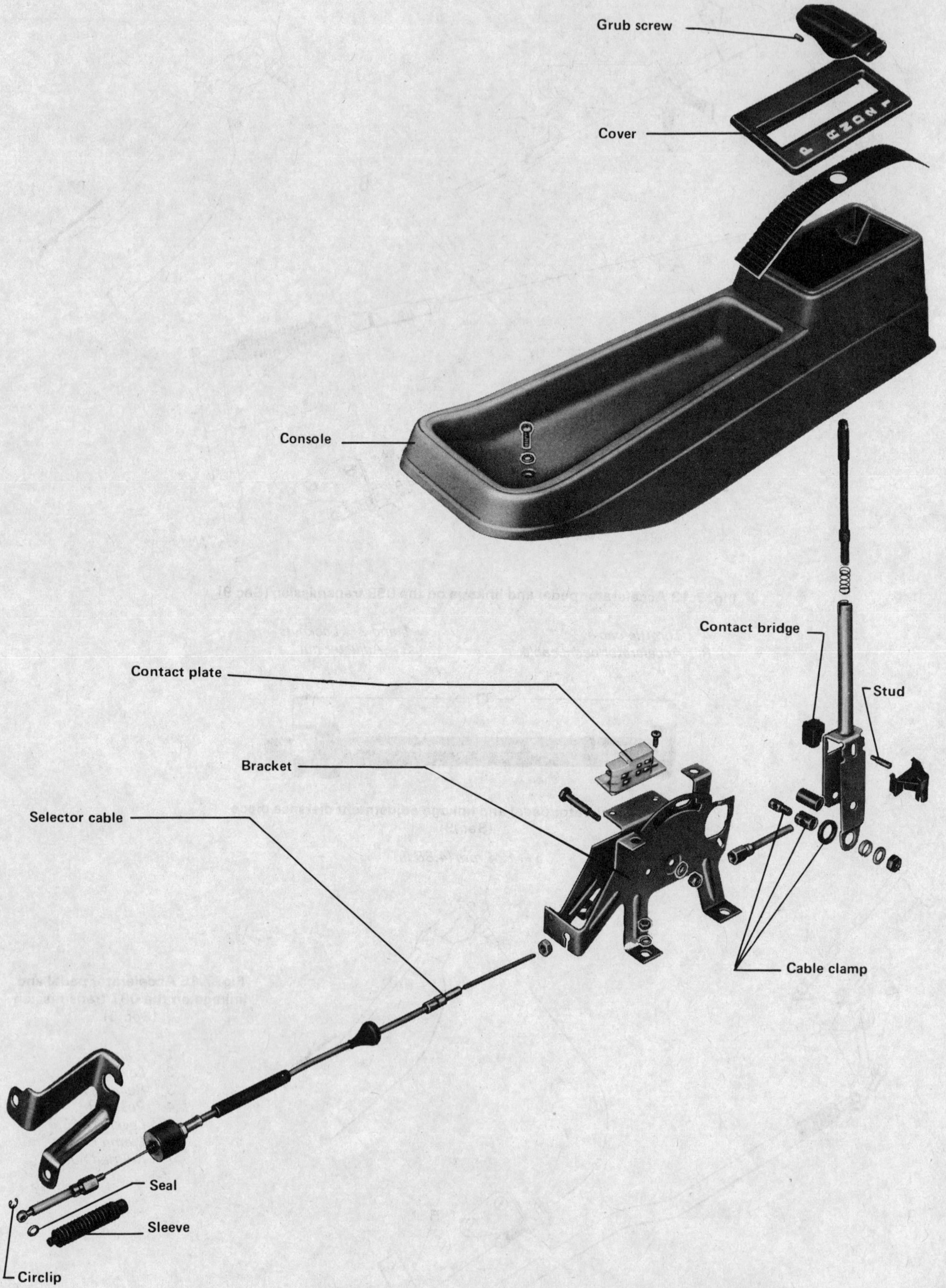

Grub screw

Cover

Console

Contact bridge

Contact plate

Stud

Bracket

Selector cable

Cable clamp

Seal

Sleeve

Circlip

Fig. 7.16 Selector lever and cable components fitted to the UK 089 transmission (Secs 10 and 11)

Other models similar

pedal rod with the bottom of the pedal. Check that the lever on the transmission is still in its idle position.

8   Remove the distance piece and refit the pedal stop, spacer and switch, as applicable.

9   Check the adjustment by depressing the accelerator pedal to the full throttle position (ie until resistance is felt). The throttle valve at the engine must be fully open without the cable kickdown spring being compressed. Now depress the accelerator pedal fully onto the stop – the kickdown spring must be compressed by 10 to 11 mm (0.40 to 0.43 in) and the lever on the transmission must contact the kickdown stop.

087 transmission

10 Check that the ball and socket linkage rod is not seized.

11 Loosen the clamp bolt on the transmission end of the pushrod.

12 With the selector lever in neutral, pull the pushrod to ensure that the throttle valve is closed, and at the same time hold the transmission lever in its idling position (ie against the pushrod).

13 Tighten the clamp bolt.

14 Working inside the car, unscrew and remove the accelerator pedal stop and spacer.

15 Make up a distance piece as shown in Fig. 7.14 using a 135 mm (5.32 in) M8 bolt, and screw it into the pedal stop nut.

16 Loosen the locknut on the accelerator pedal cable bracket on the transmission, and turn the knurled adjuster so that the bottom of the accelerator pedal just contacts the distance piece – do not confuse the pedal rod with the bottom of the pedal. Check that the lever on the transmission is still in its idle position.

17 Remove the distance piece and refit the pedal stop and spacer.

18 Check the adjustment by depressing the accelerator pedal to the full throttle position (ie until resistance is felt). The throttle valve at the engine must be fully open. Now depress the accelerator pedal fully onto the stop – the transmission lever must contact the kickdown stop. Finally disconnect the pushrod from the transmission lever – the hole must be aligned with the pin on the lever in the idle position. Refit the pushrod after making the check.

10 Selector lever and cable – removal, refitting and adjustment

1   Disconnect the battery negative lead.

2   Remove the grub screw and detach the knob from the selector lever.

3   Prise off the cover together with the blanking strip or brushes.

4   Remove the screws and withdraw the console.

5   Disconnect the wiring from the starter inhibitor switch and selector illumination bulb.

6   Unscrew the cable clamp nut, and also unscrew the nut from the floor bracket. Pull the cable clear.

7   Unscrew the nuts and remove the bracket and lever assembly from the floor.

8   Unbolt the cable bracket from the transmission, then extract the circlip and remove the cable end from the lever. Withdraw the cable from under the car.

9   Refitting is a reversal of removal, but before fitting the console adjust the cable as follows. Move the selector lever fully forwards to the P (park) position. Loosen the cable clamp nut, then move the lever on the transmission fully rearwards to the P (park) position. Tighten the cable clamp nut to the specified torque. Lightly lubricate the selector lever and cable pivots with engine oil.

11 Inhibitor switch – removal, refitting and adjustment

1   Remove the grub screw and detach the knob from the selector lever.

2   Prise off the cover together with the blanking strip or brushes.

3   Remove the screws and withdraw the console.

4   Disconnect the wiring from the starter inhibitor switch then remove the screws and withdraw the switch.

5   Refitting is a reversal of removal, but before fitting the console check that it is only possible to start the engine with the selector lever in positions N (neutral) or P (park). If necessary, reposition the switch within the elongated screw holes.

12 Fault diagnosis – automatic transmission and final drive

Symptom	Reason(s)
No drive in any gear	Fluid level too low
Erratic drive in forward gears	Fluid level too low
Dirty filter
Gear changes at above normal speed	Accelerator linkage adjustment incorrect
Dirt in governor
Gear changes at below normal speeds	Dirt in governor
Gear engagement jerky	Idle speed too high
Gear engagement delayed on upshift	Fluid level too low
Accelerator linkage adjustment incorrect
Kickdown does not operate	Accelerator linkage adjustment incorrect
Fluid dirty or discoloured	Brake bands and clutches wearing
Parking lock not effective	Selector lever out of adjustment
Parking lock defective

7

Chapter 8 Driveshafts

Contents

Specifications

Type	Double constant velocity (CV) joint, tubular driveshafts except on automatic transmission models where the right-hand driveshaft is solid

Length (excluding CV joints)

	Right-hand	Left-hand
Manual gearbox:		
With four-cylinder engine	530 mm (20.866 in)	530 mm (20.866 in)
With five-cylinder engine (except 2.2 litre 96 kW)	498.5 mm (19.626 in)	544.1 mm (21.421 in)
With five-cylinder engine (2.2 litre 96 kW)	516.3 mm (20.33 in)	562.9 mm (22.16 in)
Automatic transmission:		
With four-cylinder engine	489.7 mm (19.280 in)	589.5 mm (23.209 in)
With five-cylinder engine	483.9 mm (19.051 in)	583.0 mm (22.953 in)

CV joint lubricant	Audi G6 Grease

Torque wrench settings

	lbf ft	Nm
Inner CV joint to flange:		
except 2.2 litre 96 kW	33	45
2.2 litre 96 kW	59	80
Driveshaft nut	170	230

1 General description

Drive is transmitted from the splined final drive differential gears and drive flanges to the inner constant velocity (CV) joints. The driveshafts are either tubular or solid, as given in the Specifications, and are splined at each end to the CV joint hubs. The outer CV joints incorporate splined shafts which are attached to the front wheel hubs.

2 Driveshafts – removal and refitting

1 Prise the hub cap from the centre of the roadwheel.
2 Unscrew the driveshaft nut (photo). *This is tightened to a very high torque and no attempt to loosen it must be made unless the full weight of the car is on the roadwheels.*

3 Loosen the four bolts securing the roadwheel.
4 Jack the car and support the car securely on stands, or wood blocks.
5 Remove the roadwheel.
6 Using a socket wrench, remove the bolts from the inner driveshaft coupling and separate the driveshaft from the gearbox drive flange. Note the location of the bolt plates (photos).
7 On automatic transmission models, and when removing the right-hand driveshaft on manual gearbox models, it is necessary to disconnect the front suspension balljoint from the suspension wishbone. To do this first mark the exact position of the balljoint on the wishbone – this is important as the wheel camber setting is adjusted by moving the balljoint. Unscrew the nuts and release the balljoint.
8 Using a hub puller, press the driveshaft out of the front wheel hub, then withdraw the driveshaft.
9 Clean the splined end of the driveshaft and the wheel hub.

2.2 View of the driveshaft nut after removing the hub cap

2.6A Driveshaft inner joint coupling

2.6B Removing the bolts and plates from the driveshaft inner joint coupling

10 Refitting is a reversal of removal. However, on Coupe models with the 2.2 litre engine, apply a locking agent around the splines in a band about 5 mm (0.20 in) wide at the end of the shaft, and also apply the locking agent to the threads of the driveshaft nut. On all models tighten the nuts and bolts to the specified torque. If a suitable torque wrench is not available to tighten the driveshaft nut, tighten the nut firmly, then take the car to an Audi agent for final tightening – the front wheel camber can also be checked at the same time.

3 Driveshafts – overhaul

1 With the driveshaft removed as described in the preceding Section, remove the two clamps on the rubber boot at the inner end of the shaft and pull the boot down the shaft and off the coupling.
2 Remove the circlip from the end of the shaft, and using a suitable drift, remove the protective cap from the outer ring.

Fig. 8.1 The inner CV joints are secured with socket head bolts (Sec 2)

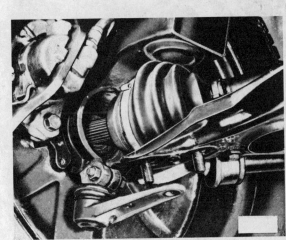

Fig. 8.2 Disconnecting the front suspension balljoint from the control arm (Sec 2)

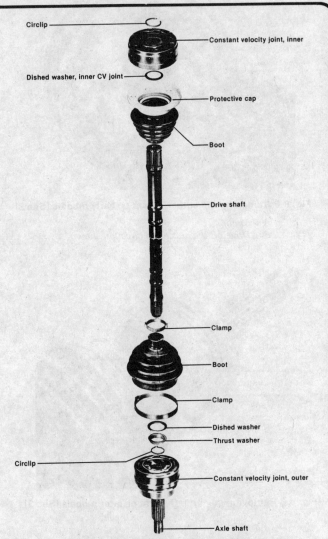

Circlip

Constant velocity joint, inner

Dished washer, inner CV joint

Protective cap

Boot

Drive shaft

Clamp

Boot

Clamp

Dished washer

Thrust washer

Circlip

Constant velocity joint, outer

Axle shaft

Fig. 8.3 Exploded view of the driveshaft (Sec 3)

8

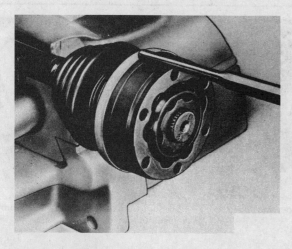

Fig. 8.4 Removing the protective cap from the inner joint (Sec 3)

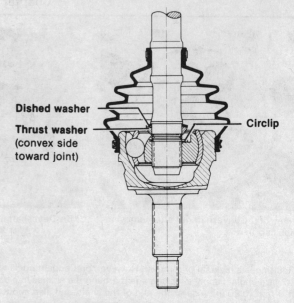

Dished washer

Thrust washer
(convex side
toward joint)

Circlip

Fig. 8.5 Cross-section of driveshaft outer joint (Sec 3)

Fig. 8.6 Removing the outer CV joint on early models (Sec 3)

A   Circlip
B   Drive off the hub in the direction shown

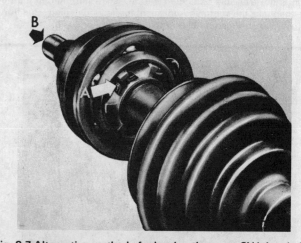

Fig. 8.7 Alternative method of releasing the outer CV joint circlip
(A) (Sec 3)

B   Direction of force

Fig. 8.8 Removing the outer CV joint on later models (Sec 3)

Fig. 8.9 Removing the cage and hub from the outer CV joint
(Sec 3)

Arrow indicates rectangular opening

3   Support the inner joint, then press the driveshaft out. Remove the dished washer or gasket, as applicable.

4   Remove the two clamps from the outer joint boot and pull the boot down the shaft.

5   On early models where the retaining circlip is visible, open the circlip and at the same time tap the outer end of the driveshaft with a mallet, or alternatively tap the inner face of the joint hub. This will dislodge the circlip from the groove in the driveshaft. On later models where the retaining circlip is not visible, strike the inner face of the outer ring with a mallet to release the hub from the circlip.

6   Withdraw the outer joint from the driveshaft together with the thrust washer and dished washer (where fitted).

7   Before starting to dismantle the outer joint, mark the position of the hub in relation to the cage and housing. Because the parts are hardened this mark will either have to be done with a grinding stone, or with paint.

8   Swivel the hub and cage and take out the balls one at a time.

9   Turn the cage until the two rectangular openings align with the housing and then remove the cage and hub.

10 Turn the hub until one segment can be pushed into one of the rectangular openings in the cage and then swivel the hub out of the cage. The parts of the joint make up a matched set and no individual parts can be replaced. If there is excessive play in the joint which is noticeable when changing from acceleration to overrun, or vice versa, a new joint must be fitted, but do not renew a joint because the parts have been polished by wear and the track of the balls is clearly visible.

11 When reassembling the joint, clean off all the old grease and use a new circlip, rubber boot and clips. Use only the special coupling grease recommended by Audi for packing the joints – see Specifications.

12 Press half a sachet of grease (45 g, 1.6 oz) into the joint and then fit the cage and hub into the housing, ensuring that it will be possible to line up the mating marks of the hub, cage, and housing after the balls have been inserted.

13 Press the balls into the hub from alternate sides; when all six have been inserted check that the mating marks on the hub, cage and housing are aligned.

14 On early models fit a new circlip into the groove of the hub. On all models squeeze the remainder of the grease into the joint so that the total amount is 90 g (3.2 oz).

15 The inner joint is dismantled in a similar way. Pivot the hub and cage and press them out of the housing as shown in Fig. 8.11.

16 Press the balls out of the cage, then align two grooves and remove the hub from the cage (Fig. 8.12).

17 When reassembling the joint, press half of the charge of grease into each side of the joint. Note that the chamfer on the splined hub must be on the larger diameter side of the outer ring. It will be necessary to pivot the joint hub when reassembling in order to align the balls with the grooves.

18 It is advisable to fit new rubber boots to the shaft; a defective boot will soon lead to the need to fit a new joint due to wear caused by grit entering the joint. Fit the boots to the shaft and put any residual grease into the boots.

19 Fit the dished washer or gasket (as applicable) to the inner end of the driveshaft and locate the protective cap on the boot. Note that the concave side of the dished washer must face the joint.

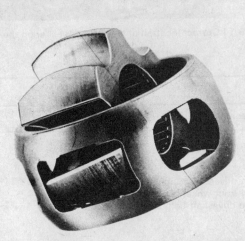

Fig. 8.10 Removing the outer CV joint hub from the cage (Sec 3)

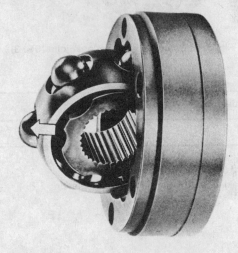

Fig. 8.11 Removing the inner joint hub and cage (Sec 3)

Fig. 8.12 Removing the inner joint hub from the cage (Sec 3)

Arrows indicate grooves

8

20 Press the inner joint onto the end of the driveshaft and secure it with a new circlip.

21 Tap the protective cap onto the outer ring.

22 Locate the dished washer (where fitted) and thrust washer on the outer end of the driveshaft, and on later models check that the retaining circlip is located in the shaft groove.

23 Using a mallet, drive the outer joint onto the driveshaft until the circlip engages the groove.

24 Fit new clamps to each end of the rubber boots, locate the boots over the joints, and tighten the clamps. If necessary the crimped type clamps can be replaced by worm drive clamps.

Fig. 8.13 Reassembling the inner joint (Sec 3)

Fig. 8.14 Correct location of the dished washer on the inner end of the driveshaft (Sec 3)

4   Fault diagnosis – driveshafts

Symptom	Reason(s)
Vibration and noise on lock	Worn driveshaft joints
Noise on taking up drive or between acceleration and overrun	Worn driveshaft joints Worn front wheel hub and driveshaft splines Loose driveshaft bolts or nut

Chapter 9 Braking system

Contents

Specifications

System type .... Four wheel hydraulic, with discs on front, and drums on rear. Twin diagonally split hydraulic circuits with vacuum servo assistance. Self-adjusting rear brakes. Load sensitive rear brake pressure regulator on some models. Cable operated handbrake on rear wheels.

General
Brake pedal free travel (maximum) .... $\frac{1}{3}$ of total travel
Handbrake free travel .... 2 teeth
Brake fluid specification .... FMVSS 116 DOT 3 or 116 DOT 4

Discs
Thickness .... 12.0 mm (0.472 in)
Wear limit .... 10.0 mm (0.394 in)
Maximum variation in thickness .... 0.02 mm (0.001 in)
Maximum run-out .... 0.06 mm (0.002 in)

Disc brake pads
Minimum pad lining thickness (excluding backplate) .... 2.0 mm (0.079 in)
Minimum pad thickness (including backplate)
    Teves .... 6.0 mm (0.236 in)
    Girling .... 7.0 mm (0.276 in)

Drums
Internal diameter:
    Models without pressure regulator .... 180.0 mm (7.087 in)
    Models with pressure regulator .... 200.0 mm (7.874 in)
Wear limit:
    Models without pressure regulator .... 181.0 mm (7.126 in)
    Models with pressure regulator .... 201.0 mm (7.913 in)
Drum radial run-out .... 0.05 mm (0.002 in)

Drum brake shoes
Minimum lining thickness .... 2.5 mm (0.098 in)

9

Torque wrench settings

Caliper to suspension strut:	lbf ft	Nm
Hexagon bolts	37	50
Serrated bolts	52	70
Guide pin bolts (Girling)	26	35
Wheel bolts	66	90
Disc guard plate	7	10
Rear brake backplate	44	60
Servo to bearing bracket	15	20
Servo bearing bracket to body	7	10
Handbrake lever	15	20

1　General description

The braking system is hydraulic with servo-assistance, and there are disc brakes on the front wheels and drum brakes on the rear. The system has a tandem master cylinder which incorporates two completely independent braking circuits, each circuit operating a front wheel and the diagonally opposite rear wheel. This ensures that if one circuit fails, the car can still be brought to rest in a straight line, even though the braking distance will be greater.

Some models incorporate a brake pressure regulator, which limits the pressure applied to the rear brake cylinders to a proportion of that applied to the front, and so prevents the rear wheels from locking.

The rear brakes are self-adjusting and incorporate a wedged key which automatically adjusts the length of the brake shoe upper pushrod on each wheel.

The handbrake operates on the rear wheels only and on some models incorporates a switch which illuminates a warning light on the instrument panel – the same light also warns of low brake fluid level.

2　Routine maintenance

1　The brake fluid level should be checked every week – the reservoir is translucent and the fluid level should be between the 'MIN' and 'MAX' marks. If necessary, top up with the specified brake fluid (photo). However, additional fluid will only be necessary if the hydraulic system is leaking, therefore the source of the leak must first be traced and rectified. Note that the level will drop slightly as the front disc pads wear, but in this case it is not necessary to top up the level.
2　Every 10 000 miles (15 000 km) or 12 months, if this occurs sooner, the hydraulic pipes and unions should be checked for chafing, leakage, cracks and corrosion. At the same time check the operation of the brake pressure regulator and check the disc pads and rear brake linings for wear. Also check the servo vacuum hose for condition and security.
3　Renew the brake fluid every 2 years.

3　Disc pads – inspection and renewal

1　Pad thickness can be checked without removing the roadwheel. Turn the wheel until the brake pad is visible through one of the openings in the wheel rim.
2　With the aid of a torch to increase visibility, measure the thickness of each brake pad including its metal backplate (photo) and compare this with the minimum value given in the Specifications. A rough guide to the amount of life remaining in brake pads which are nearing their minimum is that the rate of wear is about 1 mm (0.039 in) for every 1000 km (620 miles) driving.
3　If the brake pads are to be re-used, they must be refitted to the position from which they were taken. To ensure this, mark the pads before removing them.
4　First apply the handbrake, then jack up the front of the car and support it on axle stands. Remove the roadwheels.

Teves caliper

5　Extract the retaining spring, then use a punch to drive out the pad retaining pins.
6　Pull out the inner pad using a hooked instrument.
7　Press the floating caliper frame outwards to disengage the pad from the projection on the caliper frame and then pull out the outer pad.
8　Using two pieces of wood, lever the piston back into the cylinder. While doing this check that brake fluid will not overflow from the reservoir, and if necessary use a flexible plastic bottle to extract some fluid. **Note**: *Brake fluid is poisonous, so no attempt should be made to siphon the fluid by mouth.*
9　Check that the piston cutaway is positioned at 20° to the horizontal (see Fig. 9.4) and, if necessary, rotate the piston as required.

Girling caliper

10　Push the cylinder in the direction indicated by the arrow in Fig. 9.5 in order to move the caliper away from the pads. While doing this

2.1 Checking and topping-up the brake fluid level

3.2 Checking the disc pad wear (wheel removed)

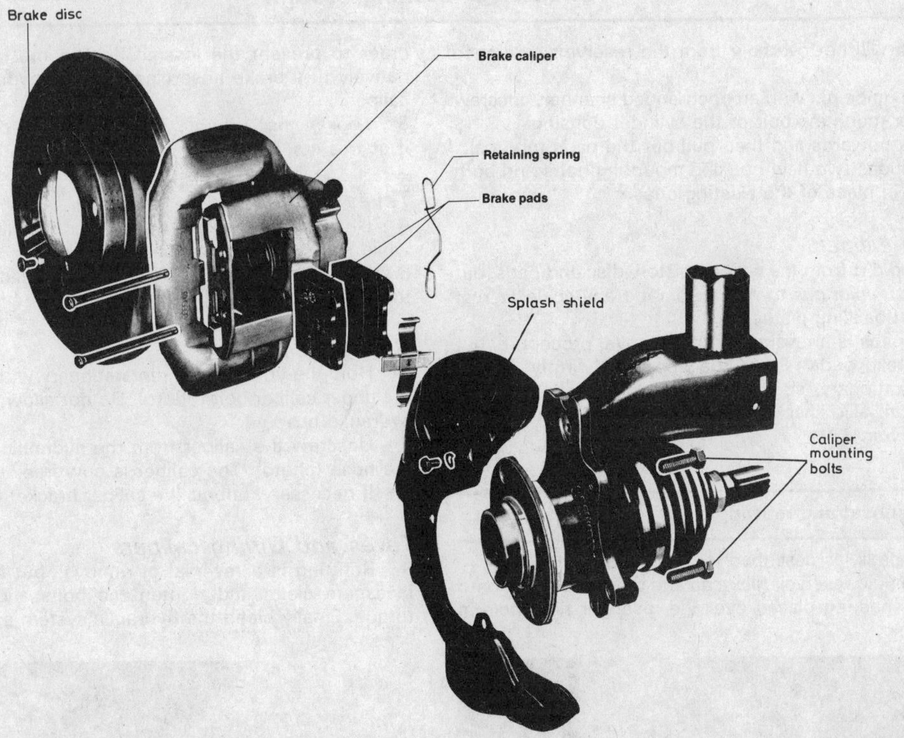

Brake disc

Brake caliper

Retaining spring

Brake pads

Splash shield

Caliper
mounting
bolts

Fig. 9.1 Teves type brake caliper and disc pads (Sec 3)

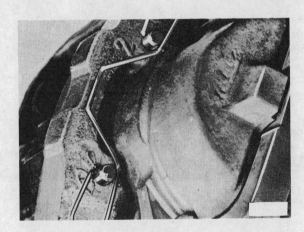

Fig. 9.2 Pin retaining spring location on the Teves type brake caliper (Sec 3)

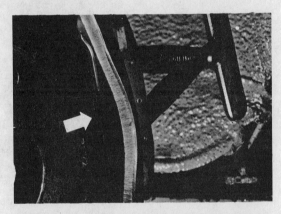

Fig. 9.3 Showing the outer pad and locating projection on the Teves type brake caliper (Sec 3)

Fig. 9.4 Checking the piston position with a 20° gauge – arrow indicates forward rotation of brake disc (Sec 3)

Fig. 9.5 Push the Girling caliper in the direction of the arrow to depress the piston and release the disc pads (Sec 3)

9

check that brake fluid will not overflow from the reservoir – refer to paragraph 8.

11   While holding the guide pin with an open-ended spanner, unscrew and remove the lower mounting bolt of the cylinder housing.

12   Pivot the housing upwards and then pull out the pads (photos).

13   The repair kit includes two new housing mounting bolts and both bolts should be used in place of the existing ones.

Teves and Girling calipers

14   Brush the dust and dirt from the caliper, piston, disc and pads, but *do not inhale it, as it is injurious to health.* Scrape any scale or rust from the disc and pad backing plates.

15   Fitting the brake pads is a reversal of the removal procedure, but on completion the brake pedal should be depressed firmly several times with the car stationary, so that the disc pads take up their normal running position. Also check and if necessary top up the brake fluid level in the reservoir.

4   Disc caliper – removal and refitting

1   Remove the disc pads, as described in Section 3.

2   Remove the brake fluid reservoir filler cap and tighten it down onto a piece of polythene sheeting placed over the reservoir filler hole in order to prevent the loss of fluid in the following procedure. Alternatively fit a brake hose clamp on the hydraulic hose attached to the caliper.

3   Loosen the hydraulic hose union, but do not attempt to unscrew it at this stage.

Teves caliper

4   Unscrew the two bolts securing the caliper to the suspension strut while supporting the caliper.

5   Unscrew the caliper from the hydraulic hose and plug the end of the hose.

Girling caliper

6   Hold the upper guide pin stationary with a spanner, then unscrew the upper caliper bolt (photo). Do not allow the caliper to hang on the hydraulic hose.

7   Unscrew the caliper from the hydraulic hose and plug the end of the hose (photo). The caliper is now free.

8   If necessary, unbolt the caliper bracket from the suspension strut.

Teves and Girling calipers

9   Refitting is a reversal of removal, but make sure that all mating faces are clean and tighten the bolts and unions to the specified torque. Finally bleed the hydraulic system as described in Section 14.

3.12A Fitted position of the disc pads

3.12B Removing a disc pad

4.6 Unscrewing the Girling caliper upper guide pin bolt

4.7 Removing the Girling caliper

5 Disc caliper – overhaul

1 Clean the exterior of the caliper, taking care not to allow any foreign matter to enter the hydraulic hose aperture.

Teves caliper

2 Press the mounting frame off the floating frame and separate the two frames.

3 Place a block of wood in the floating frame and drive out the cylinder assembly, using a soft metal drift.

4 Use a foot pump or a compressed air supply to blow the piston out of the cylinder, but support the cylinder with the piston facing downwards to avoid the risk of injury when the piston is ejected.

5 Use a blunt screwdriver to prise the seal out of the piston bore, taking great care not to scratch the bore of the cylinder.

6 Clean the caliper components thoroughly with methylated spirit and allow to dry.

7 Fit a new seal into the groove in the cylinder bore. Apply a thin coat of brake cylinder paste to the seal and to the cylinder. Then squeeze the piston into the cylinder using a vice fitted with soft jaws.

8 Rest the floating frame on the bench, then insert the brake cylinder and tap it fully into the frame.

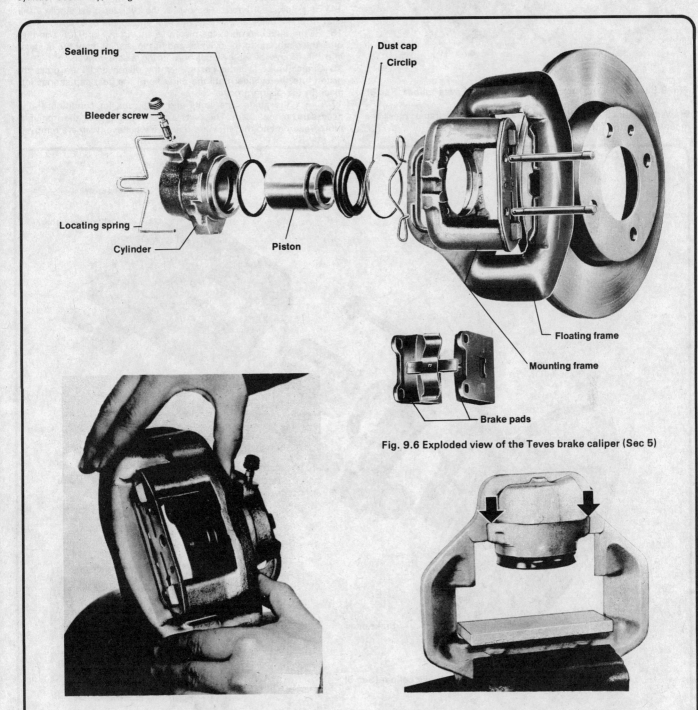

Fig. 9.6 Exploded view of the Teves brake caliper (Sec 5)

Fig. 9.7 Separating the mounting and floating frames on the Teves caliper (Sec 5)

Fig. 9.8 Removing the cylinder on the Teves caliper (Sec 5)

9

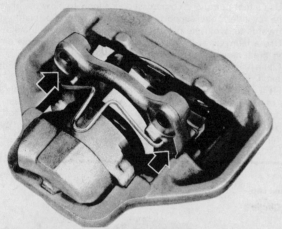

Fig. 9.9 Installing the mounting frame on the Teves caliper (Sec 5)

9 With the locating spring fitted to the mounting frame, press the mounting frame onto the floating frame.

10 Set the piston cutaway 20° to the horizontal as described in Section 3. The angle can be checked by making a simple gauge out of card.

Girling caliper

11 Use a foot pump, or a compressed air supply to blow the piston out of the cylinder, but place a block of wood inside the frame to prevent damage to the piston. Remove the dust cap.

12 Use a blunt screwdriver to prise the seal out of the piston bore, taking great care not to scratch the bore of the cylinder.

13 Clean the caliper components thoroughly with methylated spirit and allow to dry.

14 Fit a new seal into the groove in the cylinder bore. Apply a thin coat of brake cylinder paste to the seal and to the cylinder.

15 Fit the dust cap on to the piston as shown in Fig. 9.11, and then offer the piston up to the cylinder and fit the sealing lip of the dust cap into the groove of the cylinder bore, using a screwdriver.

16 Smear brake cylinder paste over the piston and then press the piston into the cylinder until the outer lip of the dust cap springs into place in the piston groove.

17 Check the guide pins, bolts and dust caps for condition and, if necessary, renew them. The bolts are self-locking and the manufacturers recommend that they are renewed whenever they are removed.

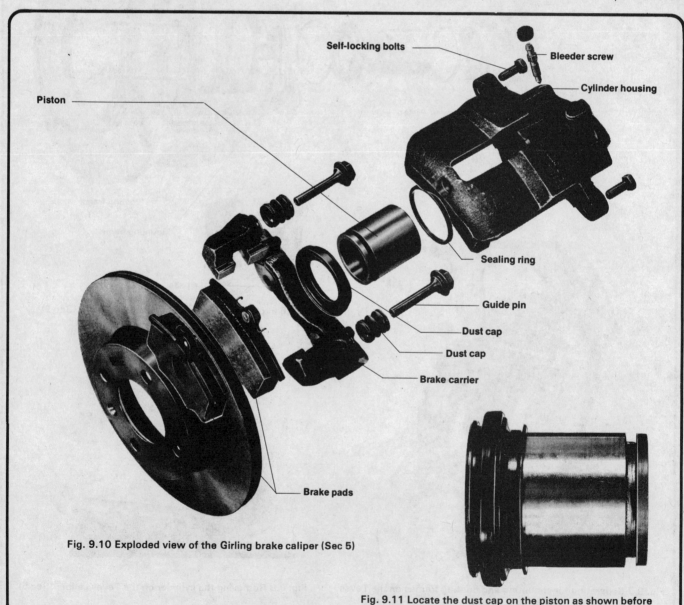

Fig. 9.10 Exploded view of the Girling brake caliper (Sec 5)

Fig. 9.11 Locate the dust cap on the piston as shown before inserting the piston in the Girling brake caliper (Sec 5)

6.2 Checking the brake disc thickness

6.4 Brake disc retaining screw location

6 Brake disc – examination, removal and refitting

1   Jack up the front of the car and support it on axle stands. Remove the roadwheel.
2   Rotate the disc and examine it for deep scoring or grooving. Light scoring is normal, but if excessive the disc should be removed and renewed, or ground by a suitably qualified engineering works. Use a micrometer in several positions to check the disc thickness (photo).
3   To remove the brake disc first remove the caliper as described in Section 4. However, do not disconnect the hydraulic hose – suspend the caliper by wire from the coil spring making sure that the hydraulic hose is not strained.
4   Remove the countersunk cross-head screw and withdraw the brake disc from the hub (photo).
5   Refitting is a reversal of removal, but make sure that the mating faces of the hub and disc are clean.

7 Rear brake shoes – inspection and renewal

1   The thickness of the rear brake linings can be checked without removing the brake drums. Remove the rubber plug which is above the handbrake cable entry on the brake backplate. Use a torch to increase visibility and check the thickness of friction material remaining on the brake shoes. If the amount remaining is close to the minimum given in the Specifications, a more thorough examination should be made by removing the brake drum.
2   Chock the front wheels, then jack up the rear of the car and support it on axle stands. Remove the rear wheels and release the handbrake.

3   Remove the cap from the centre of the brake drum by tapping it on alternate sides with a screwdriver or blunt chisel.
4   Extract the split pin and remove the locking ring.
5   Unscrew the nut and remove the thrust washer.
6   Withdraw the brake drum, making sure that the outer wheel bearing does not fall out. If the brake drum binds on the shoes, insert a small screwdriver through a wheel bolt hole and lever up the wedged key in order to release the shoes.
7   Note the position of the brake shoes and springs and mark the webs of the shoes, if necessary, to aid refitting.
8   Using pliers, depress the spring retainer caps, turn them through 90° and remove them together with the springs (photo).
9   Unhook the lower return spring from the shoes (photo).
10 Detach the bottom of the shoes from the bottom anchor, then release the top of the shoes from the wheel cylinder and swivel down to reveal the rear of the shoes (photo).
11 Disconnect the handbrake cable, then clamp the bottom of the shoes in a vice.
12 Unhook the upper return spring and the wedged key spring.
13 Separate the trailing shoe from the leading shoe and pushrod.
14 Unhook the tensioning spring and remove the pushrod from the leading shoe together with the wedged key.
15 Brush the dust from the brake drum, brake shoes, and backplate, *but do not inhale it, as it is injurious to health.* Scrape any scale or rust from the drum.
16 Measure the brake shoe lining thickness. If it is worn down to the specified minimum amount, renew all four rear brake shoes.
17 Clean the brake backplate. If there are any signs of loss of grease from the rear hub bearings, the oil seal should be renewed, with reference to Chapter 11. If hydraulic fluid is leaking from the wheel cylinder, it must be repaired or renewed, as described in Section 8. Do

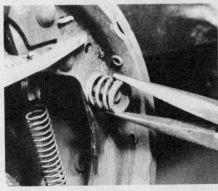

7.8 Removing the rear brake shoe retaining springs

7.9 Rear brake shoe lower return spring (arrowed)

7.10 Showing rear brake shoe fixing to wheel cylinder

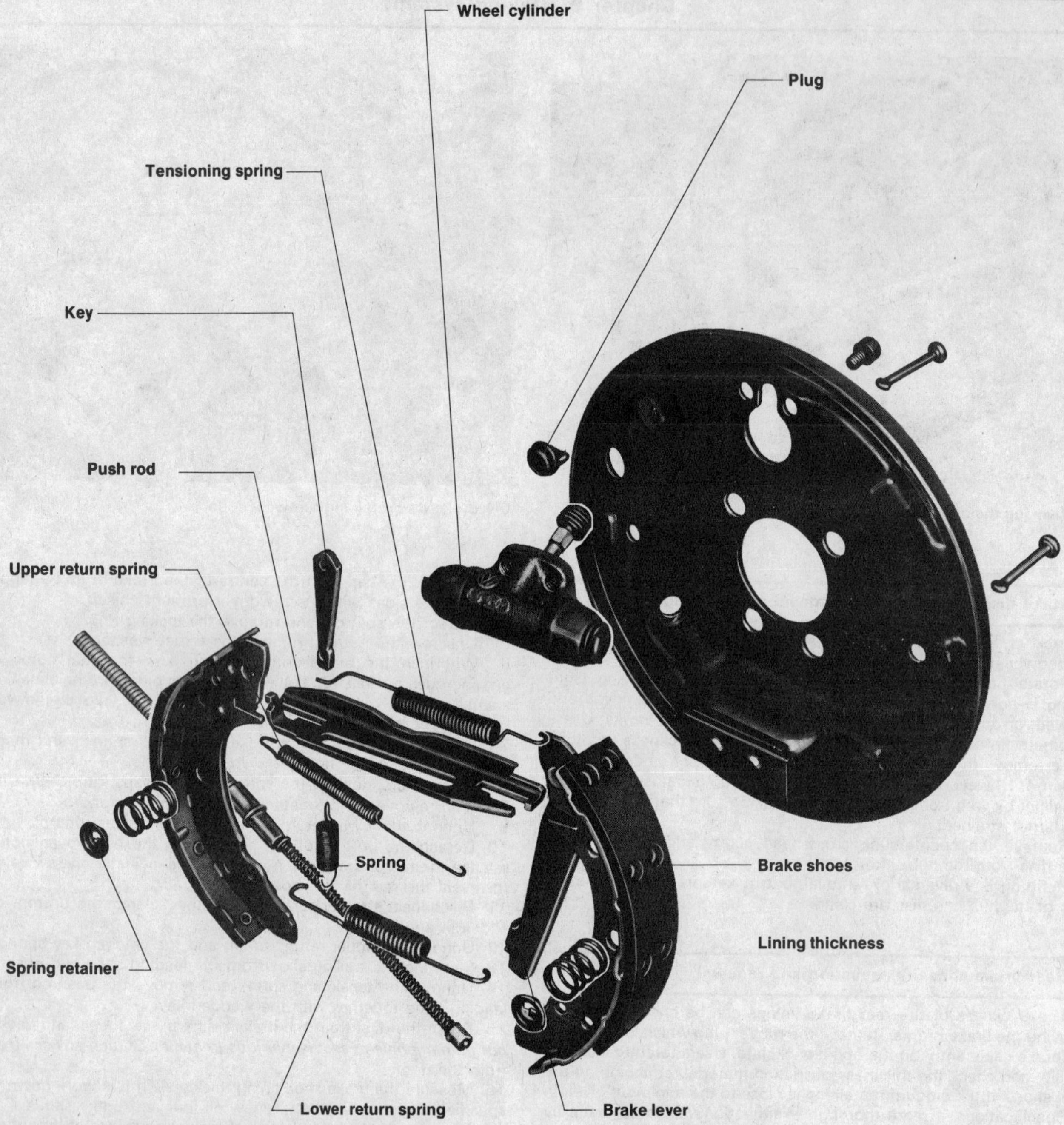

Wheel cylinder

Plug

Tensioning spring

Key

Push rod

Upper return spring

Brake shoes

Lining thickness

Spring

Spring retainer

Lower return spring

Brake lever

Fig. 9.12 Exploded view of the rear brakes (Sec 7)

Fig. 9.13 Disconnecting the handbrake cable from the brake shoes
(Sec 7)

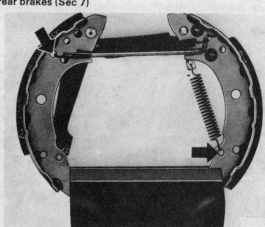

Fig. 9.14 Mount the brake shoes in a vice and unhook the springs
(Sec 7)

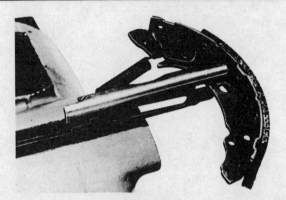

Fig. 9.15 Clamp the pushrod in a vice when refitting the leading brake shoe (Sec 7)

7.24 Rear brake self-adjusting wedged key and spring (arrowed)

not touch the brake pedal while the shoes are removed. Position an elastic band over the wheel cylinder pistons to retain them.

18 Apply a little brake grease to the contact areas of the pushrod and handbrake lever.

19 Clamp the pushrod in a vice, then hook the tensioning spring on the pushrod and leading shoe and position the shoe slot over the pushrod.

20 Fit the wedged key between the shoe and pushrod.

21 Locate the handbrake lever on the trailing shoe in the pushrod, and fit the upper return spring.

22 Connect the handbrake cable to the handbrake lever, swivel the shoes upward and locate the top of the shoes on the wheel cylinder pistons.

23 Fit the lower return spring to the shoes, then lever the bottom of the shoes onto the bottom anchor.

24 Fit the spring to the wedged key and leading shoe (photo).

25 Fit the retaining springs and caps.

26 Press the wedged key upwards to give the maximum shoe clearance (photo).

27 Fit the brake drum and adjust the wheel bearings, with reference to Chapter 11.

28 Depress the brake pedal once firmly in order to adjust the rear brakes.

29 Repeat the procedure on the remaining rear brake, then lower the car to the ground.

7.26 Rear brake shoes ready for fitting of the brake drum

---

8 Rear wheel cylinder – removal, overhaul and refitting

1 Remove the brake shoes, as described in Section 7.

2 Remove the brake fluid reservoir filler cap and tighten it down onto a piece of polythene sheeting placed over the reservoir filler hole in order to prevent the loss of fluid in the following procedure. Alternatively fit a brake hose clamp on the hydraulic hose between the rear axle and underbody.

3 Loosen the brake pipe union on the rear of the wheel cylinder (photo).

4 Using an Allen key, unscrew the wheel cylinder mounting bolts.

5 Unscrew the brake pipe union and withdraw the wheel cylinder from the backplate. Plug the end of the hydraulic pipe, if necessary.

6 Clean the exterior of the wheel cylinder, taking care not to allow any foreign matter to enter the hydraulic pipe aperture.

7 Remove the rubber boots from the ends of the cylinder and extract the two pistons and the spring between them.

8 Inspect the cylinder bore for signs of scoring and corrosion and the pistons and seals for wear. If the cylinder is satisfactory a repair kit can be used; otherwise the cylinder should be discarded and a new complete assembly fitted. If servicing a cylinder, use all the parts in the repair kit. Clean all the metal parts, using methylated spirit if necessary, *but never petrol or similar solvents*, then leave the parts to dry in the air, or dry them with a lint-free cloth.

9 Apply brake cylinder paste to the seals and fit them so that their larger diameter end is nearest to the end of the piston.

10 Smear brake cylinder paste on to the pistons and into the bore of the cylinder. Fit a piston into one end of the cylinder and then the

8.3 Brake pipe union on the rear of the rear wheel cylinder

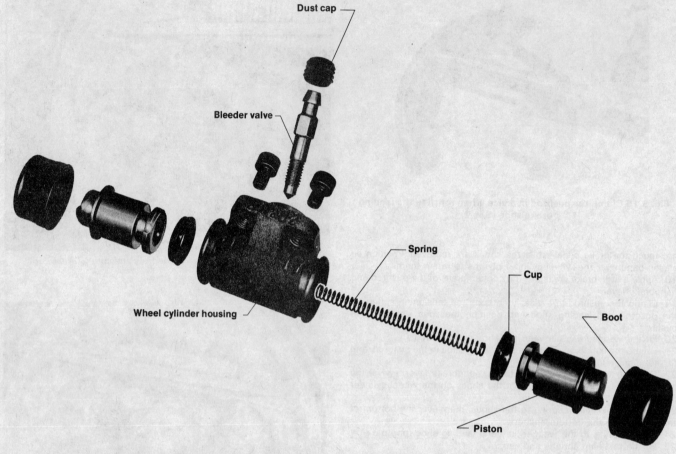

Fig. 9.16 Exploded view of the rear wheel cylinder (Sec 8)

spring and other piston into the other end. Take care not to force the pistons into the cylinders because this can twist the seals.

11 Locate the rubber boots over the pistons and into the grooves of the wheel cylinder.

12 Refitting is a reversal of removal, but bleed the hydraulic system as described in Section 14.

9 Brake drum – inspection and renovation

1 Whenever the brake drums are removed, they should be checked for wear and damage. Light scoring of the friction surface is normal, but if it is excessive, or if the internal diameter exceeds the specified wear limit, the drum and hub assembly should be renewed.

2 After a high mileage the friction surface may become oval. Where this has occurred, it may be possible to have the surface ground true by a qualified engineering works. However, it is preferable to renew the drum and hub assembly.

10 Master cylinder – removal and refitting

1 Depress the footbrake pedal several times to dissipate the vacuum in the servo unit.

2 Remove the brake fluid reservoir filler cap and draw off the fluid using a syringe or flexible plastic bottle. Take care not to spill the fluid on the car's paintwork – if some is accidentally spilled, wash it off immediately with copious amounts of cold water.

3 Refit the filler cap, but disconnect the wiring for the fluid level warning circuit.

4 Place some rags beneath the master cylinder, then unscrew the brake pipe union nuts and pull the pipes just clear of the master cylinder. Plug the ends of the pipes or cover them with masking tape.

5 Where applicable disconnect the wiring from the brake light switch.

6 Unscrew the mounting nuts and withdraw the master cylinder from the front of the servo unit. Remove the seal.

7 Refitting is a reversal of removal, but always fit a new seal. Finally bleed the hydraulic system as described in Section 14.

11 Master cylinder – overhaul

Note: *From December 1980 a sealed type master cylinder was progressively introduced – this master cylinder cannot be dismantled as the end circlip has no eyes to allow removal. Unfortunately there are no external identification marks.*

1 Empty the master cylinder and reservoir and discard the fluid.

2 Pull the reservoir off the master cylinder.

3 Remove the stop screw from the cylinder and then remove the circlip from the mouth of the bore.

4 Pull out the piston pushrod assembly, the secondary piston assembly and finally the loose spring.

5 Inspect the bore of the cylinder for signs of wear, damage and corrosion. If the cylinder is in good condition it may be re-used with a service kit, otherwise obtain a new cylinder assembly.

6 Clean all the metal parts, using methylated spirit if necessary, *but never petrol or similar solvents,* then leave the parts to dry in the air, or dry them with a clean lint-free cloth. Remove the seals.

7 Use all the parts supplied in the repair kit and moisten all components with brake fluid before fitting them. Make sure that the correct repair kit is obtained as there are two types of master cylinder – 'ATE' and 'FAG'.

8 Reassemble the secondary piston assembly in the following order. Fit the two piston seals at the larger diameter end of the piston. The piston seals are identified by their chamfer and groove (Fig. 9.18); the sealing lips of the two seals should face away from each other. Fit the cup washer, the primary cup with its lip towards the closed end of the cylinder, the support ring and finally the conical spring.

9 While holding the master cylinder body vertically with its open end

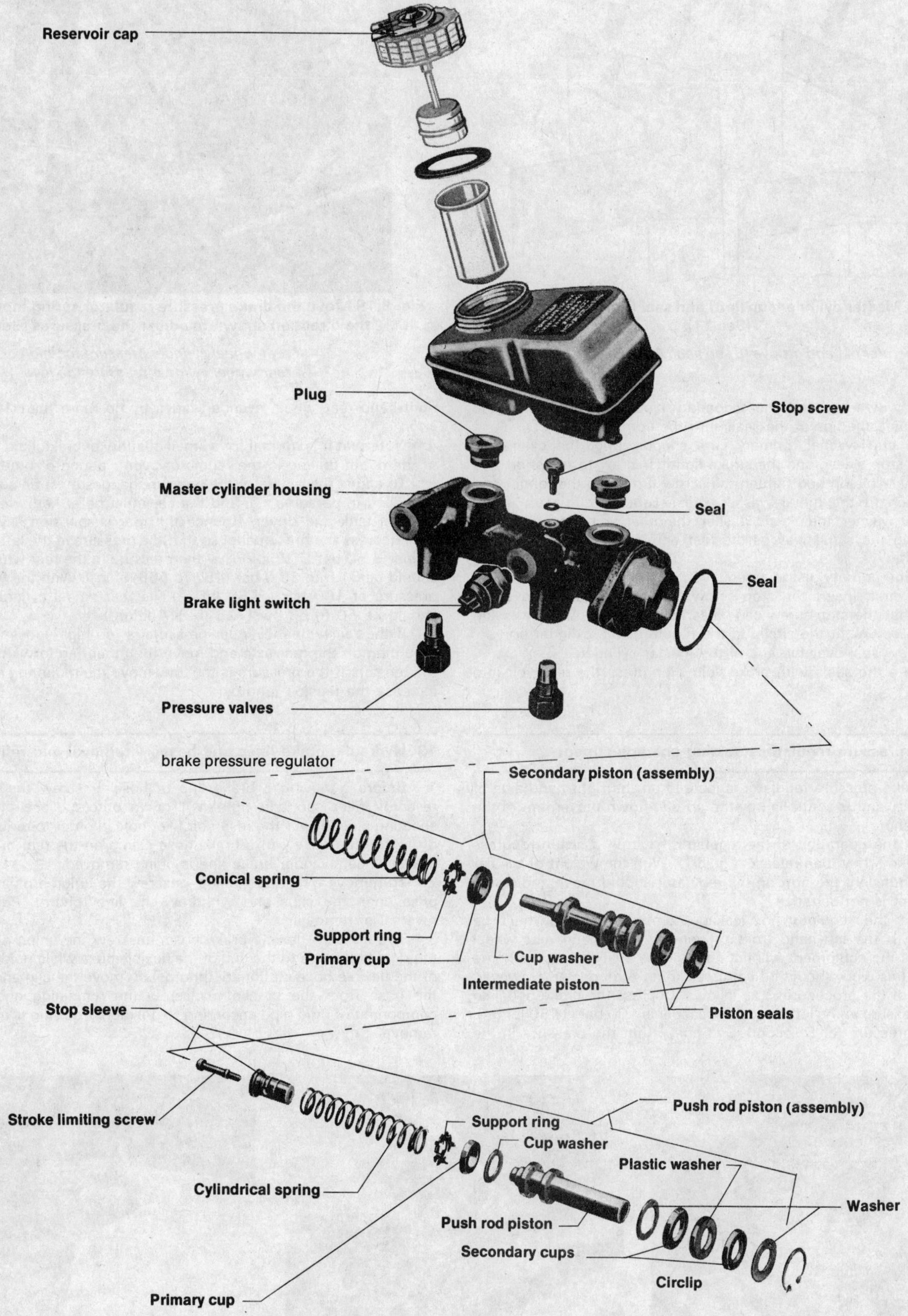

Reservoir cap

Plug

Stop screw

Master cylinder housing

Seal

Seal

Brake light switch

Pressure valves

brake pressure regulator

Secondary piston (assembly)

Conical spring

Support ring
Primary cup

Cup washer

Intermediate piston

Piston seals

Stop sleeve

Stroke limiting screw

Push rod piston (assembly)

Support ring

Cup washer

Plastic washer

Cylindrical spring

Push rod piston

Washer

Secondary cups

Primary cup

Circlip

9

Fig. 9.17 Exploded view of the master cylinder (Sec 11)

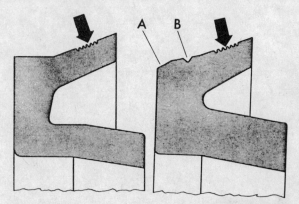

Fig. 9.18 Master cylinder cup (left) and seal (right) identification (Sec 11)

Note chamfer (A) and groove (B) on seal. Arrows show serrations

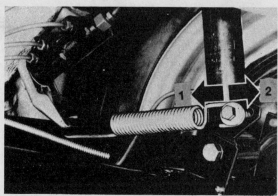

Fig. 9.19 Move the brake pressure regulator spring mounting in the direction shown to adjust the pressures (Sec 12)

1 – if rear wheel cylinder pressure too high
2 – if rear wheel cylinder pressure too low

pointing downwards, feed the secondary piston assembly into the cylinder. Guide the lips of the seals into the bore carefully.

10 Fit the cup washer, primary cup, support ring, the cylindrical spring, the stop sleeve and the stroke limiting screw to the short end of the primary piston and tighten the screw firmly. To the longer end of the piston fit the metal washer, the secondary cup with its lip towards the washer, the plastic washer, the other secondary cup, with its lip facing the same way as the first one, and finally the second metal washer.

11 Insert the primary piston assembly into the cylinder bore with the spring end first. Insert the stop screw, and if necessary move the piston so that the stop screw can be screwed in fully. After screwing in the stop screw, fit the circlip to the mouth of the cylinder bore.

12 Fit a new seal over the end of the master cylinder.

13 Lubricate the seals with brake fluid then press the reservoir into them.

right-hand rear wheel cylinder varies by no more than 10 bar (145 lbf/in^2).

4 Note that it is normal for a small quantity of brake fluid to seep out of the outlet drilling in the regulator over a period of time.

5 To adjust the regulator the pressure gauges must be connected as described in paragraph 3, and the car must be at kerb weight with a full fuel tank and driver. Bounce the rear suspension several times, then depress the brake pedal so that the pressure in the left-hand front caliper is 50 bar (725 lbf/in^2) – the pressure in the rear wheel cylinder should be 31.5 to 39.0 bar (457 to 566 lbf/in^2). With the front caliper pressure at 100 bar (1450 lbf/in^2) the rear wheel cylinder pressure should be 50 to 63 bar (725 to 914 lbf/in^2).

6 If the rear wheel cylinder pressure is too high, loosen the spring mounting on the rear axle and move the mounting forward to release the tension. If the pressure is too low, move the mounting rearward to increase the tension (photos).

12 Brake pressure regulator – testing and adjustment

1 The brake pressure regulator is located on the right-hand side of the rear axle, and is controlled by the up-and-down movement of the rear axle (photo).

2 To test the operation of the regulator, have an assistant depress the footbrake firmly then release it quickly. With the weight of the car on the suspension, the arm on the regulator should move, indicating that the unit is not seized.

3 To test the regulator for leakage, pressure gauges must be connected to the left-hand front caliper and right-hand rear wheel cylinder. As the equipment will not normally be available to the home mechanic, this work should be entrusted to an Audi dealer. However, an outline of the procedure is as follows. Depress the brake pedal so that the pressure in the left-hand front caliper is 100 bar (1450 lbf/in^2). Hold this pressure for 5 seconds and check that the pressure in the

13 Hydraulic brake lines and hoses – removal and refitting

1 Before removing a brake line or hose, unscrew the brake fluid reservoir filler cap and tighten it down onto a piece of polythene sheeting placed over the reservoir filler hole in order to reduce the loss of fluid. Alternatively fit a brake hose clamp on the rear brake hose if a rear wheel cylinder brake line is being removed.

2 To remove a rigid brake line, unscrew the union nuts at each end, prise open the clips and withdraw the line (photo). Refitting is a reversal of removal.

3 To remove a flexible brake hose, unscrew the union nut securing the rigid brake line to the end of the flexible hose while holding the end of the flexible hose stationary (photos). Remove the clip and withdraw the hose from the bracket. Unscrew the remaining end from the component or rigid pipe according to position. Refitting is a reversal of removal.

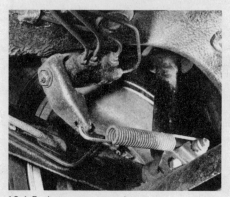

12.1 Brake pressure regulator

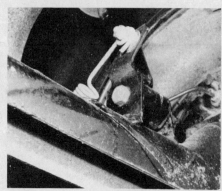

12.6A Inner view of the brake pressure regulator adjustment clamp

12.6B Outer view of the brake pressure regulator adjustment clamp

13.2 Rigid brake line clip

13.3A Front brake flexible hose connection

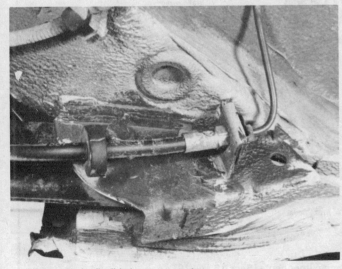

13.3B Rear brake flexible hose connection

4   Bleed the hydraulic system as described in Section 14 after fitting a rigid brake line or flexible brake hose.

14 Hydraulic system – bleeding

1   If any of the hydraulic components in the braking system have been removed or disconnected, or if the fluid level in the master cylinder has been allowed to fall appreciably, it is inevitable that air will have been introduced into the system. The removal of all this air from the hydraulic system is essential if the brakes are to function correctly and the process of removing it is known as bleeding.

2   There are a number of one-man, do-it-yourself, brake bleeding kits currently available from motor accessory shops. It is recommended that one of these kits should be used wherever possible, as they greatly simplify the bleeding operation, and also reduce the risk of expelled air and fluid being drawn back into the system.

3   If one of these kits is not available then it will be necessary to gather together a clean jar and a suitable length of clear plastic tubing which is a tight fit over the bleed screw, and also to engage the help of an assistant.

4   Before commencing the bleeding operation, check that all rigid pipes and flexible hoses are in good condition and that all hydraulic unions are tight. Take great care not to allow hydraulic fluid to come into contact with the car's paintwork, otherwise the finish will be seriously damaged. Wash off any spilled fluid immediately with cold water.

5   If hydraulic fluid has been lost from the master cylinder, due to a leak in the system, ensure that the cause is traced and rectified before proceeding further, or a serious malfunction of the braking system may occur.

6   To bleed the system, clean the area around the bleed screw at the wheel cylinder to be bled. If the hydraulic system has only been partially disconnected and suitable precautions were taken to prevent further loss of fluid, it should only be necessary to bleed that part of the system. However, if the entire system is to be bled, the following sequence must be adhered to:

(1)   Right-hand rear wheel cylinder
(2)   Left-hand rear wheel cylinder
(3)   Right-hand front caliper
(4)   Left-hand front caliper

When bleeding the rear wheel cylinders on models with a brake pressure regulator, have an assistant push the regulator lever to the rear, as shown in Fig. 9.20.

7   Remove the master cylinder filler cap and top up the reservoir. Periodically check the fluid level during the bleeding operation and top up as necessary.

8   If a one-man brake bleeding kit is being used, connect the outlet tube to the bleed screw and then open the screw half a turn. If possible postion the unit so that it can be viewed from the car, then depress the brake pedal to the floor and slowly release it. The one-way valve in the kit will prevent expelled air from returning to the system at the end of each stroke. Repeat this operation until clean hydraulic fluid, free from

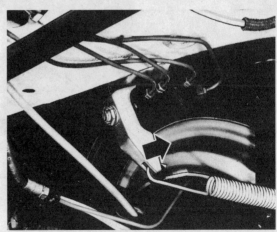

Fig. 9.20 Push the brake pressure regulator lever to the rear when bleeding the rear wheel cylinders (Sec 14)

9

air bubbles, can be seen coming through the tube. Now tighten the bleed screw and remove the outlet tube.

9   If a one-man brake bleeding kit is not available, connect one end of the plastic tubing to the bleed screw and immerse the other end in the jar containing sufficient clean hydraulic fluid to keep the end of the tube submerged (photo). Open the bleed screw half a turn and have your assistant depress the brake pedal to the floor and then slowly release it. Tighten the bleed screw at the end of each downstroke to prevent expelled air and fluid from being drawn back into the system. Repeat this operation until clean hydraulic fluid, free from air bubbles, can be seen coming through the tube. Now tighten the bleed screw and remove the plastic tube.

10 If the entire system is being bled the procedures described above should now be repeated at each wheel. Do not forget to recheck the fluid level in the master cylinder at regular intervals and top up as necessary.

11 When completed, recheck the fluid level in the master cylinder, top up if necessary, and refit the cap. Check the 'feel' of the brake pedal; this should be firm and free from any 'sponginess', which would indicate air still present in the system.

12 Discard any expelled hydraulic fluid as it is likely to be contaminated with moisture, air and dirt, which makes it unsuitable for further use.

15 Brake pedal – removal and refitting

1   The brake and clutch pedals share a common bracket assembly and pivot shaft. However, on some models the pivot shaft is fixed to the bracket and on other models it is free to move.

2   Working inside the car, extract the clip and remove the clevis pin securing the servo pushrod or intermediate pushrod to the pedal (photo). Remove the lower panel, if necessary.

3   Extract the clip from the end of the pivot shaft, unhook the return spring (where fitted) and withdraw the pedal from the shaft. On some models it is necessary to loosen the bracket mounting nuts and move the bracket to one side.

4   Check the pedal bushes for wear. If necessary drive them out from each side and press in new bushes using a soft-jawed vice.

5   Refitting is a reversal of removal, but lubricate the pivot shaft with a little multi-purpose grease.

16 Handbrake lever – removal and refitting

1   Chock the front wheels, then jack up the rear of the car and support it on axle stands.

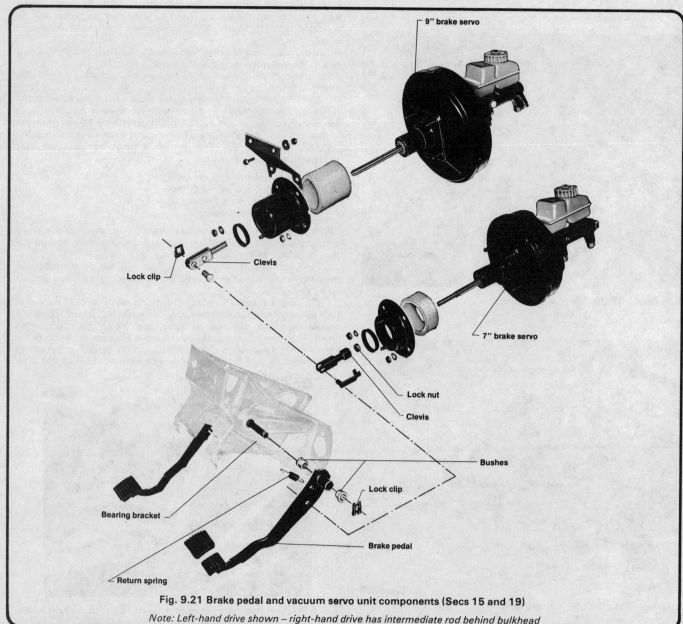

Fig. 9.21 Brake pedal and vacuum servo unit components (Secs 15 and 19)

Note: Left-hand drive shown – right-hand drive has intermediate rod behind bulkhead

14.9 Bleed tube connected to a front brake caliper

15.2 View of the upper part of the brake pedal and pushrod securing clevis pin (arrowed)

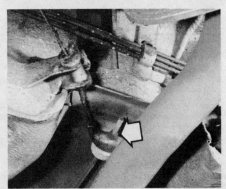

17.3 Handbrake adjustment nut (arrowed)

2   Unscrew the nut from the handbrake pullrod and remove the compensator bar.
3   Pull the rubber bellows from the underbody and off the pullrod.
4   Working inside the car, prise out the gaiter and move it up the handbrake lever.
5   Disconnect the wiring from the handbrake warning switch.
6   Unscrew the mounting bolts and withdraw the handbrake lever assembly and switch bracket.
7   Remove the central screws and withdraw the lower cover, then extract the clips, push out the clevis pin and remove the pullrod.
8   If necessary the ratchet may be dismantled by removing the clips and clevis pin or grinding off the rivet head. However, if the ratchet is known to be worn, renew the complete assembly.
9   Refitting is a reversal of removal, but lubricate the pivots and compensator bar with multi-purpose grease. Finally adjust the handbrake, as described in Section 17.

17 Handbrake – adjustment

1   Chock the front wheels, then jack up the rear of the car and support it on axle stands.
2   Fully release the handbrake lever, then firmly depress the brake pedal once.
3   Pull the handbrake lever onto the 2nd notch and check that it is just possible to turn the rear wheels by hand. If necessary, adjust the

position of the nut on the end of the pullrod beneath the car. The nut is located next to the compensator bar (photo).
4   Fully release the handbrake lever and check that both rear wheels turn freely.
5   Lower the car to the ground.

18 Vacuum servo unit – description and testing

1   The vacuum servo unit is located between the brake pedal and the master cylinder and provides assistance to the driver when the brake pedal is depressed. The unit operates by vacuum from the inlet manifold, and on some models the vacuum is increased by incorporating a vacuum booster in the vacuum supply.
2   The unit basically comprises a diaphragm and non-return valve. With the brake pedal released, vacuum is channelled to both sides of the diaphragm, but when the pedal is depressed, one side is opened to the atmosphere. The resultant unequal pressures are harnessed to assist in depressing the master cylinder pistons.
3   Normally, the vacuum servo unit is very reliable, but if the unit becomes faulty, it should be renewed. In the event of a failure, the hydraulic system is in no way affected, except that higher pedal pressures will be necessary.
4   To test the vacuum servo unit depress the brake pedal several times with the engine switched off to dissipate the vacuum. Apply moderate pressure to the brake pedal then start the engine. The pedal should move down slightly if the servo unit is operating correctly.

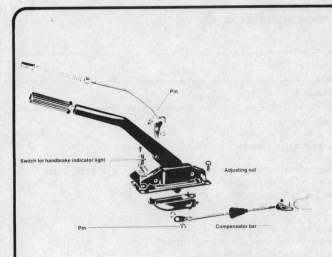

Fig. 9.22 Exploded view of the handbrake lever (Sec 16)

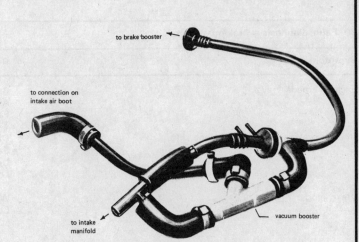

Fig. 9.23 Vacuum booster location in the vacuum servo supply on some models (Sec 18)

9

19 Vacuum servo unit – removal and refitting

1   Remove the master cylinder, as described in Section 10.
2   On right-hand drive models remove the glovebox, with reference to Chapter 12.
3   Pull the non-return valve and vacuum hose from the servo unit (photo).
4   Working inside the car disconnect the pushrod from the pedal (left-hand drive) or intermediate lever (right-hand drive) (photo). If there are two holes in the clevis, note in which one the pin is fitted.
5   Unscrew the mounting nuts and withdraw the servo unit from the bulkhead into the engine compartment.
6   Refitting is a reversal of removal. However, on models where the clevis is adjustable check the dimension shown in Fig. 9.24 and, if necessary, loosen the locknut, reposition the clevis, and re-tighten the locknut. Lubricate the clevis pin with a little molybdenum disulphide based grease. The mounting nuts are self-locking and should always be renewed.

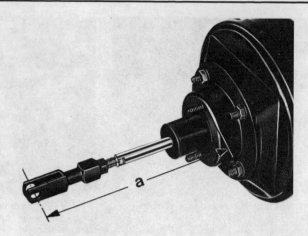

Fig. 9.24 Servo unit pushrod dimension (Sec 19)

$a = 189$ mm (7.441 in)

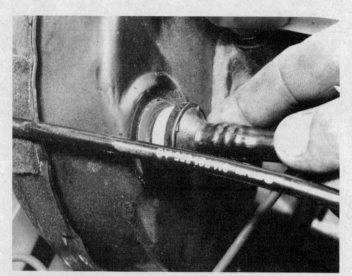

19.3 Removing the brake servo non-return valve

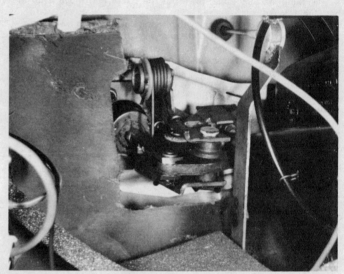

19.4 View of the intermediate brake lever on the right-hand drive models, with the glovebox removed

20 Fault diagnosis – braking system

Symptom	Reason(s)
Excessive pedal travel	Brake fluid leak Air in hydraulic system Faulty master cylinder
Uneven braking and pulling to one side	Disc pads or brake shoes contaminated with oil or brake fluid Seized wheel cylinder or caliper Unequal tyre pressures Loose suspension anchor point
Brake judder	Worn drums and/or discs Contaminated disc pad or brake shoe linings Loose suspension anchor point
Brake pedal feels 'spongy'	Air in hydraulic system Faulty master cylinder
Excessive effort to stop car	Faulty servo unit Seized wheel cylinder or caliper Contaminated disc pad or brake shoe linings

Chapter 10 Electrical system

Contents

Specifications

System type .... 12 volt, negative earth

Battery

Capacity:

    Manual gearbox models .... 36, 45 or 63 Ah

    Automatic transmission models .... 45 or 63 Ah

Note: *54 Ah batteries may be fitted to certain North American models*

Alternator

Type	Motorola or Bosch
Output	35, 45, 55, 65, 75 or 90 amp
Minimum brush length	5.0 mm (0.2 in)
Drivebelt tension (see text)	10 to 15 mm (0.4 to 0.6 in)
Stator winding resistance:	
Bosch 35 amp	0.25 to 0.28 ohm
Bosch 45 amp	0.18 to 0.20 ohm
Bosch 55 amp	0.14 to 0.16 ohm
Bosch 65 amp	0.10 to 0.11 ohm
Bosch 75 and 90 amp	0.10 ohm maximum
Motorola 35 amp	0.23 to 0.25 ohm
Motorola 55 amp	0.15 to 0.17 ohm
Motorola 65 amp	0.13 to 0.15 ohm
Motorola 45 amp with 6 wire ends	0.27 to 0.3 ohm
Motorola 45 amp with 3 wire ends	0.09 to 0.11 ohm
Diode resistance	50 to 80 ohm
Rotor winding resistance:	
Bosch	3.0 to 4.0 ohm
Motorola 35 and 55 amp	3.9 to 4.3 ohm
Motorola 45 and 65 amp	3.8 to 4.2 ohm

Starter motor

Type	Pre-engaged
Commutator minimum diameter	33.5 mm (1.32 in)
Commutator maximum run-out	0.03 mm (0.001 in)
Commutator insulation undercut	0.5 to 0.8 mm (0.02 to 0.03 in)
Minimum brush length	13.0 mm (0.5 in)

Fuses

Fusebox

No	Function	Rating (amps)
1	Low beam headlight, left	8
2	Low beam headlight, right	8
3	High beam headlight, left	8
4	High beam headlight, right	8
5	Heated rear window	16
6	Stop-lights, direction indicators	8
or	Stop-lights, hazard lights	8
7	Cigar lighter, glove compartment light, radio	8
or	Cigar lighter, radio	8
or	Cigar lighter, radio, instrument panel illumination	8
8	Instrument panel illumination	8
or	Instrument panel illumination, direction indicators	8
or	Direction indicators	8
9	Reversing lights, horn	8
or	Reversing lights, horn, automatic choke, idle cut-off valve	8
10	Heater blower	25
or	Heater blower, air conditioner, glove compartment light	25
or	Heater blower, glove compartment light	25
11	Wiper motor, and washer where fitted	8
12	Number plate lights	8
13	Parking/tail/side marker lights, right	8
14	Parking/tail/side marker lights, left	8
15	Radiator cooling fan	25

In-line fuses

No	Function	Rating (amps)
20	Fuel pump (fuel injection)	16
25	Air conditioner	25
–	Electric windows	25
–	Seat heating	16
–	Electric exterior mirror	8
–	Central door locking system	8

Bulbs

	Wattage
Headlamps:	
Standard	40/55
Halogen	55/60
High beam (Coupe)	55
Parking light	4
Direction indicators	21
Stop-light	21
Reversing light	21
Tail light	10
Foglamp (rear)	21
Foglamp (front)	55
Number plate light	10
Interior light	10
Ashtray and heater illumination	1.2
Instrument panel illumination	3
Instrument panel warning lights:	
All except charge and temperature warning lights	1.2
Charge and temperature warning lights	2
Glove compartment light	4
Luggage compartment light	5

Torque wrench settings

	lbf ft	Nm
Starter mounting	18	25
Starter bracket	15	20
Alternator pivot bolt – four-cylinder engine	15	20
Alternator pivot bolt – five-cylinder engine	21	29
Alternator adjustment bolts – four-cylinder engine	15	20
Alternator adjustment bolts – five-cylinder engine	16	22
Alternator mounting bracket – four-cylinder engine	22	30
Alternator mounting bracket – five-cylinder engine:		
Long bolt	32	43
Short bolt	16	22

Alternator pulley nut:		
Bosch	26	35
Motorola	30	40
Windscreen wiper arm	7	10
Windscreen wiper bearing	7	10
Windscreen wiper motor crank nut	7	10

1 General description

The electrical system is of 12 volt negative earth tyype. The battery is charged by a belt-driven alternator which incorporates a voltage regulator. The starter is of pre-engaged type incorporating four brushes, and on this type of motor a solenoid moves the drive pinion into engagement with the starter ring gear before the motor is energised.

Although repair procedures are given in this Chapter, it may well be more economical to renew worn components as complete units.

2 Battery – removal and refitting

1   The battery is located in the engine compartment just in front of the bulkhead (photo) on all models except North American five-cylinder models where it is located beneath the left-hand side of the rear seat.
2   Loosen the negative terminal clamp and disconnect the lead.
3   Loosen the positive terminal clamp and disconnect the lead (photo).
4   Unscrew the bolt and remove the battery holding clamp (photo).
5   Lift the battery from the platform, taking care not to spill any electrolyte.
6   Refitting is a reversal of removal, but make sure that the polarity is correct before connecting the leads, and do not overtighten the clamp bolts. **Note:** *The curved side of the holding clamp must contact the base of the batterv.*

3 Battery – maintenance

1   Where a conventional battery is fitted, the electrolyte level of each cell should be checked every month and, if necessary, topped up with distilled or de-ionized water until the separators are just covered. On some batteries the case is translucent and incorporates minimum and maximum level marks. The check should be made more often if the car is operated in high ambient temperature conditions.
2   Where a low maintenance battery is fitted it is not possible to check the electrolyte level.
3   Every 15 000 km (10 000 miles) or 12 months, whichever occurs first, disconnect and clean the battery terminals and leads. After refitting them, smear the exposed metal with petroleum jelly.
4   At the same time, inspect the battery clamp and platform for corrosion. If evident, remove the battery and clean the deposits away, then treat the affected metal with a proprietary anti-rust liquid and paint with the original colour.
5   When the battery is removed for whatever reason, it is worthwhile checking it for cracks and leakage. Cracks can be caused by topping up

the cells with distilled water in winter *after* instead of *before* a run. This gives the water no chance to mix with the electrolyte, so the former freezes and splits the battery case. If the battery case is fractured, it may be possible to repair it with a proprietary compound, but this depends on the material used for the case. If electrolyte has been lost from a cell, refer to Section 4 for details of adding a fresh solution.
6   If topping up the battery becomes excessive and the case is not fractured, the battery is being over-charged and the voltage regulator will have to be checked.
7   If the car covers a very small annual mileage, it is worthwhile checking the specific gravity of the electrolyte every three months to determine the state of charge of the battery. Use a hydrometer to make the check, and compare the results with the following table.

	Normal climates	Tropics
Discharged	1.120	1.080
Half charged	1.200	1.160
Fully charged	1.280	1.230

8   If the battery condition is suspect. first check the specific gravity of electrolyte in each cell. A variation of 0.040 or more between any cells indicates loss of electrolyre or deterioration of the internal plates.
9   A further test can be made using a battery heavy discharge meter. The battery should be discharged for a maximum of 15 seconds at a load of three times the ampere-hour capacity (at the 20 hour discharge rate). Alternatively connect a voltmeter across the battery terminals and spin the engine on the starter with the ignition disconnected (see Chapter 4), and the headlamps, heated rear window and heater blower switched on. If the voltmeter reading remains above 9.6 volts, the battery condition is satisfactory. If the voltmeter reading drops below 9.6 volts, and the battery has already been charged as described in Section 5, it is faulty and should be renewed.

4 Battery – electrolyte replenishment

1   If after fully charging the battery, one of the cells maintains a specific gravity which is 0.040 or more lower than the others, but the battery also maintains 9.6 volts during the heavy discharge test (Section 3), it is likely that electrolyte has been lost.
2   If a significant quantity of electrolyte has been lost through spillage, it will not suffice merely to refill with distilled water. Top up the cell with a mixture of 2 parts sulphuric acid to 5 parts distilled water.
3   When mixing the electrolyte, *never* add water to sulphuric acid – *always* pour the acid slowly onto the water in a glass container. *If water is added to sulphuric acid, it will explode!*
4   After topping up the cell with fresh electrolyte, recharge the battery and check the hydrometer readings again.

2.1 Battery location

2.3 Battery positive terminal and clamp

2.4 Battery holding clamp

10

5 Battery – charging

1   In winter when a heavy demand is placed on the battery, such as when starting from cold and using more electrical equipment, it is a good idea to occasionally have the battery fully charged from an external source at a rate of 10% of the battery capacity (ie 6.3 amp for a 63 Ah battery). It is not necessary to disconnect the battery leads for normal charging, *but if the battery is given a quick boost charge the leads must be disconnected.*

2   Continue to charge the battery until no further rise in specific gravity is noted over a four hour period.

3   Alternatively, a trickle charger, charging at a rate of 1.5 amp can be safely used overnight.

4   Special rapid 'boost' charges, which are claimed to restore the power of the battery in 1 to 2 hours, can be dangerous unless they are thermostatically controlled, as they can cause serious damage to the battery plates through overheating.

5   While charging the battery, ensure that the temperature of the electrolyte never exceeds 37.8°C (100°F) and loosen the vent caps (where applicable).

6 Alternator – maintenance and special precautions

1   Periodically wipe away any dirt which has accumulated on the outside of the unit, and also check that the plug is pushed firmly on the

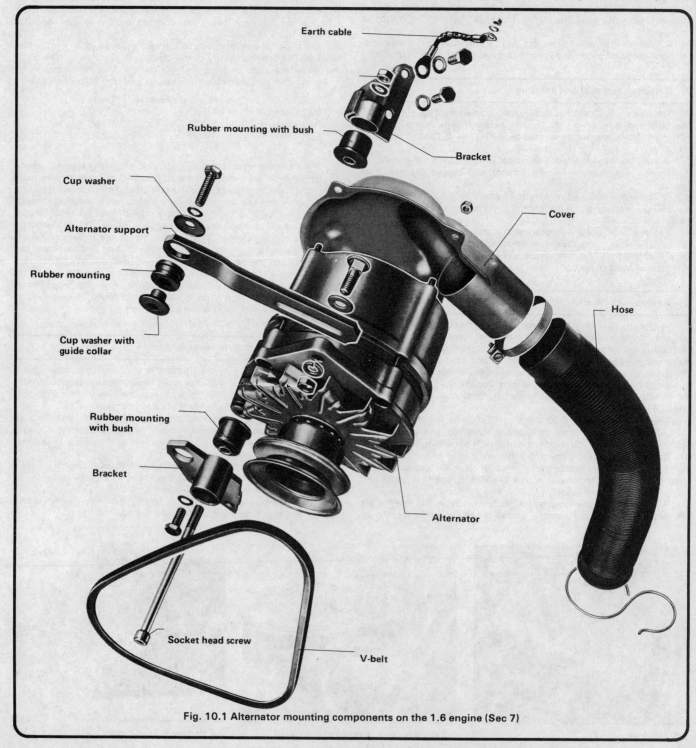

Fig. 10.1 Alternator mounting components on the 1.6 engine (Sec 7)

terminals. At the same time, check the tension of the drivebelt and adjust it if necessary as described in Section 8.

2　Take extreme care when making electrical circuit connections on the car, otherwise damage may occur to the alternator or other electrical components employing semi-conductors. Always make sure that the battery leads are connected to the correct terminals. Before using electric-arc welding equipment to repair any part of the car, disconnect the battery leads and alternator multi-plug. Never run the engine with the alternator multi-plug or a battery lead disconnected.

7　Alternator – removal and refitting

1　Disconnect the battery negative lead.

2　Loosen the alternator adjustment nuts or bolts and swivel the alternator toward the engine. If difficulty is experienced, loosen the pivot bolt.

3　Slip the drivebelt from the pulley.

4　Note the location of the wiring then disconnect it from the rear of

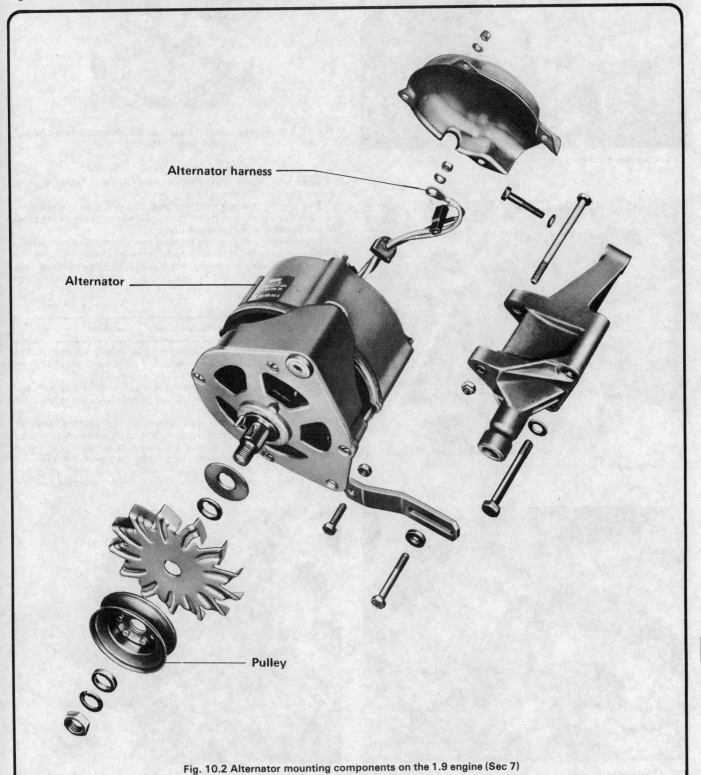

Alternator harness

Alternator

Pulley

Fig. 10.2 Alternator mounting components on the 1.9 engine (Sec 7)

10

7.4A Alternator multi-plug with clip in position

Fig. 10.3 Correct position of wiring on the alternator fitted to the 1.9 engine (Sec 7)

the alternator (photos). On some models it will first be necessary to remove the duct cover and hose.

5   Remove the link bolt and pivot bolt, and withdraw the alternator from the engine (photos). If necessary, remove the upper timing cover plug in order to remove the pivot bolt.

6   If necessary, the mounting brackets may be unbolted, and on four-cylinder engines the rubber bushes removed. When refitting the bracket on five-cylinder engines, the short bolt must be tightened first.

7   Refitting is a reversal of removal, but adjust the drivebelt as described in Section 8.

8   Alternator drivebelt – removal and adjustment

1   Every 15 000 km (10 000 miles) the alternator drivebelt should be checked for condition, and re-tensioned. If there are signs of cracking or deterioration, the drivebelt should be renewed.

2   To remove the drivebelt, loosen the adjustment nuts or bolts and swivel the alternator toward the engine. If necessary loosen the pivot bolt.

3   Slip the drivebelt from the pulleys. On models fitted with air conditioning and/or power steering, it will first be necessary to remove the drivebelts in order to remove the alternator drivebelt.

4   Fit the new drivebelt over the pulleys, then lever the alternator from the engine until the specified tension is achieved using firm thumb pressure mid-way between the pulleys (photo). Lever the

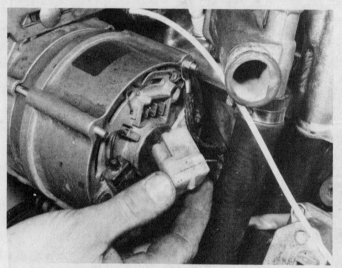

7.4B Removing the alternator multi-plug

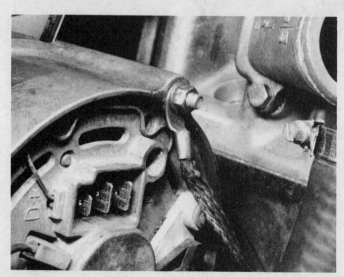

7.4C Alternator earth strap

7.5A Removing the alternator pivot bolt (upper timing cover removed in 1.6 engine)

7.5B Removing the alternator

7.5C Alternator pivot bolt plug location

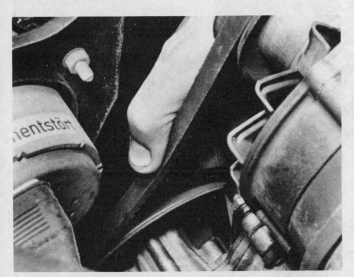

8.4A Checking the alternator drivebelt tension

8.4B Tensioning the alternator drivebelt

alternator at the pulley end to prevent any torsional damage (photo).

5   Tighten the adjustment nuts or bolts followed by the pivot bolts.

6   Run the engine for several minutes, then recheck the tension and adjust if necessary.

9   Alternator – servicing

Note: *The voltage regulator and brushes can be removed without removing the alternator. However, the following complete dismantling procedure assumes that the alternator is on the bench.*

1   Clean the exterior of the alternator.

Bosch 35A, 45A, 55A and 65A

2   Remove the screws and withdraw the voltage regulator and brushes. If the brushes are worn below the specified minimum length, they can be renewed on early models by unsoldering the leads and soldering the new brushes in position. However, on later models with a hybrid regulator it is not possible to renew the brushes.

3   Mark the end housings and stator in relation to each other.

4   Grip the pulley in a vice then unscrew the nut and withdraw the washer, pulley and fan, together with any spacers. Prise out the key.

5   Unscrew the through-bolts and tap off the front housing, together with the rotor.

6   Using a mallet or puller, remove the rotor from the front housing and remove the spacers.

7   Remove the screws and retaining plate. Drive the bearing from the front housing with a soft metal drift.

8   Using a suitable puller, remove the bearing from the slip ring end of the rotor, but take care not to damage the slip rings.

9   Remove the screw, disconnect the lead, and withdraw the suppressor condenser from the rear housing.

10 Unscrew the terminal nut(s), remove the washers, and remove the insulator from the rear housing.

11 Carefully separate the stator from the rear housing without straining the three wires. Identify each wire for location, then unsolder them using the minimum of heat to avoid damage to the diodes. Long nosed pliers may be used as a heat sink, as shown in Fig. 10.5.

12 Remove the screws and separate the diode plate from the rear housing.

13 Remove the wave washer from the rear housing.

14 Check the stator windings for a short to ground by connecting an ohmmeter or test bulb between each wire and the outer ring. Check that the internal resistance between the wires is as given in the Specifications using an ohmmeter between wires 1 and 2, then 1 and 3, and 2 and 3 – the numbering of the wires is of no importance.

15 Using the ohmmeter check that the resistance of each diode is as given in the Specifications when the ohmmeter is connected across

10

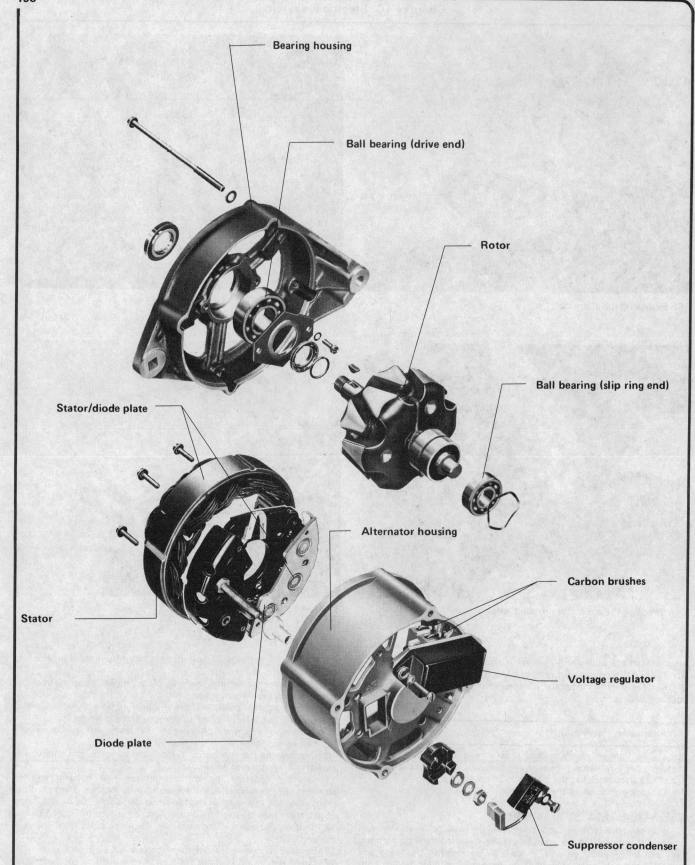

Bearing housing

Ball bearing (drive end)

Rotor

Ball bearing (slip ring end)

Stator/diode plate

Alternator housing

Carbon brushes

Stator

Voltage regulator

Diode plate

Suppressor condenser

Fig. 10.4 Exploded view of the Bosch 35A, 45A, 55A and 65A alternator (Sec 9)

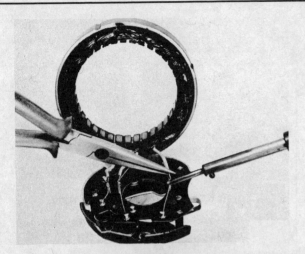

Fig. 10.5 Using pliers as a heat sink when unsoldering the stator wires (Sec 9)

ohmmeter or test bulb between each slip ring and the winding core. Check that the internal resistance of the winding is as given in the Specifications using an ohmmeter between the two slip rings.

17 Clean all the components and obtain new bearings, brushes etc, as required.

18 Reassembly is a reversal of dismantling, but when fitting the bearing to the front housing, drive it in using a metal tube *on the outer race* making sure that the open end of the bearing faces the rotor. When fitting the rear bearing to the rotor, drive it on using a metal tube *on the inner race,* making sure that the open end of the bearing faces the rear housing.

Bosch 75A and 90A

19 The procedure is identical to that described in paragraphs 2 to 18 with the following exceptions. The diode plate has two terminals protruding through the rear housing, and there are two wave washers and a plain washer in the rear housing. The rear bearing may be installed either way round as both sides are closed.

Motorola 35A, 55A and 65A

20 Remove the screws and lift the voltage regulator from the rear housing. Note the location of the wires, then disconnect them and withdraw the regulator.

21 Remove the screws and withdraw the brush holder and brushes. If the brushes are worn below the specified minimum length renew the brush holder and brushes as a complete unit.

22 Mark the end housings and stator in relation to each other.

the diode in one direction. Reverse the wires and check that there is now no resistance.

16 Check the rotor windings for a short to ground by connecting an

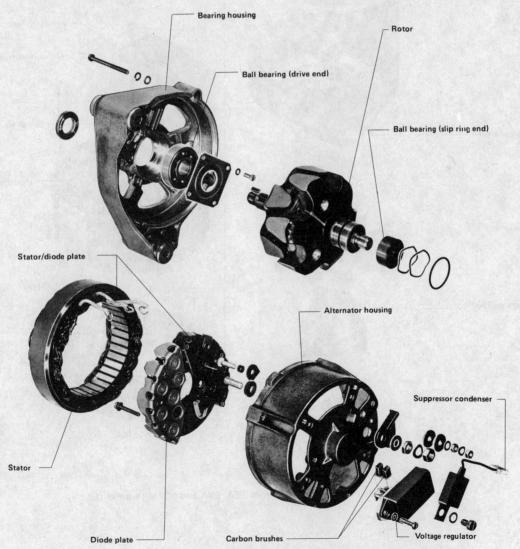

Fig. 10.6 Exploded view of the Bosch 75A and 90A alternator (Sec 9)

10

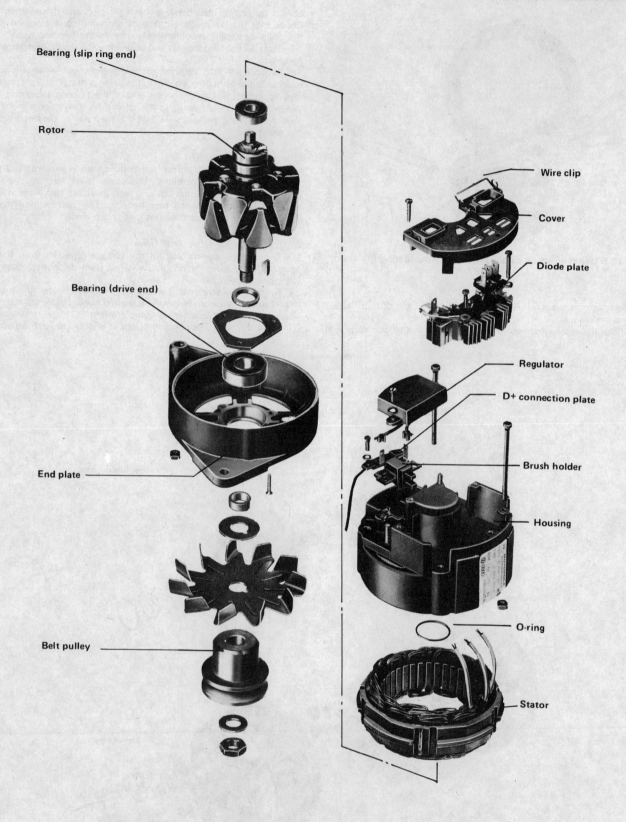

Bearing (slip ring end)

Rotor

Wire clip

Cover

Diode plate

Bearing (drive end)

Regulator

D+ connection plate

Brush holder

End plate

Housing

O-ring

Belt pulley

Stator

Fig. 10.7 Exploded view of the Motorola 35A, 55A and 65A alternator (Sec 9)

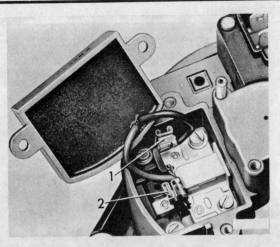

Fig. 10.8 Voltage regulator wire terminals on the Motorola 35A, 55A and 65A alternator (Sec 9)

1   Green wire (DF)   2   Red wire (D+)

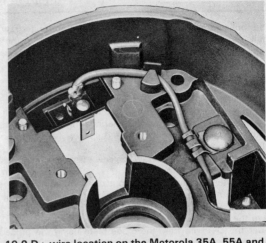

Fig. 10.9 D+ wire location on the Motorola 35A, 55A and 65A alternator (Sec 9)

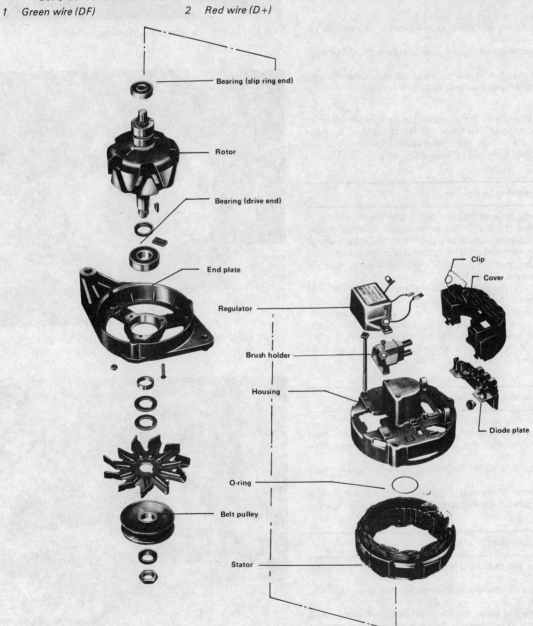

Bearing (slip ring end)

Rotor

Bearing (drive end)

End plate

Regulator

Brush holder

Housing

Clip

Cover

Diode plate

O-ring

Belt pulley

Stator

Fig. 10.10 Exploded view of the Motorola 45A alternator (Sec 9)

10

23 Grip the pulley in a vice, then unscrew the nut and withdraw the washer, pulley and fan, together with any spacers. Prise out the key.

24 Unscrew the through-bolts and nuts, and tap off the front housing, together with the rotor.

25 Remove the screws securing the bearing retaining plate to the front housing.

26 Using a mallet or puller, remove the rotor and bearing from the front housing.

27 Using a suitable puller, remove the bearings from each end of the rotor, together with the retaining plate and spacer. Take care not to damage the slip rings.

28 Remove the screws and withdraw the cover from the rear housing.

29 Identify the stator wires for location, then unsolder them from the diode plate using the minimum of heat to avoid damage to the diodes. Long nosed pliers may be used as a heat sink in a similar manner to that shown in Fig. 10.5.

30 Remove the stator from the rear housing.

31 Unsolder the D+ wire from the diode plate using the procedure described in paragraph 29.

32 Note the wire location, then remove the screws and withdraw the diode plate.

33 Remove the O-ring from the rear housing.

34 Check the stator, diodes, and rotor, as described in paragraphs 14, 15 and 16.

35 Clean all the components and obtain new bearings, brushes etc, as required.

36 Reassembly is a reversal of dismantling, but lubricate the rear housing O-ring with multi-purpose grease before fitting.

Motorola 45A

37 The procedure is identical to that described in paragraphs 20 to 36 with the following exceptions. The front bearing is retained by three small plates instead of a circular plate. The cover clips onto the rear housing. The diode plate does not include a D+ wire.

10 Starter motor – testing in the car

1   If the starter motor fails to respond when the starter switch is operated, first check that the fault is not external to the starter motor.

2   Connect a test lamp between chassis earth and the large terminal on the starter solenoid, terminal 30. This terminal is connected directly to the battery and the test lamp should light whether or not the ignition switch is operated.

3   Remove the test lamp connection from the large terminal (30) and transfer it to the smaller terminal (50) on the solenoid. The lamp should light only when the starter switch is in its *Start* position.

4   If both these tests are satisfactory the fault is in the starter motor.

5   If the starter motor is heard to operate, but the engine fails to start, check the battery terminals, the starter motor leads and the engine-to-body earth strap for cleanliness and tightness.

11 Starter motor – removal and refitting

1   Disconnect the battery negative lead.

2   Note the location of the wires on the starter solenoid, then disconnect them by removing the nut and screws, as applicable (photo).

3   Unscrew the mounting bolts and withdraw the starter motor (photo).

4   Refitting is a reversal of removal, but make sure that the mating faces are clean and tighten the mounting bolts to the specified torque.

12 Starter motor – overhaul

1   Mark the housings and mounting bracket (where fitted) in relation to each other.

2   Remove the nuts and washers and withdraw the end mounting bracket (where fitted).

3   Remove the screws and withdraw the small end cover and gasket, then extract the circlip and remove the shims. Note the exact number of shims, as they determine the shaft endfloat.

4   Unscrew the through-bolts and remove the commutator end bearing housing.

11.2 Showing the wiring to the starter solenoid

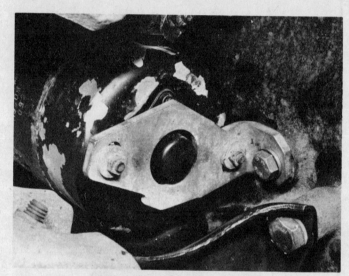
11.3A Starter motor mounting bracket on a 1.6 engine

11.3B Removing the starter motor on a 1.6 engine

Stop ring

Pinion drive

Armature

Snap ring

Intermediate
bearing

Solenoid

Carbon brushes

Bearing housing

Housing

Support plate

Brush holder plate

Bearing bush

Fig. 10.11 Exploded view of the 0.8 and 1.7 kW starter motor (Sec 12)

10

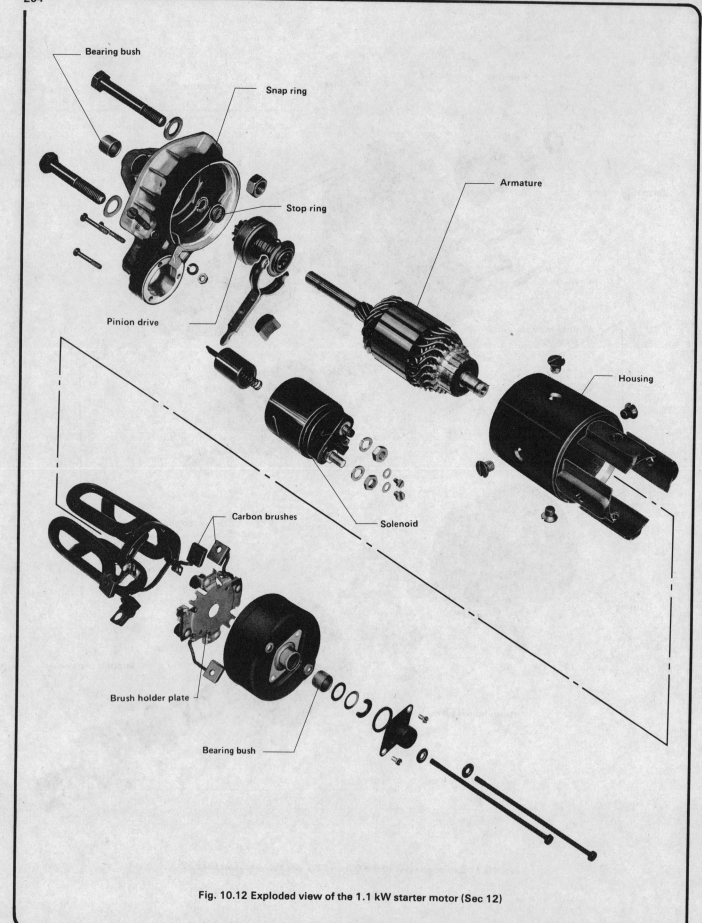

Fig. 10.12 Exploded view of the 1.1 kW starter motor (Sec 12)

5 Lift the brush springs and extract the field winding brushes.
6 Note the position of the brush holder plate in relation to the field winding housing, then withdraw the plate from the armature.
7 Unscrew the nut and disconnect the field wire from the solenoid.
8 Remove the field winding housing from the armature.
9 Unscrew the three bolts and remove the solenoid from the drive end housing. Unhook the core from the lever.
10 Unscrew and remove the lever pivot bolt and prise out the lever cover pad.
11 Remove the armature from the drive end housing and disengage the lever from the pinion drive.
12 Using a metal tube, drive the stop ring off the circlip, then extract the circlip and pull off the stop ring.
13 Withdraw the pinion drive from the armature.
14 Clean all the components in paraffin and wipe dry, then examine them for wear and damage. Check the pinion drive for damaged teeth and make sure that the one-way clutch only rotates in one direction. If the shaft bushes are worn they can be removed using a soft metal drift and new bushes installed. However, the new bushes must first be soaked in hot oil for approximately five minutes. Clean the commutator with a rag moistened with a suitable solvent. Minor scoring can be removed with fine glasspaper, but deep scoring will necessitate the commutator being skimmed in a lathe and then being undercut. Commutator refinishing is a job which is best left to a specialist.
15 Measure the length of the brushes. If less than the minimum given in Specifications, fit new brushes. Crush the old brushes to free the copper braid and file the excess solder off the braid. Fit new brushes

13.1 Fuses and relays (glovebox removed)

to the braid and hold the braid with a pair of flat nosed pliers below the carbon brush, to prevent solder from flowing down the braid. Solder the brushes on using radio quality solder and a heavy duty soldering iron of at least 250 watt rating. Check that the brushes move freely in their holders and if necessary dress the brushes with a fine file.
16 Reassembly is a reversal of the dismantling procedure, but note the following. To fit the brush assembly over the commutator, either hook the brush springs on to the edge of the brush holder, or bend pieces of wire to hold the springs off the brushes until the brush assembly has been fitted. As soon as this has been done, release the brush springs and position them so that they bear on the centres of the brushes. Apply a little molybdenum disulphide grease to the splines of the pinion drive. Fit a new circlip to the pinion end of the shaft and ensure that the circlip groove is not damaged. Any burrs on the edges of the groove should be removed with a fine file. During reassembly apply sealing compound to the points indicated in Figs. 10.13 and 10.14.

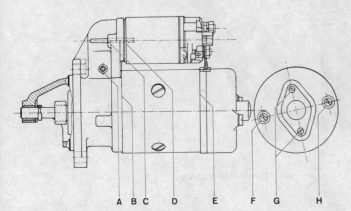

Fig. 10.13 Sealing points on the 0.8 and 1.7 kW starter motor (Sec 12)

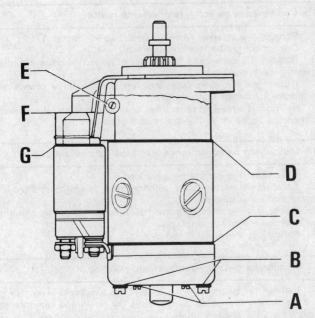

Fig. 10.14 Sealing points on the 1.1 kW starter motor (Sec 12)

13 Fuses – general

1 The fuses are located behind the left-hand side of the facia (photo). Access to them is gained by removing the curved cover inside the glovebox (right-hand drive models) or storage space (left-hand drive models).
2 The fuse and relay circuits are shown on the back of the cover, together with some spare fuses. In addition, in-line fuses are fitted to certain models, as given in the Specifications, and their location is shown in the wiring diagrams given at the end of this Chapter.
3 Always renew a fuse with one of identical rating, and never renew it more than once without finding the source of the trouble (usually a short circuit).
4 All relays are of the plug-in type. Relays cannot be repaired and if one is suspect, it should be removed and taken to an auto electrical workshop for testing.

14 Ignition switch/steering column lock – removal and refitting

1 Remove the steering column combination switch, as described in Section 15.
2 Prise the lockwasher from the inner column and remove the spring followed by the contact ring.
3 Using an Allen key, unscrew the clamp bolt from the steering lock housing and slide the housing from the outer column. Disconnect the multi-plug.
4 To remove the ignition switch, unscrew the cross-head screw inside the housing.
5 To remove the lock cylinder it will be necessary to drill a 3 mm

10

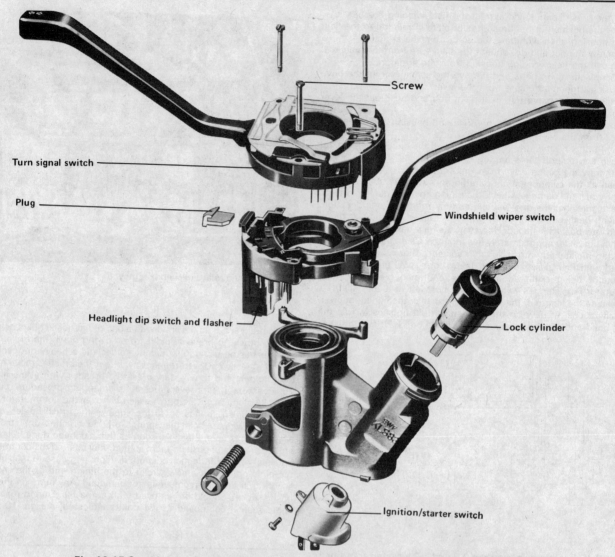

Screw

Turn signal switch

Plug

Windshield wiper switch

Headlight dip switch and flasher

Lock cylinder

Ignition/starter switch

Fig. 10.15 Combination switch and ignition switch/steering column lock components (Sec 14)

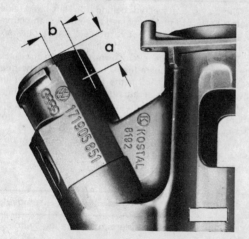

Fig. 10.16 Location for drilling hole in order to remove the lock cylinder (Sec 14)

a = 12 mm (0.472 in)   b = 10 mm (0.400 in)

(0.118 in) diameter hole in the housing at the location shown in Fig. 10.16 – the retaining pin can then be depressed and the lock cylinder removed.
6   Refitting is a reversal of removal.

15 Combination switch – removal and refitting

1   Remove the steering wheel as described in Chapter 11.
2   Disconnect the battery negative lead.
3   Remove the cross-head screws and withdraw the column shrouds (photo).
4   Disconnect the multi-plug, then remove the three screws and withdraw the combination switch.
5   Refitting is a reversal of removal, but make sure that the retaining screws are tightened firmly to ensure a good earth.

16 Instrument panel switches – removal and refitting

1   Disconnect the battery negative lead.
2   Remove the screws and withdraw the upper cover from the instrument panel (photo).
3   Disconnect the multi-plug from the relevant switch, then pull the switch from the surround (photo).
4   Refitting is a reversal of removal.

17 Handbrake switch – removal and refitting

1   Remove the gaiter from the base of the handbrake lever.
2   Disconnect the wiring, then remove the screw and withdraw the switch from the bracket (photo).
3   Refitting is a reversal of removal.

15.3A Remove the screws ...

15.3B ... and withdraw the column shrouds

16.2 Removing the instrument panel upper cover

16.3 Removing the hazard warning switch

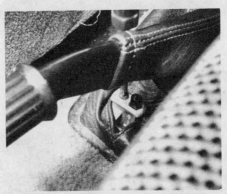
17.2 Removing the handbrake switch

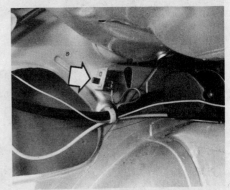
18.2 Luggage compartment switch location (arrowed)

19.3A Remove the screws ...

19.3B ... and withdraw the central console switches

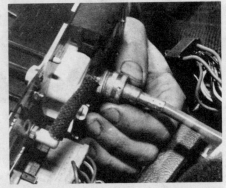
20.5 Removing the speedometer cable

18 Luggage compartment switch – removal and refitting

1 Remove the spare wheel and trim from the luggage compartment.
2 Disconnect the wiring, then remove the screw and withdraw the switch from the bracket (photo).
3 Refitting is a reversal of removal.

19 Central console switches – removal and refitting

1 Disconnect the battery negative lead.
2 Prise the two front switches from the panel.
3 Unscrew the two screws and withdraw the panel (photos).
4 Disconnect the multi-plugs and remove the switches, together with the panel.
5 Refitting is a reversal of removal.

20 Instrument panel – removal and refitting

1 Disconnect the battery negative lead.
2 Remove the steering wheel as described in Chapter 11. Although not essential, this does allow greater freedom of access.
3 Remove the screws and withdraw the upper cover.
4 Disconnect the multi-plugs from the switches and instrument panel and remove the switches.
5 Unscrew the knurled nut and disconnect the speedometer cable (photo).
6 Disconnect the vacuum tube from the econometer (photo).
7 Remove the instrument panel retaining screws using a screwdriver through the top switch apertures (photo).
8 Withdraw the instrument panel from the facia (photos).
9 Remove the screws and withdraw the surround.
10 Refitting is a reversal of removal (photo).

10

20.6 The econometer vacuum tube

20.7 Removing the instrument panel retaining screws

20.8A Instrument panel multi-plugs and speedometer cable

20.8B Front view of the instrument panel

20.8C Rear view of the instrument panel

20.10 Refitting the instrument panel showing all the multi-plugs connected

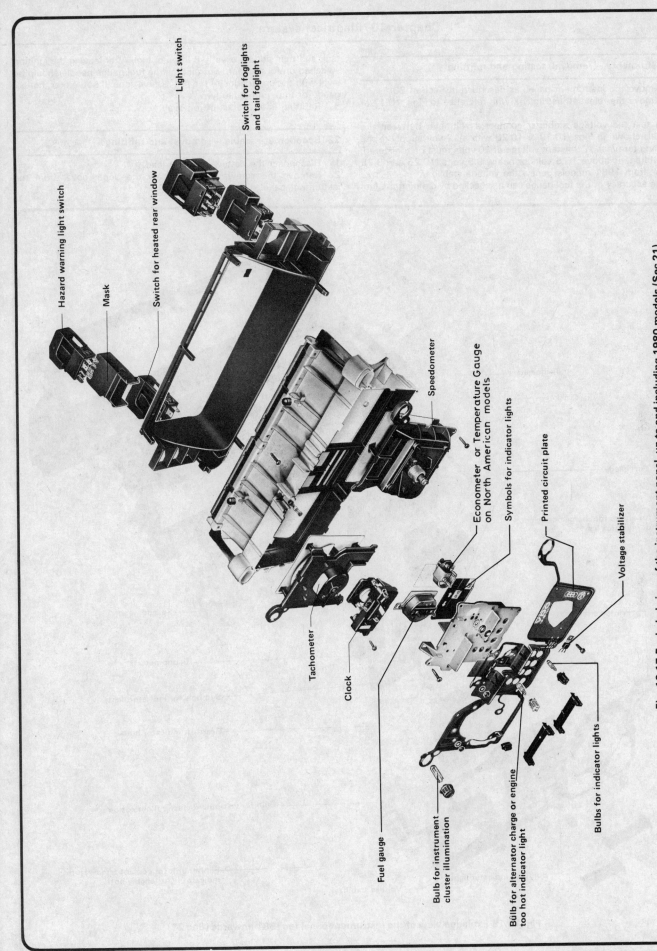

Light switch

Switch for foglights
and tail foglight

Hazard warning light switch

Mask

Switch for heated rear window

Speedometer

Econometer or Temperature Gauge
on North American models

Symbols for indicator lights

Printed circuit plate

Voltage stabilizer

Tachometer

Clock

Fuel gauge

Bulb for instrument
cluster illumination

Bulb for alternator charge or engine
too hot indicator light

Bulbs for indicator lights

Fig. 10.17 Exploded view of the instrument panel, up to and including 1980 models (Sec 21)

10

21 Instruments – removal, testing and refitting

1   Remove the instrument panel, as described in Section 20.
2   Remove the relevant instrument, with reference to Figs. 10.17 or 10.18.
3   To test the voltage stabilizer connect a voltmeter between the terminals shown in Figs. 10.19 or 10.20 with a 12 volt supply to the remaining terminal. A constant voltage of 10 volts must be registered. If the voltage is above 10.5 volts or below 9.5 volts (10.25 and 9.75 volts as from 1981 models) renew the voltage stabilizer.
4   The accuracy of the fuel gauge can be checked by draining the fuel tank and then adding exactly 8 litres of fuel. After leaving the ignition switched on for at least two minutes the fuel gauge needle should be level with the upper edge of the red reserve zone. If not, either the fuel gauge or tank unit is faulty.
5   Refitting is a reversal of removal.

22 Speedometer cable – removal and refitting

1   Disconnect the battery negative lead.
2   Remove the screws and withdraw the upper cover from the instrument panel.

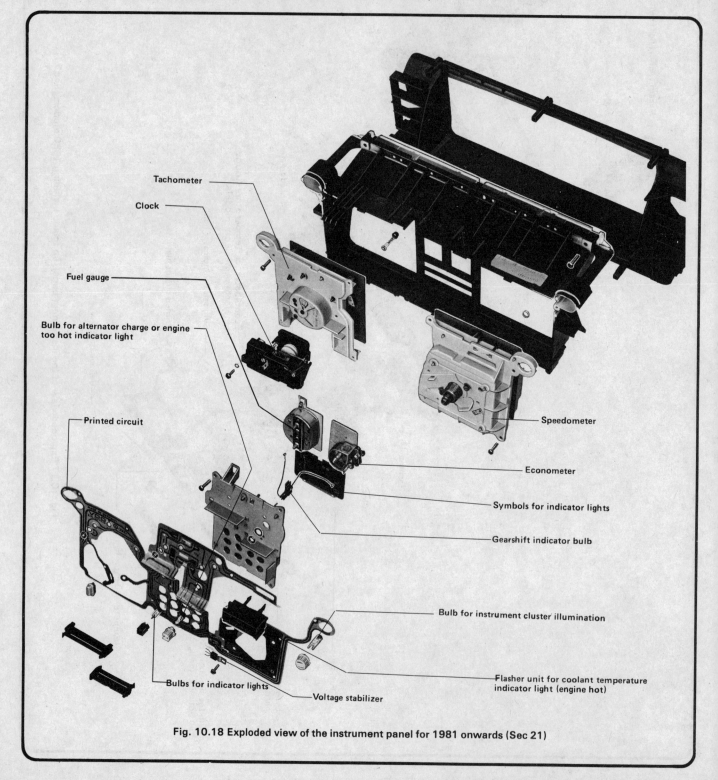

Fig. 10.18 Exploded view of the instrument panel for 1981 onwards (Sec 21)

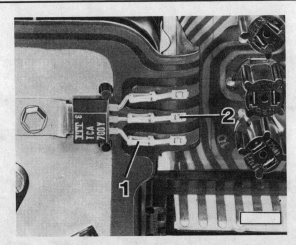

Fig. 10.19 Voltage stabilizer up to and including 1980 models (Sec 21)

1 Positive   2 Earth

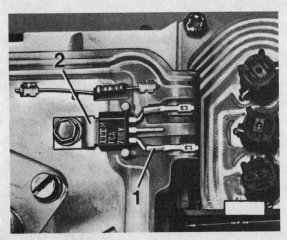

Fig. 10.20 Voltage stabilizer for 1981 onwards (Sec 21)

1 Positive   2 Earth

3 Unscrew the knurled nut and disconnect the speedometer cable.
4 Working in the engine compartment, disconnect the speedometer cable from the transmission (photos).
5 Withdraw the speedometer cable through the bulkhead into the engine compartment.
6 Refitting is a reversal of removal.

23 Headlamps and headlamp bulbs – removal and refitting

UK models
1 To remove a bulb, open the bonnet and remove the plug and rubber cap from the rear of the headlight (photos).

2 Press and twist the retaining ring or unhook the clip, and remove the headlamp bulb, but do not touch the glass if it is to be re-used (photo).
3 To remove the headlamp on Saloon models, remove the surround and front grille, and disconnect the direction indicator wiring. Loosen the front bumper mounting bolts, and press the bumper down as far as possible. Remove the sidelamp bulb (if fitted) and cross-head retaining screws and withdraw the headlamp (photo). On Coupe models it is only necessary to remove the surround and the relevant retaining ring.
4 Refitting is a reversal of removal.

North American models
5 Sealed beam units are fitted to all North American models. First

22.4A Speedometer cable fixing to the 013 gearbox

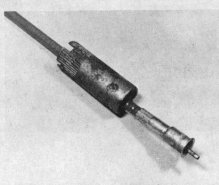

22.4B Showing the gearbox end of the speedometer cable

23.1A Removing the headlamp plug ...

23.1B ... and rubber cap

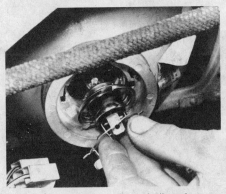

23.2 Removing the headlamp bulb and retaining ring

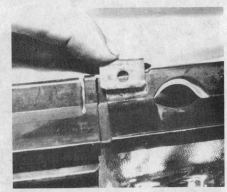

23.3A Remove the clip ...

10

23.3B ... and remove the headlamp upper trim

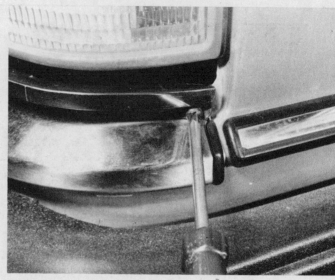

23.3C Removing the headlamp lower trim

23.3D Remove the upper screws ...

23.3E ... and lower screw ...

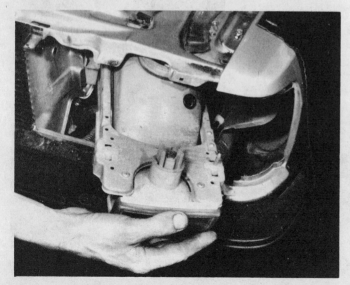

23.3F ... and withdraw the headlamp

23.3G Showing the direction indicator lamp retaining screws

Low beam headlight

Bulb for low beam
and high beam

Retainer frame

Side light bulb

Bulb for high beam

High beam headlight

Fig. 10.21 Headlamp components for UK Coupe models (Sec 23)

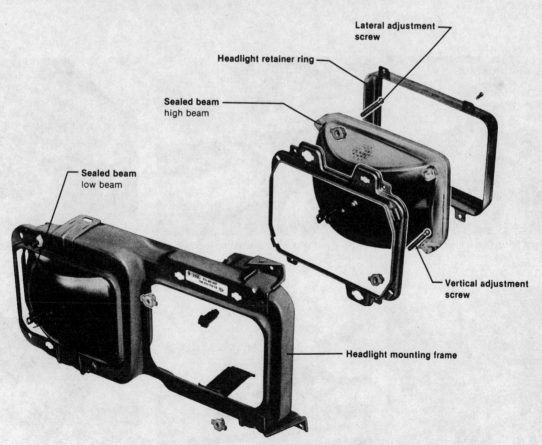

Lateral adjustment
screw

Headlight retainer ring

Sealed beam
high beam

Sealed beam
low beam

Vertical adjustment
screw

Headlight mounting frame

10

Fig. 10.22 Headlamp components for North American models (Sec 23)

remove the screws from the surround, swing it forward and lift it out. Remove the relevant retaining ring, then withdraw the headlamp and disconnect the wiring. If necessary remove the screws and withdraw the mounting frame.

6   Refitting is a reversal of removal. If the mounting frame was removed check the headlamp alignment with reference to Section 24.

24 Headlamps – alignment

1   The headlamp alignment should be checked every 15 000 km (10 000 miles) or 12 months, whichever occurs first.
2   It is recommended that the alignment is carried out by an Audi dealer using modern beam setting equipment. However, in an emergency, the following procedure will provide an acceptable light pattern.
3   Position the car on a level surface with tyres correctly inflated, approximately 10 metres (33 feet) in front of and at right-angles to a wall or garage door.
4   Draw a horizontal line on the wall or door at headlamp centre height. Draw a vertical line corresponding to the centre-line of the car, then measure off points either side of this, on the horizonal line, corresponding with the headlamp centres.
5   Switch on the main beam and check that the areas of maximum illumination coincide with the headlamp centre marks. If not, turn the adjustment screws as necessary – the upper screw controls horizontal adjustment and the lower screw height adjustment (photos).

25 Lamp bulbs – renewal

Note: *Lamp bulbs should always be renewed with ones of identical type and rating, as listed in the Specifications.*

Front sidelights (UK models)
1   Disconnect the two-pin plug from the sidelamp bulbholder on the rear of the headlamp.

2   Twist the bulbholder anti-clockwise and remove it from the headlamp (photo).
3   Push and twist the bulb to remove it.

Front direction indicators (UK models)
4   Disconnect the two-pin plug from the rear of the direction indicator.
5   Twist the bulbholder anti-clockwise and remove it.
6   Push and twist the bulb to remove it.

Front direction indicators/parking lights (North American models)
7   Remove the two screws and withdraw the lens.
8   Push and twist the bulb to remove it.
9   The bulb can only be fitted in one position because of the offset pins. Make sure that the gasket is serviceable.

Side marker light (North American models)
10 Carefully prise out the light.
11 Pull back the rubber cover and remove the bulb.

Rear lamp cluster
12 Open the boot lid. Depress the plastic clips and withdraw the bulbholder (photo).
13 Push and twist the faulty bulb to remove it.

Number plate light (UK models)
14 Prise the light out of the bumper (photo).
15 Lever out the clips and remove the cover (photo).
16 Push and twist the bulb to remove it.

Number plate light (North American models)
17 Open the boot lid and remove the light retaining screws.
18 Squeeze the plastic clips and remove the bulbholder.
19 Push and twist the bulb to remove it.

24.5A Headlight horizontal adjustment screw location

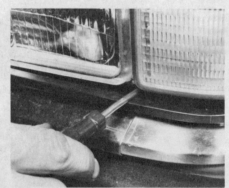
24.5B Headlight height adjustment screw location

25.2 Removing the front sidelight bulb (UK models)

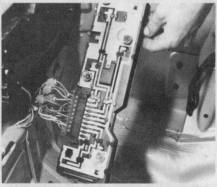
25.12 Removing the rear lamp bulbholder

25.14 Removing the number plate light

25.15 Unclipping the number plate light cover

Interior/luggage compartment light

20 Prise out the light using a screwdriver. When removing the interior light, insert the screwdriver at the opposite end to the switch (photos).

21 Remove the festoon type bulb from the spring contacts.

22 When fitting the bulb, make sure that the spring contacts are tensioned sufficiently to make good contact with the bulb.

23 Note that the luggage compartment light may be located on the rear panel or beneath the top panel.

Rear foglamp

24 Remove the screws and withdraw the surround (photo).

25 Remove the central cross-head screws and withdraw the foglamp (photo).

26 Disconnect the wiring, unhook the clip, and remove the bulbholder. Remove the bulb (photos).

27 When refitting the foglamp, adjust the beam alignment, if necessary, by turning the upper screw before fitting the surround (photo).

Instrument panel lamps

28 Remove the instrument panel, as described in Section 20.

29 Turn the bulbholder through 90° and remove it from the instrument panel (photos).

30 Pull out the wedge type bulb.

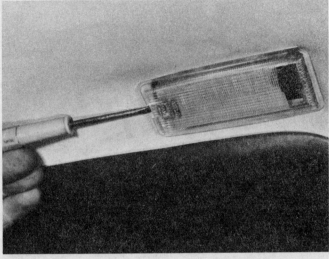

25.20A Prising out the interior light

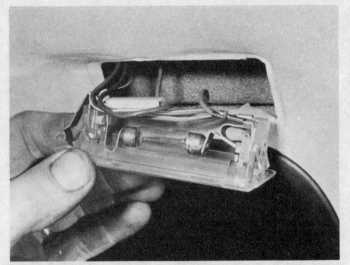

25.20B Interior light and bulb

25.20C Luggage compartment light

25.24 Removing the rear foglamp surround

25.25 Removing the rear foglamp

10

25.26A Rear foglamp bulb clip

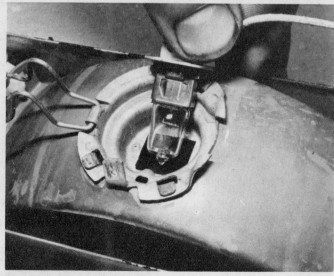

25.26B Rear foglamp bulb

25.27 Adjusting the rear foglamp beam alignment

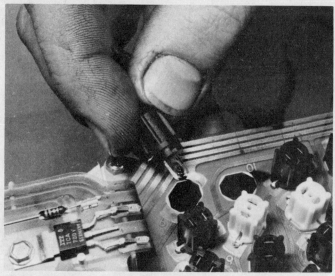

25.29A Removing an instrument panel warning light bulb

25.29B Removing an instrument panel illumination light bulb

25.31 Removing the glovebox switch/bulbholder

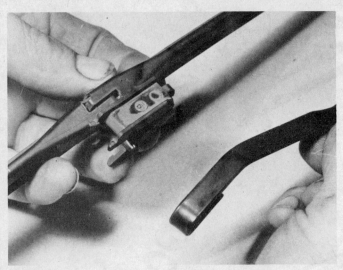

26.3 Removing a wiper blade from the wiper arm

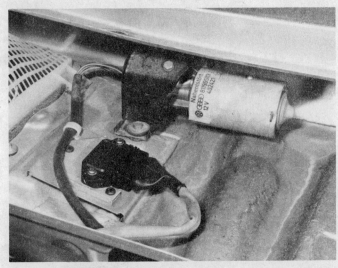

27.4 Windscreen wiper motor location

Glovebox lamp

31   Open the glovebox and prise out the switch/bulbholder (photo).
32   Push and twist the bulb to remove it.

26   Wiper blades – renewal

1   The wiper blades should be renewed when they no longer clean the windscreen effectively.
2   Lift the wiper blade and arm from the windscreen.
3   Depress the plastic clip and withdraw the blade from the hooked end of the arm (photo).
4   Insert the new blade, making sure that the plastic clip is engaged.

27   Windscreen wiper motor – removal and refitting

1   Disconnect the battery negative lead.
2   Prise the pushrods off the wiper motor crank.
3   Mark the crank in relation to the motor spindle, then unscrew the nut and remove the crank from the spindle.
4   Unbolt the wiper motor from the frame and disconnect the wiring (photo).
5   Refitting is a reversal of removal. If a new wiper motor is being fitted, switch on the ignition and run the motor for a short period

28.1 Wiper arm cover and spindle nut

before switching it off. The motor is now in its parked position and the crank should be fitted to the spindle in the position shown in Fig. 10.23.

28   Windscreen wiper arms and linkage – removal and refitting

1   Prise up the covers and unscrew the nuts securing the wiper arms to the spindles (photo).
2   Carefully lever off the wiper arms.
3   Unscrew the spindle bearing nuts and remove the rubber spacers.
4   Disconnect the battery negative lead.
5   Unscrew the wiper frame mounting bolt and withdraw the linkage assembly, at the same time disconnecting the wiring from the motor.
6   Remove the wiper motor from the frame, with reference to Section 27.
7   Prise the pushrods from the spindle arms.
8   If the spindle bearings are to be removed, saw off the rivets. After fitting the new bearings clinch the new rivets onto the wiper frame.
9   Refitting is a reversal of removal, but smear a little molybdenum disulphide grease in the pushrod ball sockets. Before fitting the wiper arms in their parked position, switch on the ignition and run the wiper motor for a short period before switching it off.

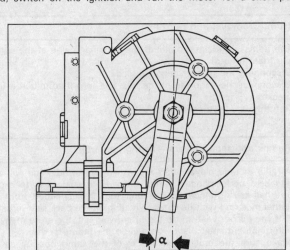

Fig. 10.23 Wiper motor crank parked position (Sec 27)

α = 8° approximately

10

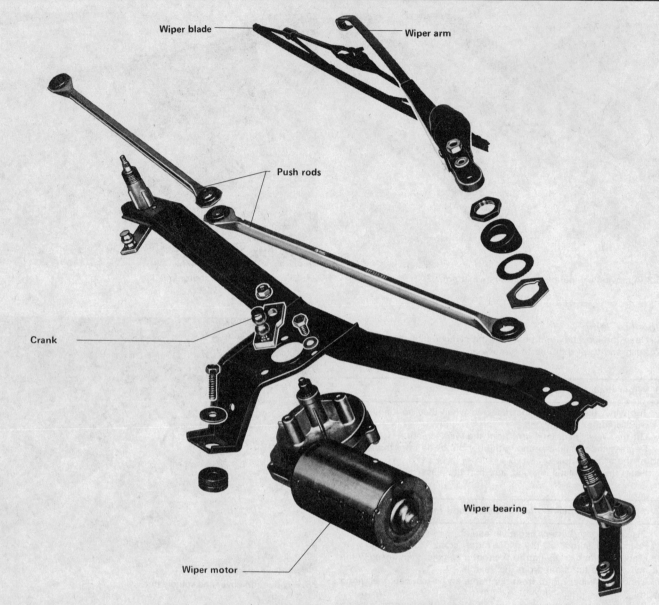

Fig. 10.24 Windscreen wiper linkage components (Sec 28)

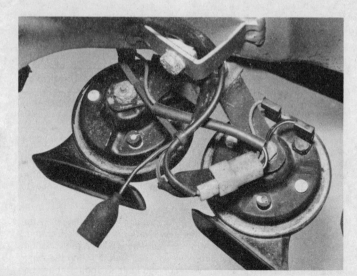

29.1 Horn location from inside engine compartment

29 Horn – removal and refitting

1   The horns are located beneath the right-hand side of the engine compartment (photo).
2   Disconnect the battery negative lead.
3   Disconnect the wiring from the relevant horn then unbolt it from the bracket.
4   Refitting is a reversal of removal.

30 Radios and tape players – fitting (general)

A radio or tape player is an expensive item to buy, and will only give its best performance if fitted properly. It is useless to expect concert hall performance from a unit that is suspended from the dashpanel by string with its speaker resting on the back seat or parcel shelf! If you do not wish to do the fitting yourself, there are many in-car entertainment specialists who will do the fitting for you.

Make sure the unit purchased is of the same polarity as the vehicle. Ensure that units with adjustable polarity are correctly set before commencing the fitting operations.

It is difficult to give specific information with regard to fitting, as final positioning of the radio/tape player, speakers and aerial is entirely a matter of personal preference. However, the following paragraphs give guidelines to follow which are relevant to all installations.

Radios

Most radios are a standardised size of 7 in wide by 2 in deep. This ensures that they will fit into the radio aperture provided in most cars. If your car does not have such an aperture, then the radio must be fitted in a suitable position either in or beneath the dashboard. Alternatively, a special console can be purchased which will fit between the dashpanel and the floor or on the transmission tunnel. These consoles can also be used for additional switches and instrumentation if required. Where no radio aperture is provided, the following points should be borne in mind before deciding exactly where to fit the unit:

(a) The unit must be within easy reach of the driver wearing a seat belt

(b) The unit must not be mounted in close proximity to an electronic tachometer, the ignition switch and its wiring, or the flasher unit and associated wiring

(c) The unit must be mounted within reach of the aerial lead, and in such a place that the aerial lead will not have to be routed near the components detailed in the preceding paragraph (b)

(d) The unit should not be positioned in a place where it might cause injury to the car occupants in an accident; for instance under the dashpanel above the driver's or passenger's legs

(e) The unit must be fitted securely

Some radios will have mounting brackets provided, together with instructions; others will need to be fitted using drilled and slotted metal strips, bent to form mounting brackets. These strips are available from most accessory shops. The unit must be properly earthed by fitting a separate earthing lead between the casing of the radio and the vehicle frame.

Use the radio manufacturers' instructions when wiring the radio into the vehicle's electrical system. If no instructions are available, refer to the relevant wiring diagram to find the location of the radio feed connection in the vehicle's wiring circuit. A 1 to 2 amp in-line fuse must be fitted in the radio's feed wire; a choke may also be necessary (see the following Section).

The type of aerial used and its fitted position, is a matter of personal preference. In general, the taller the aerial the better the reception. It is best to fit a fully retractable aerial; especially if a mechanical car-wash is used or if you live in an area where cars tend to be vandalised. In this respect, electric aerials which are raised and lowered automatically when switching the radio on or off are convenient, but are more likely to give trouble than the manual type.

When choosing a position for the aerial, the following points should be considered:

(a) The aerial lead should be as short as possible; this means that the aerial should be mounted at the front of the car

(b) The aerial must be mounted as far away from the distributor and HT leads as possible

(c) The part of the aerial which protrudes beneath the mounting point must not foul the roadwheels, or anything else

(d) If possible, the aerial should be positioned so that the coaxial lead does not have to be routed through the engine compartment

(e) The plane of the panel on which the aerial is mounted should not be so steeply angled that the aerial cannot be mounted vertically (in relation to the end-on aspect of the car). Most aerials have a small amount of adjustment available

Having decided on a mounting position, a relatively large hole will have to be made in the panel. The exact size of the hole will depend upon the specific aerial being fitted, although generally, the hole required is of $\frac{3}{4}$ in (19 mm) diameter. On metal bodied cars, a tank-cutter of the relevant diameter is the best tool to use for making the hole. This tool needs a small diameter pilot hole drilled through the panel, through which the tool clamping bolt is inserted. When the hole has been made the raw edges should be de-burred with a file and then painted to prevent corrosion.

Fit the aerial according to the manufacturer's instructions. If the aerial is very tall, or if it protrudes beneath the mounting panel for a considerable distance, it is a good idea to fit a stay beneath the aerial and the vehicle frame. This stay can be manufactured from the slotted and drilled metal strips previously mentioned. The stay should be securely screwed or bolted in place. For best reception, it is advisable to fit an earth lead between the aerial and the vehicle frame.

It will probably be necessary to drill one or two holes through bodywork panels in order to feed the aerial lead into the interior of the car. Where this is the case, ensure that the holes are fitted with rubber grommets to protect the cable and to stop possible entry of water.

Positioning and fitting of the speaker depends mainly on its type. Generally, the speaker is designed to fit directly into the aperture already provided in the car. Where this is the case, fitting the speaker is just a matter of removing the protective grille from the aperture and screwing or bolting the speaker in place. Take great care not to damage the speaker diaphragm whilst doing this. It is a good idea to fit a gasket beneath the speaker frame and the mounting panel. In order to prevent vibration, some speakers will already have such a gasket fitted.

If a pod type speaker was supplied with the radio, this can be secured to the mounting panel with self-tapping screws.

When connecting a rear mounted speaker to the radio, the wires should be routed through the vehicle beneath the carpets or floor mats, preferably along the side of the floorpan where they will not be trodden on by passengers. Make the relevant connections as directed by the radio manufacturer.

By now you will have several yards of additional wiring in the car, use PVC tape to secure this wiring out of harm's way. Do not leave electrical leads dangling. Ensure that all new electrical connections are properly made (wires twisted together will not do) and completely secure.

The radio should now be working, but before you pack away your tools it will be necessary to trim the radio to the aerial. If specific instructions are not provided by the radio manufacturer, proceed as follows: Find a station with a low signal strength on the medium-wave band, slowly turn the trim screw of the radio in or out until the loudest reception of the selected station is obtained. The set is then trimmed to the aerial.

Tape players

Fitting instructions for both cartridge and cassette stereo tape players are the same, and in general the same rules apply as when fitting a radio. Tape players are not usually prone to electrical interference like radios, although it can occur, so positioning is not so critical. If possible, the player should be mounted on an even-keel. Also it must be possible for a driver wearing a seat belt to reach the unit in order to change or turn over tapes.

For the best results from speakers designed to be recessed into a panel, mount them so that the back of the speaker protrudes into an enclosed chamber within the car (eg door interiors or the boot cavity).

To fit recessed type speakers in the front doors, first check that there is sufficient room to mount the speakers in each door without it fouling the latch or window winding mechanism. Hold the speaker against the skin of the door and draw a line around the periphery of the speaker. With the speaker removed, draw a second cutting line within the first to allow enough room for the entry of the speaker back, but at the same time providing a broad seat for the speaker flange. When you are sure that the cutting-line is correct, drill a series of holes around its periphery. Pass a hacksaw blade through one of the holes and then cut through the metal between the holes until the centre section of the panel falls out.

De-burr the edges of the hole and then paint the raw metal to prevent corrosion. Cut a corresponding hole in the door trim panel, ensuring that it will be completely covered by the speaker grille. Now drill a hole in the door edge and a corresponding hole in the door surround. These holes are to feed the speaker leads through, so fit grommets. Pass the speaker leads through the door trim, door skin and out through the holes in the side of the door and door surround. Refit the door trim panel and then secure the speaker to the door using self-tapping screws. **Note:** *If the speaker is fitted with a shield to prevent water dripping on it, ensure that this shield is at the top.*

'Pod' type speakers can be fastened to the shelf behind the rear seat, or anywhere else offering a corresponding mounting point on each side of the car. If the 'pod' speakers are mounted on each side of the shelf behind the seat, it is a good idea to drill several large diameter holes through to the boot cavity, beneath each speaker – this will improve the sound reproduction quality if they face the rear window – which then acts as a reflector – so it is worthwhile experimenting before finally fixing the speakers.

10

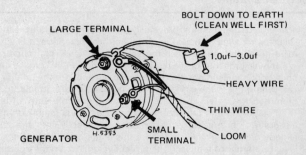

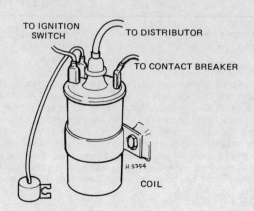

Fig. 10.25 The correct way to connect a capacitor to the alternator (Sec 31)

Fig. 10.26 The capacitor must be connected to the ignition switch side of the coil (Sec 31)

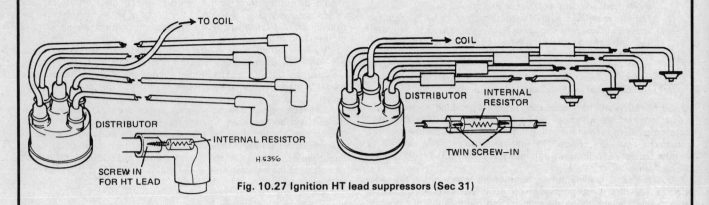

Fig. 10.27 Ignition HT lead suppressors (Sec 31)

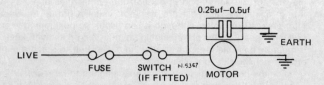

Fig. 10.28 Correct method of suppressing electric motors (Sec 31)

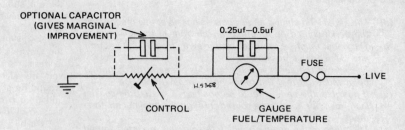

Fig. 10.29 Method of suppressing gauges and their control units (Sec 31)

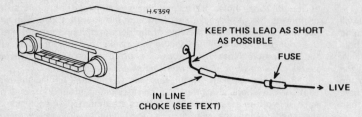

Fig. 10.30 An 'in-line' choke should be fitted into the live supply lead as close to the unit as possible (Sec 31)

31 Radios and tape players – suppression of interference (general)

To eliminate buzzes and other unwanted noises costs very little, and is not as difficult as sometimes thought. With a modicum of common sense and patience, and following the instructions in the following paragraphs, interference can be virtually eliminated.

The first cause for concern is the generator. The noise this makes over the radio is like an electric mixer and the noise speeds up when the engine is revved. (To prove the point, remove the drivebelt and try it). The remedy for this is simple; connect a 1.0 mfd to 3.0 mfd capacitor between earth (probably the bolt that holds down the generator base) and the large terminal on the alternator. This is most important for if it is connected to the small terminal, the generator will probably be damaged permanently (see Fig. 10.25).

A second common cause of electrical interference is the ignition system. Here a 1.0 mfd capacitor must be connected between earth and the SW or + terminal on the coil (see Fig. 10.26). This may stop the tick-tick sound that comes over the speaker. Next comes the spark itself.

There are several ways of curing interference from the ignition HT system. One is the use of carbon-cored HT leads as original equipment. Where copper cable is substituted then you must use resistive spark plug caps (see Fig. 10.27) of about 10 000 ohm to 15 000 ohm resistance. If, due to lack of room these cannot be used, an alternative is to use 'in-line' suppressors – if the interference is not too bad, you may get away with only one suppressor in the coil-to-distributor line. If the interference does continue (a 'clacking' noise) then modify all HT leads.

At this stage it is advisable to check that the radio and ariel are well earthed, and to see that the aerial plug is pushed well into the set and that the radio is properly trimmed (see preceding Section). In addition, check that the wire which supplies the power to the set is as short as possible. At this stage it is a good idea to check that the fuse is of the correct rating. For most sets this will be about 1 to 2 amps.

At this point, the more usual causes of interference have been suppressed. If the problem still exists, a look at the cause of interference may help to pinpoint the component generating the stray electrical discharges.

The radio picks up electromagnetic waves in the air, now some are made by regular broadcasters and some, which we do not want, are made by the car itself. The home made signals are produced by stray electrical discharges floating around in the car. Common producers of these signals are electrical motors, ie the windscreen wipers, electric screen washers, electric window winders, heater fan or an electric aerial if fitted. Other sources of interference are flashing turn signals and instruments. The remedy for these cases is shown in Fig. 10.28 for an electric motor whose interference is not too bad and Fig. 10.29 for instrument suppression. Turn signals are not normally suppressed. In recent years, radio manufacturers have included in the live line of the radio, in addition to the fuse, an in-line choke. If your circuit lacks one of these, put one in as shown in Fig. 10.30.

All the foregoing components are available from radio stores or accessory stores. If you have an electric clock fitted, this should be suppressed by connecting a 0.5 mfd capacitor directly across it as shown for a motor in Fig. 10.28.

If after all this you are still experiencing radio interference, first assess how bad it is, for the human ear can filter out unobtrusive unwanted noises quite easily. But if you are still adamant about eradicating the noise, then continue.

As a first step, a few 'experts' seem to favour a screen between the radio and the engine. This is OK as far as it goes, but the whole set is screened anyway and if interference can get past that then a small piece of aluminium is not going to stop it.

A more sensible way of screening is to discover if interference is coming down the wires. First, take the live lead; interference can get between the set and the choke (hence the reason for keeping the wires short). One remedy here is to screen the wire and this is done by buying screened wire and fitting that. The loudspeaker lead could be

screened also to prevent pick-up getting back to the radio although this is unlikely.

Without doubt, the worst source of radio interference comes from the ignition HT leads, even if they have been suppressed. The ideal way of suppressing these is to slide screening tubes over the leads themselves. As this is impractical, we can place an aluminium shield over the majority of the lead areas. In a vee or twin-cam engine this is relatively easy but for a straight engine, the results are not particularly good.

Now for the really difficult cases, here are a few tips to try out. Where metal comes into contact with metal, an electrical disturbance is caused which is why good clean connections are essential. To remove interference due to overlapping or butting panels, you must bridge the join with a wide braided earth strap (like that from the frame to the engine/transmission). The most common moving parts that could create noise and should be strapped are, in order of importance:

(a) Silencer to frame
(b) Exhaust pipe to engine block and frame
(c) Air cleaner to frame
(d) Front and rear bumpers to frame
(e) Steering column to frame
(f) Bonnet and boot lids to frame

These faults are most pronounced when the engine is idling or labouring under load. Although the moving parts are already connected with nuts, bolts, etc, these do tend to rust and corrode, this creating a high resistance interference source.

If you have a ragged sounding pulse when mobile, this could be wheel or tyre static. This can be cured by buying some anti-static powder and sprinkling inside the tyres.

If the interference takes the shape of a high pitched screeching noise that changes its note when the car is in motion and only comes now and then, this could be related to the aerial, especially if it is of the telescopic or whip type. This source can be cured quite simply by pushing a small rubber ball on top of the aerial as this breaks the electric field before it can form; but it would be much better to buy yourself a new aerial of a reputable brand. If, on the other hand, you are getting a loud rushing sound every time you brake, then this is brake static. This effect is most prominent on hot dry days and is cured only by fitting a special kit, which is quite expensive.

In conclusion, it is pointed out that it is relatively easy and therefore cheap, to eliminate 95 per cent of all noise, but to eliminate the final 5 per cent is time and money consuming. It is up to the individual to decide if it is worth it. Please remember also, that you cannot get a concert hall performance out of a cheap radio.

Finally, cassette players and eight track players are not usually affected by car noise, but in a very bad case, the best remedies are the first three suggestions plus using a 3 to 5 amp choke in the 'live' line and, in incurable cases, screening the live and speaker wires.

Note: *If your car is fitted with electronic ignition, then it is not recommended that either the spark plug resistors or the ignition coil capacitor be fitted as these may damage the system. Most electronic ignition units have built in suppression and should, therefore, not cause interference.*

32 Wiring diagrams – description

1 The wiring diagrams included at the end of this Chapter are of the current flow type where each wire is shown in the simplest line form without crossing over other wires.
2 The fuse/relay panel is at the top of the diagram and the combined letter/figure numbers appearing on the panel terminals refer to the multi-plug connector in letter form and the terminal in figure form.
3 Internal connections through electrical components are shown by a single line.
4 The encircled numbers along the bottom of the diagram indicate the earthing connecting points as given in the key.

10

33 Fault diagnosis – electrical system

Symptom	Reason(s)
Starter fails to turn engine	Battery discharged or defective
	Battery terminal and/or earth leads loose
	Starter motor connections loose
	Starter solenoid faulty
	Starter brushes worn or sticking
	Starter commutator dirty or worn
	Starter field coils earthed
	Starter armature faulty
Starter turns engine very slowly	Battery discharged
	Starter motor connections loose
	Starter brushes worn or sticking
Starter noisy	Pinion or ring gear teeth badly worn
	Mounting bolts loose
Battery will not hold charge	Plates defective
	Electrolyte level too low
	Alternator drivebelt slipping
	Alternator or regulator faulty
	Short in electrical circuit
Ignition light stays on	Alternator faulty
	Alternator drivebelt broken
Ignition light fails to come on	Warning bulb blown
	Warning light open circuit
	Alternator faulty
Instrument readings increase with engine speed	Voltage stabilizer faulty
Fuel on temperature gauge gives no reading	Wiring open circuit
	Sender unit faulty
Fuel on temperature gauge gives maximum reading all the time	Wiring short circuit
	Sender unit or gauge faulty
Lights inoperative	Bulb blown
	Fuse blown
	Switch faulty
	Wiring open circuit
	Connection corroded
Failure of component motor	Commutator dirty or burnt
	Armature faulty
	Brushes sticking or worn
	Armature shaft bearings seized
	Field coils faulty
	Fuse blown
	Wiring loose or broken
Failure of an individual component	Wiring loose or broken
	Fuse blown
	Switch faulty
	Component faulty

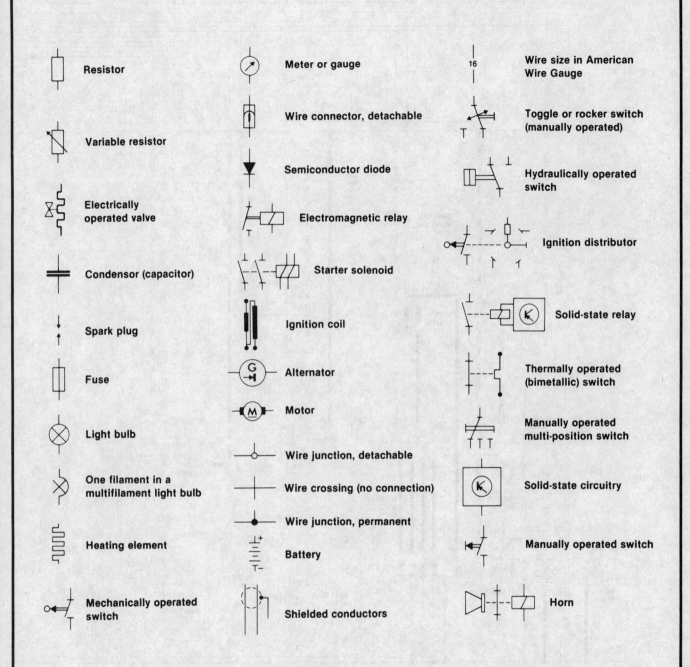

Fig. 10.31 Key to symbols for wiring diagrams

Color Code

Black	— BK	Green	— G
Brown	— BR	Light Green	— LT. G
Clear	— CL	Blue	— BL
Red	— R	Violet	— V
Yellow	— Y	Gray	— GY
		White	— W

10

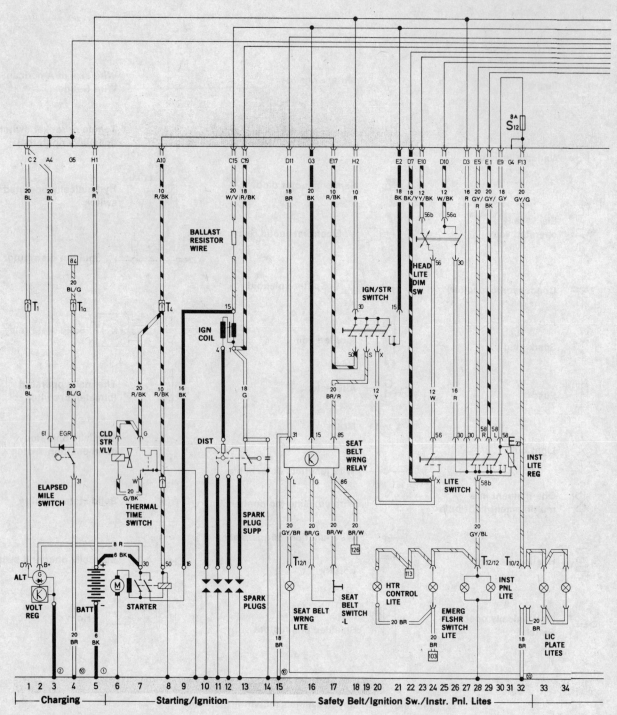

NOTE: All wire sizes American Wire Gauge

Description	Current Track	Description	Current Track	Description	Current Track
Alternator	1, 2	Battery	5	Clock	87
Alternator indicator light	83	Brake control light	88	Cold start valve	6
Ashtray light	121	Brake control light diode	88	Control pressure regulator	124
Auxiliary air regulator	123	Brake fluid level warning switch	90	Coolant temperature gauge	80
Back-up light, left	93	Brake light, left	76	Coolant temperature sender	79
Back-up light, right	92	Brake light, right	73	Distributor	10-13
Back-up light switch	91	Brake light switch 1 and 2	73, 74	Door switch, left front, with buzzer contact	126
Ballast resistor wire	12	Cigarette lighter	119	Door switch, left rear	128
		Cigarette lighter light	110	Door switch, right front	125

Fig. 10.32 Wiring diagrams for 1980 North American four-cylinder models

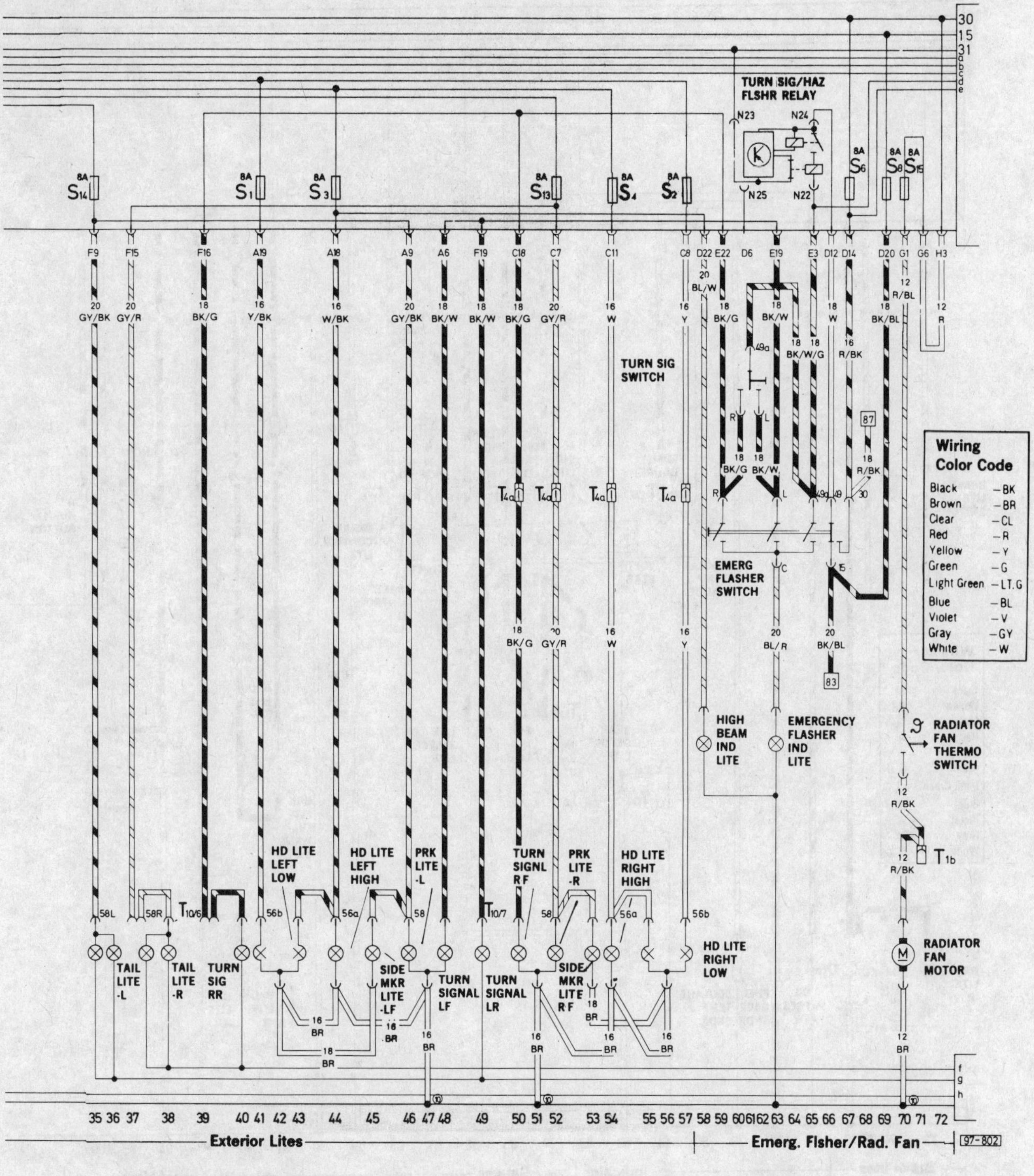

TURN SIG/HAZ
FLSHR RELAY

N23   N24

K

N25   N22

S_{14} S_1 S_3 S_{13} S_4 S_2 S_6 S_8 S_{15}

F9 F15 F16 A19 A18 A9 A6 F19 C18 C7 C11 C8 D22 E22 D6 E19 E3 D12 D14 D20 G1 G6 H3

20 20 18 16 18 20 18 18 18 20 16 16 20 18   18 18 18 18   12
GY/BK GY/R BK/G Y/BK W/BK GY/BK BK/W BK/W BK/G GY/R W Y BK/G BK/W W BK/BL R/BL R
BL/W   18 18   16
                                                            BK/W/G   R/BK

TURN SIG
SWITCH

87

18
BK/G BK/W   R/BK
R   L   R

18 18
BK/G BK/W

T_{4a} T_{4a} T_{4a} T_{4a}

R   L   49a 49   30

EMERG
FLASHER
SWITCH

C

15

83

18 20 16 16   20 20
BK/G GY/R W Y   BL/R BK/BL

**Wiring
Color Code**

Black — BK
Brown — BR
Clear — CL
Red — R
Yellow — Y
Green — G
Light Green — LT.G
Blue — BL
Violet — V
Gray — GY
White — W

HIGH
BEAM
IND
LITE

EMERGENCY
FLASHER
IND
LITE

RADIATOR
FAN
THERMO
SWITCH

12
R/BK

12
R/BK T_{1b}

58L 58R $T_{10/6}$ 56b 56a 58 $T_{10/7}$ 58 56a 56b

HD LITE
LEFT
LOW

HD LITE
LEFT
HIGH

PRK
LITE
-L

TURN
SIGNL
RF

PRK
LITE
-R

HD LITE
RIGHT
HIGH

M   RADIATOR
    FAN
    MOTOR

HD LITE
RIGHT
LOW

TAIL
LITE
-L

TAIL
LITE
-R

TURN
SIG
RR

SIDE
MKR
LITE
-LF

TURN
SIGNAL
LF

TURN
SIGNAL
LR

SIDE
MKR
LITE
RF

16 16 18 16 16 16 18 12
BR BR BR BR BR BR BR BR

f
g
h

35 36 37 38 39 40 41 42 43 44 45 46 47 48 49 50 51 52 53 54 55 56 57 58 59 60 61 62 63 64 65 66 67 68 69 70 71 72

Exterior Lites —————————————————————   Emerg. Flsher/Rad. Fan   97-802

Description	Current Track	Description	Current Track	Description	Current Track
Door switch right rear	124	Fresh air fan switch	99	Headlight, high beam, right	54
EGR elapsed mileage switch	4	Fuel gauge	81	Headlight, left	41-43
EGR indicator light	84	Fuel gauge sender	78	Headlight, right	55, 57
Emergency flasher indicator light	63	Fuel injection fuse	122	Heater control light	20
Emergency flasher switch	59-67	Fuel pump	122	High beam indicator light	58
Emergency flasher switch light	24	Fuel pump relay	122-124	Horns	94-97
Fresh air fan motor	99	Headlight dimmer switch	24	Horn button	96
Fan motor series resistor	99	Headlight, high beam, left	44	Horn relay	94, 95

10

Fig. 10.32 Wiring diagram for 1980 North American four-cylinder models (continued)

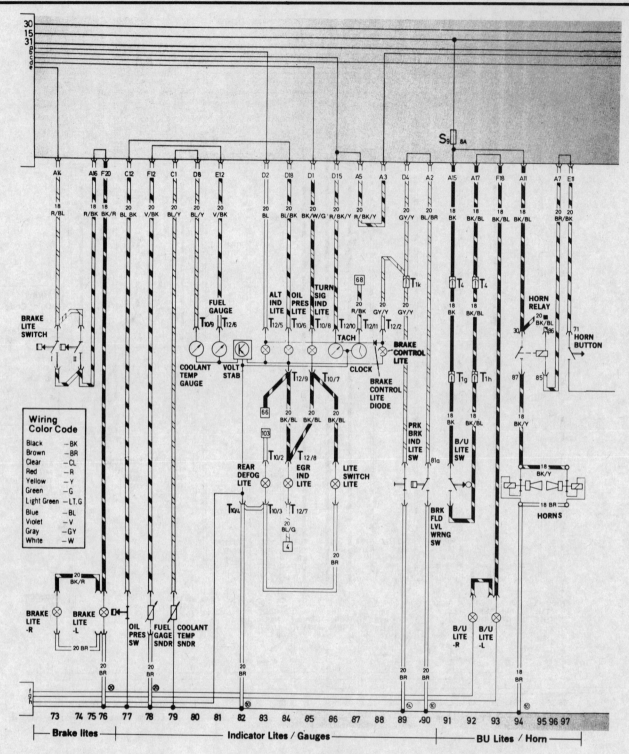

NOTE: All wire sizes American Wire Gauge

Description	Current Track	Description	Current Track	Description	Current Track
Ignition coil	**12**	Load reduction relay	**98-100**	Parking light, right	**52**
Ignition/starter switch	**18-21**	Oil pressure light	**84**	Radiator fan motor	**70**
Instrument panel lights	**27, 29**	Oil pressure switch	**77**	Radiator fan thermo switch	**70**
Instrument panel light regulator	**31**	Oil temperature gauge	**120**	Rear defogger light	**83**
Interior light	**126**	Oil temperature gauge light	**112**	Rear defogger switch	**102**
Light switch	**24-30**	Oil temperature sender	**120**	Rear window defogger	**104**
Light switch light	**86**	Parking brake indicator light switch	**89**	Seat belt buckle switch, left	**17**
License plate lights	**33-34**	Parking light, left	**46**	Seat belt warning system light	**15**

Fig. 10.32 Wiring diagram for 1980 North American four-cylinder models (continued)

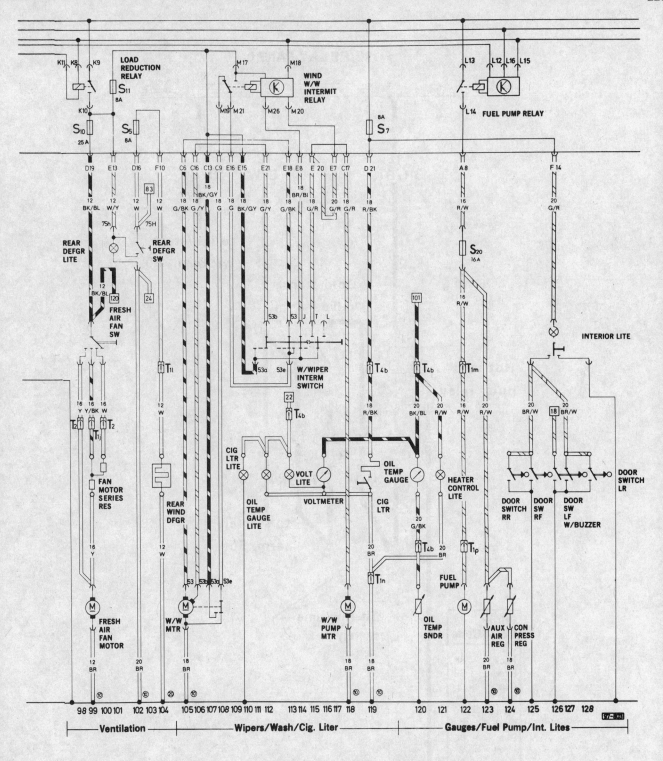

Fig 10.32 Wiring diagram for 1980 North American four-cylinder models (continued)

Description	Current Track	Description	Current Track	Description	Current Track
Seat belt warning system relay	15-17	Thermal time switch	7	Voltage regulator	1, 2
Side marker light, left front	45	Turn signal/hazard flasher relay	60-65	Voltage stabilizer	82
Side marker light, right front	53	Turn signal indicator light	85	Voltmeter	116
Spark plug suppressors	10-13	Turn signal, left front	48	Voltmeter light	113
Spark plugs	10-13	Turn signal, left rear	49	Windshield washer pump motor	118
Starter	6-8	Turn signal, right front	50	Windshield wiper/washer intermittant relay	108-113
Tachometer	86	Turn signl, right rear	40	Windshield wiper intermittant switch	111-116
Tail light, left	35, 36	Turn signal switch	60-62	Windshield wiper motor	105
Tail light, right	37, 38				

10

228

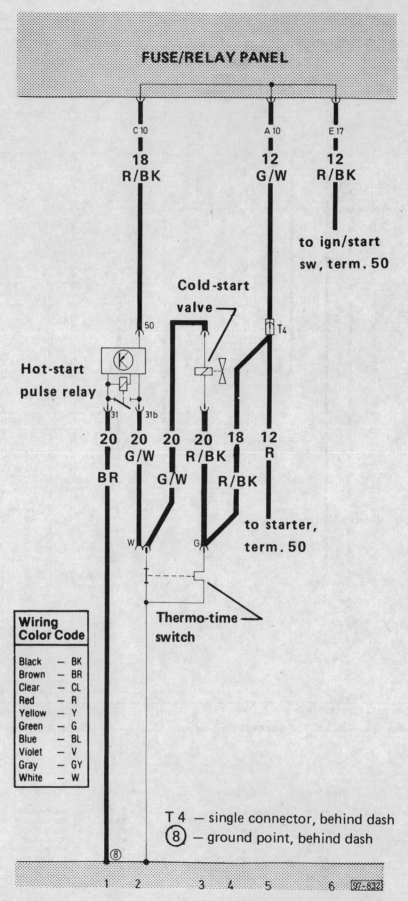

Fig. 10.33 Additional wiring diagram for hot start relay (North American models)

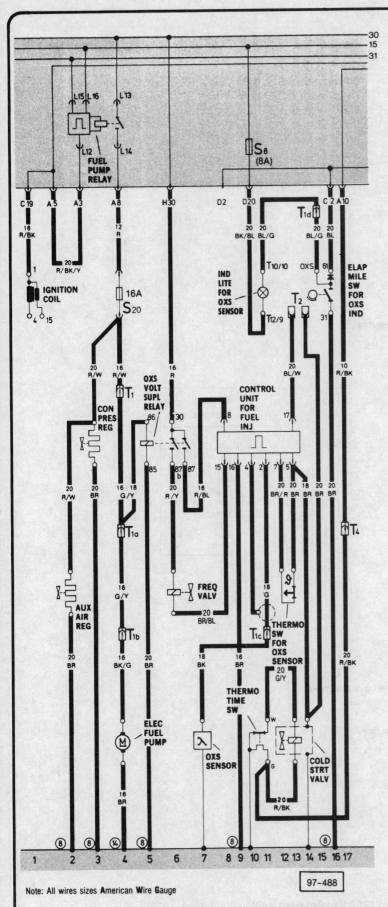

Description — **Current Track**

Description	Current Track
Auxiliary air regulator	2
Cold start valve	12–14
Control pressure regulator	3
Control unit for fuel injector	8–13
Elapsed mileage switch for OXS indicator	15, 16
Electric fuel pump	4
Frequency valve	6
Fuel pump relay	2–4
Fuse for fuel pump (in-line above fuse/relay panel)	4
Fuse in fuse/relay panel	10
Ignition coil	1
Indicator light for OXS sensor	11
OXS voltage supply relay	5, 6
Oxygen sensor-OXS	7
Thermoswitch for oxygen sensor system	12, 13
Thermo-time switch for cold start valve	10, 11

Wire connectors

T1 — single, below dashboard on left	4
T1a — single, in engine compartment (connection for OXS voltage supply relay)	4
T1b — single, engine compartment, left side	4
T1c — single, behind dashboard	11
T1d — single, trunk, left side	15
T2 — double, engine compartment (test connection for dwell meter)	13
T4 — 4 point, below dashboard	17

8 — ground connector, behind dashboard

14 — ground connector, under rear seat

Wiring Color Code

Black	— BK
Brown	— BR
Clear	— CL
Red	— R
Yellow	— Y
Green	— G
Light Green	— LT.G
Blue	— BL
Violet	— V
Gray	— GY
White	— W

Note: All wires sizes American Wire Gauge

97-488

Fig. 10.34 Wiring diagram for 1980 oxygen sensor system (California)

10

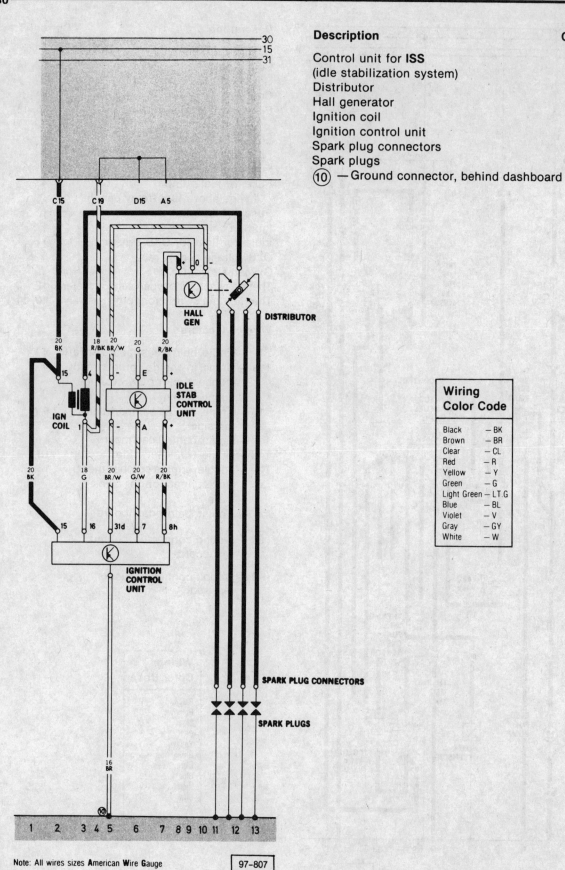

Description | **Current Track**

Control unit for **ISS**
(idle stabilization system) — 5–7
Distributor — 11–13
Hall generator — 8–10
Ignition coil — 3
Ignition control unit — 2–7
Spark plug connectors — 11–13
Spark plugs — 11–13
⑩ —Ground connector, behind dashboard — 5

Wiring Color Code

Black	— BK
Brown	— BR
Clear	— CL
Red	— R
Yellow	— Y
Green	— G
Light Green	— LT.G
Blue	— BL
Violet	— V
Gray	— GY
White	— W

Note: All wires sizes American Wire Gauge

97–807

Fig. 10.35 Wiring diagram for 1980 transistorised ignition (California)

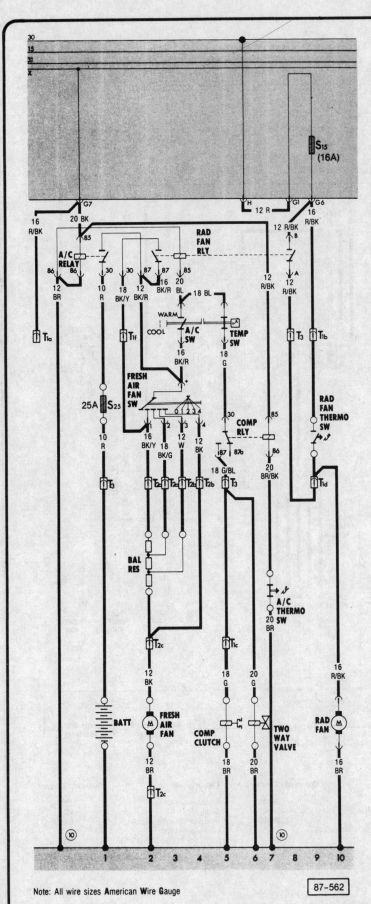

Description	Current Track
Air conditioner micro switch	3
Air conditioner relay	1, 2
Air conditioner thermo switch	7
Ballast resistor for fresh air fan	2
Battery	1
Compressor clutch	5
Compressor relay	5–7
Fresh air fan	2
Fresh air fan switch	2–4
Fuse, on fuse/relay panel	9
Fuse, in-line above fuse/relay panel	1
Radiator fan	10
Radiator fan relay	3–9
Radiator fan thermo switch	9
Temperature switch	5
Two-way valve	6

Wire connectors

T1 — single, on fuse/relay panel
T1b — single, behind dashboard
T1c — single, near A/C compressor
T1d — single, engine compartment
T1f — single, behind dashboard
T2a — double, behind dashboard
T2b — double, behind dashboard
T2c — double, near fresh air fan
T3 — 3 point, behind dashboard
⑩ — ground strap, near fuse/relay panel

Wiring Color Code	
Black	— BK
Brown	— BR
Clear	— CL
Red	— R
Yellow	— Y
Green	— G
Light Green	— LT.G
Blue	— BL
Violet	— V
Gray	— GY
White	— W

Note: All wire sizes American Wire Gauge

87-562

Fig. 10.36 Wiring diagram for 1980 air conditioner (North American models)

10

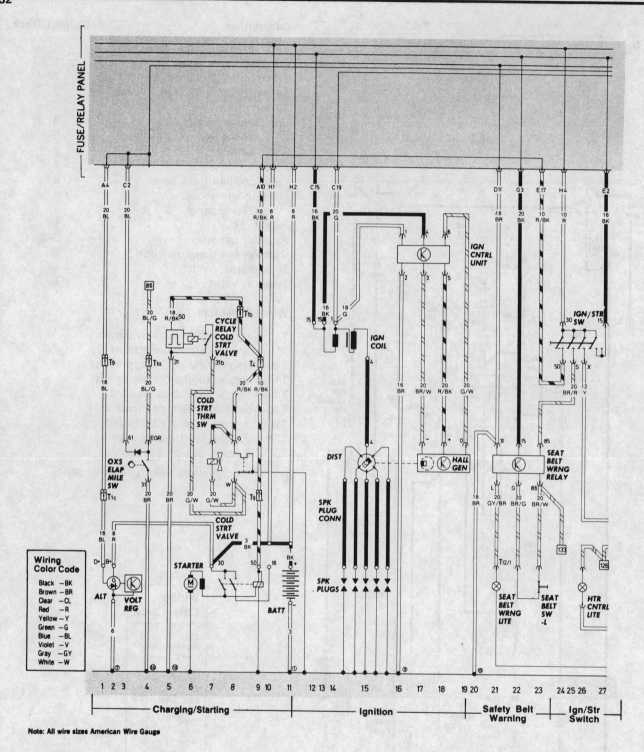

Note: All wire sizes American Wire Gauge

Description	Current Track	Description	Current Track	Description	Current Track
Alternator	2	Blower motor	102-103	Cigarette lighter	128
Alternator indicator light	85	Blower series resistor	102-103	Clock	90
Ashtray light	130	Blower switch	101-103	Cold-start thermo switch	8
Auxiliary-air regulator	124	Brake-fluid level warning switch	93	Cold-start valve	7
Back-up light, left	96	Brake light, left	78	Control-pressure regulator	122
Back-up light, right	95	Brake light, right	75	Coolant-temperature gauge	82
Back-up light switch	94	Brake light switch 1	75	Coolant-temperature sender unit	5-7
Battery	11	Brake light switch 2	76	Cycle relay for cold-start valve	81

Fig. 10.37 Wiring diagram for 1980 North American five-cylinder models

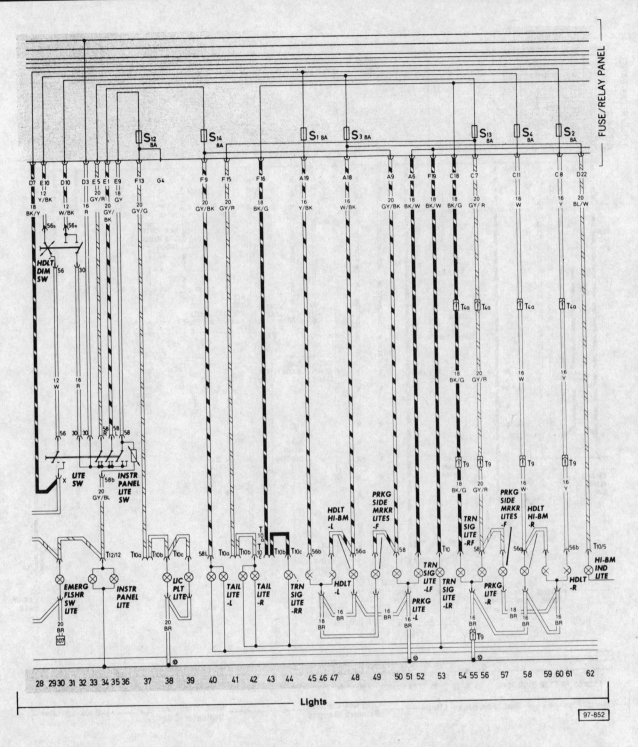

Fig. 10.37 Wiring diagram for 1980 North American five-cylinder models (continued)

Description	Current Track	Description	Current Track	Description	Current Track
Distributor	15	Emergency-flasher switch light	30	Hall generator (TIS)	17-19
Door switch, left front with buzzer contact	133-134	Fuel gauge	83	Headlight dimmer switch	29-32
Door switch, left rear	135	Fuel gauge sender unit	80	Headlight, high beam, left	48
Door switch, right front	132	Fuel pump	121	Headlight, high beam, right	58
Door switch, right rear	131	Fuel pump relay	121-123	Headlight, left	45-47
Emergency-flasher light	62	Fuses S-17—S-15 Fuses on fuse/relay panel	-	Headlight, right	59-61
Emergency-flasher switch	63-70	S-31—Fuse for electric fuel pump	121	Heater-control light	26
				High-beam indicator light	62

10

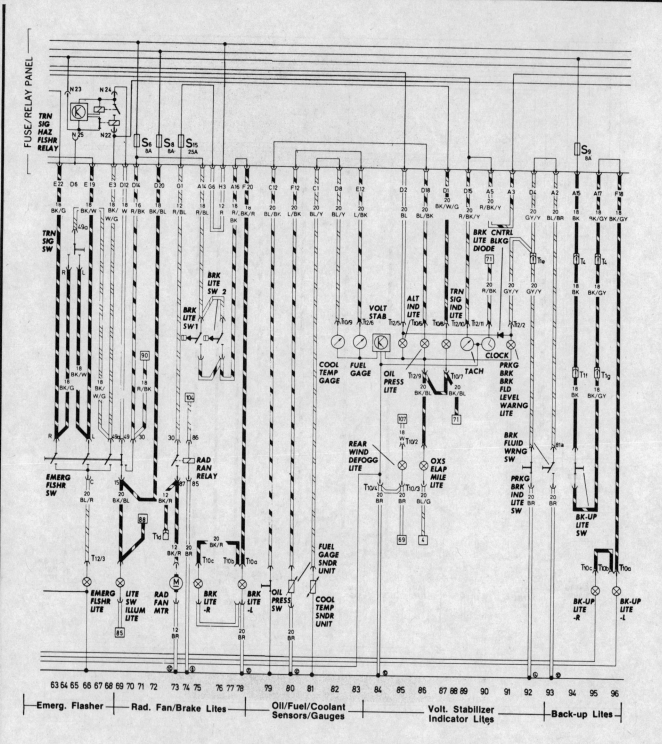

Fig. 10.37 Wiring diagram for 1980 North American five-cylinder models (continued)

Description	Current Track	Description	Current Track	Description	Current Track
Horn button	97	Load-reduction relay	101-102	Parking-brake/Brake-fluid level	
Horn relay	97-98	Oil-pressure light	86	warning light	91
Horns	99-100	Oil-pressure switch	79	Parking light, left	50
Ignition coil	12-15	Oil-temperature gauge	129	Parking light, right	56
Ignition-control unit	16-18	Oil-temperature gauge light	125	Parking, side-marker lights, front	49-57
Ignition/starter switch	36	Oil-temperature sender unit	129	Radiator-fan motor	73
License-plate light	38-39	OXS elasped mileage light	86	Radiator-fan relay	73-74
Light switch	30-35	OXS elasped mileage switch	3-4	Radiator thermo switch	104
Light-switch illumination light	69			Rear defogger	108

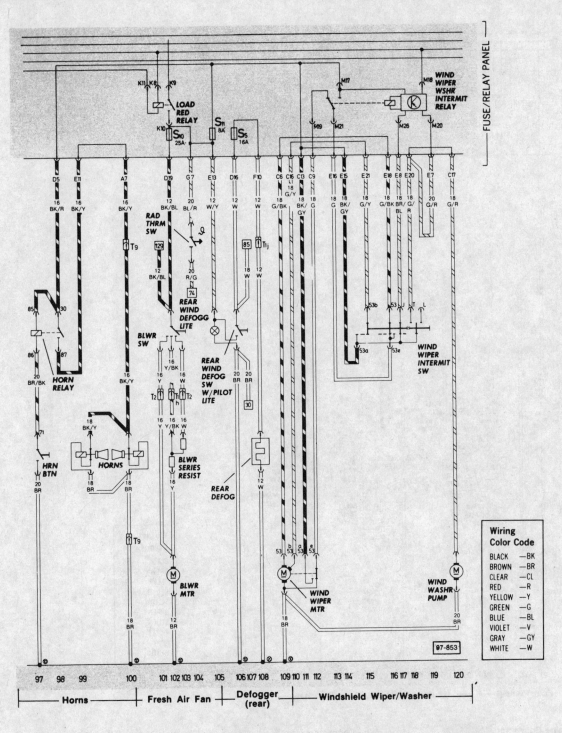

Fig. 10.37 Wiring diagram for 1980 North American five-cylinder models (continued)

Description	Current Track	Description	Current Track	Description	Current Track
Rear-window defogger light	85	Tachometer	88	Voltage regulator	2
Rear-window defogger switch with pilot light	106	Tail light, left	40	Voltage stabilizer	127
		Tail light, right	42	Voltmeter	84
Seat-belt switch, left	23	Turn-signal/hazard flasher relay	64-68	Voltmeter light	126
Seat-belt warning system light	21	Turn-signal indicator light	87	Windshield-washer pump	120
Seat-belt warning system relay	21-23	Turn-signal light, left front	52	Windshield-wiper intermittent switch	115-118
Spark-plug connectors	15	Turn-signal light, left rear	53	Windshield-wiper motor	109-112
Spark plugs	15	Turn-signal light, right front	54	Windshield-wiper/washer	
		Turn-signal light, right rear	44	intermittent relay	113-119

10

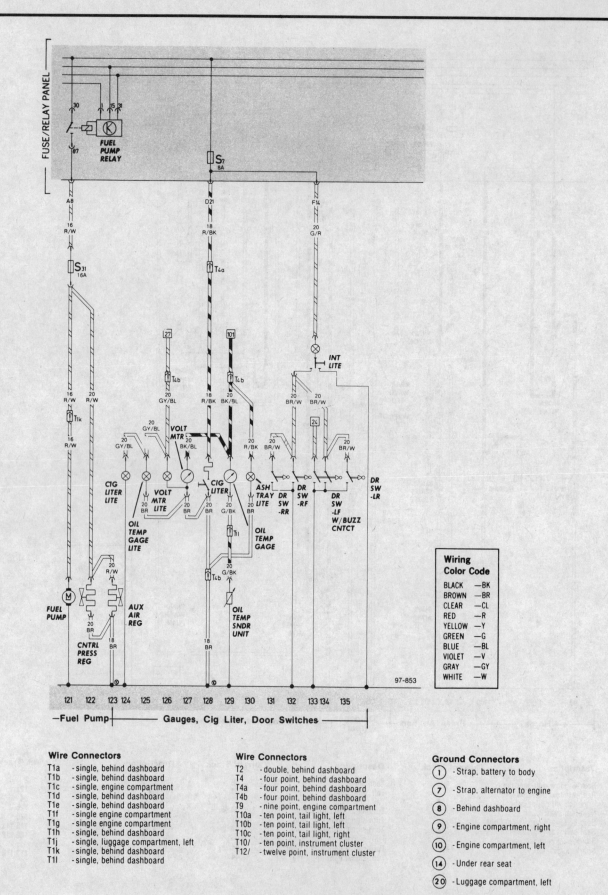

Fig. 10.37 Wiring diagram for 1980 North American five-cylinder models (continued)

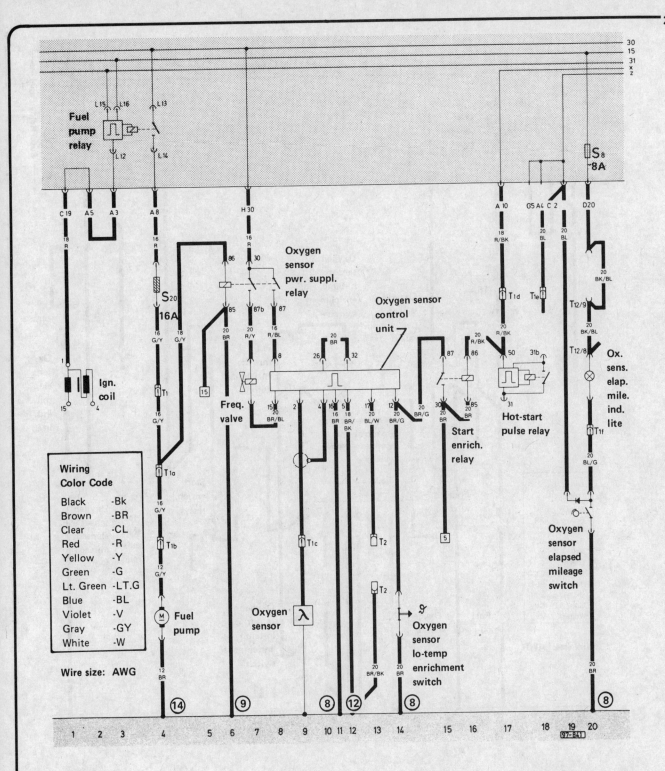

Fig. 10.38 Additional wiring diagram for 1980 oxygen sensor system (North American models)

Wiring Color Code

Black	-Bk
Brown	-BR
Clear	-CL
Red	-R
Yellow	-Y
Green	-G
Lt. Green	-LT.G
Blue	-BL
Violet	-V
Gray	-GY
White	-W

Wire size: AWG

Wire connectors:

T1   — single, behind dash
T1a   — single, behind dash
T1b   — single, trunk, right
T1c   — single, trunk, left
T1d   — single, behind dash

T1e   — single, behind dash
T1f   — single, behind dash
T2   — double, engine comp.
        (test conn. for OXS)
T12   — twelve point, on dash

Ground connectors:

⑧   — behind dash
⑨   — engine comp., left
⑫   — engine block
⑭   — under rear seat

10

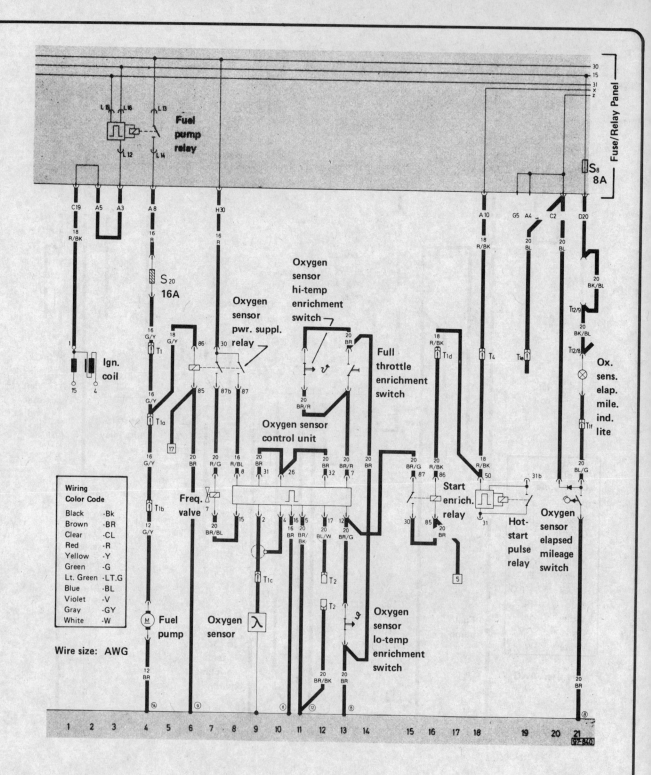

Fig. 10.39 Wiring diagram for 1980 oxygen sensor system on North American five-cylinder models

Wire connectors:

T 1 — single, behind dash
T 1a — single, behind dash
T 1b — single, trunk, right side
T 1c — single, trunk, left side
T 1d — single, behind dash
T 1e — single, behind dash

T 1f — single, behind dash
T 22 — double, engine comp.
    (test conn. for OXS)
T 4 — four point, behind dash
T 12 — twelve point on dash

Ground connectors:

⑧ — behind dash
⑨ — engine comp., left
⑫ — engine block
⑭ — under rear seat

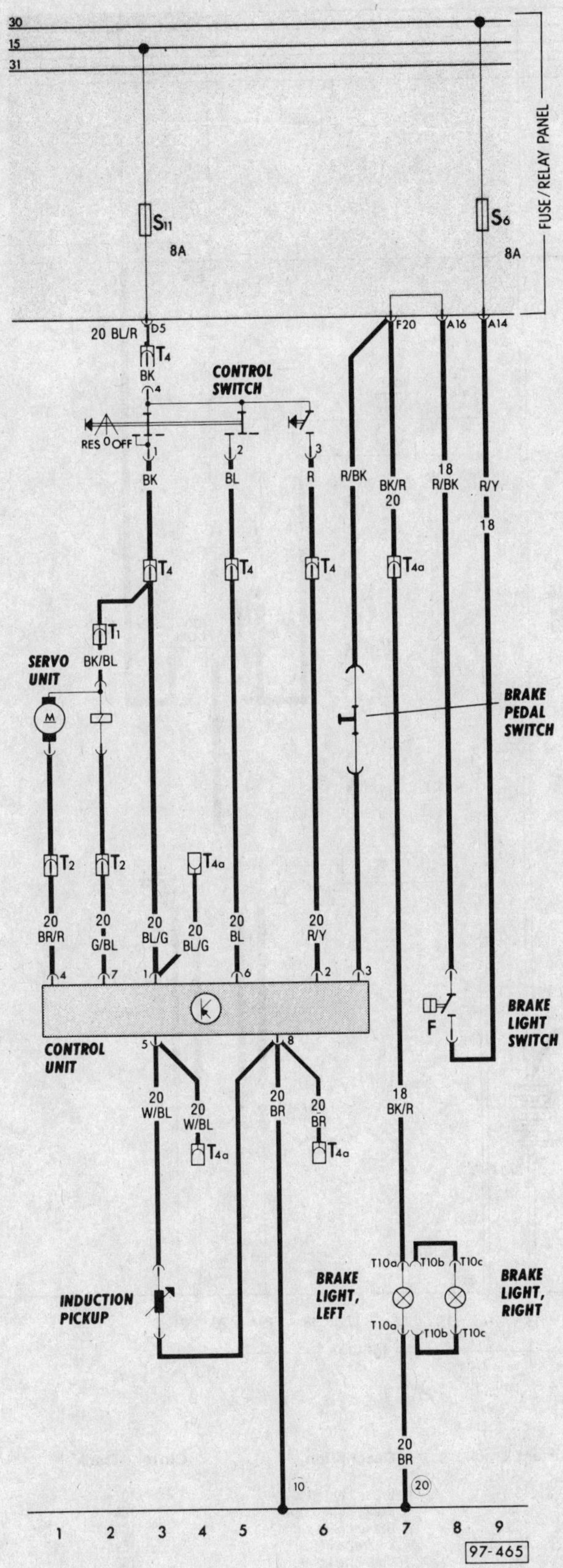

Wire Connectors

T1 — single, behind dashboard
T1a — single, behind dashboard
T2 — double, behind dashboard
T4 — four point, behind dashboard
T4a — four point, (test connection only for production)
T10a — ten point
T10b — ten point
T10c — ten point

Ground Connectors

(10) — near Fuse/Relay Panel
(20) — luggage comp. left rear

Wiring Color Code	
Black	— BK
Brown	— BR
Clear	— CL
Red	— R
Yellow	— Y
Green	— G
Light Green	— LT.G
Blue	— BL
Violet	— V
Gray	— GY
White	— W

FUSE / RELAY PANEL

S11 8A   S6 8A

20 BL/R   D5

CONTROL SWITCH

RES OFF

SERVO UNIT

BRAKE PEDAL SWITCH

BRAKE LIGHT SWITCH

CONTROL UNIT

INDUCTION PICKUP

BRAKE LIGHT, LEFT   BRAKE LIGHT, RIGHT

10

|97-465|

Fig. 10.40 Wiring diagram for 1980 cruise control (North American models)

10

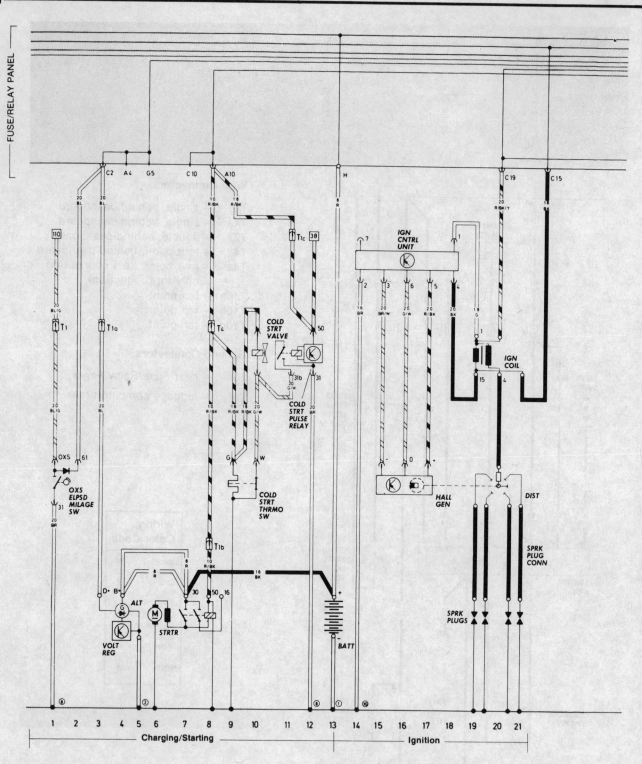

Fig. 10.41 Wiring diagram for 1981 North American four-cylinder models

Note: All wire sizes American Wire Gauge

Description	Current Track	Description	Current Track	Description	Current Track
Alternator	4	Battery	13	Brake light, left	102
Alternator indicator light	115	Blower	135	Brake light, right	100
Antenna connection	156	Blower series resistor	135	Brake-light switch	100
Auxiliary air regulator	23	Blower switch	135-137	Cigarette lighter	159
Back-up light, left	129	Blower switch light	134	Cigarette lighter light	160
Back-up light, right	127	Brake control light blocking diode	122	Clock	121
Back-up light switch	127	Brake-fluid-level warning switch	126	Cold-start pulse relay	11, 12

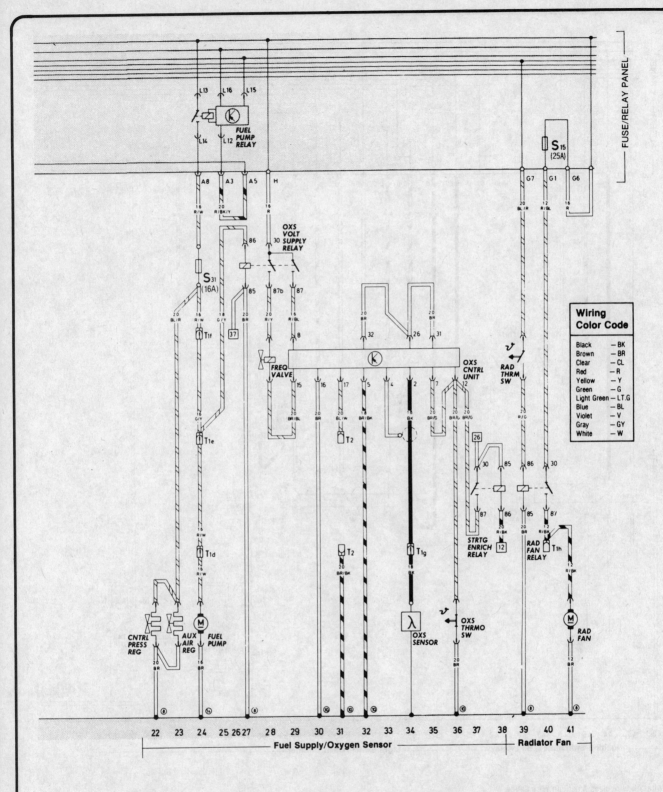

Fig. 10.41 Wiring diagram for 1981 North American four-cylinder models (continued)

Description	Current Track	Description	Current Track	Description	Current Track
Cold-start thermo switch	9, 10	Coolant-temperature gauge	106	Door switch, left rear	172
Cold-start valve	10	Coolant-temperature sender	106	Door switch, right front	169
Control-pressure regulator	22	Defogger light	109	Door switch, right rear	168
Coolant over-temperature warning light	116	Defogger switch	138, 139	Emergency-flasher light	118
		Distributor	19-21	Emergency-flasher switch	91-97
Coolant over-temperature warning light blocking diode	116	Door switch, left front (with buzzer contact)	170, 171	Emergency-flasher switch light	89
				Frequency valve	28

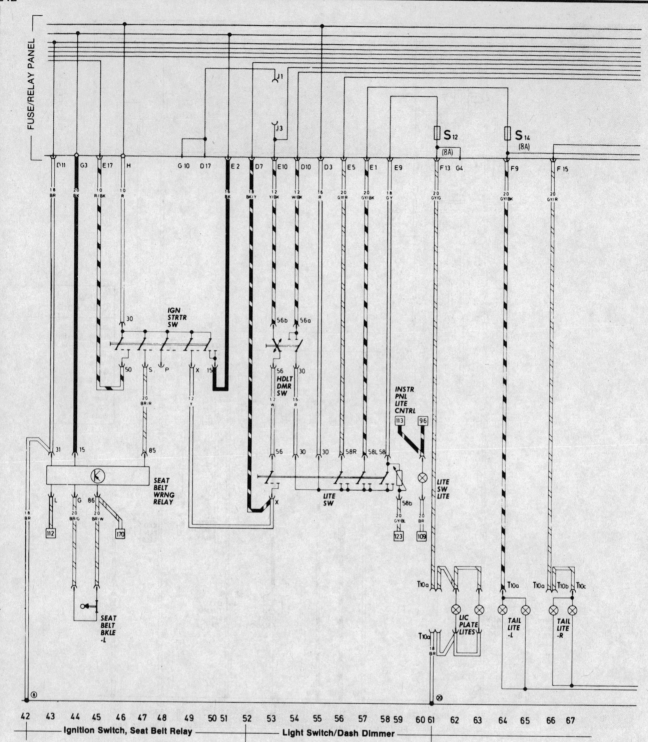

Note: All wire sizes American Wire Gauge

Description	Current Track	Description	Current Track	Description	Current Track
Fuel gauge	107	Glove-box light	163	High-beam indicator light	119
Fuel-gauge sender	104	Hall generator	15-17	Horns	133, 134
Fuel pump	24	Headlight dimmer switch	53-54	Horn button	132
Fuel pump fuse 16A		Headlight, highbeam, left	73	Horn relay	131-132
(in-line above fuse/relay panel)		Headlight, highbeam, right	84	Ignition coil	19
Fuel pump relay	24-27	Headlight, left	70-72	Ignition control unit	14-18
Fuses on fuse/relay panel (S1 - S15)		Headlight, right	87	Ignition/starter switch	46-50

Fig. 10.41 Wiring diagram for 1981 North American four-cylinder models (continued)

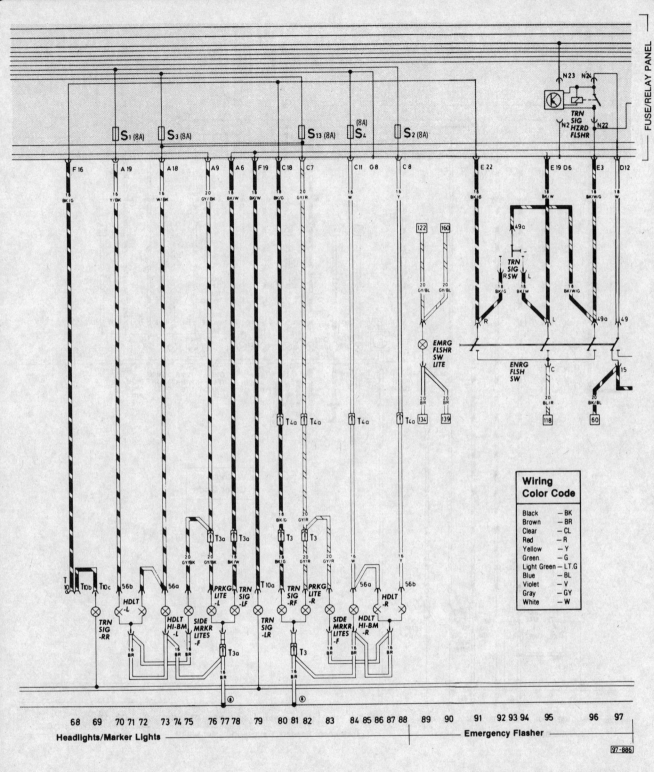

Fig. 10.41 Wiring diagram for 1981 North American four-cylinder models (continued)

Description	Current Track	Description	Current Track	Description	Current Track
Instrument-panel light	123	Luggage-compartment light	174	Over-temp warning light flasher	117
Instrument-panel light control	59	Luggage-compartment light switch	174	OXS control unit	29-36
Interior light	172	Oil-pressure light	114	OXS elapsed mileage switch	1, 2
License-plate lights	62.63	Oil-pressure switch	103	OXS indicator light	110
Light switch	53-58	Oil-temperature gauge	165	OXS sensor	34
Light switch light	60	Oil-temperature gauge light	162	OXS thermo switch	36
Load-reduction relay	122.123	Oil-temperature sender	167	OXS voltage-supply relay	27-29

10

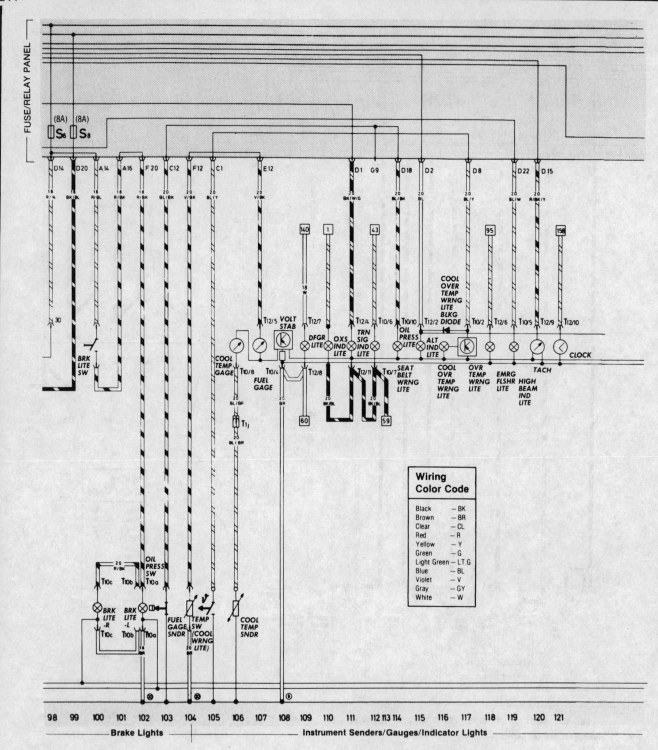

Note: All wire sizes American Wire Gauge

Description	Current Track	Description	Current Track	Description	Current Track
Parking-brake/brake-fluid warning light	124	Radiator thermo switch	39	Spark plugs	19-21
Parking-brake indicator light switch	125	Radio	157	Spark plug connectors	19-21
Parking light, left	76	Rear defogger	141	Starter	6-8
Parking light, right	82	Seat belt buckle, left	45	Starting enrichment relay	37-38
Radiator fan	41	Seat belt warning light	112	Tachometer	120
Radiator fan relay	39-40	Seat belt warning relay	43-47	Tail light, left	64, 65
		Side-marker lights, front	75, 83	Tail light, right	66, 67

Fig. 10.41 Wiring diagram for 1981 North American four-cylinder models (continued)

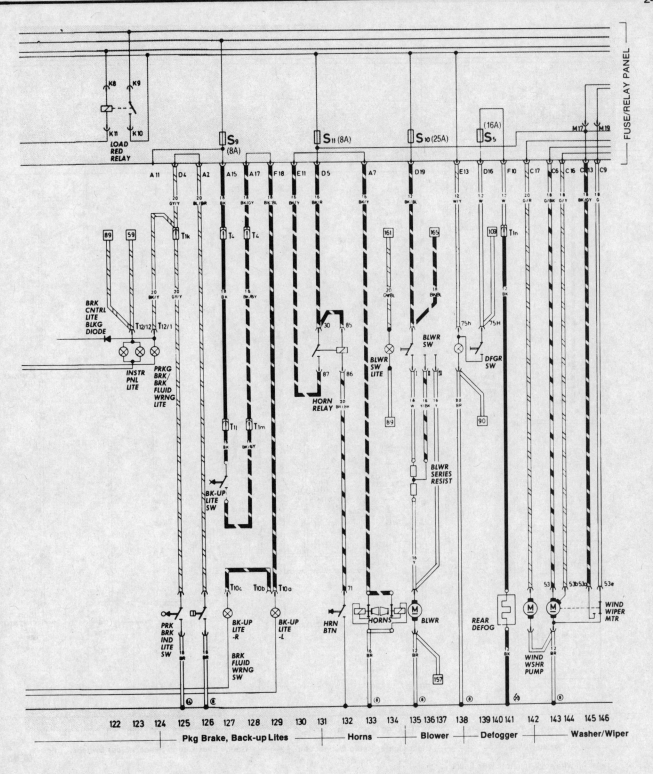

Fig. 10.41 Wiring diagram for 1981 North American four-cylinder models (continued)

Description	Current Track	Description	Current Track	Description	Current Track
Temperature switch (for coolant warning light)	105	Turn-signal, right rear	69	Windshield-wiper intermittent switch	150-154
		Turn-signal switch	92-94	Windshield-wiper motor	143-146
Turn-signal/hazard flasher	95, 96	Voltage regulator	4	Windshield-wiper/washer intermittent relay	147-150
Turn-signal indicator light	111	Voltage stabilizer	108		
Turn-signal, left front	78	Voltmeter	164		
Turn-signal, left rear	79	Voltmeter light	161		
Turn-signal, right front	80	Windshield-washer pump	142		

10

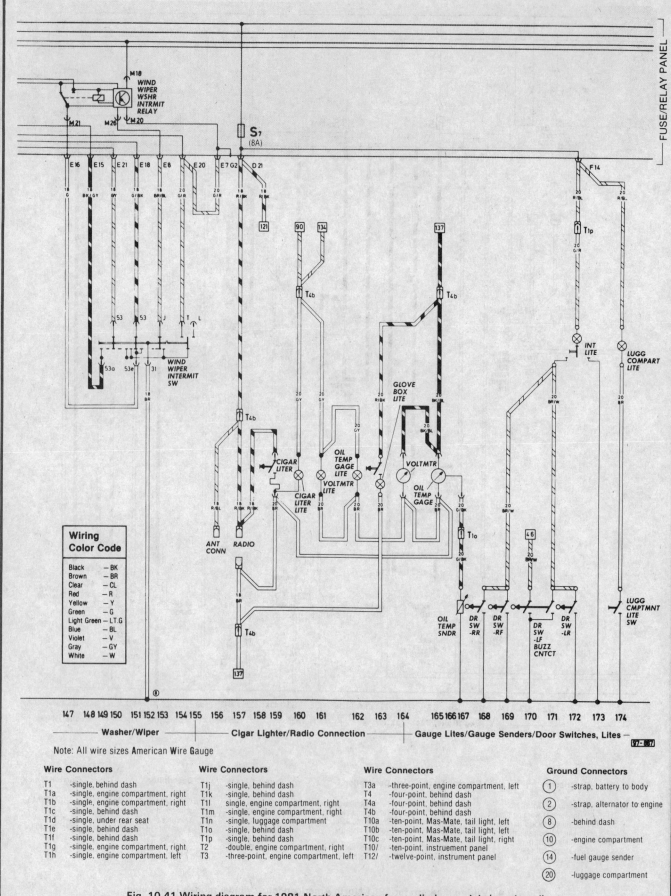

Fig. 10.41 Wiring diagram for 1981 North American four-cylinder models (continued)

Note: All wire sizes American Wire Gauge

Wiring Color Code

Black	— BK
Brown	— BR
Clear	— CL
Red	— R
Yellow	— Y
Green	— G
Light Green	— LT.G
Blue	— BL
Violet	— V
Gray	— GY
White	— W

Wire Connectors

T1	-single, behind dash
T1a	-single, engine compartment, right
T1b	-single, engine compartment, right
T1c	-single, behind dash
T1d	-single, under rear seat
T1e	-single, behind dash
T1f	-single, behind dash
T1g	-single, engine compartment, right
T1h	-single, engine compartment, left

Wire Connectors

T1j	-single, behind dash
T1k	-single, behind dash
T1l	single, engine compartment, right
T1m	-single, engine compartment, right
T1n	-single, luggage compartment
T1o	-single, behind dash
T1p	-single, behind dash
T2	-double, engine compartment, right
T3	-three-point, engine compartment, left

Wire Connectors

T3a	-three-point, engine compartment, left
T4	-four-point, behind dash
T4a	-four-point, behind dash
T4b	-four-point, behind dash
T10a	-ten-point, Mas-Mate, tail light, left
T10b	-ten-point, Mas-Mate, tail light, left
T10c	-ten-point, Mas-Mate, tail light, right
T10/	-ten-point, instrument panel
T12/	-twelve-point, instrument panel

Ground Connectors

①	-strap, battery to body
②	-strap, alternator to engine
⑧	-behind dash
⑩	-engine compartment
⑭	-fuel gauge sender
⑳	-luggage compartment

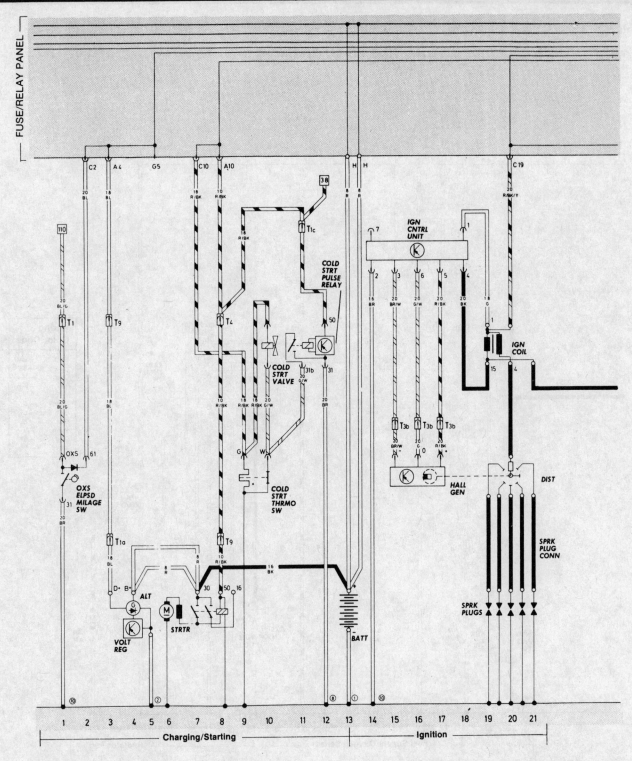

Fig. 10.42 Wiring diagram for 1981 North American five-cylinder models

Note: All wire sizes American Wire Gauge

Description	Current Track	Description	Current Track	Description	Current Track
Alternator	4	Battery	13	Brake light, left	102
Alternator indicator light	115	Blower	135	Brake light, right	100
Antenna connection	156	Blower series resistor	135	Brake-light switch	100
Auxiliary air regulator	23	Blower switch	135-137	Cigarette lighter	159
Back-up light, left	129	Blower switch light	134	Cigarette lighter light	160
Back-up light, right	127	Brake control light blocking diode	122	Clock	121
Back-up light switch	127	Brake-fluid-level warning switch	126	Cold-start pulse relay	11, 12

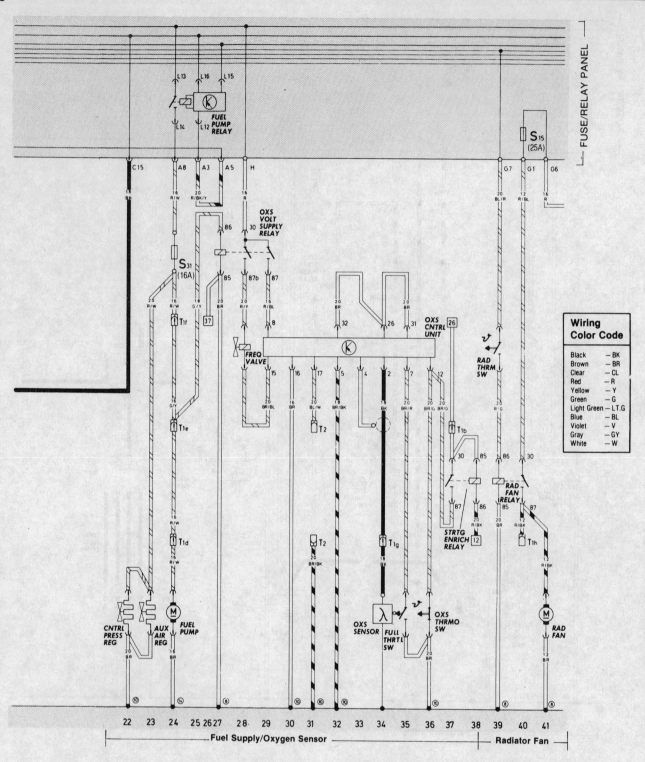

Fig. 10.42 Wiring diagram for 1981 North American five-cylinder models (continued)

Description	Current Track	Description	Current Track	Description	Current Track
Cold-start thermo switch	9, 10	Coolant-temperature gauge	106	Door switch, left rear	172
Cold-start valve	10	Coolant-temperature sender	106	Door switch, right front	169
Control-pressure regulator	22	Defogger light	109	Door switch, right rear	168
Coolant over-temperature		Defogger switch	138, 139	Emergency-flasher light	118
warning light	116	Distributor	19-21	Emergency-flasher switch	91-97
Coolant over-temperature warning		Door switch, left front		Emergency-flasher switch light	89
light blocking diode	116	(with buzzer contact)	170, 171	Frequency valve	28

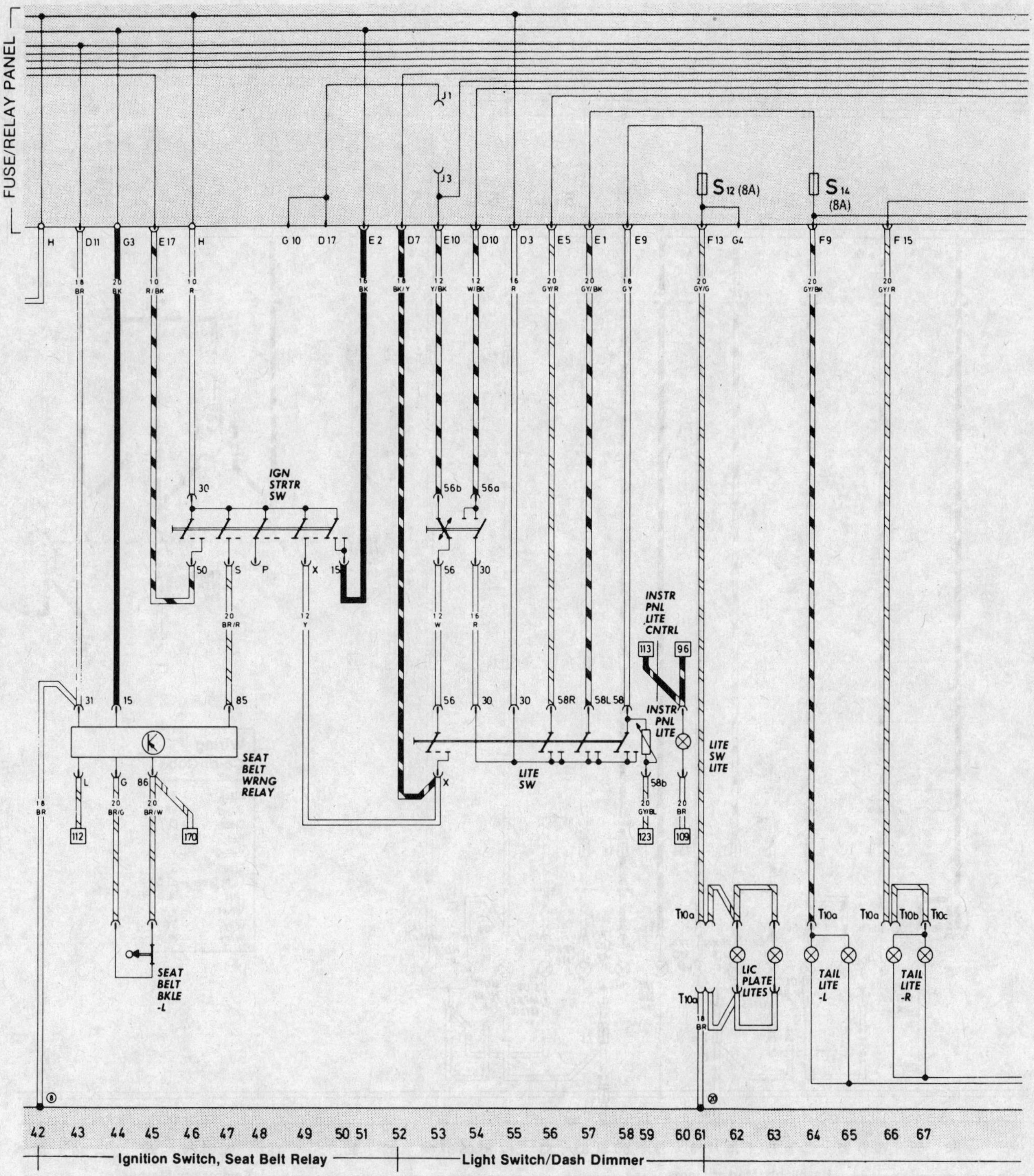

FUSE/RELAY PANEL

J1

J3

S₁₂ (8A)   S₁₄ (8A)

| H | D11 | G3 | E17 | H | G 10 | D17 | E 2 | D7 | E10 | D10 | D3 | E5 | E1 | E9 | F 13 | G4 | F9 | F 15 |

18 BR | 20 BK | 10 R/BK | 10 R | 16 BK | 16 BK/Y | 12 Y/BK | 12 W/BK | 16 R | 20 GY/R | 20 GY/BK | 18 GY | 20 GY/G | 20 GY/BK | 20 GY/R

IGN STRTR SW

30   56b   56a

50 S P   X 15   56   30

IGN
STRTR
SW

20 BR/R   12 Y   12 W   16 R

85

31   15   56   30   30   58R   58L 58

INSTR PNL LITE CNTRL

113   96

INSTR PNL LITE

K

SEAT BELT WRNG RELAY

LITE SW LITE

L G 86
18 BR | 20 BR/G | 20 BR/W

112   170

LITE SW

58b

20 GY/BL   20 BR

123   109

SEAT BELT BKLE -L

T10a

LIC PLATE LITES

T10a   T10a T10b T10c

TAIL LITE -L   TAIL LITE -R

T10a
18 BR

| 42 | 43 | 44 | 45 | 46 | 47 | 48 | 49 | 50 | 51 | 52 | 53 | 54 | 55 | 56 | 57 | 58 | 59 | 60 | 61 | 62 | 63 | 64 | 65 | 66 | 67 |

Ignition Switch, Seat Belt Relay ——— Light Switch/Dash Dimmer

Note: All wire sizes American Wire Gauge

Description	Current Track	Description	Current Track	Description	Current Track
Fuel gauge	107	Fuses on fuse/relay panel (S1 - S15)		Headlight, right	87
Fuel-gauge sender	104	Glove-box light	163	High-beam indicator light	119
Fuel pump	24	Hall generator	15-17	Horns	133, 134
Fuel pump fuse 16A		Headlight dimmer switch	53-54	Horn button	132
(in-line above fuse/relay panel)		Headlight, highbeam, left	73	Horn relay	131-132
Fuel pump relay	24-27	Headlight, highbeam, right	84	Ignition coil	19
Full-throttle enrichment switch	9, 10	Headlight, left	70-72	Ignition control unit	14-18

10

Fig. 10.42 Wiring diagram for 1981 North American five-cylinder models (continued)

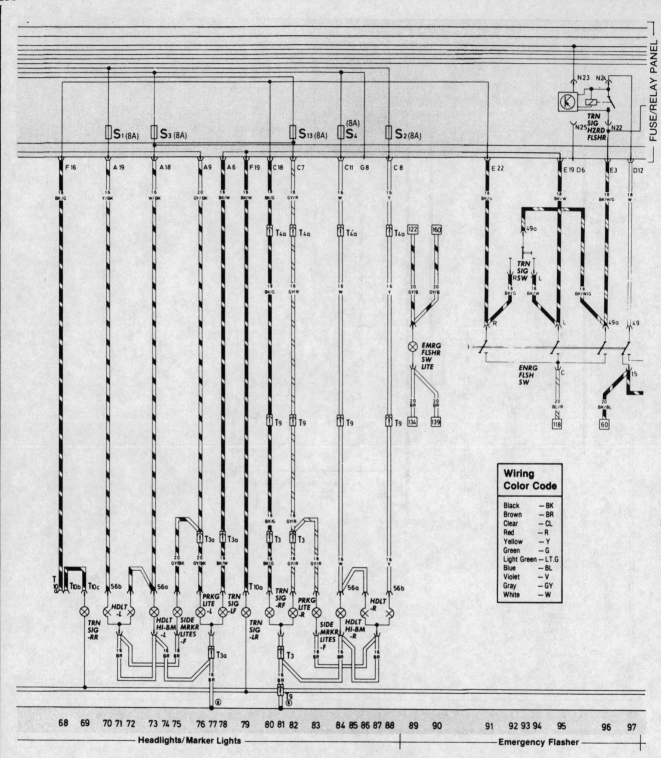

Fig. 10.42 Wiring diagram for 1981 North American five-cylinder models (continued)

Description	Current Track	Description	Current Track	Description	Current Track
Ignition/starter switch	46-50	Load-reduction relay	122,123	Oil-temperature sender	167
Instrument-panel light	123	Luggage-compartment light	174	Over-temp warning light flasher	117
Instrument-panel light control	59	Luggage-compartment light switch	174	OXS control unit	29-36
Interior light	172	Oil-pressure light	114	OXS elapsed mileage switch	1, 2
License-plate lights	62,63	Oil-pressure switch	103	OXS indicator light	110
Light switch	53-58	Oil-temperature gauge	165	OXS sensor	34
Light switch light	60	Oil-temperature gauge light	162	OXS thermo switch	36

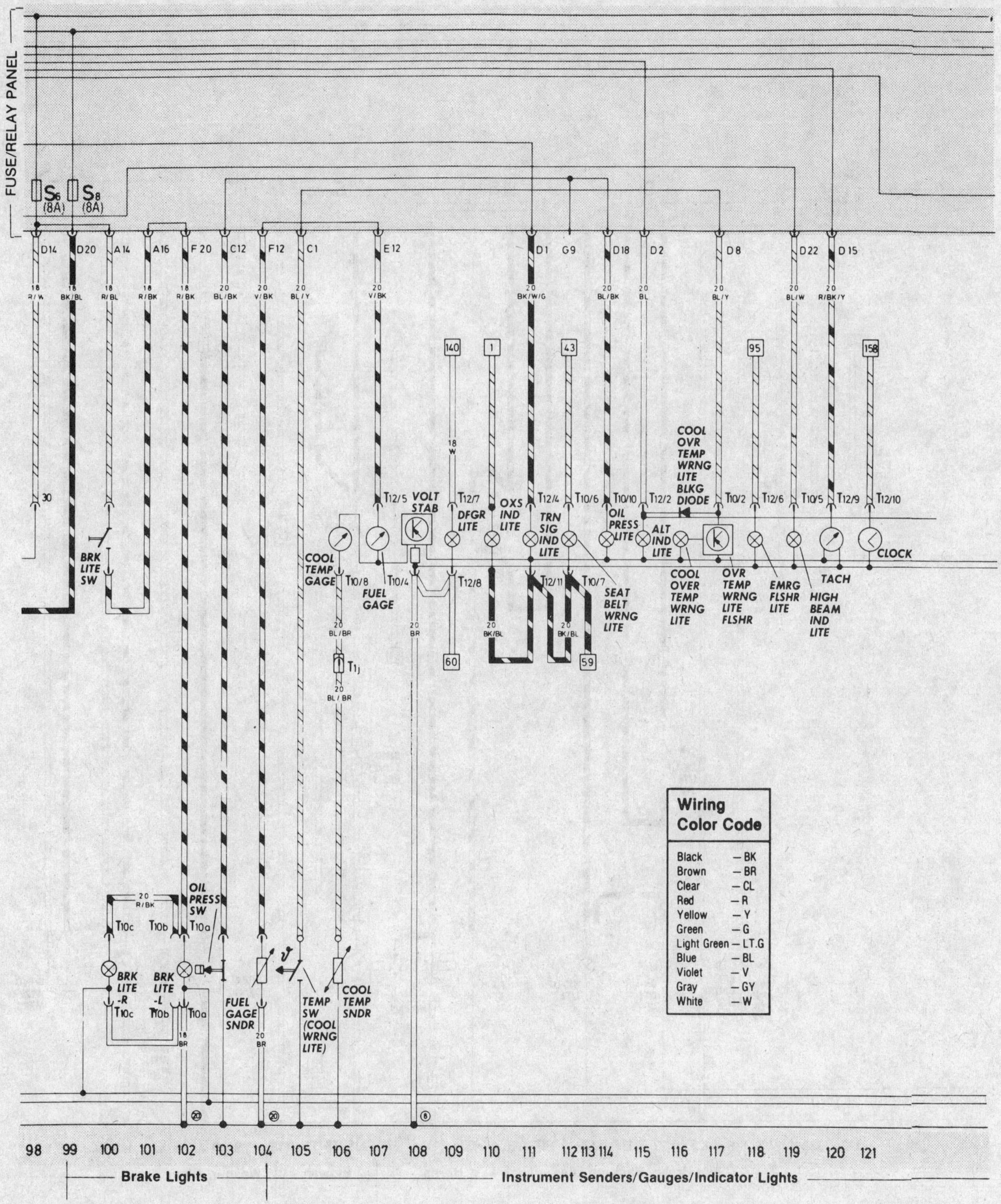

Description	Current Track	Description	Current Track	Description	Current Track
OXS voltage-supply relay	27-29	Radiator fan relay	39-40	Side-marker lights, front	75, 83
Parking-brake/brake-fluid warning light	124	Radiator thermo switch	39	Spark plugs	19-21
Parking-brake indicator light switch	125	Radio	157	Spark plug connectors	19-21
Parking light, left	76	Rear defogger	141	Starter	6-8
Parking light, right	82	Seat belt buckle, left	45	Starting enrichment relay	37-38
Radiator fan	41	Seat belt warning light	112	Tachometer	120
		Seat belt warning relay	43-47	Tail light, left	64, 65
				Tail light, right	66, 67

10

Fig. 10.42 Wiring diagram for 1981 North American five-cylinder models (continued)

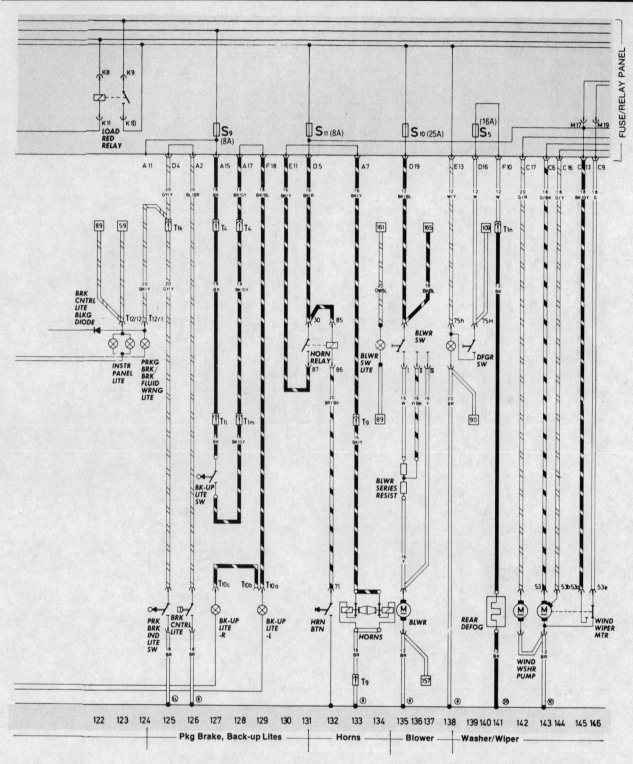

Description	Current Track	Description	Current Track	Description	Current Track
Temperature switch (for coolant warning light)	105	Turn-signal, right rear	69	Windshield-wiper intermittent switch	150-154
		Turn-signal switch	92-94	Windshield-wiper motor	143-146
Turn-signal/hazard flasher	95, 96	Voltage regulator	4	Windshield-wiper/washer intermittent relay	147-150
Turn-signal indicator light	111	Voltage stabilizer	108		
Turn-signal, left front	78	Voltmeter	164		
Turn-signal, left rear	79	Voltmeter light	161		
Turn-signal, right front	80	Windshield-washer pump	142		

Fig. 10.42 Wiring diagram for 1981 North American five-cylinder models (continued)

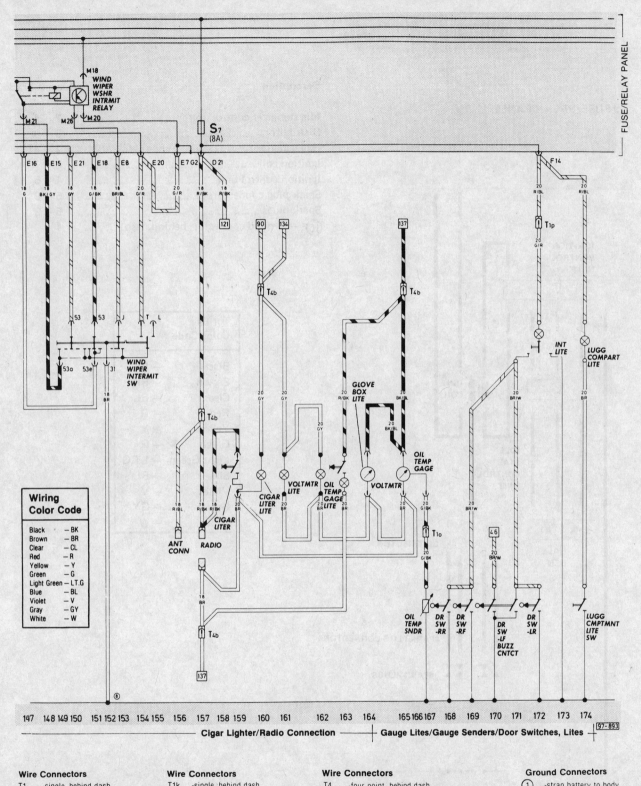

Fig. 10.42 Wiring diagram for 1981 North American five-cylinder models (continued)

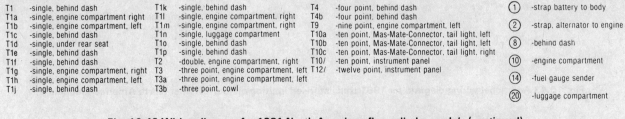

Wiring Color Code

Black	– BK
Brown	– BR
Clear	– CL
Red	– R
Yellow	– Y
Green	– G
Light Green	– LT.G
Blue	– BL
Violet	– V
Gray	– GY
White	– W

Cigar Lighter/Radio Connection — Gauge Lites/Gauge Senders/Door Switches, Lites

Wire Connectors

T1 -single, behind dash
T1a -single, engine compartment right
T1b -single, engine compartment, left
T1c -single, behind dash
T1d -single, under rear seat
T1e -single, behind dash
T1f -single, behind dash
T1g -single, engine compartment, right
T1h -single, engine compartment, left
T1j -single, behind dash

Wire Connectors

T1k -single, behind dash
T1l -single, engine compartment, right
T1m -single, engine compartment, right
T1n -single, luggage compartment
T1o -single, behind dash
T1p -single, behind dash
T2 -double, engine compartment, right
T3 -three point, engine compartment, left
T3a -three point, engine compartment, left
T3b -three point, cowl

Wire Connectors

T4 -four point, behind dash
T4b -four point, behind dash
T9 -nine point, engine compartment, left
T10a -ten point, Mas-Mate-Connector, tail light, left
T10b -ten point, Mas-Mate-Connector, tail light, left
T10c -ten point, Mas-Mate-Connector, tail light, right
T10/ -ten point, instrument panel
T12/ -twelve point, instrument panel

Ground Connectors

① -strap battery to body
② -strap, alternator to engine
⑧ -behind dash
⑩ -engine compartment
⑭ -fuel gauge sender
⑳ -luggage compartment

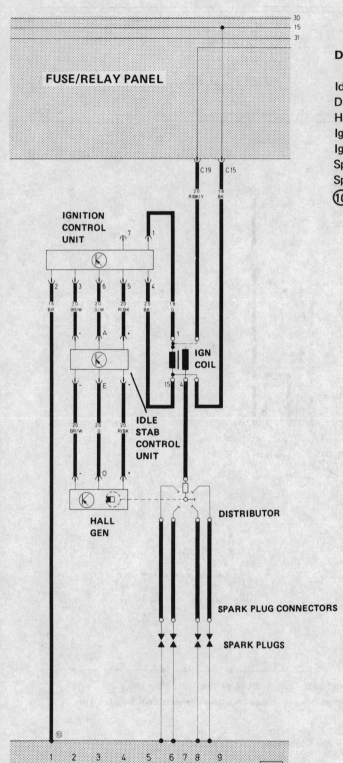

FUSE/RELAY PANEL

IGNITION CONTROL UNIT

IGN COIL

IDLE STAB CONTROL UNIT

HALL GEN

DISTRIBUTOR

SPARK PLUG CONNECTORS

SPARK PLUGS

Description	Current Track
Idle stabilizer control unit	2 — 4
Distributor	5 — 9
Hall generator	2 — 4
Ignition coil	6 — 7
Ignition control unit	1 — 5
Spark plug connectors	5 — 9
Spark plugs	5 — 9
⑩ — Ground connector, behind dash	1

Wiring Color Code

Black	— BK
Brown	— BR
Clear	— CL
Red	— R
Yellow	— Y
Green	— G
Light Green	— LT.G
Blue	— BL
Violet	— V
Gray	— GY
White	— W

Note: All wire sizes American Wire Gauge

Fig. 10.43 Additional wiring diagram for 1981 transistorised ignition on four-cylinder North American models

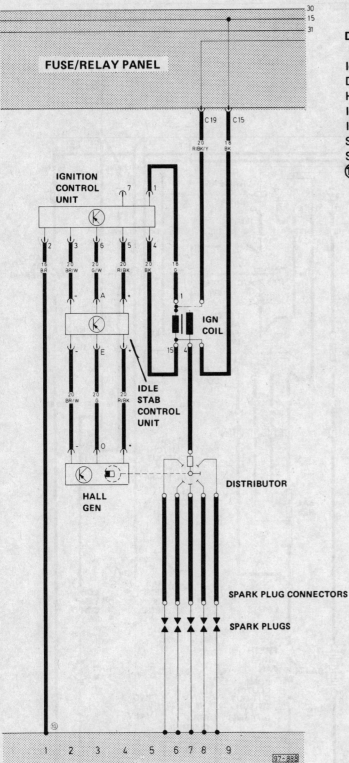

FUSE/RELAY PANEL

Description	Current Track
Idle stabilizer control unit	2 – 4
Distributor	5 – 9
Hall generator	2 – 4
Ignition coil	6 – 7
Ignition control unit	1 – 5
Spark plug connectors	5 – 9
Spark plugs	5 – 9
⑩ – Ground connector, behind dash	1

Wiring Color Code

Black	– BK
Brown	– BR
Clear	– CL
Red	– R
Yellow	– Y
Green	– G
Light Green	– LT.G
Blue	– BL
Violet	– V
Gray	– GY
White	– W

Note: All wire sizes American Wire Gauge

Fig. 10.44 Additional wiring diagram for 1981 transistorised ignition on five-cylinder North American models

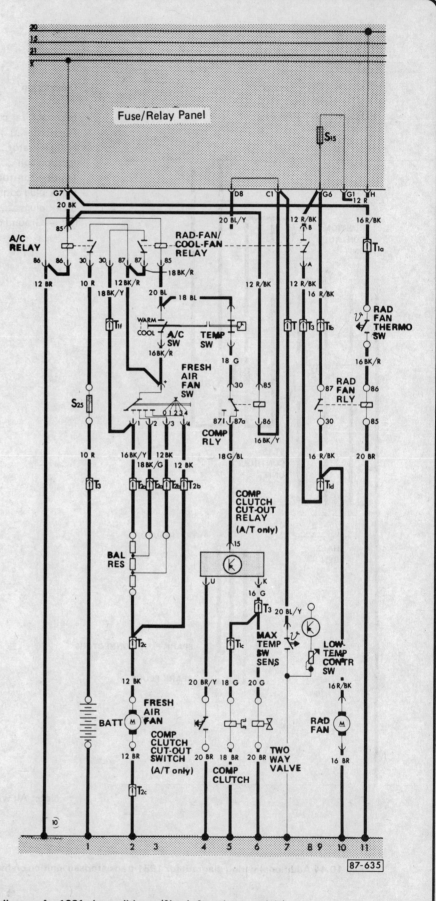

Wire Connectors

Single

T - on fuse/relay panel
T1a - on fuse/relay panel
T1b - behind dash
T1c - near compressor
T1d - in engine compartment
T1f - behind dash

Double

T2a - behind dash
T2b - behind dash
T2c - near fresh air fan

3-point

T3 - behind dash

Ground Connections

⑩ - ground strap, near fuse/relay panel

Fig. 10.45 Wiring diagram for 1981 air conditioner (North American models)

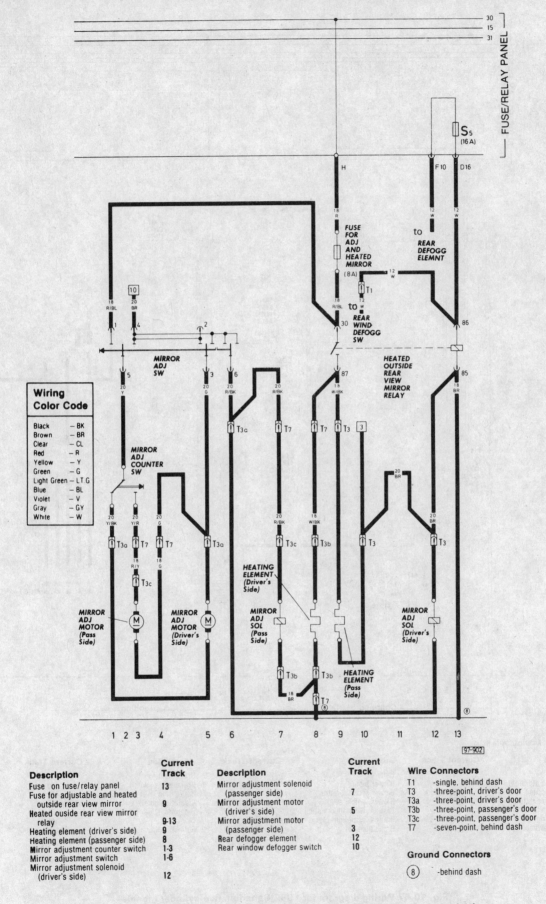

Description	Current Track	Description	Current Track
Fuse on fuse/relay panel	13	Mirror adjustment solenoid (passenger side)	7
Fuse for adjustable and heated outside rear view mirror	9	Mirror adjustment motor (driver's side)	5
Heated ouside rear view mirror relay	9-13	Mirror adjustment motor (passenger side)	3
Heating element (driver's side)	9	Rear defogger element	12
Heating element (passenger side)	8	Rear window defogger switch	10
Mirror adjustment counter switch	1-3		
Mirror adjustment switch	1-6		
Mirror adjustment solenoid (driver's side)	12		

Wire Connectors

T1	-single, behind dash
T3	-three-point, driver's door
T3a	-three-point, driver's door
T3b	-three-point, passenger's door
T3c	-three-point, passenger's door
T7	-seven-point, behind dash

Ground Connectors

(8) -behind dash

10

Fig. 10.46 Wiring diagram for electric exterior mirror (North American models)

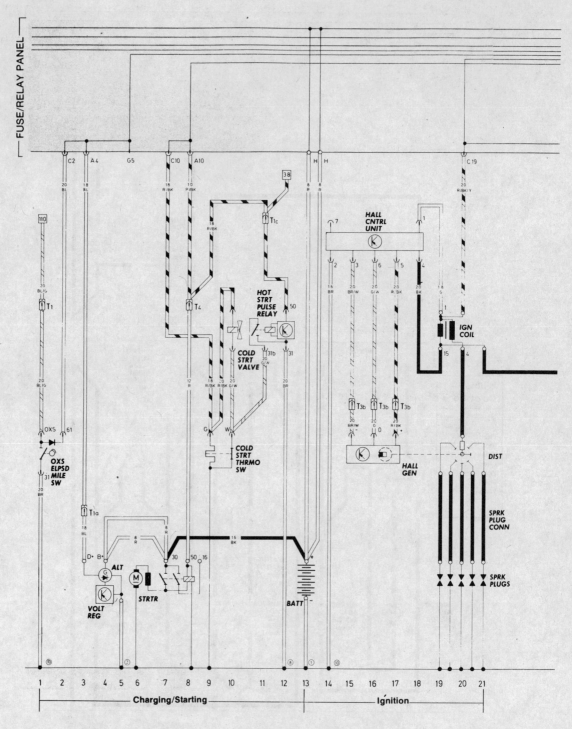

All wire sizes American Wire Gauge

Description	Current Track	Description	Current Track	Description	Current Track
Alternator	4	Battery	13	Brake light, right	100
Alternator indicator light	116	Blower motor	140	Brake lights switch	100
Antenna connection	162	Blower series resistor	140	Brake fluid level warning light	131
Auxiliary air regulator	23	Blower switch	140-142	Cigarette lighter	165
Backup light, left	134	Blower-switch illumination light	139	Cigarette lighter light	166
Backup light, right	132	Brake control-light blocking diode	127	Clock	126
Backup light switch	132	Brake light, left	102	Cold-start thermoswitch	9,10

Fig. 10.47 Wiring diagram for 1982 Canadian five-cylinder models

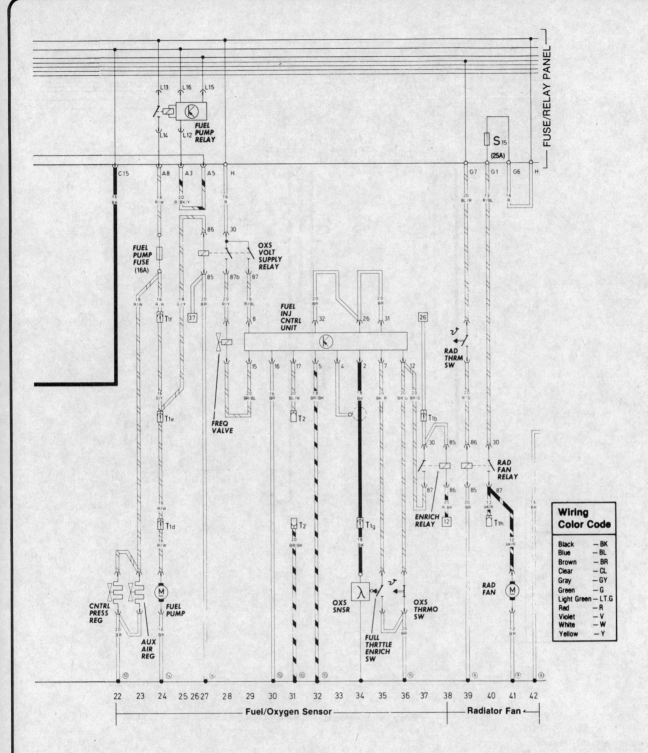

Wiring Color Code	
Black	— BK
Blue	— BL
Brown	— BR
Clear	— CL
Gray	— GY
Green	— G
Light Green	— LT.G
Red	— R
Violet	— V
White	— W
Yellow	— Y

Fuel/Oxygen Sensor — current tracks 22 through 38

Radiator Fan — current tracks 39 through 42

Description	Current Track	Description	Current Track	Description	Current Track
Cold-start valve	10	Coolant over-temperature warning light blocking diode	120	Distributor	19-21
Control-pressure regulator	22			Door switch, left front, with buzzer contact	175,176
Coolant over-temperature warning flasher	121	Coolant-temperature warning light switch	105	Door switch, left rear	177
Coolant over-temperature warning light	120	Coolant-temperature gauge	106	Door switch, right front	174
		Coolant-temperature sender	106	Door switch, right rear	173

10

Fig. 10.47 Wiring diagram for 1982 Canadian five-cylinder models (continued)

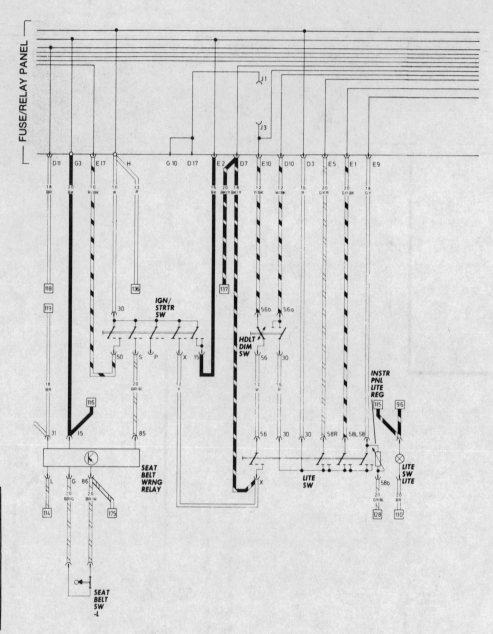

Wiring Color Code

Black	— BK
Blue	— BL
Brown	— BR
Clear	— CL
Gray	— GY
Green	— G
Light Green	— LT.G
Red	— R
Violet	— V
White	— W
Yellow	— Y

43 44 45 46 47 48 49 50 51 52 53 54 55 56 57 58 59 60

Safety Belt Warning/Igniton Switch/Light Switch

All wire sizes American Wire Gauge

Description	Current Track	Description	Current Track	Description	Current Track
Emergency-flasher light	122	Fuel-injection control unit	29-36	Hall control unit	14-18
Emergency-flasher switch	91-97	Fuel pump	24	Hall generator	15-17
Emergency-flasher switch light	89	Fuel-pump fuse	24	Headlight dimmer switch	53,54
Enrichment relay	37,38	Fuel-pump relay	24-27	Headlight high beam, left	73
Frequency valve	28	Full throttle enrichment switch	35	Headlight high beam, right	84
Fuel gauge	107	Fuses (S1-S15) in fuse/relay panel	-	Headlight, left	70-72
Fuel gauge sender	104	Glove-compartment light	169	Headlight, right	86-88
				High-beam indicator light	123

Fig. 10.47 Wiring diagram for 1982 Canadian five-cylinder models (continued)

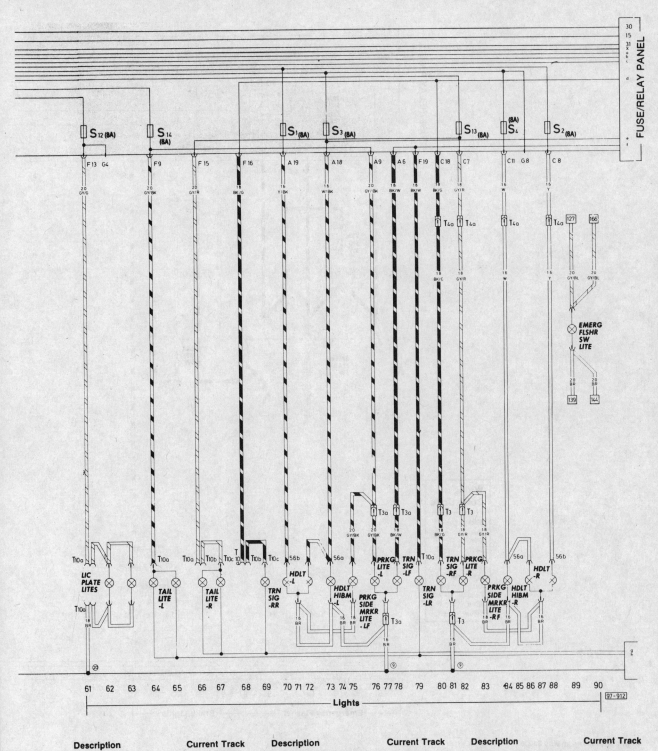

Description	Current Track	Description	Current Track	Description	Current Track
Horns	138,139	Instrument-panel-light regulator	59	Luggage-compartment light switch	179
Horn button	137	Interior ight	177	Oil-pressure light	117
Horn relay	136,137	License-plate light	62,63	Oil-pressure light control unit	116-119
Hot-start pulse relay	11,12	Light switch	53-58	Oil-pressure sender	166
Ignition coil	19-20	Light switch light	60	Oil-pressure switch	103
Ignition/starter switch	46-50	Load-reduction relay	127,128	Oil-temperature gauge	171
Instrument-panel lights	128	Luggage-compartment light	179		

Fig. 10.47 Wiring diagram for 1982 Canadian five-cylinder models (continued)

10

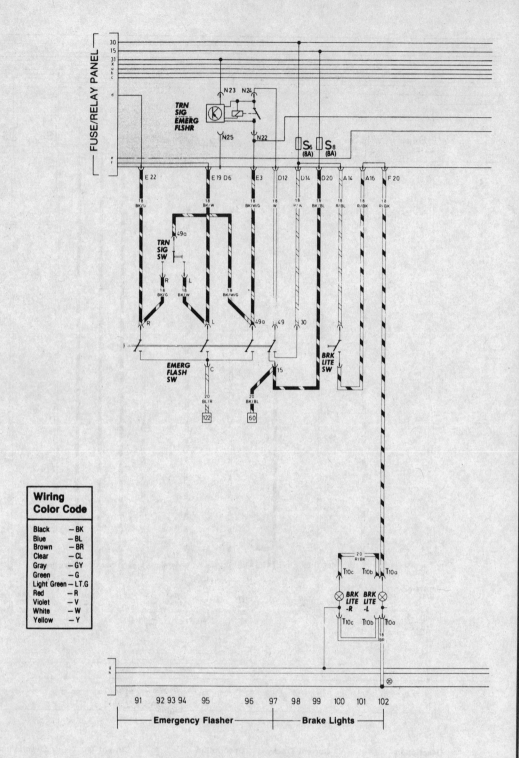

Description	Current Track	Description	Current Track	Description	Current Track
Oil-temperature gauge light	168	Parking brake/brake fluid warning		Radiator-fan relay	39-40
Oil-temperature sender	172	light	129	Radiator-fan	41
OXS elapsed mileage switch	1,2	Parking-brake indicator switch	130	Radiator thermoswitch	39
OXS indicator light	110	Parking light, left	76	Radio connection	163
OXS sensor	34	Parking light, right	82	Radio light	159
OXS thermoswitch	36	Parking side-marker lights, front	75,83	Rear defogger light	109
OXS voltage-supply relay	27-29				

Fig. 10.47 Wiring diagram for 1982 Canadian five-cylinder models (continued)

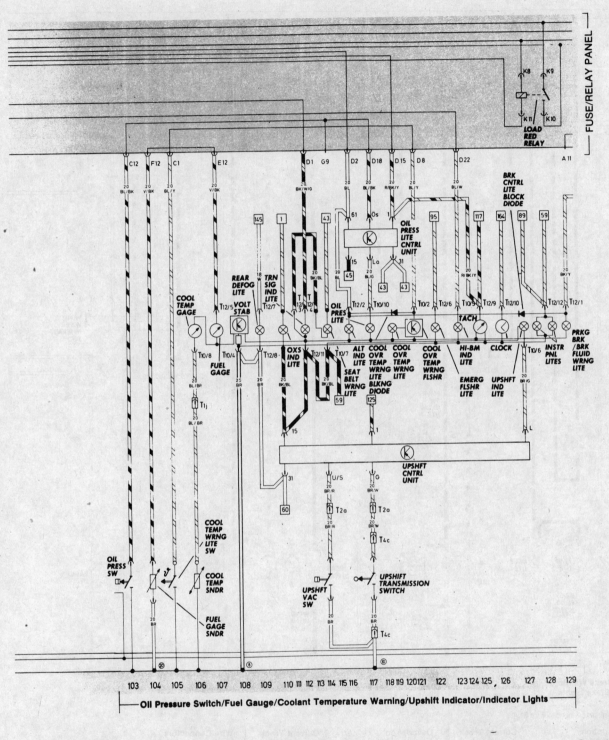

Fig. 10.47 Wiring diagram for 1982 Canadian five-cylinder models (continued)

Oil Pressure Switch/Fuel Gauge/Coolant Temperature Warning/Upshift Indicator/Indicator Lights

Description	Current Track	Description	Current Track	Description	Current Track
Rear defogger	146	Spark-plug connector	19-21	Turn-signal indicator light	112
Rear defogger switch	143,144	Starter	6-8	Turn signal, left front	78
Safety-belt switch, left	45	Tachometer	125	Turn signal, left rear	79
Safety-belt warning light	114	Tail light, left	64,65	Turn signal, right front	80
Safety-belt warning relay	43-47	Tail light, right	66,67	Turn signal, right rear	69
Spark-plugs	19-21	Turn-signal/ emergency flasher	95,96	Turn signal switch	92-94

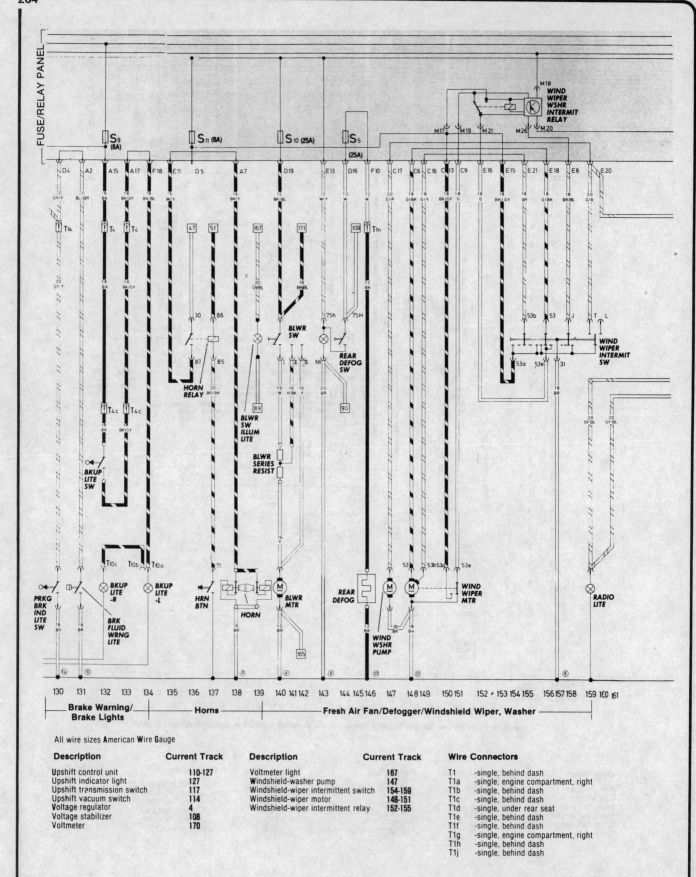

Fig. 10.47 Wiring diagram for 1982 Canadian five-cylinder models (continued)

All wire sizes American Wire Gauge

Description	Current Track	Description	Current Track	Wire Connectors	
Upshift control unit	110-127	Voltmeter light	167	T1	-single, behind dash
Upshift indicator light	127	Windshield-washer pump	147	T1a	-single, engine compartment, right
Upshift transmission switch	117	Windshield-wiper intermittent switch	154-159	T1b	-single, behind dash
Upshift vacuum switch	114	Windshield-wiper motor	148-151	T1c	-single, behind dash
Voltage regulator	4	Windshield-wiper intermittent relay	152-155	T1d	-single, under rear seat
Voltage stabilizer	108			T1e	-single, behind dash
Voltmeter	170			T1f	-single, behind dash
				T1g	-single, engine compartment, right
				T1h	-single, behind dash
				T1j	-single, behind dash

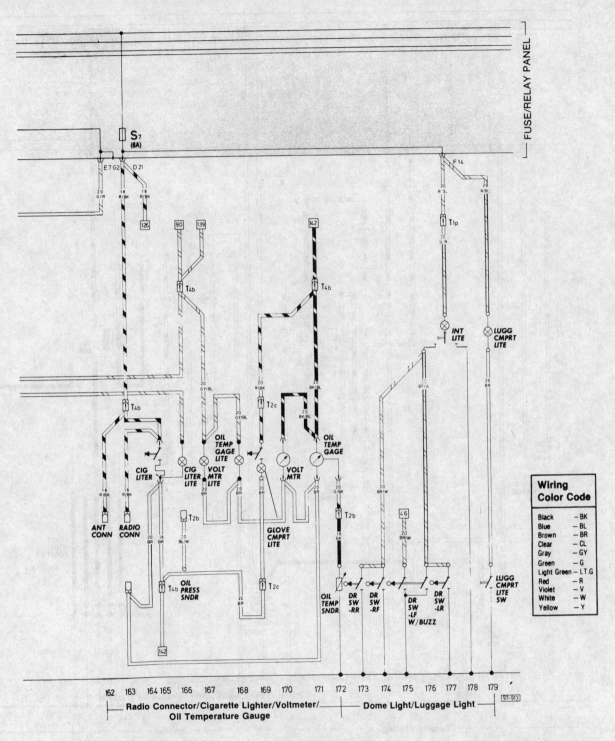

Fig. 10.47 Wiring diagram for 1982 Canadian five-cylinder models (continued)

Wiring Color Code

Black	– BK
Blue	– BL
Brown	– BR
Clear	– CL
Gray	– GY
Green	– G
Light Green	– LT.G
Red	– R
Violet	– V
White	– W
Yellow	– Y

Radio Connector/Cigarette Lighter/Voltmeter/Oil Temperature Gauge — Dome Light/Luggage Light

Wire Connectors

T1k -single, behind dash
T1n -single, luggage compartment
T1p -single, behind dash
T2 -double, engine compartment, right
T2a -double, behind dash
T2b -double, behind dash
T2c -double, behind dash
T3 -three-point, engine compartment, right
T3a -three-point, engine compartment, left
T3b -three-point, cowl

Wire Connectors

T4 -four-point, behind dash
T4a -four-point, behind dash
T4b -four-point, behind dash
T4c -four-point, engine compartment, right
T10a -ten-point, Mas-Mate, tail light, left
T10b -ten-point, Mas-Mate, tail light, left
T10c -ten-point, Mas-Mate, tail light, right
T10/ -ten-point, instrument panel
T12/ -twelve point, instrument panel

Ground Connectors

① -strap, battery to body
② -strap, alternator to engine
⑧ -behind dash
⑨ -engine compartment, left
⑩ -engine compartment, right
⑭ -fuel gauge sender
⑳ -luggage compartment

10

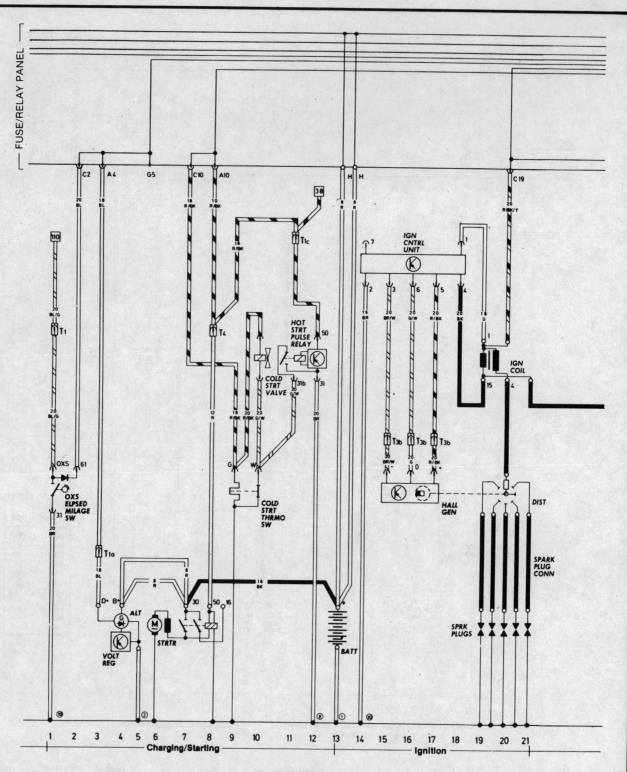

Note: All wire sizes American Wire Gauge

Description	Current Track	Description	Current Track	Description	Current Track
Alternator	4	Blower motor	140	Brake light, left	102
Alternator indicator light	116	Blower series resistor	140	Brake light, right	100
Antenna connection	177	Blower switch	140-142	Brake light switch	100
Auxiliary air regulator	23	Blower switch illumination		Cigarette lighter	176
Back-up light, left	134	light	139	Cigarette lighter illumination	
Back-up light, right	132	Brake control light blocking		light	175
Back-up light switch	132	diode	127	Clock	126
Battery	13	Brake fluid level warning		Cold-start thermoswitch	9-10
		light	131		

Fig. 10.48 Wiring diagram for 1982 Audi 4000 Coupe (North American models)

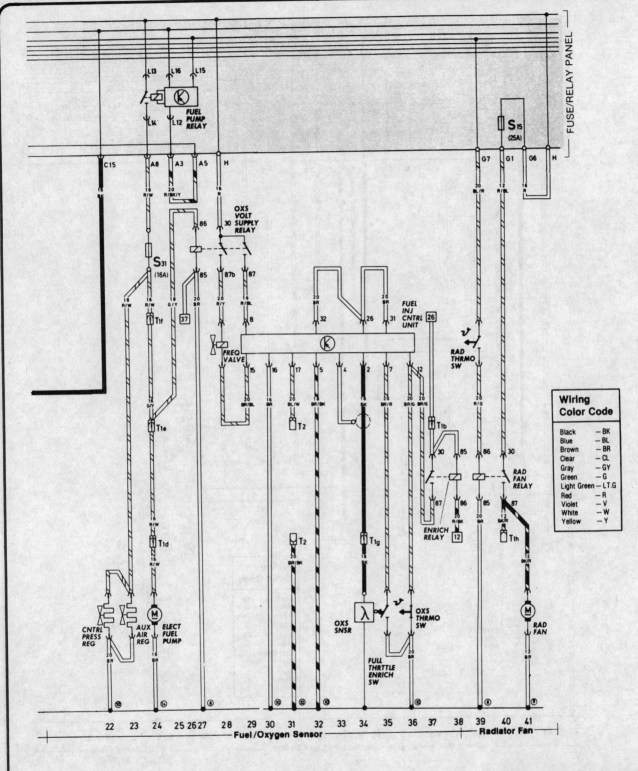

Description	Current Track	Description	Current Track	Description	Current Track
Cold start valve	10	Coolant over-temperature warning light blocking diode	119	Door switch, left rear	183
Control pressure regulator	22			Door switch, right front	180
Control unit for oil pressure warning light	116-119	Coolant over-temperature warning light flasher	121	Door switch, right rear	179
Coolant temperature gauge	106	Coolant warning light temperature switch	105	Electric fuel pump	24
Coolant temperature sender unit	106	Distributor	19-21	Emergency flasher light	122
		Door switch left front, with buzzer contact	181, 182	Emergency flasher switch	91-97
Coolant over-temperature warning light	119			Emergency flasher switch illumination light	89

Fig. 10.48 Wiring diagram for 1982 Audi 4000 Coupe (North American models) (continued)

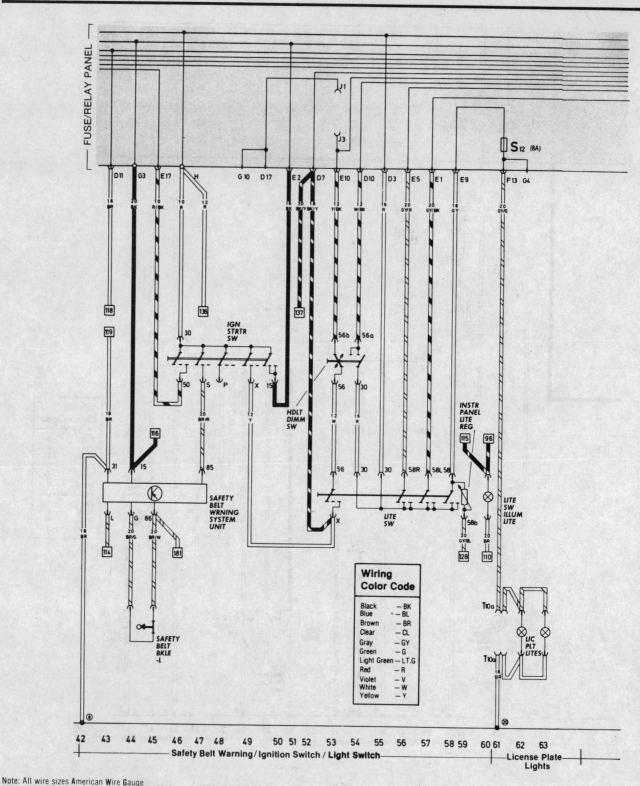

Note: All wire sizes American Wire Gauge

Description	Current Track	Description	Current Track	Description	Current Track
Enrichment relay	37, 38	Fuse for electric fuel pump		Headlight, high beam, right	84
Frequency valve	28	(S31)	24	Headlight, left	70, 72
Fuel gauge	107	Fuses (S1-S15) in fuse/relay		Headlight, right	86, 88
Fuel gauge sender unit	104	panel		High beam indicator light	123
Fuel injection control unit	29-36	Glove compartment light	167	Horn Button	137
Fuel pump relay	24-27	Hall generator	15-17	Horn relay	136, 137
Full-throttle enrichment		Headlight dimmer switch	53-54	Horns	138, 139
switch	35	Headlight, high beam, left	73	Hot-start pulse relay	11-12

Fig. 10.48 Wiring diagram for 1982 Audi 4000 Coupe (North American models) (continued)

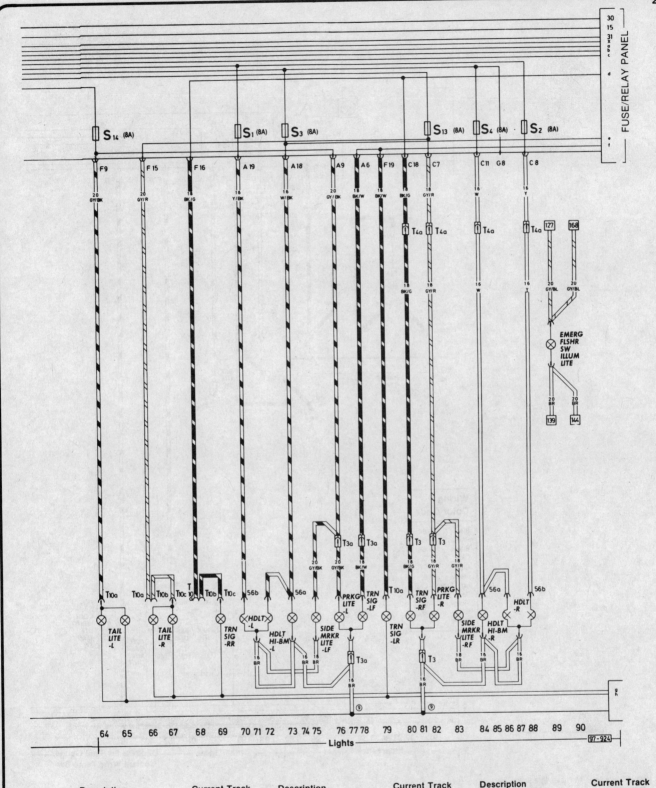

Description	Current Track	Description	Current Track	Description	Current Track
Ignition coil	19	Light switch illumination light	60	Oil pressure light	117
Ignition control unit	14-18			Oil pressure sender unit	166
Ignition/starter switch	46-50	Load reduction relay	127-128	Oil pressure switch	103
Instrument panel light	128	Luggage compartment light	185	Oil temperature gauge	161
Instrument panel light regulator	59	Luggage-compartment light switch	185	Oil temperature gauge illumination light	170
Interior light	183	Oil pressure gauge	165	Oil temperature sender unit	160
License plate lights	62, 63	Oil pressure gauge illumination light	172	OXS elapsed mileage switch	1, 2
Light switch	53-58				

10

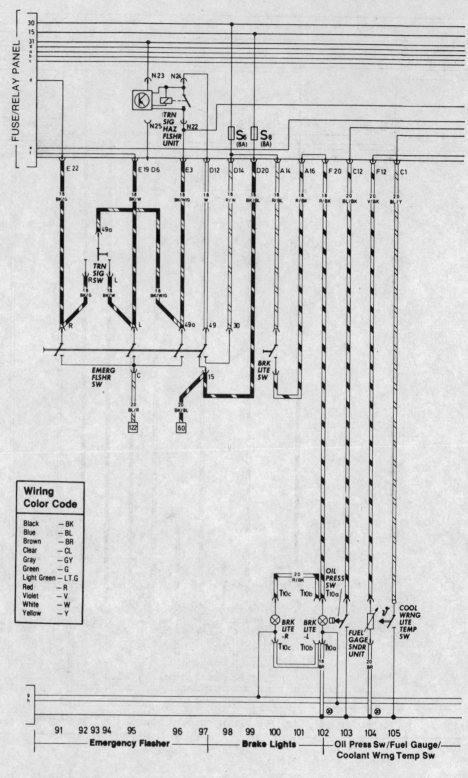

Fig. 10.48 Wiring diagram for 1982 Audi 4000 Coupe (North American models) (continued)

Note: All wire sizes American Wire Gauge

Description	Current Track	Description	Current Track	Description	Current Track
OXS indicator light	110	Parking light, left	76	Rear defogger light	109
OXS-sensor	34	Parking light, right	82	Rear defogger switch	143, 144
OXS-thermoswitch	36	Radiator fan	41	Safety-belt buckle, left	45
OXS voltage supply relay	27-29	Radiator fan relay	39, 40	Safety-belt warning	
Parking brake/brake		Radiator thermoswitch	39	system light	114
fluid warning light	129	Radio	177, 178	Safety-belt warning	
Parking brake indicator		Radio illumination light	173	system unit	43-47
light switch	130	Rear defogger element	146	Shift control indicator light	127

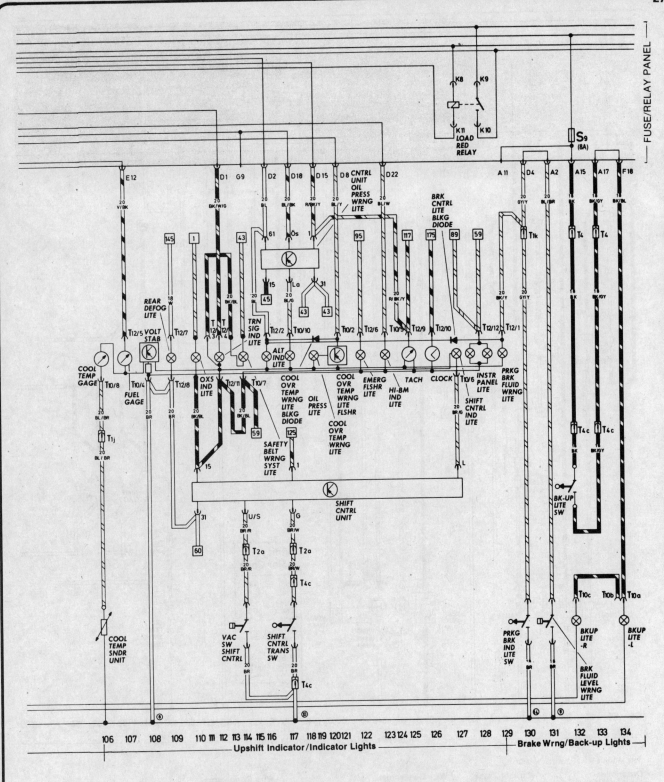

Fig. 10.48 Wiring diagram for 1982 Audi 4000 Coupe (North American models) (continued)

Description	Current Track	Description	Current Track	Description	Current Track
Shift control transmission switch	117	Tail light, left	64, 65	Turn signal, right rear	69
Shift control unit	110-127	Tail light, right	66, 67	Turn signal switch	92-94
Side marker lights, front	75-83	Turn-signal emergency flasher unit	95, 96	Vacuum switch for shift control	114
Spark plug connectors	19-21	Turn signal indicator light	112	Voltage stabilizer	108
Spark plugs	19-21	Turn signal, left front	78	Voltage regulator	4
Starter	6-8	Turn signal, left rear	79	Voltmeter	163
Tachometer	125	Turn signal, right front	80		

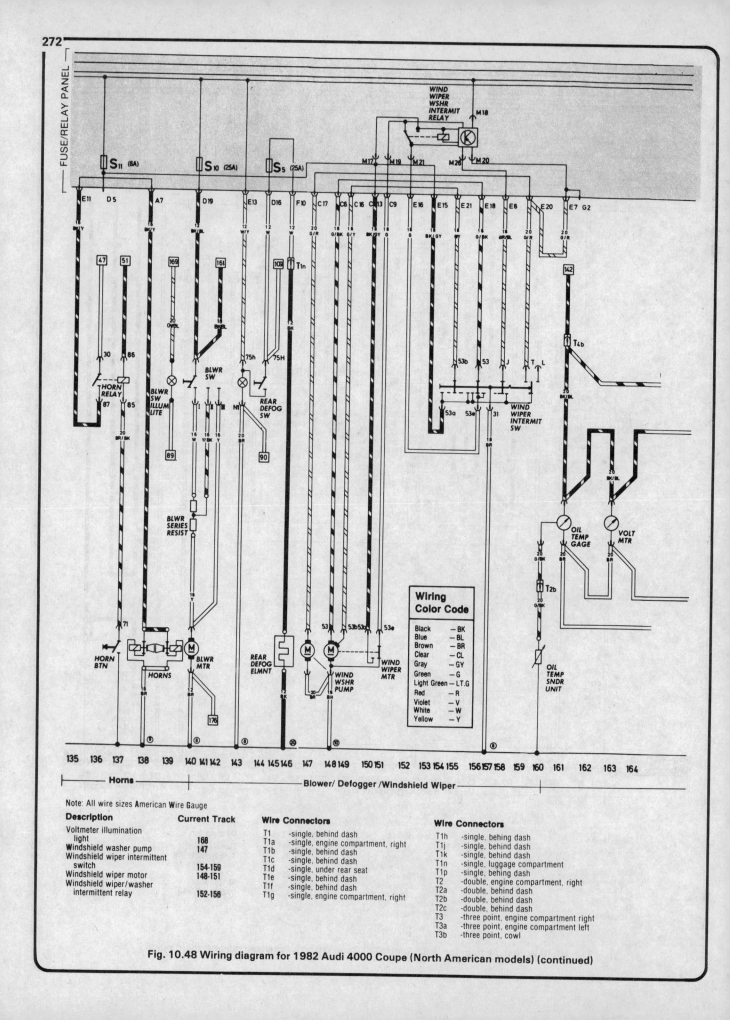

Fig. 10.48 Wiring diagram for 1982 Audi 4000 Coupe (North American models) (continued)

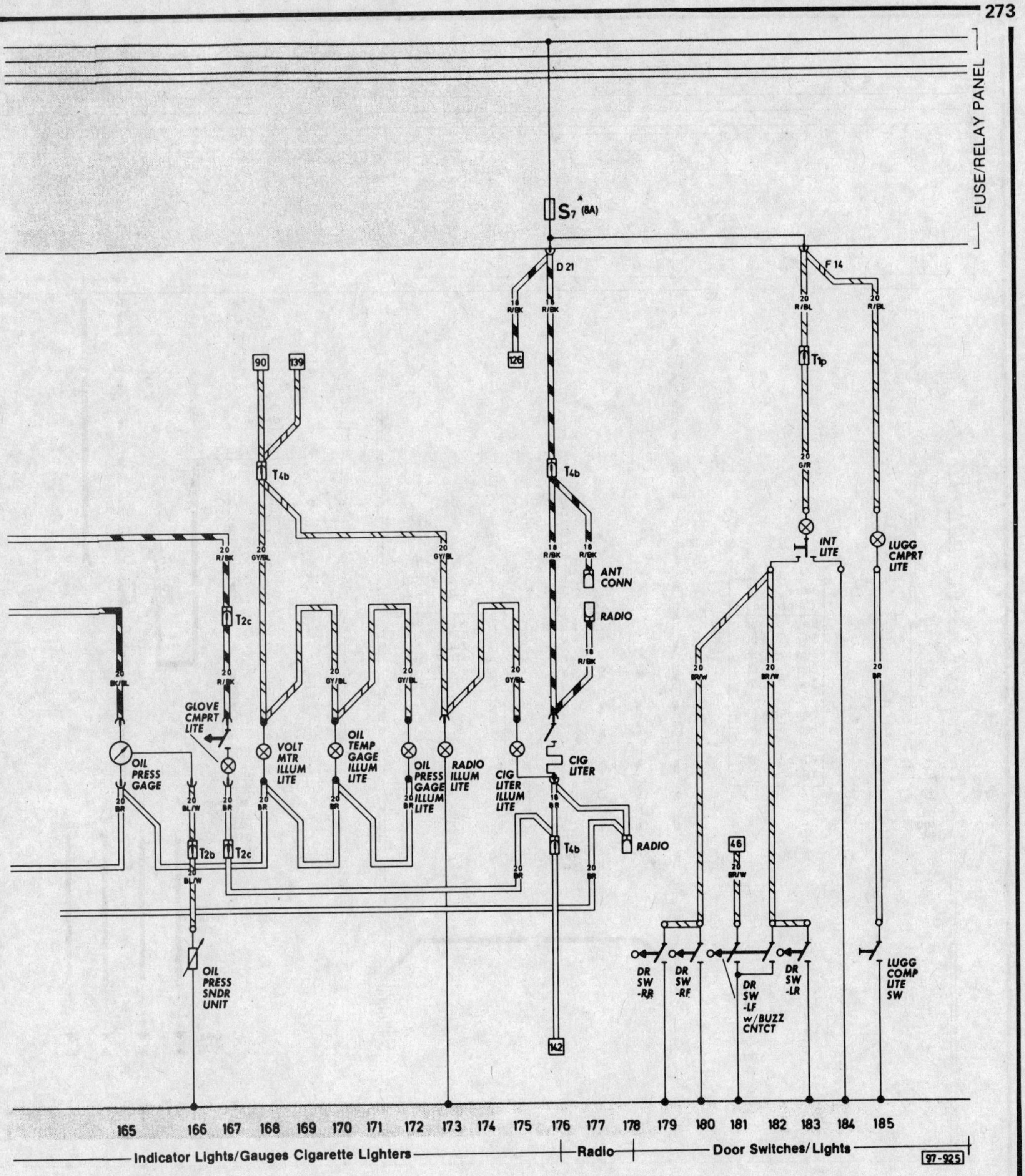

Fig. 10.48 Wiring diagram for 1982 Audi 4000 Coupe (North American models) (continued)

165 166 167 168 169 170 171 172 173 174 175 176 177 178 179 180 181 182 183 184 185

Indicator Lights/Gauges Cigarette Lighters — Radio — Door Switches/Lights

Wire Connectors

T4 -four point, behind dash
T4a -four point, behind dash
T4b -four point, behind dash
T4c -four point, engine compartment, right
T10a -ten point, Mas-Mate-connector, tail light, left
T10b -ten point, Mas-Mate-connector, tail light, left
T10c -ten point, Mas-Mate-connector, tail light, right
T10/ -ten point, instrument panel
T12/ -twelve point, instrument panel

Ground Connectors

1 -strap, battery to body
2 -strap, alternator to engine
8 -behind dash
9 -engine compartment, left

Ground Connectors

10 -engine compartment, right
14 -fuel gauge sender unit
20 -luggage compartment

10

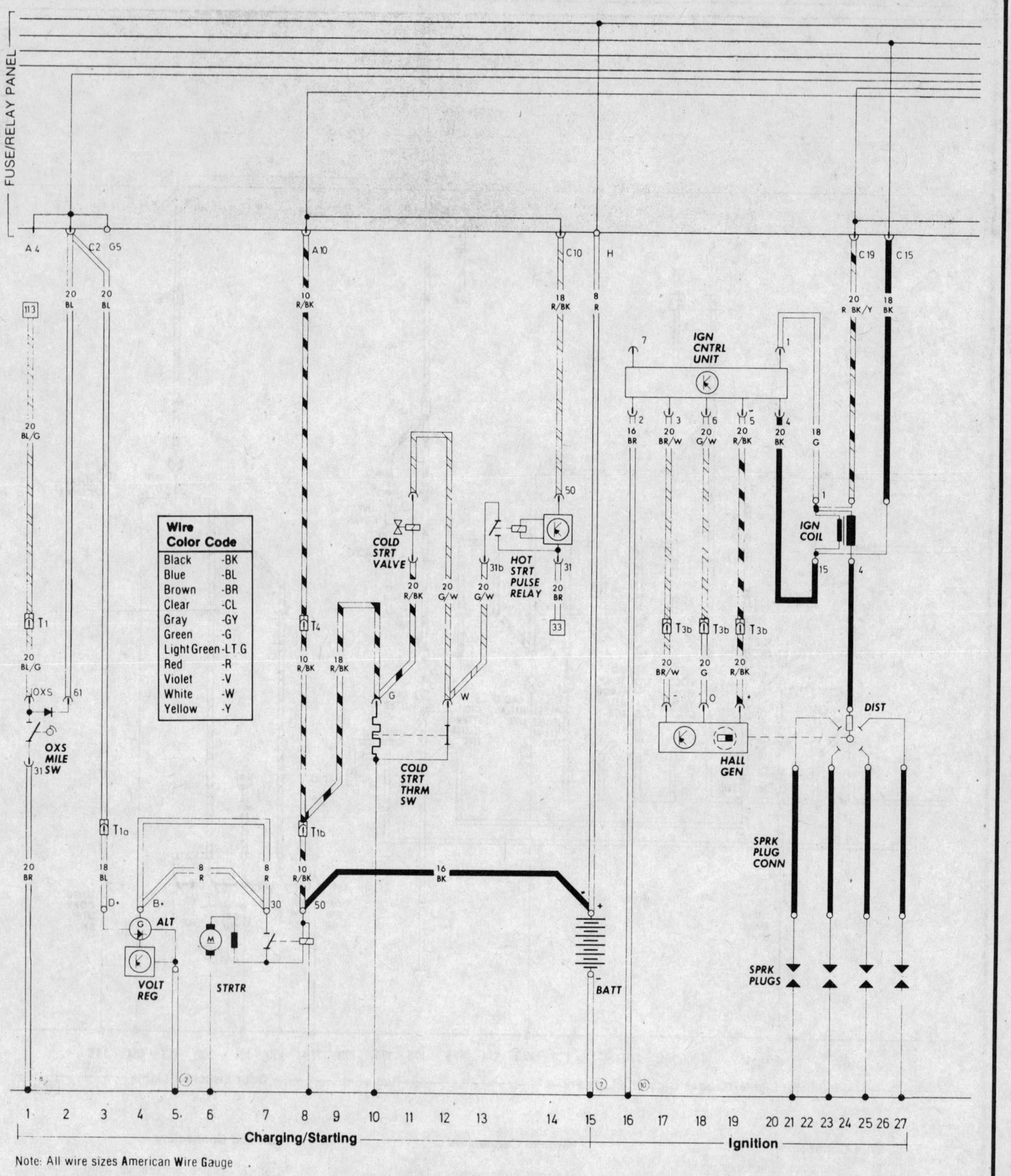

Wire Color Code

Black	-BK
Blue	-BL
Brown	-BR
Clear	-CL
Gray	-GY
Green	-G
Light Green	-LT.G
Red	-R
Violet	-V
White	-W
Yellow	-Y

Charging/Starting   Ignition

Note: All wire sizes American Wire Gauge

Description	Current Track	Description	Current Track	Description	Current Track
Alternator	4	Back-up light, right	136	Blower switch	145-147
Alternator indicator light	121	Back-up light switch	136	Blower switch illumination light	143
Antenna connection	180	Battery	45	Brake fluid level warning light	135
Auxiliary air regulator	29	Blower motor	145	Brake light, left	105
Back-up light, left	138	Blower series resistor	145	Brake light, right	103
				Brake light switch	103

Fig. 10.49 Wiring diagram for 1982 North American four-cylinder models

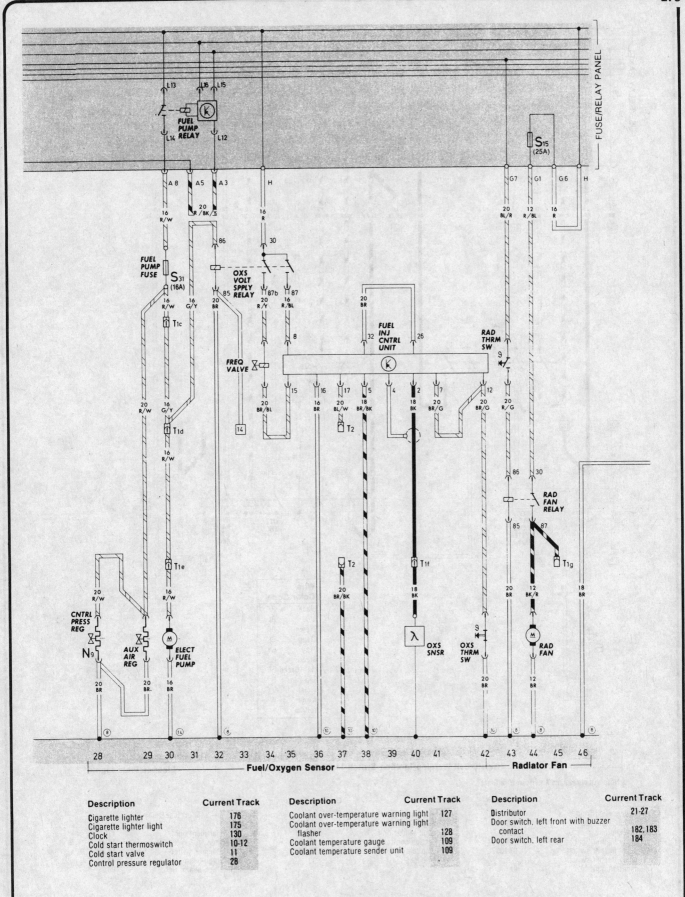

Fig. 10.49 Wiring diagram for 1982 North American four-cylinder models (continued)

Description	Current Track	Description	Current Track	Description	Current Track
Cigarette lighter	176	Coolant over-temperature warning light	127	Distributor	21-27
Cigarette lighter light	175	Coolant over-temperature warning light flasher	128	Door switch, left front with buzzer contact	182, 183
Clock	130			Door switch, left rear	184
Cold start thermoswitch	10-12	Coolant temperature gauge	109		
Cold start valve	11	Coolant temperature sender unit	109		
Control pressure regulator	28				

10

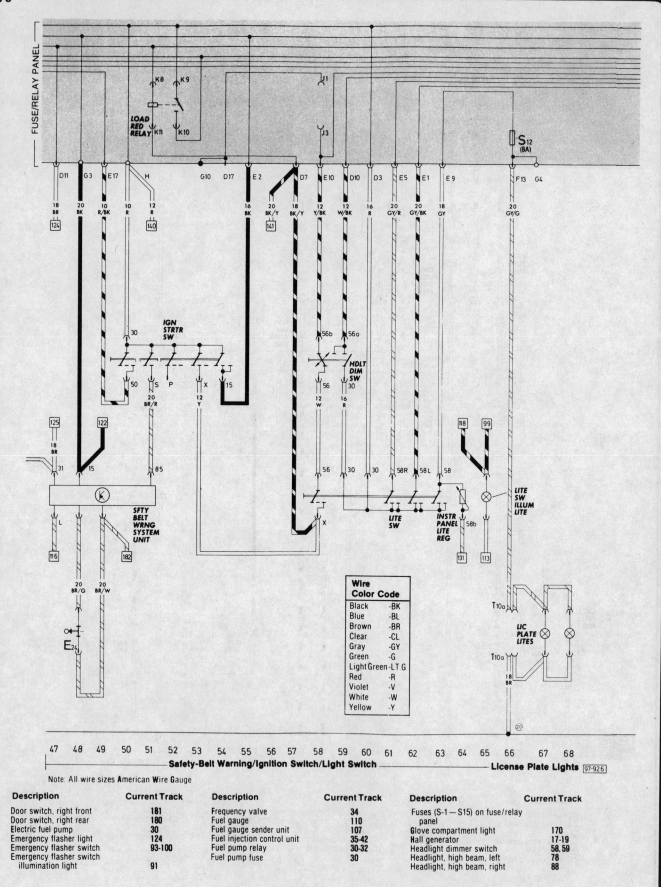

───── Safety-Belt Warning/Ignition Switch/Light Switch ───── ── License Plate Lights ── 97-926

Note: All wire sizes American Wire Gauge

Description	Current Track	Description	Current Track	Description	Current Track
Door switch, right front	181	Frequency valve	34	Fuses (S-1 — S15) on fuse/relay	
Door switch, right rear	180	Fuel gauge	110	panel	
Electric fuel pump	30	Fuel gauge sender unit	107	Glove compartment light	170
Emergency flasher light	124	Fuel injection control unit	35-42	Hall generator	17-19
Emergency flasher switch	93-100	Fuel pump relay	30-32	Headlight dimmer switch	58.59
Emergency flasher switch		Fuel pump fuse	30	Headlight, high beam, left	78
illumination light	91			Headlight, high beam, right	88

Fig. 10.49 Wiring diagram for 1982 North American four-cylinder models (continued)

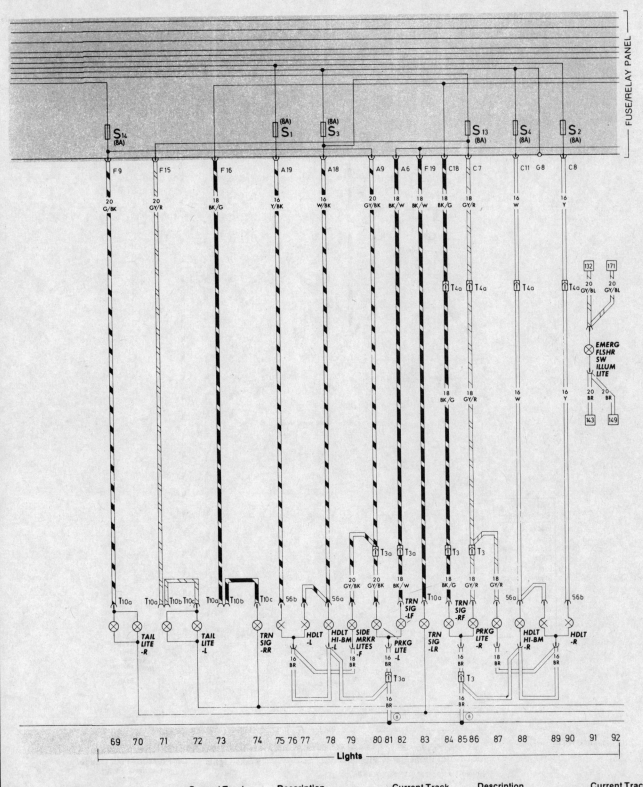

Fig. 10.49 Wiring diagram for 1982 North American four-cylinder models (continued)

Description	Current Track	Description	Current Track	Description	Current Track
Headlight, left	76	Horn relay	140, 141	Interior light	184
Headlight, right	89	Ignition coil	24	License plate lights	67, 68
High beam indicator light	129	Ignition control unit	16-21	Light switch	58-63
Hot start pulse relay	13, 14	Ignition/starter switch	50-54	Light switch illumination light	65
Horns	142-144	Instrument panel light	131, 132	Load reduction relay	51, 52
Horn button	141	Instrument panel light regulator	64	Luggage compartment light	186

10

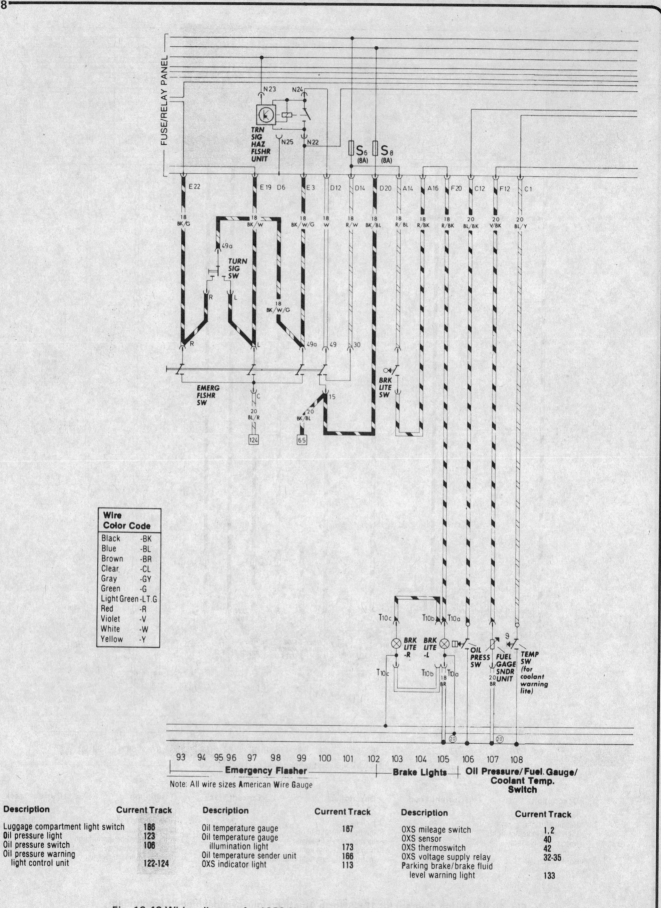

Fig. 10.49 Wiring diagram for 1982 North American four-cylinder models (continued)

Wire Color Code

Black	-BK
Blue	-BL
Brown	-BR
Clear	-CL
Gray	-GY
Green	-G
Light Green	-LT.G
Red	-R
Violet	-V
White	-W
Yellow	-Y

Note: All wire sizes American Wire Gauge

Description	Current Track	Description	Current Track	Description	Current Track
Luggage compartment light switch	166	Oil temperature gauge	167	OXS mileage switch	1,2
Oil pressure light	123	Oil temperature gauge illumination light	173	OXS sensor	40
Oil pressure switch	106			OXS thermoswitch	42
Oil pressure warning light control unit	122-124	Oil temperature sender unit	166	OXS voltage supply relay	32-35
		OXS indicator light	113	Parking brake/brake fluid level warning light	133

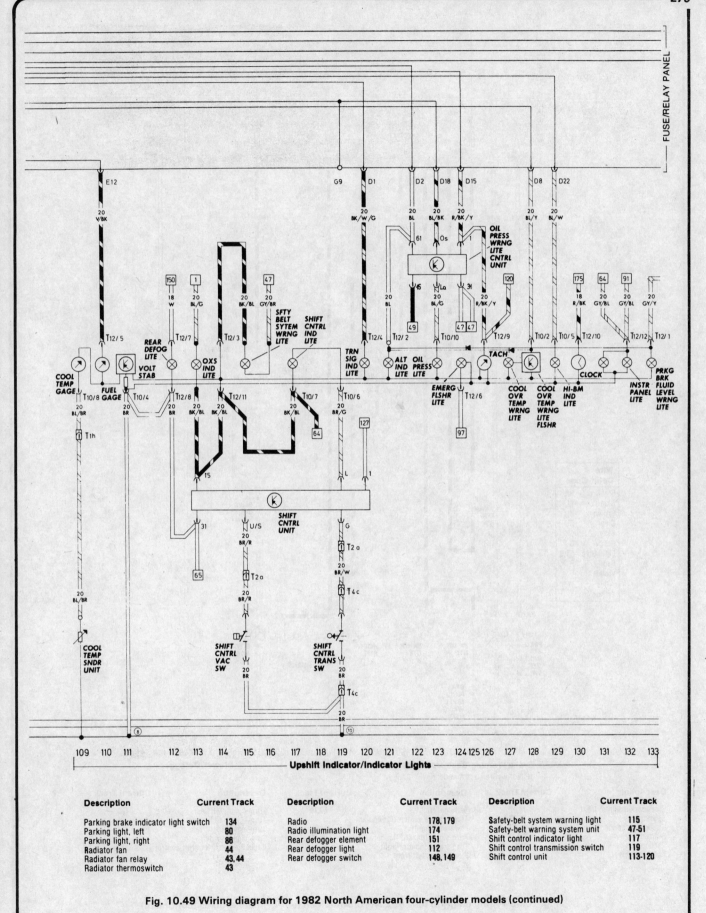

Fig. 10.49 Wiring diagram for 1982 North American four-cylinder models (continued)

Description	Current Track	Description	Current Track	Description	Current Track
Parking brake indicator light switch	134	Radio	178, 179	Safety-belt system warning light	115
Parking light, left	80	Radio illumination light	174	Safety-belt warning system unit	47-51
Parking light, right	86	Rear defogger element	151	Shift control indicator light	117
Radiator fan	44	Rear defogger light	112	Shift control transmission switch	119
Radiator fan relay	43, 44	Rear defogger switch	148, 149	Shift control unit	113-120
Radiator thermoswitch	43				

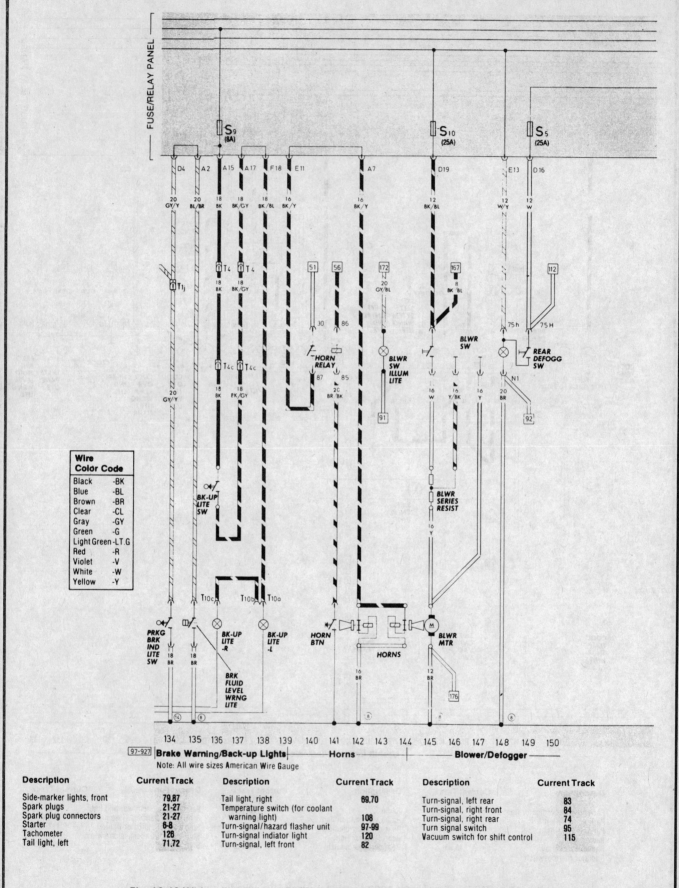

Fig. 10.49 Wiring diagram for 1982 North American four-cylinder models (continued)

Description	Current Track	Description	Current Track	Description	Current Track
Side-marker lights, front	79,87	Tail light, right	69,70	Turn-signal, left rear	83
Spark plugs	21-27	Temperature switch (for coolant warning light)	108	Turn-signal, right front	84
Spark plug connectors	21-27			Turn-signal, right rear	74
Starter	6-8	Turn-signal/hazard flasher unit	97-99	Turn signal switch	95
Tachometer	126	Turn-signal indiator light	120	Vacuum switch for shift control	115
Tail light, left	71,72	Turn-signal, left front	82		

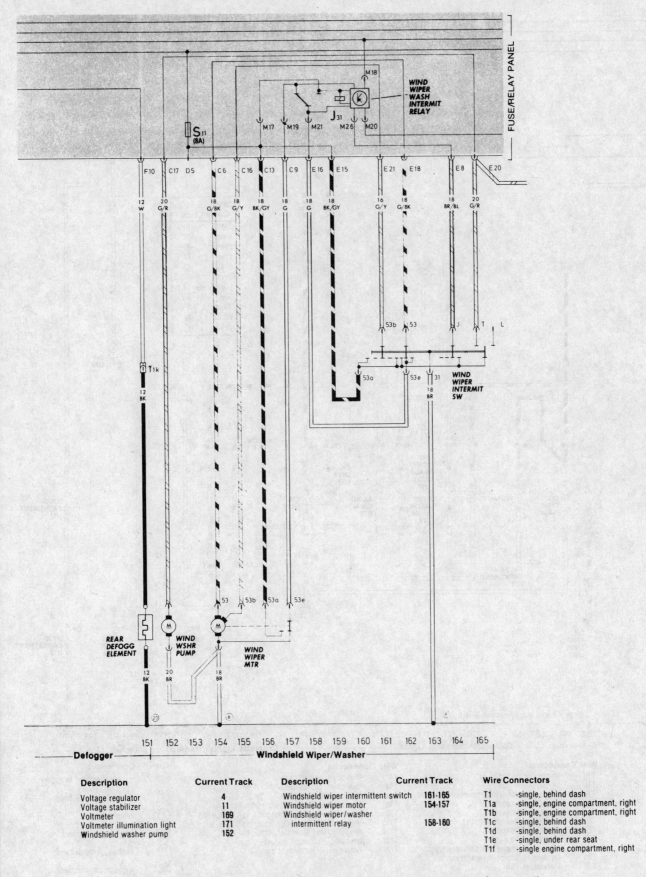

Fig. 10.49 Wiring diagram for 1982 North American four-cylinder models (continued)

Description	Current Track	Description	Current Track	Wire Connectors	
Voltage regulator	4	Windshield wiper intermittent switch	161-165	T1	-single, behind dash
Voltage stabilizer	11	Windshield wiper motor	154-157	T1a	-single, engine compartment, right
Voltmeter	169	Windshield wiper/washer		T1b	-single, engine compartment, right
Voltmeter illumination light	171	intermittent relay	158-160	T1c	-single, behind dash
Windshield washer pump	152			T1d	-single, behind dash
				T1e	-single, under rear seat
				T1f	-single engine compartment, right

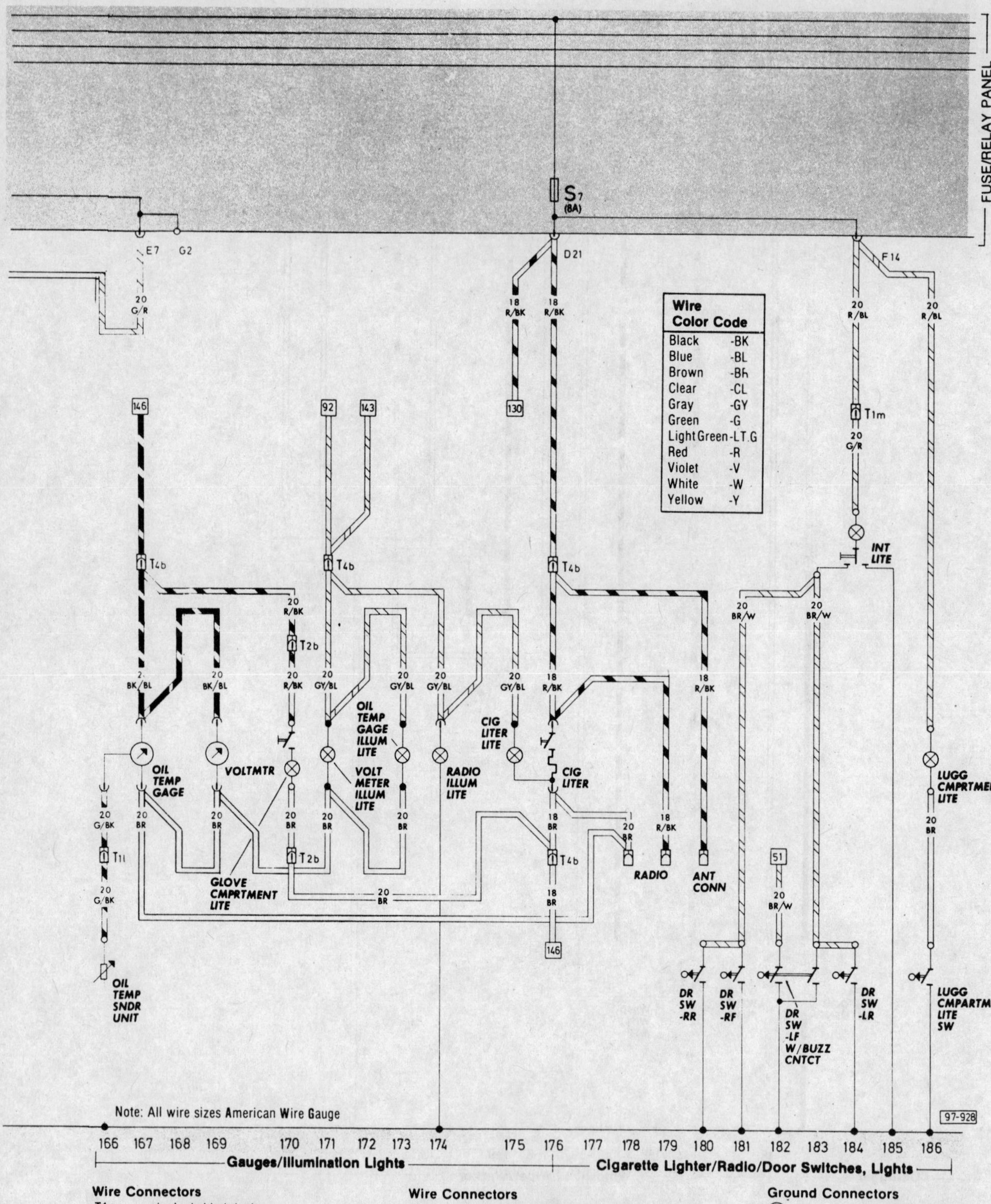

FUSE/RELAY PANEL

S7
(8A)

E7 G2

20
G/R

D21

18
R/BK

18
R/BK

Wire Color Code

Black	-BK
Blue	-BL
Brown	-Bʰ
Clear	-CL
Gray	-GY
Green	-G
Light Green	-LT.G
Red	-R
Violet	-V
White	-W
Yellow	-Y

F14

20
R/BL

20
R/BL

146

92

143

130

T4b

T4b

T4b

T1m

20
G/R

INT LITE

20
R/BK

T2b

20
R/BK

20
GY/BL

20
GY/BL

20
GY/BL

18
R/BK

18
R/BK

20
BR/W

20
BR/W

2.
BK/BL

20
BK/BL

OIL TEMP GAGE ILLUM LITE

VOLT METER ILLUM LITE

RADIO ILLUM LITE

CIG LITER LITE

OIL TEMP GAGE

VOLTMTR

CIG LITER

LUGG CMPRTMENT LITE

20
G/BK

20
BR

20
BR

20
BR

20
BR

20
BR

18
BR

18
BR

20
BR

T11

GLOVE CMPRTMENT LITE

T2b

20
BR

RADIO

ANT CONN

20
BR

51

20
BR/W

T4b

20
G/BK

18
BR

146

OIL TEMP SNDR UNIT

DR SW -RR

DR SW -RF

DR SW -LF W/BUZZ CNTCT

DR SW -LR

LUGG CMPARTMENT LITE SW

Note: All wire sizes American Wire Gauge

97-928

166 167 168 169 170 171 172 173 174   175 176 177 178 179 180 181 182 183 184 185 186

|— Gauges/Illumination Lights —| |— Cigarette Lighter/Radio/Door Switches, Lights —|

Wire Connectors

T1g	-single, behind dash
T1j	-single, behind dash
T1k	-single, luggage compartment
T1l	-single, behind dash
T1m	-single, behind dash
T2	-double, engine compartment, right
T2a	-double, behind dash
T2b	-double, behind dash
T3	-three-point, engine compartment, right
T3a	-three-point, engine compartment, left
T3b	-three-point, cowl

Wire Connectors

T4	-four-point, behind dash
T4a	-four-point, behind dash
T4b	-four-point, behind dash
T4c	-four-point, engine compartment, right
T10a	-ten-point, Mas-Mate-Connector, tail light, left
T10b	-ten-point, Mas-Mate-Connector, tail light, left
T10c	-ten-point, Mas-Mate-Connector, tail light, right
T10/	-ten-point, instrument panel
T12/	-twelve point, instrument panel

Ground Connectors

②	-strap, alternator to engine
⑦	-strap, battery to body
⑧	-behind dash
⑩	-engine compartment, right
⑭	-fuel gauge sender unit
⑳	-luggage compartment

Fig. 10.49 Wiring diagram for 1982 North American four-cylinder models (continued)

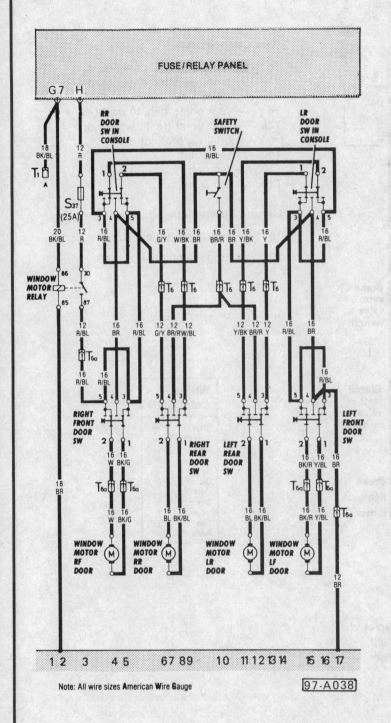

Description	Current Track
Fuse, behind dashboard	3
Motor for power window, left front door	15
Motor for power window, left rear door	12
Motor for power window, right front door	4
Motor for power window, right rear door	7
Relay for window motors	2,3
Safety switch, in switch plate	10
Window switch on left rear door	11–14
Window switch on right rear door	6–9
Window switch, left front door, in switch plate	15,16
Window switch, right front door, in switch plate	4,5
Window switch, left rear door, in switch plate	15,16
Window switch, right rear door, in switch plate	4,5

T1 — Wire connector, single, on dashboard wiring harness

T6 — Wire connector, 6-point, behind dashboard

T6a — Wire connector, 6-point, behind switch plate

Color Code

Black	— BK	Green	— G
Brown	— BR	Blue	— BL
Red	— R	Violet	— V
Orange	— O	Gray	— GY
Yellow	— Y	White	— W

Note: All wire sizes American Wire Gauge

97-A038

10

Fig. 10.50 Wiring diagram for Audi 4000 power windows (North American models)

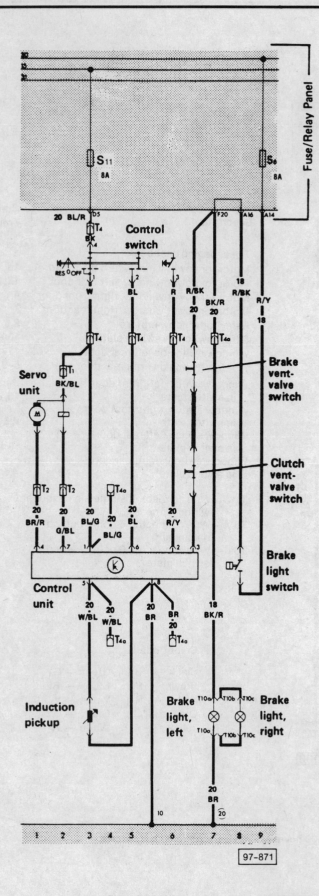

Wire Connectors

T1   — single, behind dashboard
T1a   — single, behind dashboard
T2   — double, behind dashboard
T4   — four point, behind dashboard
T4a   — four point (test connection
        only for production)
T10a — ten point
T10b — ten point
T10c — ten point

Ground Connectors

10   — near Fuse/Relay Panel
20   — luggage comp. left rear

Wiring Color Code	
Black	— BK
Brown	— BR
Clear	— CL
Red	— R
Yellow	— Y
Green	— G
Light Green	— LT.G
Blue	— BL
Violet	— V
Gray	— GY
White	— W

97-871

Fig. 10.51 Wiring diagram for 1981/82 cruise control(North American models)

Chapter 11 Suspension and steering

Refer to Chapter 13 for Specifications and information applicable to 1983 through 1987 models

Contents

Specifications

Front suspension
Type .... Independent, with coil spring struts incorporating telescopic shock absorbers, lower wishbones and anti-roll bar

Rear suspension
Type .... Transverse torsion axle incorporating trailing arms, Panhard rod, telescopic shock absorbers with externally mounted coil springs

Steering
Type .... Rack-and-pinion, tie-rods connected to coupling attached to rack, power assistance or steering damper fitted to some models

Front wheel alignment
Total toe-out .... + 10' ± 10' (1.0 ± 1.0 mm/0.04 ± 0.04 in)
Toe angle difference, left and right, at 20° lock .... –50' ± 30'
Camber .... –40' ± 30'
Maximum camber difference between sides .... 30'
Castor .... +30' ± 30'
Maximum castor difference between sides .... 30'

Rear wheel alignment
Camber .... –1° ± 20'
Maximum camber difference between sides .... 30'
Total toe-out .... +20' ± 20'
Maximum toe-out difference between sides .... 25'

Wheels
Type .... Pressed steel or light alloy
Size .... 5J x 13, 5½J x 13 or 6J x 14

11

Tyres

Size:

UK models	155 SR 13, 165 SR 13, 175/70 SR 13, 175/70 HR 13, 185/60 HR 14
North American models	175/70 SR 13, 185/60 HR 14

	Four-cylinder models	Five-cylinder models
Pressures — lbf/in² (bar) cold tyres:		
UK models:		
185/60 HR 14	23 (1.6)	26 (1.8)
except 185/60 HR 14	25 (1.7)	26 (1.8)
Spare	36 (2.5)	36 (2.5)
North American models	25 (1.7)	25 (1.7)
Spare	36 (2.5)	36 (2.5)

Note: *Increase pressures by 1.5 lbf/in² (0.1 bar) for fully loaded car, and by 3.0 lbf/in² (0.2 bar) for winter tyres.*

Torque wrench settings

Front suspension

	lbf ft	Nm
Strut to body	44	60
Strut bearing to piston rod	37	50
Shock absorber screw cap	110	150
Suspension balljoint to strut	37	50
Suspension balljoint to wishbone	48	65
Wishbone to subframe	44	60
Subframe to body	52	70
Anti-roll bar	18	25

Rear suspension

Panhard rod	59	80
Trailing arm to body	74	100
Shock absorber to rear axle	44	60
Shock absorber to body	15	20
Brake backplate/stub axle	44	60

Steering

Flange tube:		
Manual	18	25
Power-assisted	22	30
Steering wheel	30	40
Steering gear to body:		
Long version	15	20
Short version	26	35
Steering gear to wheel housing	15	20
Damper to steering gear	30	40
Tie-rod to short steering gear	26	35
Tie-rod to coupling	33	45
Coupling to rack	33	45
Damper bracket to steering gear	15	20
Tie-rod end to strut	22	30
Tie-rod end locknut	30	40
Tie-rod clamp	11	15
Steering lock	7	10

Wheels

Wheel bolts	66	90

1 General description

The front suspension is of independent type, incorporating coil spring struts and lower wishbones. The struts are fitted with telescopic shock absorbers and both front suspension units are mounted on a subframe. An anti-roll bar is fitted to the lower wishbones.

The rear suspension comprises a transverse torsion axle with trailing arms rubber bushed to the body. The axle is attached to the lower ends of the shock absorbers, which act as struts, since they incorporate mountings for the coil springs. Side-to-side movement of the axle is controlled by a Panhard rod.

The steering is of rack-and-pinion type mounted on the bulkhead. The tie-rods are attached to a single coupling which is itself bolted to the steering rack. Power assistance is fitted to some models, and a steering damper may be fitted to some models with manual steering.

2 Front suspension strut — removal and refitting

1 Prise the cap from the centre of the roadwheel, then unscrew the driveshaft nut. *This is tightened to a very high torque and no attempt to loosen it must be made unless the full weight of the car is on the roadwheels.*

2 Loosen the four bolts securing the roadwheel.

3 Jack up the car and support the body securely on stands, or wood blocks.

4 Remove the roadwheel.

5 Remove the brake caliper with reference to Chapter 9, but do not disconnect the hydraulic hose. Support the caliper on a stand without straining the hose.

6 Detach the hose bracket from the strut.

7 Unscrew and remove the suspension balljoint clamp bolt, noting that its head faces forward.

8 Using a balljoint removing tool, as described in Section 13, unscrew the nut and disconnect the tie-rod end from the strut/wheel bearing housing.

9 Unscrew the anti-roll bar mounting bolts and remove the bar, with reference to Section 5.

10 Remove the driveshaft nut, then push the wishbone down from the strut.

11 Using a hub puller, press the driveshaft out of the front wheel hub.

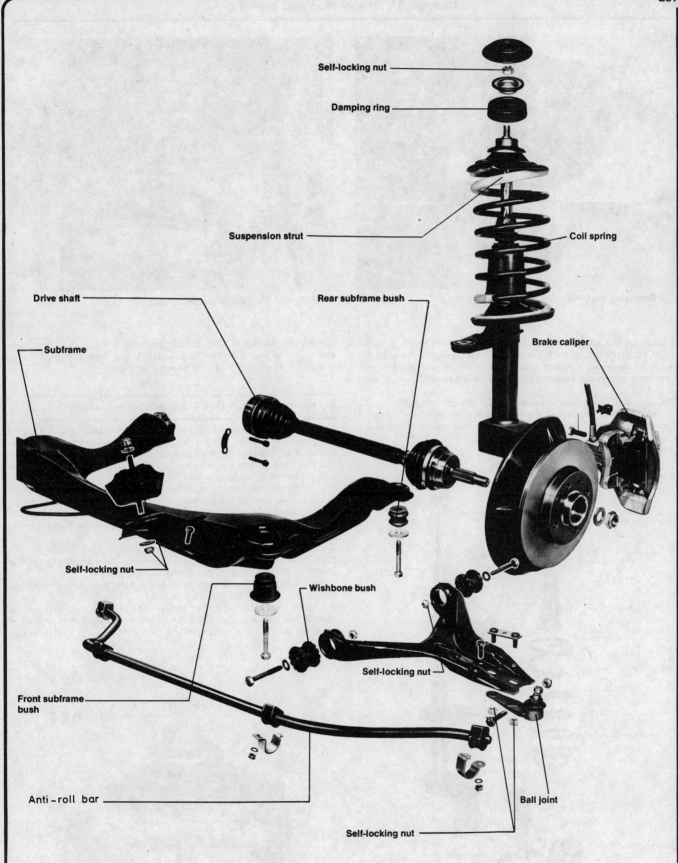

Self-locking nut

Damping ring

Suspension strut

Coil spring

Drive shaft

Rear subframe bush

Brake caliper

Subframe

Self-locking nut

Wishbone bush

Self-locking nut

Front subframe bush

Ball joint

Anti-roll bar

Self-locking nut

Fig. 11.1 Exploded view of the front suspension (Secs 2, 5 and 6)

11

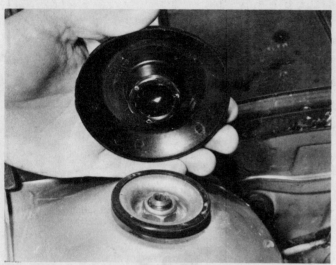

2.12 Removing the front suspension strut dust cap

2.13 View of the front suspension strut

12 Support the suspension strut from below, then, working in the engine compartment, pull off the dust cap and unscrew the nut from the top of the shock absorber piston rod (photo). It will be necessary to hold the piston rod stationary with an Allen key while unscrewing the nut.

13 Lower the suspension strut from under the car (photo).

14 Refitting is a reversal of removal. However, refer to Chapter 8 when installing the driveshaft, Chapter 9 when installing the brake

caliper, and Section 5 when installing the anti-roll bar. Tighten all nuts and bolts to the specified torque. The upper rubber damping ring should be dusted with talcum powder before fitting.

3 Front suspension strut – dismantling and reassembly

1 Do not attempt to dismantle the suspension strut unless a spring compressor has been fitted. If you have no special compressor, take the strut to a garage for dismantling.

2 With the spring compressor in place on the spring, clamp the wheel bearing housing in a vice.

3 Compress the spring until the upper spring retainer is free of tension, then remove the slotted nut from the top of the piston rod. To do this, a special tool is available (Fig. 11.3). However it is possible to hold the piston rod stationary with an Allen key, and use a peg spanner to unscrew the slotted nut.

4 Remove the strut bearing, followed by the spring retainer.

5 Lift the coil spring from the strut with the compressor still in position. Mark the top of the spring for reference.

6 Withdraw the bump stop components from the piston rod, noting their order of removal.

7 Move the shock absorber piston rod up and down through its complete stroke and check that the resistance is even and smooth. If there are any signs of seizing or lack of resistance, or if fluid has been

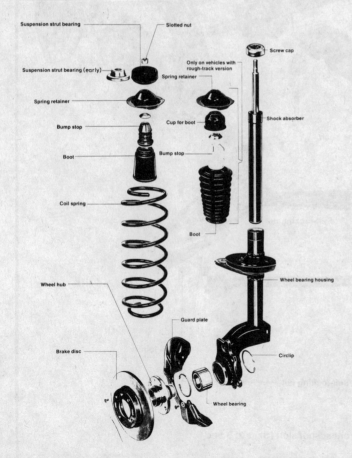

Fig. 11.2 Exploded view of the front suspension strut for 1980 models onwards (Sec 3)

Suspension strut bearing
Slotted nut
Suspension strut bearing (early)
Only on vehicles with rough-track version
Spring retainer
Screw cap
Spring retainer
Shock absorber
Bump stop
Cup for boot
Boot
Bump stop
Coil spring
Boot
Wheel bearing housing
Wheel hub
Guard plate
Circlip
Brake disc
Wheel bearing

VW 524

Fig. 11.3 Using the special tool to unscrew the slotted nut from the front suspension. A peg spanner and Allen key will suffice if necessary – see text (Sec 3)

leaking excessively, the shock absorber should be renewed. To do this, unscrew the screw cap using a hexagon box spanner, or the special Audi tool No 40-201 A. The cap is very tight, so the tool used must fit accurately.

8   Pull the shock absorber from the strut.

9   If the strut wheel bearing housing is to be renewed, remove the wheel bearing as described in Section 4, then fit the bearing and hub to the new housing, with reference to the same Section.

10   Clean all the components, in particular the shock absorber recess in the wheel bearing housing. Note that the coil springs are normally colour coded, and therefore new springs must always bear the same code as those removed. Check the strut bearing for wear, and if necessary renew it – if the old type bearing is fitted, it may well be worthwhile fitting the modified type.

11   Reassembly is a reversal of removal, but tighten the screw cap and slotted nut to the specified torques.

4   Front hub and bearing – removal and refitting

1   Remove the front suspension strut as described in Section 2.

2   Remove the cross-headed screw and tap the brake disc from the hub.

3   Remove the screws and withdraw the splash guard.

4   Support the wheel bearing housing with the hub facing downward, and press or drive out the hub, using a suitable mandrel. The bearing inner race will remain on the hub, and therefore, once removed, it is not possible to re-use the bearing. Use a puller to remove the inner race from the hub.

Fig. 11.4 Using a puller to remove the wheel bearing inner race from the front hub (Sec 4)

5   Extract the circlips, then, while supporting the wheel bearing housing, press or drive out the bearing, using a mandrel on the outer race.

6   Clean the recess in the housing, then smear it with a little general purpose grease.

7   Fit the outer circlip, then support the wheel bearing housing and press or drive in the new bearing, using a metal tube *on the outer race only*.

8   Fit the inner circlip making sure that it is correctly seated.

9   Position the hub with its bearing shoulder facing upward, then press or drive on the bearing and housing, using a metal tube *on the inner race only*.

10   Refit the splash guard and brake disc, then refit the front suspension strut, as described in Section 2.

5   Anti-roll bar – removal and refitting

1   Jack up the front of the car and support it on axle stands. Apply the handbrake.

2   Unscrew the nuts and extract the front mounting clamps which secure the anti-roll bar to the subframe (photo).

3   Unscrew the nuts and extract the side mounting clamps which secure the anti-roll bar to the suspension wishbones (photo). Withdraw the anti-roll bar from under the car.

4   Refitting is a reversal of removal, but make sure that the anti-roll bar is fitted the correct way round, with the offset away from the wishbones (Fig. 11.5). Initially, the mounting bolts must be only partially tightened. Then the car should be lowered to the ground and 'bounced' a few times to settle the mountings, before fully tightening the bolts to the specified torque with the full weight of the car on its wheels.

6   Front suspension wishbone – removal, overhaul and refitting

1   Remove the anti-roll bar as described in Section 5.

2   Remove the relevant roadwheel.

3   Unscrew and remove the suspension balljoint clamp bolt, noting that its head faces forward.

4   Tap the wishbone downward to release the balljoint from the strut.

Fig. 11.5 Offset position with correctly fitted anti-roll bar (Sec 5)

5.2 Anti-roll bar front mounting (arrowed)

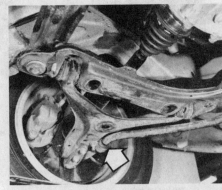

5.3 Front suspension wishbone and anti-roll bar side mounting clamp (arrowed)

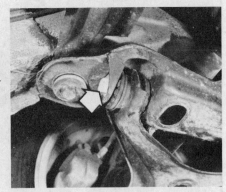

6.5 Front suspension wishbone pivot bolt (arrowed)

11

5   Unscrew and remove the pivot bolts from the subframe, noting the position of their heads, then lower the wishbone and withdraw it (photo).

6   Check the balljoint for excessive wear, and check the pivot bushes for deterioration. Also examine the wishbone for damage and distortion. If necessary, the balljoint and bushes should be renewed.

7   To renew the balljoint, first outline its exact position on the wishbone. This is important as the holes in the wishbone are elongated to allow camber adjustment. Unscrew the nuts and remove the balljoint and clamp plate. Fit the new balljoint in the exact outline, and tighten the nuts.

8   To renew the pivot bushes, use a long bolt together with a metal tube and washers to pull each bush from the wishbone eyes. Fit the new bushes using the same method, but first dip them in soapy water.

9   Refitting the wishbone is a reversal of removal, but delay tightening the pivot bolts until the weight of the car is on the suspension. Refer to Section 5 when refitting the anti-roll bar. Have the front wheel camber angle checked and, if necessary, adjusted by an Audi dealer.

7   Rear axle – removal and refitting

1   Jack up the rear of the car, and support it with axle stands positioned beneath the underbody. Chock the front wheels and remove the rear wheels.

2   Unhook the rubber mounting rings and lower the rear exhaust silencer as far as possible. Support the silencer on an axle stand.

3   Unscrew the nut from the handbrake lever rod and remove the compensator bar.

4   Prise the handbrake cable guide bushes from the underbody brackets, and remove the cables form the rear brackets.

5   Remove the brake fluid reservoir filler cap and tighten it down onto a piece of polythene sheeting placed over the reservoir filler hose in order to prevent the loss of fluid. Alternatively fit brake hose clamps to both rear brake hoses.

6   Disconnect both rear brake hoses from the trailing arms by unscrewing the rigid brake line union nuts, while holding the hose end unions stationary with a spanner. Remove the clamp plates.

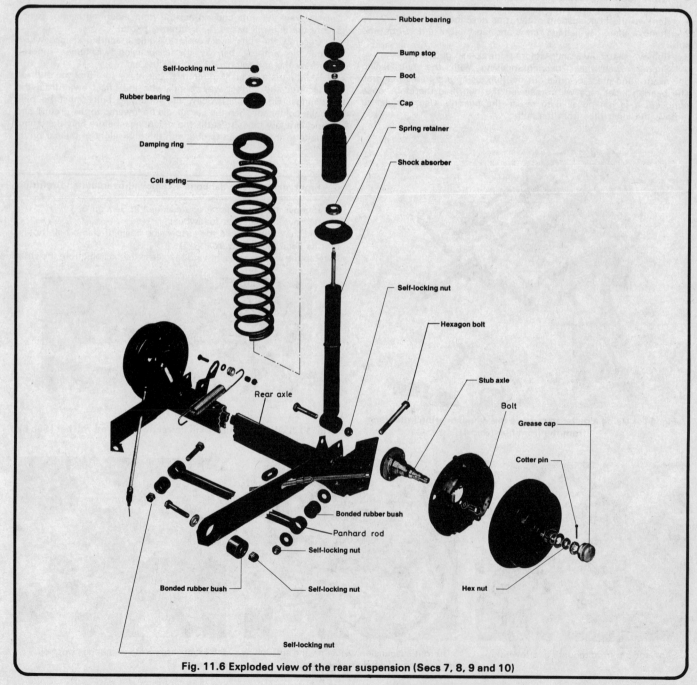

Fig. 11.6 Exploded view of the rear suspension (Secs 7, 8, 9 and 10)

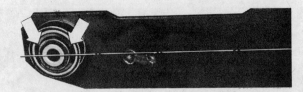

Fig. 11.7 Correctly installed position of the rear suspension trailing arm pivot bushes (Sec 7)

7 Loosen the nuts on the pivot bolts at the front of the trailing arms.
8 Unhook the brake pressure regulator spring from the rear axle.
9 Unbolt the Panhard rod from the rear axle.
10 Support the rear axle with a trolley jack, and place axle stands beneath the trailing arms.
11 Unscrew and remove the rear shock absorber lower mounting bolts.
12 Unscrew the nuts and remove the pivot bolts from the trailing arms.
13 With the help of an assistant if necessary, lower the rear axle to the ground while guiding the handbrake cable over the exhaust pipe.
14 If necessary, remove the stub axles, with reference to Section 10; also remove the brake lines and handbrake cables, if required. The pivot bushes may be renewed using a long bolt and nut, metal tube, and packing washers, but make sure that the bush gaps are in line with the trailing arms and press the bushes in flush.
15 Refitting is a reversal of removal, but delay tightening the rear axle, shock absorber and Panhard rod mounting bolts until the weight of the car is on the suspension. Bleed the hydraulic system and adjust the handbrake cable, as described in Chapter 9.

8 Rear suspension strut/shock absorber – removal and refitting

1 Open the boot lid, and detach the trim from the fuel tank.
2 Unscrew the nut from the top of the shock absorber piston rod and remove the dished washer and rubber bearing (photo).
3 Jack up the rear of the car using a trolley jack beneath the rear axle, and support the car with axle stands positioned beneath the underbody. Chock the front wheels.
4 Lower the rear axle until the coil spring is no longer under tension, then unscrew and remove the shock absorber lower mounting bolt. The shock absorber can now be lowered from the car, together with the coil spring and damping ring (photo).
5 Remove the damping ring, coil spring, bump stop components, and spring retainer from the shock absorber, but mark the position of the retainer if the shock absorber is to be re-used. **Note:** *Both shock absorbers should not be disconnected from the rear axle at the same time, as the rear brake hydraulic hoses may be damaged.*

6 Clean all the components, and examine them for wear and damage. Note that the coil springs are normally colour coded, and therefore new springs must always bear the same code as those removed. With the shock absorber vertical, move the piston rod up and down through its complete stroke and check that the resistance is even and smooth. If there are any signs of seizing, or lack of resistance, or if fluid has been leaking excessively, the shock absorber should be renewed. Renew all components as necessary.
7 Before fitting new shock absorbers check their action when vertical – after being stored on their sides for some time, it is necessary to operate the piston rods through several full strokes, in order to purge any trapped air.
8 Refitting is a reversal of removal, but position the spring retainer as shown in Fig. 11.8, and dust the upper rubber bearings with talcum powder before fitting them. Delay tightening the shock absorber lower mounting bolt to the specified torque until the weight of the car is on the suspension.

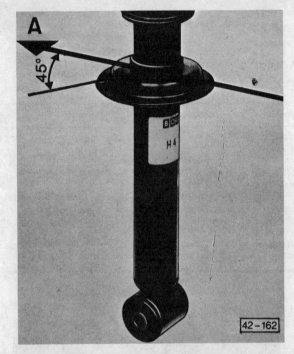

Fig. 11.8 Correctly installed position of the spring retainer on the rear shock absorber (Sec 8)

A – front of car

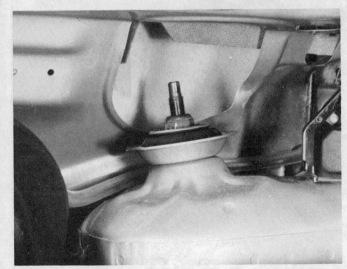

8.2 Rear suspension strut upper mounting

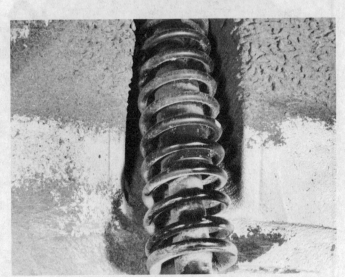

8.4 View of the rear suspension coil spring

11

9.2A Panhard rod-to-body mounting

9.2B Panhard rod-to-rear axle mounting

9   Panhard rod – removal, overhaul and refitting

1   Jack up the rear of the car and support it on axle stands. Chock the front wheels.
2   Unscrew and remove the bolts attaching the Panhard rod to the underbody and rear axle, noting which way round the bolts are fitted (photos). Withdraw the Panhard rod.
3   Examine the rod and bushes for damage and deterioration. If necessary, the bushes can be renewed, using a long bolt together with a metal tube and washers – dip the new bushes in soapy water before installing them.
4   Refitting is a reversal of removal, but delay tightening the mounting bolts until the weight of the car is on the suspension.

10   Rear wheel bearings and stub axle – removal, refitting and adjustment

1   Chock the front wheels, then jack up the rear of the car and support it on axle stands. Remove the rear roadwheel, and release the handbrake.
2   Remove the cap from the centre of the brake drum by tapping it on alternate sides with a screwdriver or blunt chisel (photo).
3   Extract the split pin and remove the locking ring.
4   Unscrew the nut and remove the thrust washer (photos).
5   Withdraw the drake drum, making sure that the outer wheel bearing does not fall out (photo). If the brake drum binds on the shoes, insert a small screwdrivber through a wheel bolt hole and lever up the

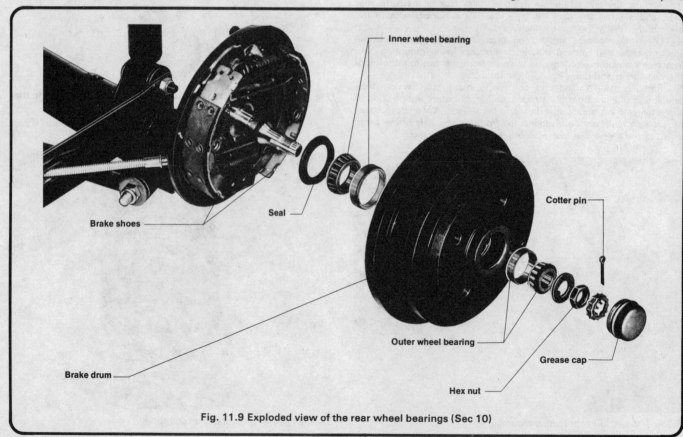

Inner wheel bearing

Seal

Brake shoes

Cotter pin

Outer wheel bearing

Grease cap

Brake drum

Hex nut

Fig. 11.9 Exploded view of the rear wheel bearings (Sec 10)

10.2 Removing the rear hub bearing cap

wedged key in order to release the shoes – refer to Chapter 9, if necessary.

6   Remove the outer wheel bearing inner race and rollers from the brake drum/hub.

7   Lever the oil seal from the inner side of the brake drum/hub and withdraw the inner wheel bearing inner race and rollers (photo).

8   Using a soft metal drift, drive the outer races from each side of the brake drum/hub.

9   Clean the bearings and brake drum/hub with parafffin, and also wipe the stub axle clean. Examine the tapered rollers, inner and outer races, brake drum/hub, and stub axle for wear and damage. If the bearing surfaces are pitted, renew them. Obtain a new oil seal.

10 Pack the bearing cages and tapered rollers with a lithium based grease, and also pack the grease into the brake drum/hub inner cavity.

11 Using a length of metal tube, drive the outer races fully into the brake drum/hub.

12 Insert the inner bearing inner race and rollers, then locate the oil seal with the sealing lip facing inward, and drive it in with a block of wood until flush. Smear a little grease on the oil seal lip then wipe clean the outer face of the seal.

13 To remove the stub axle, first remove the rear brake shoes, with reference to Chapter 9.

14 Remove the brake fluid reservoir filler cap, and tighten it down onto a piece of polythene sheeting over the reservoir filler hole in order

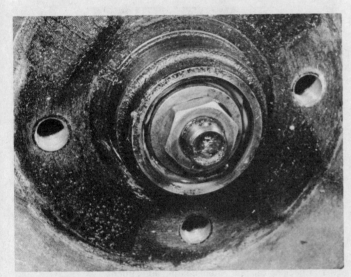

10.4A Remove the rear hub bearing nut ...

10.4B ... and thrust washer

10.5 Removing the rear brake drum

10.7 Rear wheel bearing oil seal

11

to prevent the loss of fluid in the following procedure. Alternatively fit a brake hose clamp on the hydraulic hose between the rear axle and underbody.

15   Unscrew the brake pipe union on the rear of the wheel cylinder.

16   Unscrew the bolts and withdraw the brake backplate and stub axle from the rear axle mounting plate, at the same time disconnecting the handbrake cable.

17   Refitting the stub axle is a reversal of the removal procedure, but make sure that the mating faces are clean. Tighten the bolts to the specified torque. Refit the rear brake shoes with reference to Chapter 9.

18   Locate the brake drum/hub on the stub axle and fit the outer wheel bearing, followed by the thrust washer and nut (photo).

19   Tighten the nut firmly while turning the drum/hub, then back off the nut until the thrust washer can *just* be moved by pressing on it with a screwdriver. Do not lever or twist the screwdriver in an attempt to move the thrust washer (photo).

20   Fit the locking ring without moving the nut, and install a new split pin.

21   Tap the grease cap onto the drum/hub.

22   If the stub axle has been removed, bleed the brake hydraulic system as described in Chapter 9, then depress the footbrake pedal firmly to set the rear brake shoes.

23   Refit the roadwheel and lower the car to the ground.

11   Steering wheel – removal and refitting

1   Pull the horn bar from the centre of the steering wheel – the retainers are quite strong and quite an effort is required to release the bar.

2   Disconnect the horn wiring and withdraw the bar (photo).

3   Set the front wheel in the straight-ahead position, and the turn signal lever in neutral.

4   Mark the steering wheel and inner column in relation to each other, then unscrew and remove the retaining nut and washer (photo).

5   Withdraw the steering wheel from the inner column splines. If it is tight, ease it off by rocking from side to side.

6   Refitting is a reversal of removal, but align the previously made marks, and tighten the retaining nut to the specified torque. Make sure that the turn signal lever is in neutral, otherwise the switch arm may be damaged.

12   Steering column – removal, overhaul and refitting

1   Remove the steering wheel as described in Section 11.

2   Remove the trim panel covering the steering column.

3   Disconnect the battery negative lead.

10.18 Fitting the rear hub outer bearing

10.19 Checking the rear wheel bearing adjustment

11.2 Disconnecting the wire from the horn bar

11.4 Steering wheel retaining nut

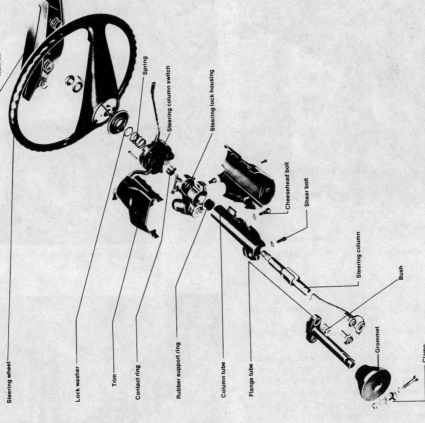

Horn bar

Steering wheel

Lock washer

Trim

Contact ring

Rubber support ring

Column tube

Flange tube

Spring

Steering column switch

Steering lock housing

Cheesehead bolt

Shear bolt

Steering column

Bush

Grommet

Clamp

Fig. 11.10 Exploded view of the steering column (Secs 11 and 12)

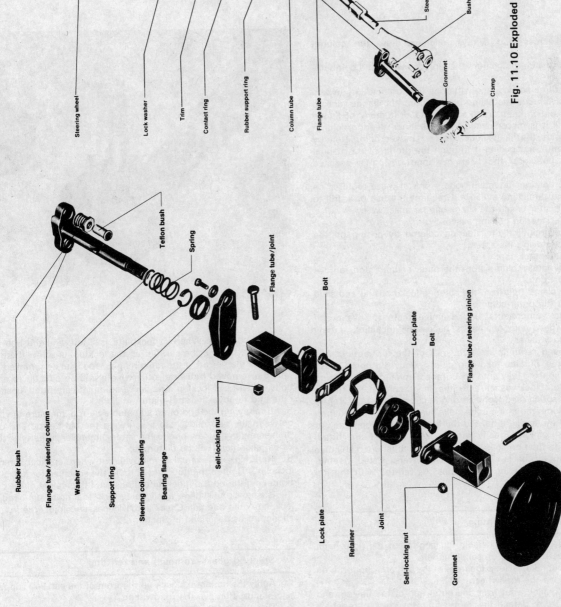

Rubber bush

Flange tube / steering column

Washer

Support ring

Steering column bearing

Bearing flange

Self-locking nut

Teflon bush

Spring

Flange tube / joint

Bolt

Lock plate

Retainer

Joint

Self-locking nut

Grommet

Lock plate

Bolt

Flange tube / steering pinion

Fig 11.11 Steering column flange tube components on models with power assisted steering (Sec 12)

11

12.7 Disconnecting the flange tube from the inner steering column

13.3A Using a separator tool to remove the tie-rod from the strut

4   Remove the cross-head screws, and withdraw the column shrouds.
5   Disconnect the multi-plugs from the ignition switch and combination switch.
6   Remove the three screws, and withdraw the combination switch.
7   Unscrew and remove the clamp bolt securing the flange tube to the steering gear pinion, then, using a soft metal drift, drive the flange tube upward until it is disconnected from the inner steering column (photo). If necessary the flange tube can be removed completely by removing the clamp and pulling it through the grommet on manual steering, or by unbolting the bearing flange on power-assisted steering.
8   Unscrew the column mounting bolts – one of these requires an Allen key, and the remaining shear-bolt requires the use of a drill to remove the head, after which the shank can be unscrewed.
9   Withdraw the steering column assembly.
10   Commence dismantling the steering column by prising off the lockwasher and removing the spring.
11   Lever off the contact ring.
12   Withdraw the inner column from the outer column, and remove the rubber support ring.
13   Unscrew the clamp bolt from the steering lock housing and slide the housing from the outer column.
14   Clean all the components, and examine them for wear and damage. Obtain new components as necessary, including a new shear-bolt and lockwasher.
15   Reassembly and refitting are a reversal of the dismantling and removal procedures, but the following points should be noted. Push the steering lock housing fully onto the outer column before tightening the bolt. Press the lockwasher onto the inner column so that it compresses the spring and contact ring against the stop. Before tightening the column mounting bolts make sure that the inner column is fully entered in the flange tube, and the flange tube is connected to the steering gear pinion. Except where Teflon sleeves are fitted, lubricate the flange tube brushes with a little molybdenum disulphide grease. If the flange tube is dismantled on power-assisted steering models, note that the bearing flange must be refitted with the lug towards the centre of the car.

13.3B Steering tie-rod end

types of coupling. Where a lockplate is fitted, and the bolt head is toward the front of the car, flatten the locktab, unscrew the bolt, and withdraw the tie-rod. If the remaining tie-rod is to be removed as well, refit the removed bolt first, otherwise it will be difficult to enter the bolts. Where self-locking nuts and a stud plate are fitted, unscrew the nuts and remove the stud plate.
5   If renewing the end of an adjustable tie-rod, measure the distance between the two ends before screwing the old tie-rod end out, and then screw in the new one to the same dimension, otherwise the front wheel alignment will be disturbed.
6   Refitting is a reversal of removal, but where applicable renew the lockplate. Tighten the nuts and bolts to the specified torque, but delay tightening the tie-rod inner mountings until the weight of the car is on the suspension. Where applicable, lock the bolts by bending the lockplate onto one flat. Check and, if necessary, adjust the front wheel alignment as described in Section 22.

13 Tie-rod – removal and refitting

1   The left-hand tie-rod is adjustable for length, but the right-hand tie-rod may not be adjustable on some models.
2   Apply the handbrake, jack up the front of the car, and support it on axle stands. Remove the roadwheel.
3   Unscrew the balljoint nut from the outer end of the tie-rod, and use a separator tool to detach the tie-rod from the strut (photos).
4   The inner end of the tie-rod may be attached by two different

14 Steering gear – removal and refitting

1   Apply the handbrake, jack up the front of the car, and support it on axle stands. Remove the roadwheels.
2   Disconnect the inner ends of the tie-rods with reference to Section 13, paragraph 4.

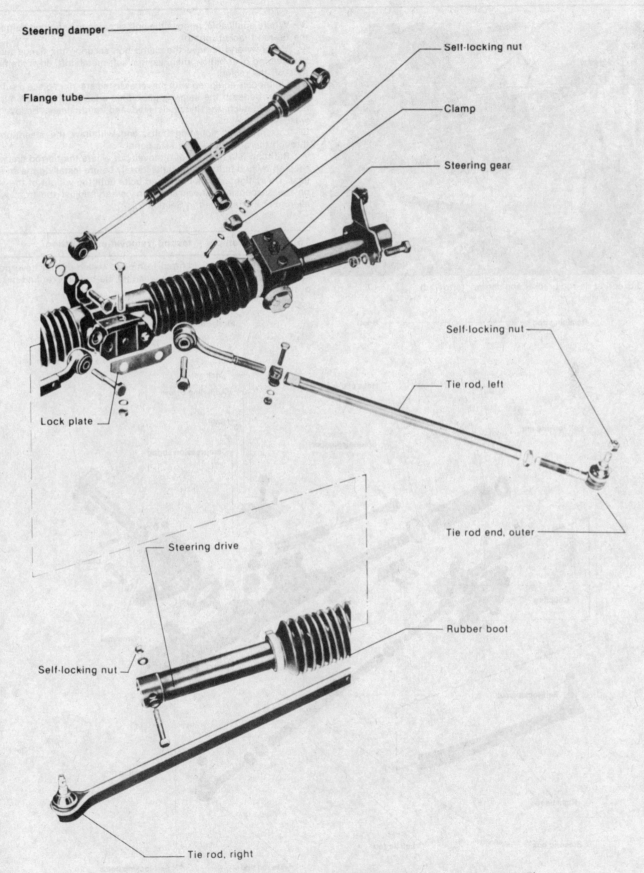

Steering damper

Flange tube

Self-locking nut

Clamp

Steering gear

Lock plate

Self-locking nut

Tie rod, left

Tie rod end, outer

Steering drive

Rubber boot

Self-locking nut

Tie rod, right

Fig. 11.12 Manual steering gear (long type) components (Secs 13, 14, 15, 16 and 17)

Left-hand drive shown

14.3 Steering tie-rod bracket and damper (arrowed)

3 Where applicable, remove the bolt securing the steering damper to the tie-rod bracket (photo).
4 Unscrew and remove the clamp bolt securing the flange tube to the steering gear pinion, then, using a soft metal drift, drive the flange tube off the pinion.
5 On models equipped with power assisted steering, place a suitable container beneath the steering gear, then unscrew the union nut and bolt, and detach the hydraulic feed and return lines. Recover the washers.
6 Unscrew the mounting bolts, and withdraw the steering gear through the aperture in the side panel.
7 Refitting is a reversal of removal, but where the tie-rod bracket is secured by two bolts, fit the bolts loosely before installing the steering gear. Delay tightening all nuts and bolts until the weight of the car is on the suspension. Check and, if necessary, adjust the front wheel alignment as described in Section 22.

15 Steering damper – testing, removal and refitting

1 A steering damper is fitted to models which do not have power steering, and it is connected between the tie-rod bracket and the side of the engine compartment.

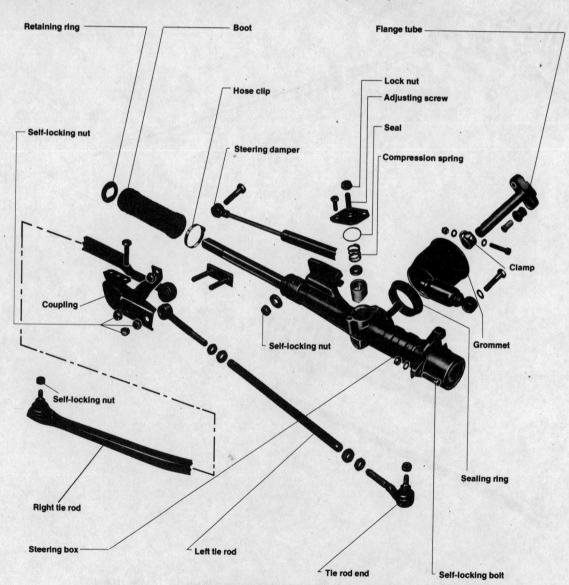

Fig. 11.13 Exploded view of the manual steering gear (short type) (Secs 14, 15, 16 and 17)

Left-hand drive shown

2   Repair of the steering damper is not possible. If the steering is sensitive to road shocks, remove the damper and check its operation. The damper is attached by a bolt at each end.

3   Test the damper by moving the piston in and out by hand, over the whole range of its travel. If the movement is not smooth and with a uniform resistance, fit a new damper.

16 Steering gear bellows – renewal

Central bellows type

1   Remove the steering gear, as described in Section 14.

2   Remove the tie-rod bracket, then release the clips and slide off the bellows.

3   Smear the rack with steering gear grease, then fit the new bellows and clips. If necessary, worm drive clips may be fitted in place of the crimped type. Fit the tie-rod bracket.

4   Refit the steering gear as described in Section 14.

End bellows type

5   Unbolt the tie-rod bracket from the end of the steering rack.

6   Prise the bellows from the retaining ring, then remove the ring.

7   Release the clip and slide off the bellows.

8   Smear the rack with steering gear grease, then fit the new

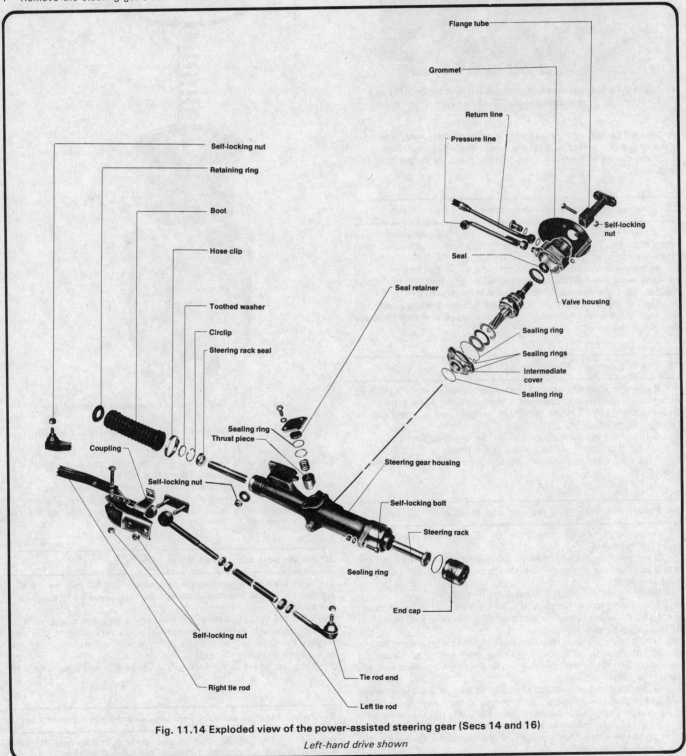

Fig. 11.14 Exploded view of the power-assisted steering gear (Secs 14 and 16)

Left-hand drive shown

Fig. 11.15 Manual steering gear adjustment locknut (1) and adjusting screw (2) (Sec 17)

bellows, clip, and ring. If necessary, a worm drive clip may be fitted in place of the crimped type, with the screw toward the bulkhead.
9   Refit the tie-rod bracket, and tighten the bolts to the specified torque.

17 Steering gear (manual) – adjustment

1   If there is any undue slackness in the steering gear, resulting in noise or rattles, the steering gear should be adjusted as follows, with reference to Fig. 11.15.
2   Loosen the locknut and, with the wheels in the straight-ahead position, turn the adjusting screw until it just touches the thrust washer. On some models an Allen key will be required.
3   Tighten the locknut while holding the adjusting screw stationary.
4   Turn the steering from lock to lock, and make sure that there are no tight spots.

18 Power steering – filter renewal

1   If any component in the steering system is renewed, or if the fluid in the steering system is changed, a new filter should be fitted.
2   The filter is fitted in the bottom of the fluid reservoir and can be renewed as follows.
3   Remove the reservoir cover and lift out the spring.
4   Lift off the filter cover and take out the filter.
5   Fit a new filter and sealing ring using a reversal of the removal procedure.

19 Power steering – fluid draining and refilling

1   Disconnect the feed hose from the steering fluid reservoir and drain the reservoir.
2   Disconnect the return hose from the reservoir and put its open end into a jar. Turn the steering wheel from lock to lock to expel as much fluid as possible.
3   Discard the fluid which has been drained off.
4   After fitting a new filter (Section 18), ensure that all hoses are in place and their clips tightened, and then fill the system with fresh fluid of the approved specification.
5   Fill the reservoir to the top with fluid and then start the engine and switch off as soon as it fires, repeating the starting and stopping sequence several times; this will cause fluid to be drawn into the system quickly.
6   Watch the level of fluid and keep adding fluid so that the reservoir is never sucked dry. When the fluid ceases to drop as a result of the start/stop sequence, start the engine and allow it to run at idling speed.
7   Turn the steering from lock to lock several times, being careful not to leave the wheels on full lock because this will cause the pressure in the system to build up.

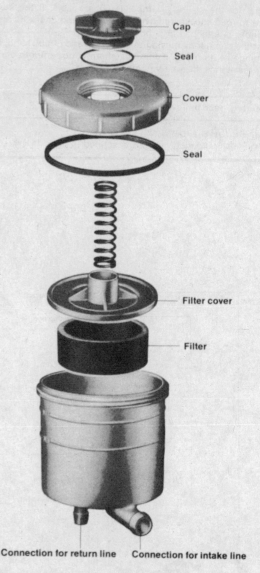

Fig. 11.16 Power steering filter components (Sec 18)

8   Watch the level of the fluid in the reservoir and add fluid if necessary to keep the level at the MAX mark.
9   When the level stops falling and no more air bubbles appear in the reservoir, switch the engine off and fit the reservoir cap. The level of fluid will rise slightly when the engine is switched off, but the rise should not exceed 10 mm (0.39 in).

20 Power steering – checking for fluid leaks

1   With the engine running, turn the steering to full lock on one side and hold it in this position to allow maximum pressure to build up in the system.
2   With the steering still at full lock, check all joints and unions for signs of leaks, and tighten if necessary. To check the steering rack seal, remove the inner end of the rack bellows from the steering gear, and pull it back to reveal the seal.
3   Turn the wheel to full lock on the other side and again check for leaks.

21 Power steering pump – servicing and drivebelt adjustment

Note: *The pump may be either of cast iron or light alloy type. With the latter type it is not possible to renew the oil seal or bearing.*

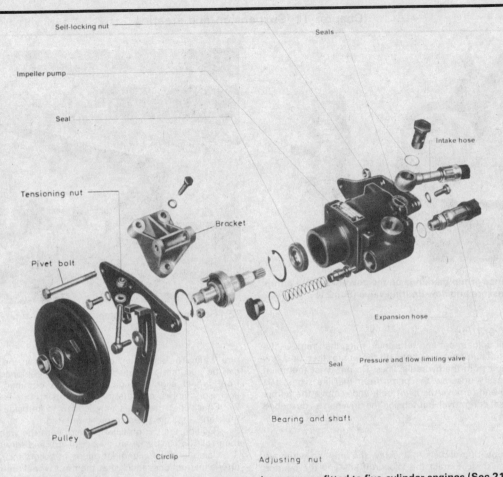

Self-locking nut

Seals

Impeller pump

Seal

Intake hose

Tensioning nut

Bracket

Pivet bolt

Expansion hose

Seal

Pressure and flow limiting valve

Pulley

Bearing and shaft

Circlip

Adjusting nut

Fig. 11.17 Exploded view of the cast iron power steering pump as fitted to five-cylinder engines (Sec 21)

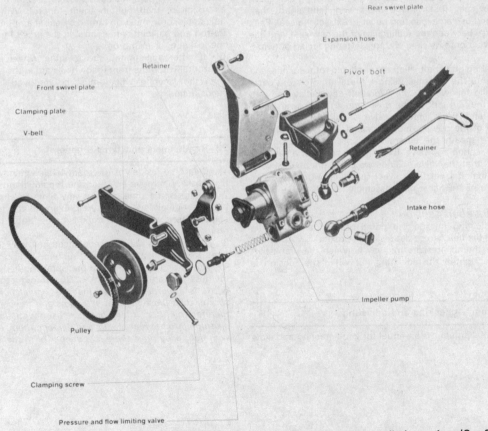

Rear swivel plate

Expansion hose

Retainer

Pivot bolt

Front swivel plate

Clamping plate

V-belt

Retainer

Intake hose

Pulley

Impeller pump

Clamping screw

Pressure and flow limiting valve

Fig. 11.18 Exploded view of the light alloy power steering pump as fitted to four-cylinder engines (Sec 21)

11

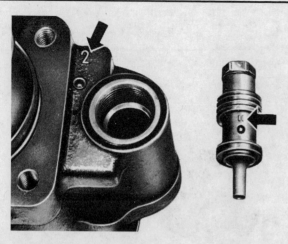

Fig. 11.19 Tolerance group markings on the power steering pump and pressure and flow limiting valve (Sec 21)

22.4 Steering tie-rod adjustment and locking nuts

Removing and refitting

1   First loosen the adjustment and tensioning nuts, then remove the drivebelt. Place a suitable container beneath the pump, then unscrew the union nut or bolt from the hydraulic lines. Do not twist the union nut line – if necessary unscrew the pump from the line when it is removed. Unscrew and remove the pivot bolt, and remove the pump. Refitting is a reversal of removal, but tension the drivebelt as described in paragraph 6.

Servicing

2   To remove the bearing and shaft, unscrew the nut, and withdraw the pulley from the shaft. Extract the Woodruff key and the bearing circlip. Temporarily refit the pulley nut, then grip it in a soft-jawed vice, and use a mallet to drive the pump housing off the bearing and shaft.
3   To remove the seal, first remove the bearing and shaft, then extract the circlip and use an expanding puller to extract the seal. Pack multi-purpose grease between the sealing lips of the new seal, and use a metal tube to drive it onto its seat, with the lettering facing outward. Refit the circlip.
4   To refit the bearing and shaft, align the shaft and rotor splines, and drive the bearing into the housing, using a metal tube on the outer race. Refit the circlip followed by the Woodruff key, pulley and nut. Where applicable, the 'Z' mark on the pulley must face forward.
5   The pressure and flow limiting valve should be checked if intermittent failure of the power steering occurs. To do this, place a suitable container beneath the pump, then unscrew the plug and remove the washer, spring and valve. Examine the spring and valve for damage, and check that the valve drillings are clear. If a new valve is fitted, make sure that it is of the correct tolerance group (see Fig. 11.19). Always fit a new washer on reassembly.

Adjusting the drivebelt tension

6   Loosen the adjusting nut on the pump bracket, and turn the tensioning nut until the belt can be depressed approximately 10.0 mm (0.4 in) under firm thumb pressure midway between the crankshaft and pump pulleys. Tighten the adjusting nut when the tension is correct.

---

22   Wheel alignemnt – checking and adjusting

1   Accurate wheel alignment is essential for good steering and slow

tyre wear. The alignment details are given in the Specifications and can be accurately checked by a suitably equipped garage. However, front wheel alignment gauges can be obtained from most motor accessory stores, and the method of using one is as follows.
2   Check that the car is only loaded to kerbside weight, with a full fuel tank, and the tyres correctly inflated.
3   Position the car on level ground, with the wheels straight-ahead, then roll the car backwards 12 ft (4 m), and forwards again.
4   Using a wheel alignment gauge in accordance with the manufacturer's instructions, check that the front wheel toe-out dimension is as given in the Specifications. If adjustment is necessary, loosen the locknuts or clamp bolts, as applicable, and turn the tie-rod (or tie-rods) as required, then tighten them (photo). Where both tie-rods are adjustable, both must be turned by equal amounts. Make sure that the tie-rod end balljoints are central in the arcs of travel before tightening the locknuts or clamp bolts.
5   If, after adjustment, the steering wheel spokes are no longer horizontal when the front roadwheels are in the straight ahead position then the steering wheel must be removed (see Section 11) and repositioned.

---

23   Roadwheels and tyres – general

1   Clean the insides of the roadwheels whenever they are removed. If necessary, remove any rust and repaint them, where applicable.
2   At the same time, remove any flints or stones which may have become embedded in the tyres. Examine the tyres for damage and splits. Where the depth of tread is amost down to the legal minimum, renew them.
3   The wheels should be rebalanced half way through the life of the tyres to compensate for loss of rubber.
4   Check and adjust the tyre pressures regularly, and make sure that the dust caps are correctly fitted. Do not forget to check the spare tyre.
5   *It is important to note that the wheel bolts for steel rims are shorter than those for light alloy rims and the correct bolt length must therefore be fitted. If long bolts are used with steel rims, the bolts will protrude into the rear brakes and damage them. If short bolts are used with light alloy rims, there is a danger of the wheels becoming loose.*

24 Fault diagnosis – suspension and steering

Symptom	Reason(s)
Excessive play in steering	Worn steering gear Worn tie-rod end balljoints Worn tie-rod bushes Incorrect rack adjustment Worn suspension balljoints
Wanders, or pulls to one side	Incorrect wheel alignment Worn tie-rod end balljoints Worn suspension balljoints Uneven tyre pressures Weak shock absorber Broken or weak coil spring
Heavy or stiff steering	Seized steering or suspension balljoint Incorrect wheel alignment Low tyre pressures Leak of lubricant in steering gear Power steering faulty (where applicable) Power steering pump drivebelt broken (where applicable)
Wheel wobble and vibration	Roadwheels out of balance Roadwheels damaged Weak shock absorbers Worn wheel bearings
Excessive tyre wear	Incorrect wheel alignment Weak shock absorbers Incorrect tyre pressures Roadwheels out of balance

Chapter 12 Bodywork and fittings

Contents

1 General description

The body is of unitary all-steel construction, and incorporates computer calculated impact crumple zones at the front and rear, with a central safety cell passenger compartment. During manufacture the body is undersealed and treated with cavity wax injection. In addition all open box members are sealed.

There are two body styles, the four-door Saloon and the three-door Coupe, and there are a number of trim options on the Saloon version.

2 Maintenance – bodywork and underframe

1   The general condition of a vehicle's bodywork is the one thing that significantly affects its value. Maintenance is easy but needs to be regular. Neglect, particularly after minor damage, can lead quickly to further deterioration and costly repair bills. It is important also to keep watch on those parts of the vehicle not immediately visible, for instance the underside, inside all the wheel arches and the lower part of the engine compartment.

2   The basic maintenance routine for the bodywork is washing – preferably with a lot of water, from a hose. This will remove all the loose solids which may have stuck to the vehicle. It is important to flush these off in such a way as to prevent grit from scratching the finish. The wheel arches and underframe need washing in the same way to remove any accumulated mud which will retain moisture and tend to encourage rust. Paradoxically enough, the best time to clean the underframe and wheel arches is in wet weather when the mud is thoroughly wet and soft. In very wet weather the underframe is usually cleaned of large accumulations automatically and this is a good time for inspection.

3   Periodically, it is a good idea to have the whole of the underframe of the vehicle steam cleaned, engine compartment included, so that a thorough inspection can be carried out to see what minor repairs and renovations are necessary. Steam cleaning is available at many garages and is necessary for removal of the accumulation of oily grime

which sometimes is allowed to become thick in certain areas. If steam cleaning facilities are not available, there are one or two excellent grease solvents available which can be brush applied. The dirt can then be simply hosed off.

4   After washing paintwork, wipe off with a chamois leather to give an unspotted clear finish. A coat of clear protective wax polish will give added protection against chemical pollutants in the air. If the paintwork sheen has dulled or oxidised, use a cleaner/polisher combination to restore the brilliance of the shine. This requires a little effort, but such dulling is usually caused because regular washing has been neglected. Always check that the door and ventilator opening drain holes and pipes are completely clear so that water can be drained out (photo). Bright work should be treated in the same way as

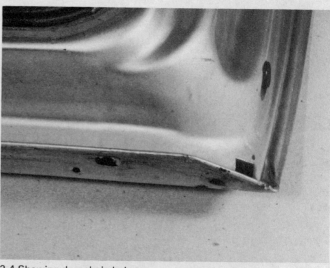

2.4 Showing door drain holes

paintwork. Windscreens and windows can be kept clear of the smeary film which often appears, by adding a little ammonia to the water. If they are scratched, a good rub with a proprietary metal polish will often clear them. Never use any form of wax or other body or chromium polish on glass.

3 Maintenance – upholstery and carpets

1 Mats and carpets should be brushed or vacuum cleaned regularly to keep them free of grit. If they are badly stained remove them from the vehicle for scrubbing or sponging and make quite sure they are dry before refitting. Seats and interior trim panels can be kept clean by wiping with a damp cloth. If they do become stained (which can be more apparent on light coloured upholstery) use a little liquid detergent and a soft nail brush to scour the grime out of the grain of the material. Do not forget to keep the headlining clean in the same way as the upholstery. When using liquid cleaners inside the vehicle do not over-wet the surfaces being cleaned. Excessive damp could get into the seams and padded interior causing stains, offensive odours or even rot. If the inside of the vehicle gets wet accidentally it is worthwhile taking some trouble to dry it out properly, particularly where carpets are involved. *Do not leave oil or electric heaters inside the vehicle for this purpose.*

4 Minor body damage – repair

The photographic sequences on pages 310 and 311 illustrate the operations detailed in the following sub-sections.

Repair of minor scratches in bodywork

If the scratch is very superficial, and does not penetrate to the metal of the bodywork, repair is very simple. Lightly rub the area of the scratch with a paintwork renovator, or a very fine cutting paste, to remove loose paint from the scratch and to clear the surrounding bodywork of wax polish. Rinse the area with clean water.

Apply touch-up paint to the scratch using a fine paint brush; continue to apply fine layers of paint until the surface of the paint in the scratch is level with the surrounding paintwork. Allow the new paint at least two weeks to harden: then blend it into the surrounding paintwork by rubbing the scratch area with a paintwork renovator or a very fine cutting paste. Finally, apply wax polish.

Where the scratch has penetrated right through to the metal of the bodywork, causing the metal to rust, a different repair technique is required. Remove any loose rust from the bottom of the scratch with a penknife, then apply rust inhibiting paint to prevent the formation of rust in the future. Using a rubber or nylon applicator fill the scratch with bodystopper paste. If required, this paste can be mixed with cellulose thinners to provide a very thin paste which is ideal for filling narrow scratches. Before the stopper-paste in the scratch hardens, wrap a piece of smooth cotton rag around the top of a finger. Dip the finger in cellulose thinners and then quickly sweep it across the surface of the stopper-paste in the scratch; this will ensure that the surface of the stopper-paste is slightly hollowed. The scratch can now be painted over as described earlier in this Section.

Repair of dents in bodywork

When deep denting of the vehicle's bodywork has taken place, the first task is to pull the dent out, until the affected bodywork almost attains its original shape. There is little point in trying to restore the original shape completely, as the metal in the damaged area will have stretched on impact and cannot be reshaped fully to its original contour. It is better to bring the level of the dent up to a point which is about $\frac{1}{8}$ in (3 mm) below the level of the surrounding bodywork. In cases where the dent is very shallow anyway, it is not worth trying to pull it out at all. If the underside of the dent is accessible, it can be hammered out gently from behind, using a mallet with a wooden or plastic head. Whilst doing this, hold a suitable block of wood firmly against the outside of the panel to absorb the impact from the hammer blows and thus prevent a large area of the bodywork from being 'belled-out'.

Should the dent be in a section of the bodywork which has a double skin or some other factor making it inaccessible from behind, a different technique is called for. Drill several small holes through the

metal inside the area – particularly in the deeper section. Then screw long self-tapping screws into the holes just sufficiently for them to gain a good purchase in the metal. Now the dent can be pulled out by pulling on the protruding heads of the screws with a pair of pliers.

The next stage of the repair is the removal of the paint from the damaged area, and from an inch or so of the surrounding 'sound' bodywork. This is accomplished most easily by using a wire brush or abrasive pad on a power drill, although it can be done just as effectively by hand using sheets of abrasive paper. To complete the preparation for filling, score the surface of the bare metal with a screwdriver or the tang of a file, or alternatively, drill small holes in the affected area. This will provide a really good 'key' for the filler paste.

To complete the repair see the Section on filling and re-spraying.

Repair of rust holes or gashes in bodywork

Remove all paint from the affected area and from an inch or so of the surrounding 'sound' bodywork, using an abrasive pad or a wire brush on a power drill. If these are not available a few sheets of abrasive paper will do the job just as effectively. With the paint removed you will be able to gauge the severity of the corrosion and therefore decide whether to renew the whole panel (if this is possible) or to repair the affected area. New body panels are not as expensive as most people think and it is often quicker and more satisfactory to fit a new panel than to attempt to repair large areas of corrosion.

Remove all fittings from the affected area except those which will act as a guide to the original shape of the damaged bodywork (eg headlamp shells etc). Then, using tin snips or a hacksaw blade, remove all loose metal and any other metal badly affected by corrosion. Hammer the edges of the hole inwards in order to create a slight depression for the filler paste.

Wire brush the affected area to remove the powdery rust from the surface of the remaining metal. Paint the affected area with rust inhibiting paint; if the back of the rusted area is accessible treat this also.

Before filling can take place it will be necessary to block the hole in some way. This can be achieved by the use of zinc gauze or aluminium tape.

Zinc gauze is probably the best material to use for a large hole. Cut a piece to the approximate size and shape of the hole to be filled, then position it in the hole so that its edges are below the level of the surrounding bodywork. It can be retained in position by several blobs of filler paste around its periphery.

Aluminium tape should be used for small or very narrow holes. Pull a piece off the roll and trim it to the approximate size and shape required, then pull off the backing paper (if used) and stick the tape over the hole; it can be overlapped if the thickness of one piece is insufficient. Burnish down the edges of the tape with the handle of a screwdriver or similar, to ensure that the tape is securely attached to the metal underneath.

Bodywork repairs – filling and re-spraying

Before using this Section, see the Sections on dent, deep scratch, rust holes and gash repairs.

Many types of bodyfiller are available, but generally speaking those proprietary kits which contain a tin of filler paste and a tube of resin hardener are best for this type of repair. A wide, flexible plastic or nylon applicator will be found invaluable for imparting a smooth and well contoured finish to the surface of the filler.

Mix up a little filler on a clean piece of card or board – measure the hardener carefully (follow the maker's instructions on the pack) otherwise the filler will set too rapidly or too slowly.

Using the applicator apply the filler paste to the prepared area; draw the applicator across the surface of the filler to achieve the correct contour and to level the filler surface. As soon as a contour that approximates to the correct one is achieved, stop working the paste – if you carry on too long the paste will become sticky and begin to 'pick up' on the applicator. Continue to add thin layers of filler paste at twenty-minute intervals until the level of the filler is just proud of the surrounding bodywork.

Once the filler has hardened, excess can be removed using a metal plane or file. From then on, progressively finer grades of abrasive paper should be used, starting with a 40 grade production paper and finishing with 400 grade wet-and-dry paper. Always wrap the abrasive paper around a flat rubber, cork, or wooden block – otherwise the surface of the filler will not be completely flat. During the smoothing of the filler surface the wet-and-dry paper should be periodically rinsed

12

in water. This will ensure that a very smooth finish is imparted to the filler at the final stage.

At this stage the 'dent' should be surrounded by a ring of bare metal, which in turn should be encircled by the finely 'feathered' edge of the good paintwork. Rinse the repair area with clean water, until all of the dust produced by the rubbing-down operation has gone.

Spray the whole repair area with a light coat of primer – this will show up any imperfections in the surface of the filler. Repair these imperfections with fresh filler paste or bodystopper, and once more smooth the surface with abrasive paper. If bodystopper is used, it can be mixed with cellulose thinners to form a really thin paste which is ideal for filling small holes. Repeat this spray and repair procedure until you are satisfied that the surface of the filler, and the feathered edge of the paintwork are perfect. Clean the repair area with clean water and allow to dry fully.

The repair area is now ready for final spraying. Paint spraying must be carried out in a warm, dry, windless and dust free atmosphere. This condition can be created artificially if you have access to a large indoor working area, but if you are forced to work in the open, you will have to pick your day very carefully. If you are working indoors, dousing the floor in the work area with water will help to settle the dust which would otherwise be in the atmosphere. If the repair area is confined to one body panel, mask off the surrounding panels; this will help to minimise the effects of a slight mis-match in paint colours. Bodywork fittings (eg chrome strips, door handles etc) will also need to be masked off. Use genuine masking tape and several thicknesses of newspaper for the masking operations.

Before commencing to spray, agitate the aerosol can thoroughly, then spray a test area (an old tin, or similar) until the technique is mastered. Cover the repair area with a thick coat of primer; the thickness should be built up using several thin layers of paint rather than one thick one. Using 400 grade wet-and-dry paper, rub down the surface of the primer until it is really smooth. While doing this, the work area should be thoroughly doused with water, and the wet-and-dry paper periodically rinsed in water. Allow to dry before spraying on more paint.

Spray on the top coat, again building up the thickness by using several thin layers of paint. Start spraying in the centre of the repair area and then, using a circular motion, work outwards until the whole repair area and about 2 inches of the surrounding original paintwork is covered. Remove all masking material 10 to 15 minutes after spraying on the final coat of paint.

Allow the new paint at least two weeks to harden, then, using a paintwork renovator or a very fine cutting paste, blend the edges of the paint into the existing paintwork. Finally, apply wax polish.

5   Major body damage – repair

Where serious damage has occurred or large areas need renewal due to neglect, it means that complete new panels will need welding in, and this is best left to professionals. If the damage is due to impact,

it will also be necessary to completely check the alignment of the bodyshell, and this can only be carried out accurately by an Audi dealer using special jigs. If the body is left misaligned, it is primarily dangerous as the car will not handle properly, and secondly, uneven stresses will be imposed on the steering, suspension and possibly transmission, causing abnormal wear, or complete failure, particularly to such items as the tyres.

6   Door rattles – tracing and rectification

1   The most common cause of door rattles is a striker plate which is worn, loose, or misaligned, but other causes may be:

   (a) *Loose door handles, window winder handles, door hinges, or door stays*
   (b) *Loose, worn or misaligned door lock components*
   (c) *Loose, or worn remote control mechanism*
   (d) *Loose window glass*

2   If the striker catch is worn, as a result of door rattles, fit a new striker before adjusting the door.
3   If door hinges are worn significantly, new hinges should be fitted.

7   Front door trim panel – removal and refitting

1   Unscrew and remove the locking knob.
2   Remove any retaining screws from the perimeter of the panel – on some models it will be necessary to prise off a plastic cap to expose the screw.
3   Remove the cross-head screws from the armrest, swivel it approximately 90° around the top mounting and withdraw it from the panel (photo).
4   On models with manually operated windows, fully close the window and note the position of the regulator handle. Prise the plastic cover from the centre of the handle, remove the screw, and pull off the handle, together with the bezel.
5   Prise the finger plate from the door lock interior remote control, remove the screw, and withdraw the escutcheon (photos).
6   Where necessary remove the triangular cover from the front of the panel (photo).
7   With a wide-bladed screwdriver, release the trim panel retaining clips from the door and withdraw the trim panel.
8   Carefully remove the waterproof sheeting.
9   Refitting is the reverse of removal. Make sure that the panel clips are aligned with the holes before tapping them in with the palm of the hand.

8   Front and rear door locks – removal and refitting

1   Using an Allen key unscrew and remove the two lock retaining

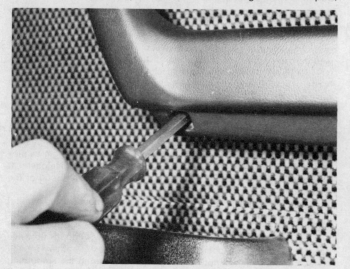

7.3 Removing the armrest

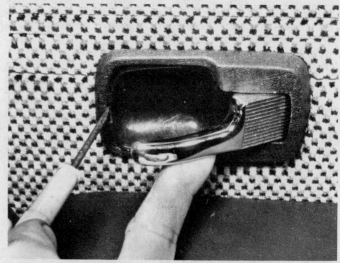

7.5A Prise out the finger plate ...

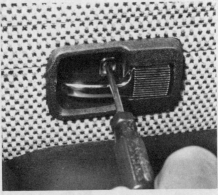

7.5B ... and remove the interior door handle escutcheon

7.6 Removing the front door trim cover

8.1 Front door lock

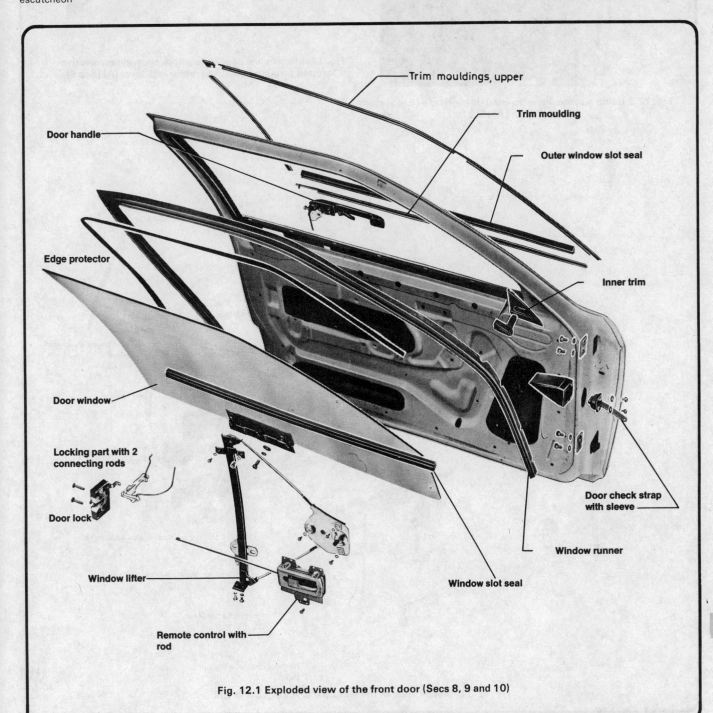

Fig. 12.1 Exploded view of the front door (Secs 8, 9 and 10)

Trim mouldings, upper

Trim moulding

Outer window slot seal

Door handle

Inner trim

Edge protector

Door window

Locking part with 2 connecting rods

Door lock

Door check strap with sleeve

Window lifter

Window runner

Window slot seal

Remote control with rod

12

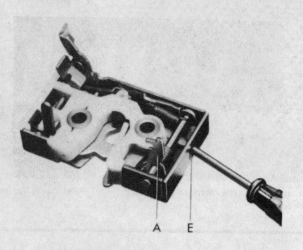

Fig. 12.4 Inner view of rear door lock showing screwdriver inserted through hole (E) to retain lock lever (A) (Sec 8)

Fig. 12.2 Using a screwdriver inserted through hole (E) to return the lock lever (A) (Sec 8)

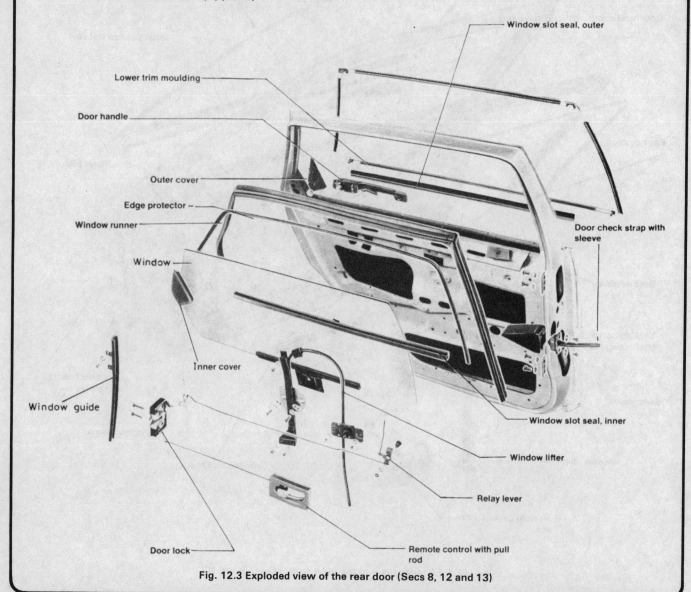

Window slot seal, outer

Lower trim moulding

Door handle

Outer cover

Edge protector

Window runner

Window

Inner cover

Window guide

Door check strap with sleeve

Window slot seal, inner

Window lifter

Relay lever

Door lock

Remote control with pull rod

Fig. 12.3 Exploded view of the rear door (Secs 8, 12 and 13)

screws (photo) and withdraw the lock approximately 10 to 12 mm (0.4 to 0.5 in).

2 Insert a screwdriver through the hole in the bottom of the lock to retain the lock lever in the 90° position.

3 Unhook the remote control rod from the lock lever.

4 Pull the lock out of the sleeve and disconnect the operating rod.

5 Refitting is a reversal of removal.

9 Front door exterior handle – removal and refitting

1 Remove the front door lock as described in Section 8.

2 Prise the plastic insert from the handle, starting from the front.

3 Remove the handle retaining screws, one from the front of the handle and the other from the edge of the door.

4 Press the operating rod out of the cam, and withdraw the exterior handle, together with the rod.

5 Refitting is a reversal of removal.

10 Front door – dismantling and reassembly

1 Remove the trim panel, door lock and exterior handle, as described in Sections 7, 8 and 9.

2 On models with power windows and door locks remove the relevant components with reference to Sections 27 and 28.

3 Remove the trim moulding below the window. To do this on Saloon models unscrew the rear screw and lever off the moulding. On Coupe models it will also be necessary to unscrew the front screw after pushing the seal (Fig. 12.6) to one side.

4 Prise the upper trim mouldings from the door.

5 Pull the inner window seal from the flange, with the windows fully open.

6 Remove the outer window seal by twisting out the plastic clips.

7 Position the window so that the lower channel is in the inner door panel aperture, then unscrew the retaining bolts, tilt the window, and remove it from the door.

8 Remove the screws and withdraw the inner remote control handle and rod (photo).

9 Unbolt and remove the window regulator and channel (where applicable).

10 Remove the lock relay mechanism.

11 Prise out the window channel and protector.

12 Remove the screws and withdraw the door check strap.

13 Reassembly is a reversal of dismantling.

11 Rear door trim panel – removal and refitting

1 Unscrew and remove the locking knob.

2 Remove the cross-head screws and withdraw the armrest.

3 On models with manually operated windows, fully close the

10.8 Removing the front door inner remote control handle (central door locking type)

window and note the position of the regulator handle. Prise the plastic cover from the centre of the handle, remove the screw, and pull off the handle, together with the bezel.

4 Prise the finger plate from the door lock interior remote control, remove the screw, and withdraw the escutcheon.

5 With a wide-bladed screwdriver, release the trim panel retaining clips from the door and withdraw the trim panel.

6 Carefully remove the waterproof sheeting.

7 Refitting is a reversal of removal. Make sure that the panel clips are aligned with the holes before tapping them in with the palm of the hand.

12 Rear door exterior handle – removal and refitting

1 Prise the plastic insert from the handle, starting from the front.

2 Remove the handle retaining screws, one from the front of the handle and the other from the edge of the door. The handle can now be withdrawn from the door.

3 Refitting is a reversal of removal.

13 Rear door – dismantling and reassembly

1 Remove the door lock, trim panel and exterior handle as described in Sections 8, 11 and 12.

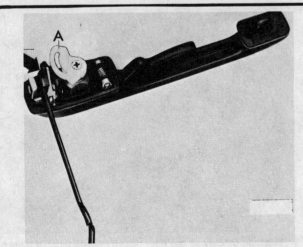

Fig. 12.5 Front door exterior handle showing cam (A) and rod retaining clip (arrowed) (Sec 9)

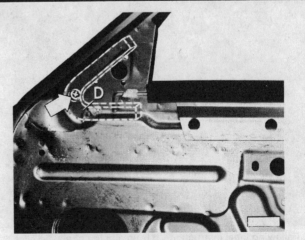

Fig. 12.6 Front door trim moulding screw location (arrowed) showing seal (D) on Coupe models (Sec 10)

12

These photos illustrate a method of repairing simple dents. They are intended to supplement *Body repair - minor damage* in this Chapter and should not be used as the sole instructions for body repair on these vehicles.

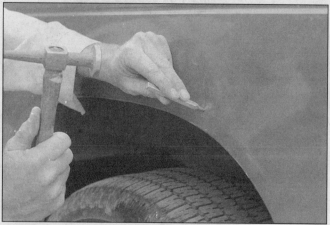

1   If you can't access the backside of the body panel to hammer out the dent, pull it out with a slide-hammer-type dent puller. In the deepest portion of the dent or along the crease line, drill or punch hole(s) at least one inch apart . . .

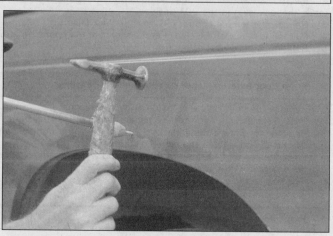

2   . . . then screw the slide-hammer into the hole and operate it. Tap with a hammer near the edge of the dent to help 'pop' the metal back to its original shape. When you're finished, the dent area should be close to its original contour and about 1/8-inch below the surface of the surrounding metal

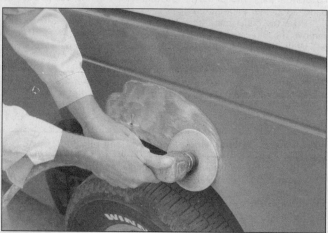

3   Using coarse-grit sandpaper, remove the paint down to the bare metal. Hand sanding works fine, but the disc sander shown here makes the job faster. Use finer (about 320-grit) sandpaper to feather-edge the paint at least one inch around the dent area

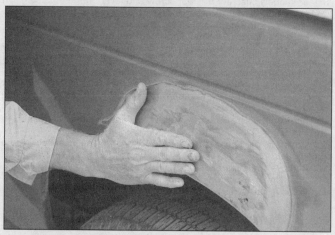

4   When the paint is removed, touch will probably be more helpful than sight for telling if the metal is straight. Hammer down the high spots or raise the low spots as necessary. Clean the repair area with wax/silicone remover

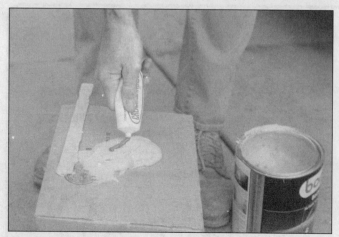

5   Following label instructions, mix up a batch of plastic filler and hardener. The ratio of filler to hardener is critical, and, if you mix it incorrectly, it will either not cure properly or cure too quickly (you won't have time to file and sand it into shape)

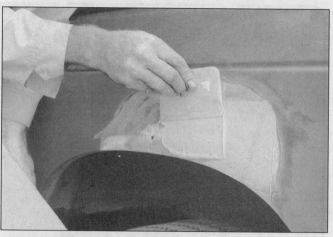

6   Working quickly so the filler doesn't harden, use a plastic applicator to press the body filler firmly into the metal, assuring it bonds completely. Work the filler until it matches the original contour and is slightly above the surrounding metal

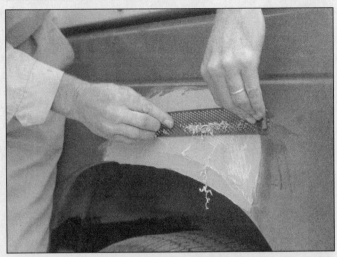

7   Let the filler harden until you can just dent it with your fingernail. Use a body file or Surform tool (shown here) to rough-shape the filler

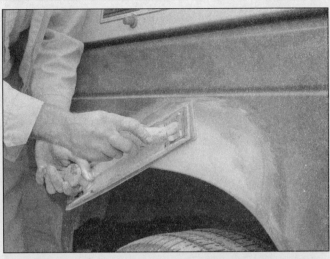

8   Use coarse-grit sandpaper and a sanding board or block to work the filler down until it's smooth and even. Work down to finer grits of sandpaper - always using a board or block - ending up with 360 or 400 grit

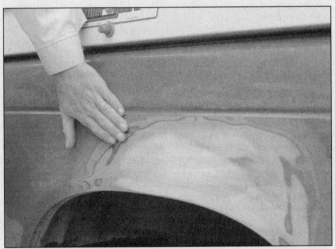

9   You shouldn't be able to feel any ridge at the transition from the filler to the bare metal or from the bare metal to the old paint. As soon as the repair is flat and uniform, remove the dust and mask off the adjacent panels or trim pieces

10   Apply several layers of primer to the area. Don't spray the primer on too heavy, so it sags or runs, and make sure each coat is dry before you spray on the next one. A professional-type spray gun is being used here, but aerosol spray primer is available inexpensively from auto parts stores

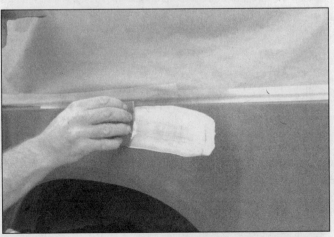

11   The primer will help reveal imperfections or scratches. Fill these with glazing compound. Follow the label instructions and sand it with 360 or 400-grit sandpaper until it's smooth. Repeat the glazing, sanding and respraying until the primer reveals a perfectly smooth surface

12   Finish sand the primer with very fine sandpaper (400 or 600-grit) to remove the primer overspray. Clean the area with water and allow it to dry. Use a tack rag to remove any dust, then apply the finish coat. Don't attempt to rub out or wax the repair area until the paint has dried completely (at least two weeks)

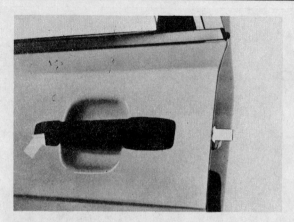

Fig. 12.7 Rear door exterior handle screw locations (arrowed) (Sec 12)

Fig. 12.8 Removing the rear door window through the slot (arrowed) (Sec 13)

2   On models with power windows and door locks remove the relevant components with reference to Sections 27 and 28.
3   Prise the upper trim mouldings from the door.
4   Unscrew the end screws and prise off the lower trim moulding below the window.
5   Prise off the inner corner cover, unscrew the nut, and remove the outer corner plate.
6   Remove the outer window seal by twisting out the plastic clips.
7   Pull the inner window seal from the clips and flange, with the window fully open.
8   Close the window, then remove the rear window channel by unscrewing the retaining screws and withdrawing it downward. Access to the middle screw is by prising out the grommet.
9   Position the window so that the window channel screws are aligned with the holes and remove the screws. Lift the window from the door while guiding it through the slot at the rear of the window aperture.
10 Prise out the window channel and protector.
11 Unbolt and remove the window regulator and channel.
12 Remove the screws and withdraw the inner remote control handle and rod.
13 Unscrew the nut and withdraw the lock relay rods and lever.
14 Remove the screws and withdraw the door check strap.
15 Reassembly is a reversal of dismantling.

14 Doors – removal and refitting

1   Remove the trim panel as described in Section 7 or 11.
2   If the same door is being refitted, mark round the hinges on the door, using a pencil or a fine tipped ballpoint pen. This simplifies realignment of the door.
3   Remove the circlip from the pin in the door check strap and tap out the pin (photo). Fit the pin and circlip back into the clevis to prevent their being lost.
4   With an assistant supporting the weight of the door, or with the bottom of the door propped, remove the screws from the hinges and take the door off.
5   Refitting is a reversal of removal. If the same door is refitted, screw the screws in until they are just tight and line the hinges up with the marks made prior to removal. If using a different door, screw the hinge screws in until they are just tight, close the door and push it into the position which aligns its edge with the body contour. Move the door up or down or sideways as necessary to give an even gap between the edge of the door and the body pillars. When door alignment is correct, tighten the hinge screws fully. If necessary, adjust the striker as described in the following Section.

15 Door striker – adjustment

1   Mark round the door striker (photo) with a pencil, or a fine ballpoint pen.
2   Fit a spanner to the hexagon on the striker and unscrew the striker about one turn so that the striker moves when tapped with a soft-headed hammer.
3   Tap the striker towards the inside of the car if the door rattles, or towards the outside of the car if the door fits too tightly, but be careful to keep the striker in the same horizontal line, unless it also requires vertical adjustment. Only move the striker a small amount at a time;

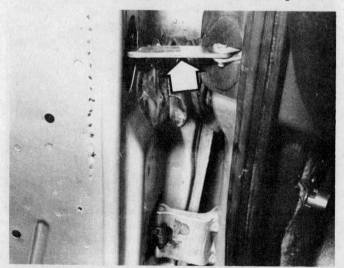

14.3 Door check strap (arrowed)

15.1 Front door striker

the actual amount moved can be checked by reference to the pencil mark made before the striker was loosened.

4 When a position has been found in which the door closes firmly, but without difficulty, tighten the striker.

16 Bonnet – removal, refitting and adjustment

1 Support the bonnet in its open position, and place some cardboard or rags beneath the corners by the hinges.
2 Disconnect the windscreen washer pipe from the bonnet (photo).
3 Mark the location of the hinges with a pencil (photo).
4 With the help of an assistant, unscrew the nuts and withdraw the bonnet from the car.
5 Refitting is a reversal of removal, but adjust the hinges to their original positions so that the bonnet is level with the surrounding bodywork. If necessary the front of the bonnet height may be adjusted by screwing the striker located beneath the bonnet in or out (photo).

17 Bonnet lock cable – removal, refitting and adjustment

1 On Saloon models remove the headlights and surrounds, as described in Chapter 10.
2 On Coupe models lever off the clips and pull the trim strip from the

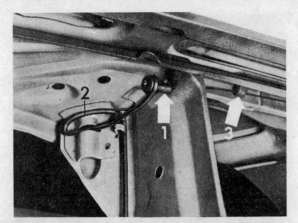

Fig. 12.9 Bonnet lock cable location on Saloon models (Sec 17)

1 Clamp	3 Guide
2 Lever	

radiator grille, then remove the screws and withdraw the headlight surround.
3 Unscrew the clamp bolt and disconnect the cable from the nipple, then release the cable from the lever and guide sleeves (photo).

16.2 Windscreen washer pipe location on the bonnet

16.3 A bonnet hinge

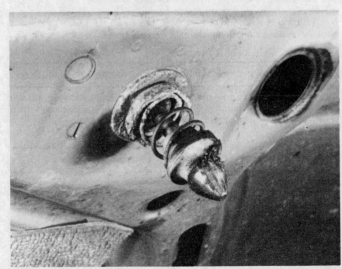

16.5 Bonnet striker

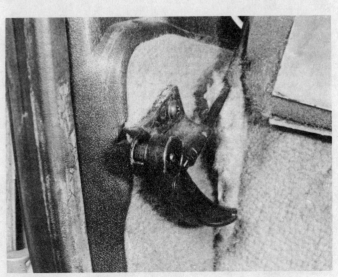

17.3 Bonnet lock lever

12

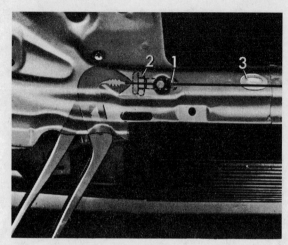

Fig. 12.10 Adjusting the bonnet lock cable on Coupe models
(Sec 17)

1   Clamp   3   Guide
2   Lever

4   Refitting is a reversal of removal, but adjust the cable by pulling it
taut with a pair of pliers, at the same time pressing the nipple against
the lever, then tighten the clamp bolt. **Do not**, however, pretension the
locking lever.

18 Boot lid – removal, refitting and adjustment

1   Support the boot lid in its open position, and place some
cardboard or rags beneath the corners by the hinges.
2   Disconnect the wiring loom and power lock hose, as necessary,
then mark the location of the hinges with a pencil (photo).
3   With the help of an assistant, unscrew the nuts and withdraw the
boot lid from the car.
4   Refitting is a reversal of removal, but adjust the hinges to their
original positions so that the boot lid is level with the surrounding
bodywork.

19 Boot lid torsion bars – removal and refitting

1   Support the boot lid in its open position.
2   Remove the rear seat, backrest, and parcel shelf.
3   Using a screwdriver, lever the torsion bar rubber bushes from the
rear panel.
4   Push the torsion bars rearward and use pliers to remove their ends
from the mountings.

18.2 A boot lid hinge

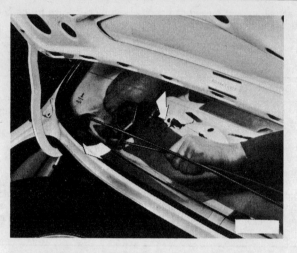

Fig. 12.11 Removing the boot lid torsion bars (Sec 19)

5   Withdraw the torsion bars from the car.
6   Refitting is a reversal of removal.

20 Tailgate – removal, refitting and adjustment

1   Disconnect the battery negative lead.
2   Open the tailgate and support it.
3   Disconnect the cable for the rear light cluster.
4   Detach the gas-filled struts from the tailgate by levering down the
spring clip and pulling the socket from the ball.
5   Mark the location of the hinges with a pencil, then, with the help
of an assistant, unscrew the nuts and withdraw the tailgate from the
car.
6   Refitting is a reversal of removal, but adjust the hinges to their
original positions. Use the adjustment of the hinges on the tailgate to
position the tailgate in relation to the rear panel, and the adjustment
of the hinges on the roof panel to position the tailgate in relation to the
side panels.

21 Tailgate cable – removal and refitting

1   Remove the rear seat and backrest.
2   Remove the screws and withdraw the side trim panel and pocket.
3   Unscrew the cable clamp bolt and disconnect the cable and clip.
4   Disconnect the cable from the tailgate lock.
5   Unclip the cable from the side panel.
6   Refitting is a reversal of removal, but make sure that all slack is
removed before tightening the cable clamp bolt.

22 Windscreen and rear window glass – removal and refitting

The windscreen and rear window are directly bonded to the
metalwork, and the removal and fitting of this glass should be left to
your Audi dealer or a specialist glass replacement company.

23 Sunroof – removal, refitting and adjustment

Sunroof without wind deflector
1   Tilt the sunroof using the crank.
2   Pull the finger eyes inwards and disconnect the sunroof from the
guide blocks.
3   Withdraw the sunroof rearwards until the sliding blocks can be
disengaged from the guides, then lift the sunroof from the car.
4   Refitting is a reversal of removal. However, if the sunroof does not
run parallel, remove the drive and set both guide blocks with the levers
in their highest position, then refit the drive. To adjust the front seal

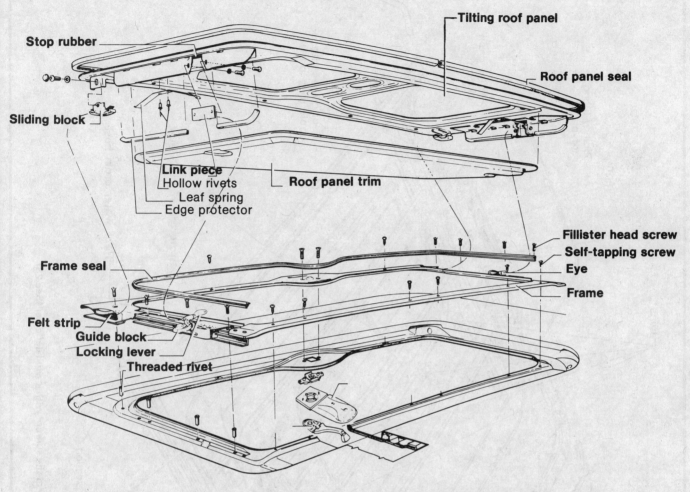

Fig. 12.12 Exploded diagram of the sunroof without a wind deflector (Sec 23)

tension, remove the seal then close the sunroof and check that the front gap is between 3.6 and 4.0 mm (0.14 and 0.16 in). If not, loosen the support lever screws and move the levers as necessary. The front and rear height of the sunroof can also be adjusted by repositioning the mountings.

Sunroof with wind deflector

5   Tilt the sunroof using the crank.
6   Prise the panel trim down then, using a 300 mm (11.8 in) long hooked piece of wire, unhook the trim spring.
7   Close the sunroof, release the trim at the front, and push back the trim.
8   Disconnect the right-hand tilt mechanism, and remove the connecting rods and left-hand tilt mechanism (photo).

9   Prise the lockwasher off the retainer pin and remove the guide lever.
10   Remove the screws from the front guide and sunroof.
11   Crank the sunroof forward until the rear guide pins are released, then withdraw the sunroof from the car.
12   Refitting is a reversal of removal. The height of the sunroof can be adjusted by loosening the mountings.

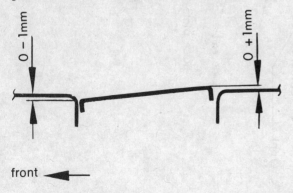

Fig. 12.13 Sunroof adjustment dimensions (Sec 23)

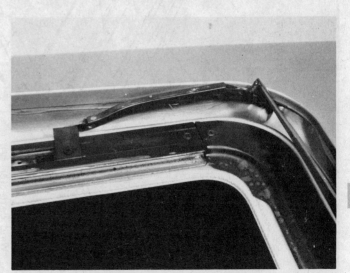

23.8 Sunroof mechanism

12

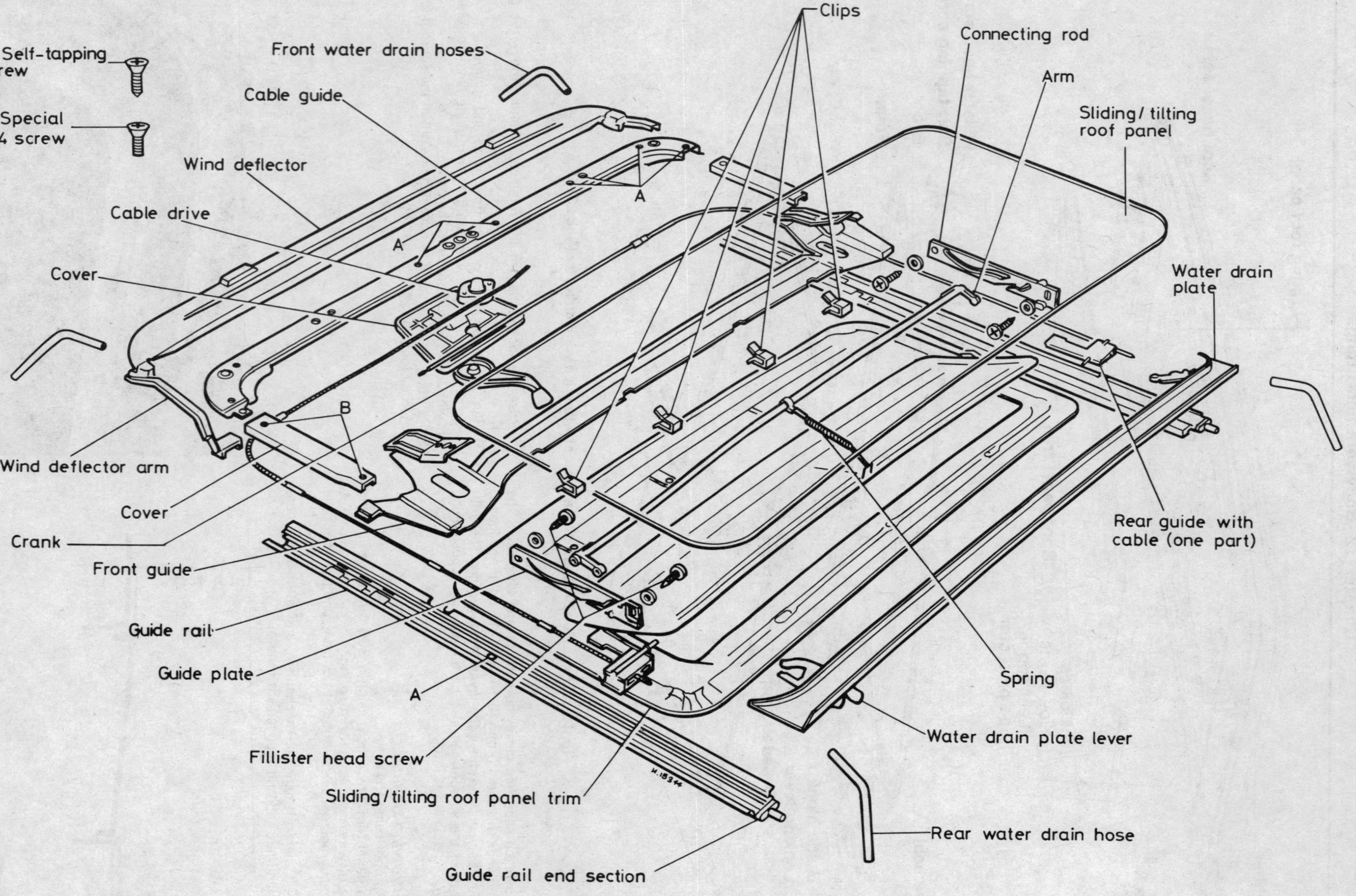

Water drain plate

Rear guide with cable (one part)

Sliding/tilting roof panel

Connecting rod

Arm

Clips

Spring

Water drain plate lever

Rear water drain hose

Front water drain hoses

Cable guide

Wind deflector

Cable drive

Guide rail end section

A

A

Sliding/tilting roof panel trim

Fillister head screw

Guide plate

Guide rail

Front guide

Crank

Cover

Wind deflector arm

Cover

B

A-Self-tapping screw

B-Special M 4 screw

Fig. 12.14 Exploded view of the sunroof with a wind deflector (Sec 23)

24.2A Front bumper mounting bolt

24 Bumpers – removal and refitting

1   Disconnect the direction indicator/rear number plate wiring and headlight washer equipment from the bumper, as applicable.
2   Unscrew and remove the centre mounting bolts located on the front underframe or in the rear luggage compartment (photos).
3   Slide the bumper from the side guides, keeping the bumper parallel to the front of the car.
4   If necessary, remove the screws and withdraw the corner sections, then unclip the cover from the bumper.
5   Refitting is a reversal of removal.

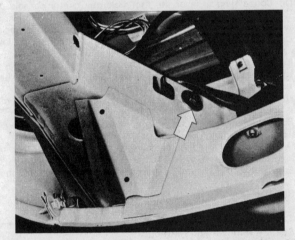
Fig. 12.15 Location of a front bumper mounting bolt (Sec 24)

Fig. 12.17 Location of the front bumper corner section retaining screws (Sec 24)

Fig. 12.16 Removing the front bumper (Sec 24)

24.2B Rear bumper mounting nuts

25 Facia – removal and refitting

1   Remove the instrument panel as described in Chapter 10.
2   On Saloon models remove the screws from the front of the central console.
3   Remove the screws securing the shelf to the facia on the driver's side.
4   Remove the screws and withdraw the glovebox and side trim (photo).

Fig. 12.18 Glovebox retaining screw locations on Saloon models
(Sec 25)
Left-hand drive shown

Fig. 12.19 Console retaining screw locations on Coupe models
(Sec 25)

1   *Gear lever trim*   2   *Console*

25.4 Removing the facia side trim

5   On Coupe models lever the trim from the centre console, and remove the trim screws from around the gear lever. Remove the remaining screws and withdraw the console slighty from the facia.
6   On Saloon models remove the screws and withdraw the lower facia panel downwards.
7   Remove the trim from the instrument panel surround.
8   Unscrew the bolts securing the sides of the facia to the bulkhead, and also remove the centre support screw.
9   Unclip the centre double vent and remove it from the instrument panel aperture.
10 Push the centre fresh air hose down slightly, then unscrew the facia central mounting nut.
11 Working in the engine compartment, unscrew the two nuts securing the facia to the bulkhead.
12 Ease the facia from the bulkhead, and withdraw it through the door aperture.
13 Refitting is a reversal of removal.

26 Seats – removal and refitting

Front seat
1   Push the seat fully forward.
2   Remove the screw where fitted, then pull the trim piece from the seat runner.
3   Pull the cap from the seat runner side member.
4   At the front of the seat unscrew the stop nut.
5   Pull up the lever and slide the seat off the rear of the runners. Remove the seat through the door aperture.
6   Refitting is a reversal of removal.

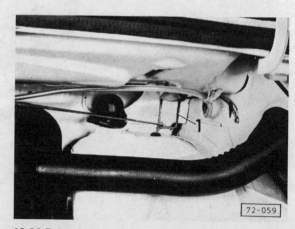

Fig. 12.20 Releasing a rear seat backrest upper hook (1) (Sec 26)

Rear seat

7   Lift out the rear seat cushion.
8   To remove the backrest, have an assistant press down on the backrest, then release the upper hooks from the rear luggage compartment, using a length of welding wire.
9   Lift the backrest and remove it through the door aperture.
10 Refitting is a reversal of removal.

27 Central door locking system – general

1   Certain models are equipped with a central door locking system which automatically locks all doors and the rear tailgate/boot lid in unison with the manual locking of either front door. On early models the system is operated by vacuum from the engine, but a separate pump is fitted to some later models.
2   Any fault in the system is most likely to be caused by a leak in one of the hoses, in which case the hose and connections should be checked and repaired as necessary. Access to the appropriate actuator is generally fairly straightforward after removal of the relevant trim panel. Typical access to the boot lid actuator is shown in the photo sequence. With the later type system, a fault may be in the pump

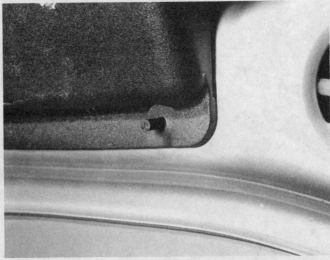

27.2A To remove the boot lid locking actuator pull out the pins ...

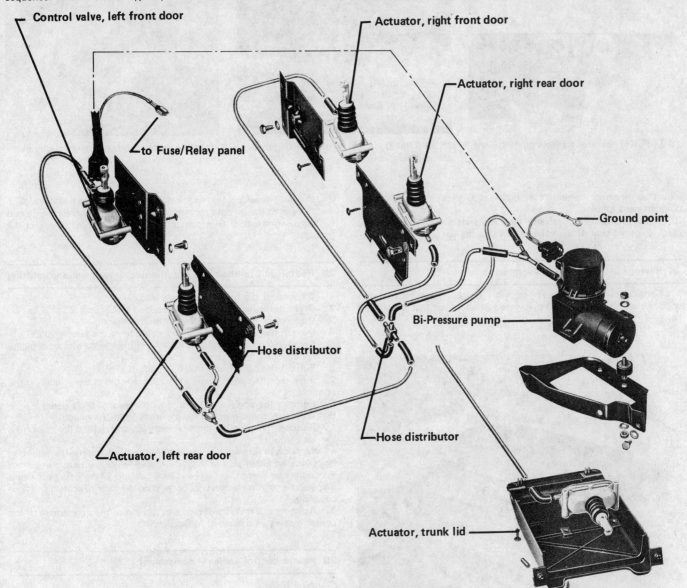

Fig. 12.21 Central door locking system components (late type) (Sec 27)

Left-hand drive shown

27.2B ... remove the screws ...

27.2C ... and remove the actuator

27.2D Central door locking system pump (later models)

28.3A Power operated window guide channel

28.3B Regulator cable connection on power operated windows

28.3C Removing a power operated window motor

which is located behind the right-hand trim in the luggage compartment (photo).

3   When fitting a check valve on the early system make sure that the black coloured side of the valve is towards the vacuum source.

28 Power operated windows – general

1   Certain models are equipped with power (electric) operated windows which can be raised or lowered when the ignition is switched on.

28.3D Removing the power operated window guide channel and cable

2   If a fault develops, first check that the system fuse has not blown.
3   Access to the electric motors and regulator mechanism is gained by removing the door trim panels as described in Sections 7 or 11 (photos).

29 Heater unit (without air conditioning) – removal and refitting

1   Disconnect the battery negative lead.
2   Drain the cooling system as described in Chapter 2.
3   Disconnect the heater hoses at the bulkhead.
4   Detach the temperature control cable from the heater valve.
5   Remove the central console and the left and right trim from below the facia.
6   Pull off the heater and fresh air control knobs.
7   Prise out the control panel, then remove the screws securing the controls.
8   Remove the screws and withdraw the central facia panel.
9   Disconnect and remove the air ducts from the heater.
10 Remove the large heater retaining clip, and detach the cowl from the air plenum.
11 Working in the engine compartment remove the heater mounting bolts located either side of the motor, then lower the heater unit from inside the car. Since there will still be a quantity of water in the heater, place some polythene sheeting, or rags, on the floor to protect the floor covering.
12 Refitting is a reversal of removal, but check the adjustment of the control cables as described in Section 30.

30 Heater control cables – adjustment

Control flap
1   Check that the outer cable is in contact with the stop shoulder and firmly secured with the clip.
2   Remove the clip at the control flap end, then close the flap and fit

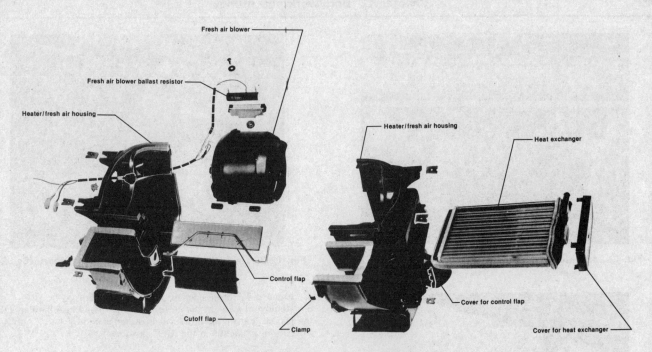

Fresh air blower

Fresh air blower ballast resistor

Heater/fresh air housing

Heater/fresh air housing

Heat exchanger

Control flap

Cutoff flap

Clamp

Cover for control flap

Cover for heat exchanger

Fig. 12.22 Exploded view of the heater (Sec 29)

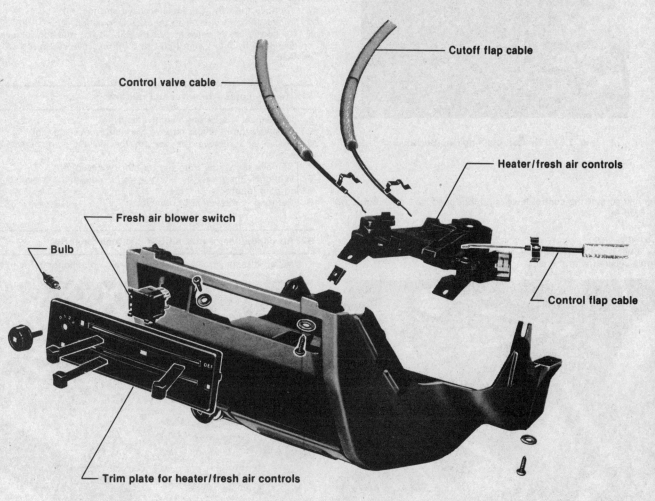

Control valve cable

Cutoff flap cable

Heater/fresh air controls

Fresh air blower switch

Bulb

Control flap cable

Trim plate for heater/fresh air controls

Fig. 12.23 Heater controls (Sec 29)

12

Fig. 12.24 Heater control retaining screw locations (Sec 29)

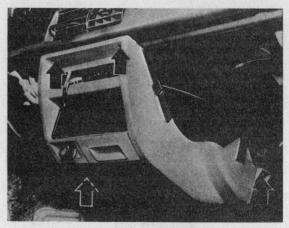

Fig. 12.25 Heater control facia panel screw locations (Sec 29)

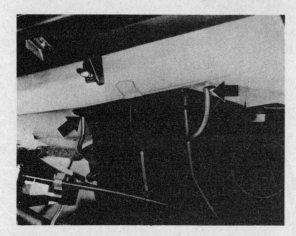

Fig. 12.26 Heater retaining clip (Sec 29)

4   Move the control lever to the 'DEF' position.
5   Remove the clip at the cut-off flap end, then close the flap and fit the clip so that the control lever is pretensioned by 1 to 2 mm (0.04 to 0.08 in) while still in the 'DEF' position.

Heater valve

6   Check that the outer cable is in contact with the stop shoulder and firmly secured with the clip.
7   Remove the clip at the heater valve end (photo).
8   Move the control lever to the 'COLD' position.
9   Close the heater valve and fit the clip so that the control lever is pretensioned by 1 to 2 mm (0.04 to 0.08 in) while still in the 'COLD' position.

31 Heater motor – removal and refitting

1   Disconnect the battery negative lead.
2   Unscrew the nuts and remove the motor cover (photo).
3   Unclip and remove the resistor leaving the wires connected (photo).
4   Remove the screw from the resistor holder (photo).
5   Withdraw the motor by tilting it on its side, then disconnect the wiring plug (photo).
6   Refitting is a reversal of removal.

32 Air conditioner – precautions and maintenance

1   Never disconnect any part of the air conditioner refrigeration

the clip so that the control lever is pretensioned by 1 to 2 mm (0.04 to 0.08 in).

Cut-off flap

3   Check that the outer cable is in contact with the stop shoulder and firmly secured with the clip.

30.7 Heater valve (arrowed)

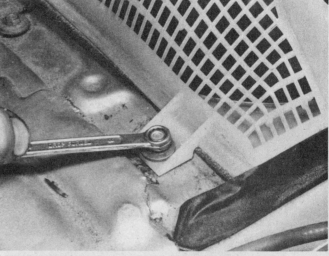

31.2 Removing the heater motor cover

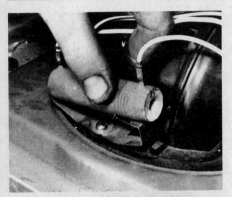

31.3 Removing the heater motor resistor

31.4 Removing the heater motor resistor holder

31.5 Removing the heater motor

circuit unless the system has been discharged by your Audi dealer or a qualified refrigeration engineer.

2   Where the compressor or condenser obstruct other mechanical operations such as engine removal, then it is permissible to unbolt their mountings and move them to the limit of their flexible hose deflection, but not to disconnect the hoses. If there is still insufficient room to carry out the required work then the system must be discharged before disconnecting and removing the assemblies.

3   The system will, of course, have to be recharged on completion.

4   Regularly check the condenser for clogging with flies or dirt. Hose clean with water or compressed air.

5   Regularly check the tension of the compressor drivebelt. The belt deflection should be about 10 mm (0.39 in) at the centre point of its longest run. If adjustment is required, the quantity of spacers between the crankshaft pulley halves must be either increased to reduce the tension, or decreased to increase the tension. Access to the pulley is gained by removing the intake grille. The spacers must be positioned either side of the inner pulley half, as necessary.

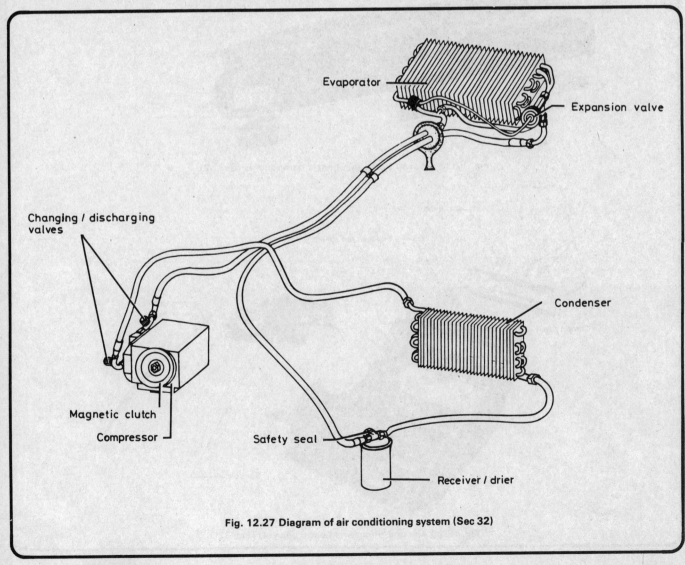

Fig. 12.27 Diagram of air conditioning system (Sec 32)

12

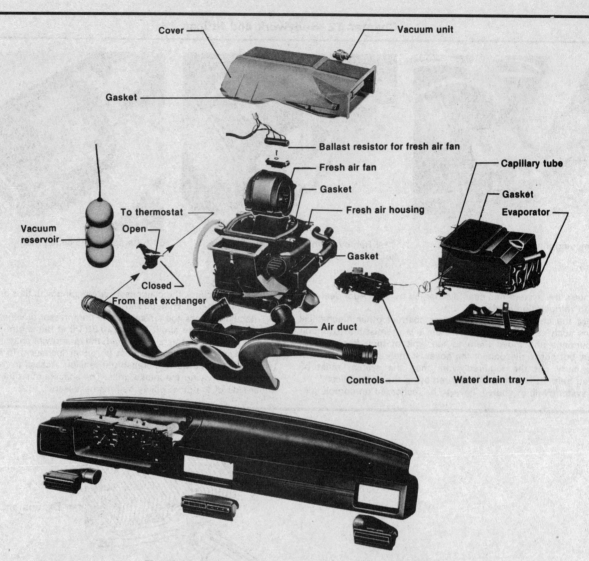

Cover — Vacuum unit

Gasket

Ballast resistor for fresh air fan

Fresh air fan

Gasket

Capillary tube

Fresh air housing

Gasket

Evaporator

To thermostat

Open

Vacuum reservoir

Closed

From heat exchanger

Gasket

Air duct

Controls

Water drain tray

Fig. 12.28 Air conditioner and heater components (Sec 32)

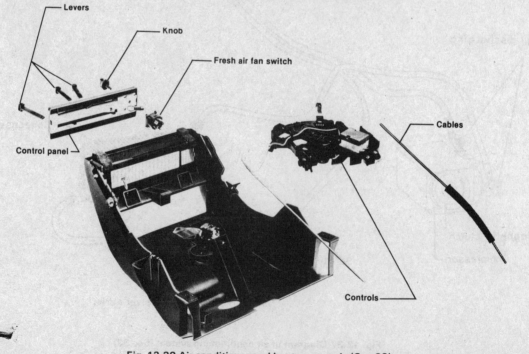

Levers

Knob

Fresh air fan switch

Cables

Control panel

Controls

Fig. 12.29 Air conditioner and heater controls (Sec 32)

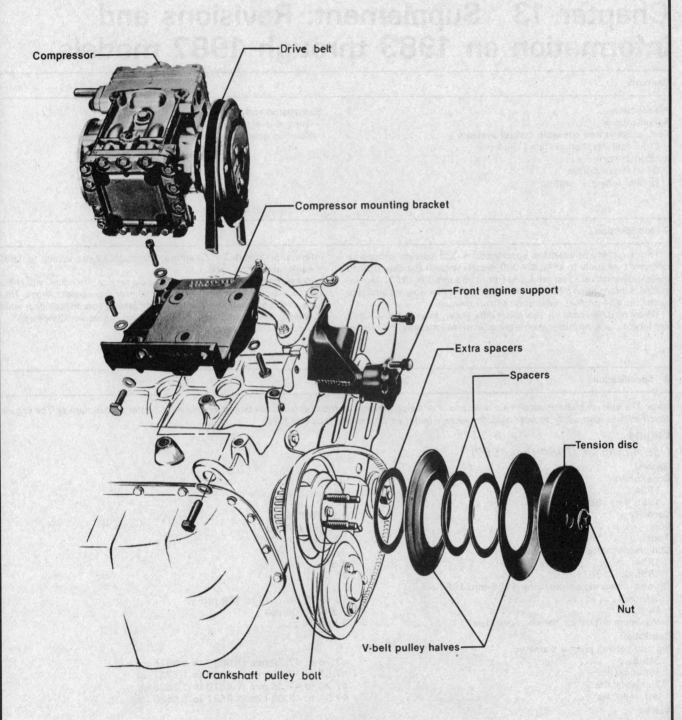

Fig. 12.30 Air conditioner compressor components (Sec 32)

Compressor

Drive belt

Compressor mounting bracket

Front engine support

Extra spacers

Spacers

Tension disc

Nut

V-belt pulley halves

Crankshaft pulley bolt

12

Chapter 13 Supplement: Revisions and information on 1983 through 1987 models

Contents

1 Introduction

This supplement contains specifications and service procedure changes that apply to all Audi 4000 models (except the Quattro and diesel-powered vehicles) produced from 1983 through 1987. Also included is information related to previous models that was not available at the time of original publication of this manual.

Where no differences (or very minor differences) exist between 1982 and later models, no information is given. In those instances, the original information included in Chapters 1 through 12, pertaining to 1982 models, should be used.

We recommend that before beginning a service procedure, you check this supplement for any new specifications or procedure changes. Take note of this supplementary information and be sure to include it while following the original procedure in one of the earlier Chapters.

2 Specifications

Note: *The following specifications are revisions of or supplementary to those listed at the beginning of each Chapter of this manual. The original specifications also apply to later models unless alternative figures are included here.*

Engine

1.8L 4-cylinder (1984 thru 1987)

General

Code letters
1984	JN
1985 thru 1987	MG
Capacity	1.8L (109 cu in)
Bore	81 mm (3.19 in)
Stroke	86.4 mm (3.40 in)

Compression ratio
1984	8.5:1
1985 thru 1987	10.0:1

Cylinder compression pressure (1985 thru 1987 only)
Standard	10 to 13 bar (145 to 189 psi)
Minimum	7.5 bar (109 psi)
Maximum difference between cylinders	3 bar (44 psi)

Crankshaft

Big end bearing journal diameter
Standard	47.76 to 47.78 mm (1.8817 to 1.8825 in)
1st undersize	47.51 to 47.53 mm (1.8719 to 1.8727 in)
2nd undersize	47.26 to 47.28 mm (1.8620 to 1.8628 in)
3rd undersize	47.01 to 47.03 mm (1.8522 to 1.8530 in)

Valves
Lifter type	Hydraulic
Valve clearances	Not adjustable

Torque specifications

Cylinder head bolts

	Nm	lb-ft
Step 1	40	29
Step 2	60	43
Step 3	An additional 1/2-turn (180°) in one movement	

5-cylinder (1984 thru 1987)

General
Code letters (4000 Coupe GT)	KX
Capacity	2.22L (136 cu in)
Bore	81 mm (3.19 in)

Stroke	86.4 mm (3.40 in)
Compression ratio	8.5:1
Cylinder compression pressure (1985 thru 1987 only)	
Standard	9 to 12 bar (130 to 174 psi)
Minimum	7 bar (102 psi)
Maximum difference between cylinders	3 bar (44 psi)

Crankshaft

Big end bearing journal diameter	
Standard	47.76 to 47.78 mm (1.8699 to 1.8825 in)
1st undersize	47.51 to 47.53 mm (1.8719 to 1.8727 in)
2nd undersize	47.26 to 47.28 mm (1.8620 to 1.8628 in)
3rd undersize	47.01 to 47.03 mm (1.8522 to 1.8530 in)

Valves

Lifter type	Hydraulic
Valve clearances	Not adjustable

Brakes (1984 and later models, except 1984 Coupe and all 4000/4000S Sedan models [see Chapter 9])

Discs (Coupe GT, 4000 CS and 4000 5-cylinder Sedans)

Thickness	20 mm (0.787 in)
Wear limit	18 mm (0.709 in)
Maximum variation in thickness	0.01 mm (0.0003 in)
Maximum runout	0.03 mm (0.001 in)

Suspension and steering

Torque specifications

Stabilizer bar (anti-roll bar)	Nm	lb-ft
Clamp bolt nut (earlier design)	20	14
Clamp (from late 1985 on)		
Studs	35	26
Self-locking nuts	35	26
Link rod nut	20	14

3 Fuel, exhaust and emission control systems

CIS-E fuel injection system (1984 on)

General description

The CIS-E system differs from its CIS predecessor in several ways. First, it receives data from sensors whose output signals are processed by an electronic control unit (aside from an oxygen sensor, which enables the control unit to determine the correct fuel/air mixture, the CIS system has no data gathering capability or computer control of any variable other than fuel/air mixture in relation to exhaust gas CO content).

Another difference between CIS and CIS-E systems is that an electro-hydraulic pressure actuator has been added to the mixture control unit. This device influences the injection quantity (the mixture control unit in a CIS system is strictly a mechanical-hydraulic device).

The CIS-E system performs five major functions:

1) Measures air flow and monitors such operating data as engine speed, temperature and selected load conditions (idle, full load).
2) Provides mechanical-hydraulic control of fuel injection quantity (just like CIS).
3) Continuously injects fuel.
4) Handles electronic control of mixture enrichment for starting, post-start phase, warm-up, acceleration/full load and wide open throttle.
5) Provides ancillary functions such as deceleration fuel shutoff, engine speed limit, Lambda control (oxygen sensor), etc.

The fuel supply system and the means by which fuel is metered are basically similar to their analogues in the CIS system. For example, the CIS and CIS-E systems have virtually identical cold starting and idle systems. But sometimes, under certain operating conditions, the engine's fuel requirements deviate markedly from the norm. Thanks to sensors that monitor engine temperature and throttle position (load signal), the E system is able to deal with these situations effectively.

Post-start phase and warm-up

For example, during the post-start phase and warm-up, mixture enrichment is based on engine temperature which is measured by a temperature sensor. The electronic control unit processes this signal and, via an electromagnetically-influenced stop in the pressure actuator, alters the pressure in the differential pressure valves in the fuel distributor, metering more fuel. Because the post-start phase and warm-up are now under the control of the computer, the warm-up regulator used on CIS vehicles has been omitted from vehicles with CIS-E.

Acceleration conditions

The mixture control unit of the CIS-E system also differs slightly from the all-mechanical unit of a CIS system. The lever arm of the air flow sensor plate on the CIS-E system is equipped with a potentiometer. When the vehicle accelerates, the sensor plate rises and the potentiometer sends a signal to the control unit, which processes the information.

Full-load conditions

During full-load, wide open throttle (WOT) conditions, an engine designed to run on lean mixtures under less than full-load conditions needs mixture enrichment. A full-load contact switch on the throttle valve indicates this condition to the control unit, which enriches the mixture.

Deceleration fuel shutoff

Fuel flow is cut off during deceleration by a fuel shutoff system that relies on information gained from engine temperature and speed sensors. When the engine is warm, switching points are set as low as possible to reduce fuel consumption. At lower temperatures, the thresholds are raised so that engine will not stall when the clutch pedal is depressed (manual transaxle) or the accelerator is released (automatic transaxle).

Mechanical component checks, adjustments and replacement

With the exception of the new electronic components described above, the rest of the CIS-E system is quite similar to the older CIS system. However, checks, adjustments to or replacement of many of these components may involve tampering with electronic components which cannot be serviced by the home mechanic. To avoid disturbing the delicate adjustments of these electronic components, it is recommended that the CIS-E system be serviced by an authorized Audi dealer service department.

Electronic component checks, adjustments and replacement

Because special VW or Siemens wire harness adapters and test equipment are required to check and/or adjust the electronic components (potentiometer, throttle valve switch, etc.) of the CIS-E fuel injection system, it is impossible for the home mechanic to check, adjust or replace these components. It is recommended that you take your vehicle to an authorized Audi dealer service department if one of these components malfunctions.

13

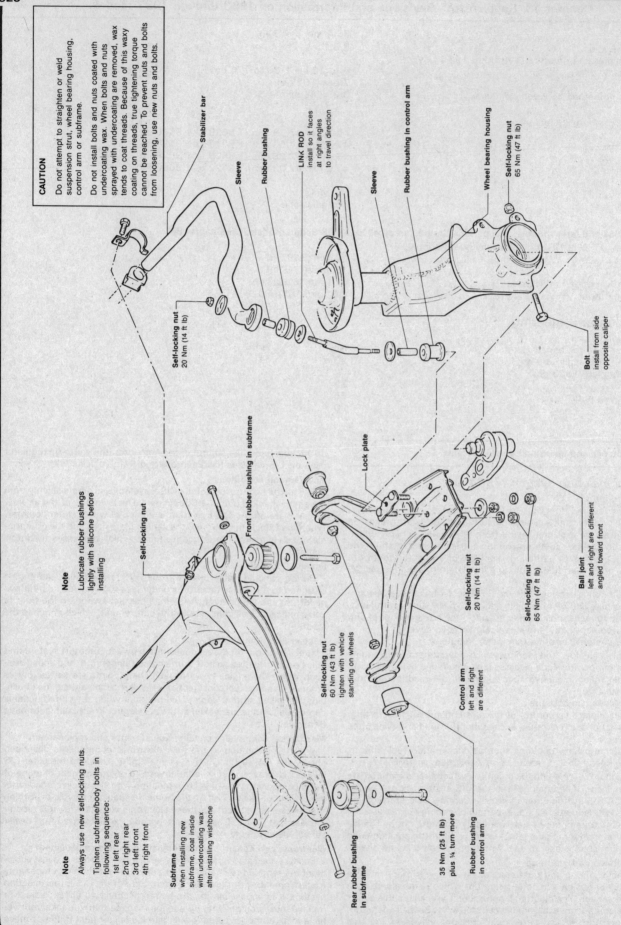

CAUTION

Do not attempt to straighten or weld suspension strut, wheel bearing housing, control arm or subframe.

Do not install bolts and nuts coated with undercoating wax. When bolts and nuts sprayed with undercoating are removed, wax tends to coat threads. Because of this waxy coating on threads, true tightening torque cannot be reached. To prevent nuts and bolts from loosening, use new nuts and bolts.

Stabilizer bar

Sleeve

Rubber bushing

LINK ROD
install so it faces at right angles to travel direction

Sleeve

Rubber bushing in control arm

Wheel bearing housing

Self-locking nut
65 Nm (47 ft lb)

Self-locking nut
20 Nm (14 ft lb)

Bolt
install from side opposite caliper

Note

Always use new self-locking nuts.

Tighten subframe/body bolts in following sequence:
1st left rear
2nd right rear
3rd left front
4th right front

Subframe
when installing new subframe, coat inside with undercoating wax after installing wishbone

Note

Lubricate rubber bushings lightly with silicone before installing

Self-locking nut

Front rubber bushing in subframe

Lock plate

Self-locking nut
60 Nm (43 ft lb)
tighten with vehicle standing on wheels

Self-locking nut
20 Nm (14 ft lb)

Self-locking nut
65 Nm (47 ft lb)

Ball joint
left and right are different angled toward front

Control arm
left and right are different

35 Nm (25 ft lb)
plus ¼ turn more

Rubber bushing in control arm

Rear rubber bushing in subframe

Fig. 13.1   Exploded view of stabilizer (anti-roll) bar with link rod

Idle speed/ignition timing/idle mixture checking/adjusting

Idle speed, ignition timing and idle mixture must all be checked and adjusted simultaneously. Because this procedure requires special VW or Siemens test equipment, it is beyond the scope of the home mechanic. If your vehicle should require any of these services, it is recommended that you take it to a dealer service department.

Fuel pressure check

Since a special fuel pressure gauge adapter is required, fuel pressure checking is beyond the scope of the home mechanic.

4 Ignition system

General description

The transistorized coil ignition (TCI) systems employed on 1983 and 1984 4-cylinder and all 5-cylinder engines from 1983 on are basically similar to earlier units. However, there are a few differences.

Later model (1985 through 1987) vehicles powered by 4-cylinder CIS-E engines do not use centrifugal and vacuum advance. Instead, advance is determined electronically from dynamic conditions by a control unit (computer). Ignition timing is also determined by the control unit, which receives signals from several sensors, including an idle switch, full throttle switch, knock sensor, Hall sender and manifold vacuum sensor.

Ignition timing — setting

The ignition timing procedure on CIS-E equipped vehicles is basically the same procedure as the one outlined in Chapter 4 for earlier CIS equipped vehicles. However, if it is necessary to adjust the idle speed, you must take the vehicle to an Audi dealer service department because idle speed and CO mixture adjustment, which is often affected by idle speed, require special VW and/or Siemens test equipment. It is recommended, therefore, that the vehicle be taken to an Audi dealer service department for timing the ignition as well, since all three procedures are interrelated.

5 Suspension and steering

General description

Although basically similar to earlier front suspension designs, later models incorporate a stabilizer link rod between the stabilizer bar and the control arm (see Fig. 13.1). The stabilizer bar on later versions (late 1985 on) of the new design is attached to the frame with a slightly different clamp design (see Fig. 13.2). Neither change, however, makes much difference with respect to stabilizer bar, wishbone or strut removal.

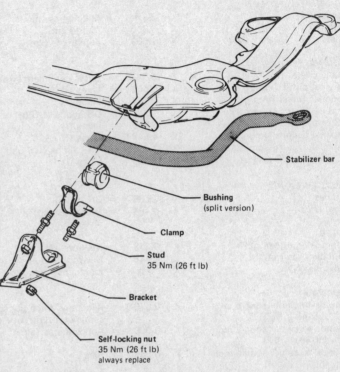

Fig. 13.2 Exploded view of late 1985 on stabilizer bar clamp design

- Stabilizer bar
- Bushing (split version)
- Clamp
- Stud 35 Nm (26 ft lb)
- Bracket
- Self-locking nut 35 Nm (26 ft lb) always replace

Steering gear (manual) — adjustment

1 Audi 4000 vehicles from VIN no. DA-087-236 on require a different steering gear adjustment procedure than the one described in Chapter 11.

2 With the wheels in the straight-ahead position, turn the adjustment bolt clockwise approximately 20-degrees.

3 Road test the vehicle.

4 If the steering is too heavy, turn the bolt slightly counterclockwise. If the steering is too loose. turn the bolt clockwise slightly.

13

Conversion factors

Length (distance)

Inches (in)	X	25.4	= Millimetres (mm)	X 0.0394	= Inches (in)
Feet (ft)	X	0.305	= Metres (m)	X 3.281	= Feet (ft)
Miles	X	1.609	= Kilometres (km)	X 0.621	= Miles

Volume (capacity)

Cubic inches (cu in; in³)	X	16.387	= Cubic centimetres (cc; cm³)	X 0.061	= Cubic inches (cu in; in³)
Imperial pints (Imp pt)	X	0.568	= Litres (l)	X 1.76	= Imperial pints (Imp pt)
Imperial quarts (Imp qt)	X	1.137	= Litres (l)	X 0.88	= Imperial quarts (Imp qt)
Imperial quarts (Imp qt)	X	1.201	= US quarts (US qt)	X 0.833	= Imperial quarts (Imp qt)
US quarts (US qt)	X	0.946	= Litres (l)	X 1.057	= US quarts (US qt)
Imperial gallons (Imp gal)	X	4.546	= Litres (l)	X 0.22	= Imperial gallons (Imp gal)
Imperial gallons (Imp gal)	X	1.201	= US gallons (US gal)	X 0.833	= Imperial gallons (Imp gal)
US gallons (US gal)	X	3.785	= Litres (l)	X 0.264	= US gallons (US gal)

Mass (weight)

Ounces (oz)	X	28.35	= Grams (g)	X 0.035	= Ounces (oz)
Pounds (lb)	X	0.454	= Kilograms (kg)	X 2.205	= Pounds (lb)

Force

Ounces-force (ozf; oz)	X	0.278	= Newtons (N)	X 3.6	= Ounces-force (ozf; oz)
Pounds-force (lbf; lb)	X	4.448	= Newtons (N)	X 0.225	= Pounds-force (lbf; lb)
Newtons (N)	X	0.1	= Kilograms-force (kgf; kg)	X 9.81	= Newtons (N)

Pressure

Pounds-force per square inch (psi; lbf/in²; lb/in²)	X	0.070	= Kilograms-force per square centimetre (kgf/cm²; kg/cm²)	X 14.223	= Pounds-force per square inch (psi; lbf/in²; lb/in²)
Pounds-force per square inch (psi; lbf/in²; lb/in²)	X	0.068	= Atmospheres (atm)	X 14.696	= Pounds-force per square inch (psi; lbf/in²; lb/in²)
Pounds-force per square inch (psi; lbf/in²; lb/in²)	X	0.069	= Bars	X 14.5	= Pounds-force per square inch (psi; lbf/in²; lb/in²)
Pounds-force per square inch (psi; lbf/in²; lb/in²)	X	6.895	= Kilopascals (kPa)	X 0.145	= Pounds-force per square inch (psi; lbf/in²; lb/in²)
Kilopascals (kPa)	X	0.01	= Kilograms-force per square centimetre (kgf/cm²; kg/cm²)	X 98.1	= Kilopascals (kPa)
Millibar (mbar)	X	100	= Pascals (Pa)	X 0.01	= Millibar (mbar)
Millibar (mbar)	X	0.0145	= Pounds-force per square inch (psi; lbf/in²; lb/in²)	X 68.947	= Millibar (mbar)
Millibar (mbar)	X	0.75	= Millimetres of mercury (mmHg)	X 1.333	= Millibar (mbar)
Millibar (mbar)	X	0.401	= Inches of water (inH₂O)	X 2.491	= Millibar (mbar)
Millimetres of mercury (mmHg)	X	0.535	= Inches of water (inH₂O)	X 1.868	= Millimetres of mercury (mmHg)
Inches of water (inH₂O)	X	0.036	= Pounds-force per square inch (psi; lbf/in²; lb/in²)	X 27.68	= Inches of water (inH₂O)

Torque (moment of force)

Pounds-force inches (lbf in; lb in)	X	1.152	= Kilograms-force centimetre (kgf cm; kg cm)	X 0.868	= Pounds-force inches (lbf in; lb in)
Pounds-force inches (lbf in; lb in)	X	0.113	= Newton metres (Nm)	X 8.85	= Pounds-force inches (lbf in; lb in)
Pounds-force inches (lbf in; lb in)	X	0.083	= Pounds-force feet (lbf ft; lb ft)	X 12	= Pounds-force inches (lbf in; lb in)
Pounds-force feet (lbf ft; lb ft)	X	0.138	= Kilograms-force metres (kgf m; kg m)	X 7.233	= Pounds-force feet (lbf ft; lb ft)
Pounds-force feet (lbf ft; lb ft)	X	1.356	= Newton metres (Nm)	X 0.738	= Pounds-force feet (lbf ft; lb ft)
Newton metres (Nm)	X	0.102	= Kilograms-force metres (kgf m; kg m)	X 9.804	= Newton metres (Nm)

Power

Horsepower (hp)	X	745.7	= Watts (W)	X 0.0013	= Horsepower (hp)

Velocity (speed)

Miles per hour (miles/hr; mph)	X	1.609	= Kilometres per hour (km/hr; kph)	X 0.621	= Miles per hour (miles/hr; mph)

Fuel consumption*

Miles per gallon, Imperial (mpg)	X	0.354	= Kilometres per litre (km/l)	X 2.825	= Miles per gallon, Imperial (mpg)
Miles per gallon, US (mpg)	X	0.425	= Kilometres per litre (km/l)	X 2.352	= Miles per gallon, US (mpg)

Temperature

Degrees Fahrenheit = (°C x 1.8) + 32

Degrees Celsius (Degrees Centigrade; °C) = (°F - 32) x 0.56

*It is common practice to convert from miles per gallon (mpg) to litres/100 kilometres (l/100km), where mpg (Imperial) x l/100 km = 282 and mpg (US) x l/100 km = 235

Index

Haynes Automotive Manuals

NOTE: New manuals are added to this list on a periodic basis. If you do not see a listing for your vehicle, consult your local Haynes dealer for the latest product information.

ACURA
12020 Integra '86 thru '89 & Legend '86 thru '90
12021 Integra '90 thru '93 & Legend '91 thru '95

AMC
Jeep CJ - see JEEP (50020)
14020 Concord/Hornet/Gremlin/Spirit '70 thru '83
14025 (Renault) Alliance & Encore '83 thru '87

AUDI
15020 4000 all models '80 thru '87
15025 5000 all models '77 thru '83
15026 5000 all models '84 thru '88

AUSTIN
Healey Sprite - see MG Midget (66015)

BMW
*18020 3/5 Series '82 thru '92
18021 3 Series including Z3 models '92 thru '98
18025 320i all 4 cyl models '75 thru '83
18050 1500 thru 2002 except Turbo '59 thru '77

BUICK
*19010 Buick Century '97 thru '02
Century (FWD) - see GM (38005)
*19020 Buick, Oldsmobile & Pontiac Full-size (Front wheel drive) '85 thru '02
19025 Buick Oldsmobile & Pontiac Full-size (Rear wheel drive) '70 thru '90
19030 Mid-size Regal & Century '74 thru '87
Regal - see GENERAL MOTORS (38010)
Skyhawk - see GM (38030)
Skylark - see GM (38020, 38025)
Somerset - see GENERAL MOTORS (38025)

CADILLAC
21030 Cadillac Rear Wheel Drive '70 thru '93
Cimarron, Eldorado & Seville - see GM (38015, 38030, 38031)

CHEVROLET
10305 Chevrolet Engine Overhaul Manual
*24010 Astro & GMC Safari Mini-vans '85 thru '03
24015 Camaro V8 all models '70 thru '81
24016 Camaro all models '82 thru '92
Cavalier - see GM (38015)
Celebrity - see GM (38005)
24017 Camaro & Firebird '93 thru '02
24020 Chevelle, Malibu, El Camino '69 thru '87
24024 Chevette & Pontiac T1000 '76 thru '87
Citation - see GENERAL MOTORS (38020)
24032 Corsica/Beretta all models '87 thru '96
24040 Corvette all V8 models '68 thru '82
24041 Corvette all models '84 thru '96
24045 Full-size Sedans Caprice, Impala, Biscayne, Bel Air & Wagons '69 thru '90
24046 Impala SS & Caprice and Buick Roadmaster '91 thru '96
24047 Lumina '90 thru '94 - see GM (38010)
*24048 Lumina & Monte Carlo '95 thru '03
Lumina APV - see GM (38035)
24050 Luv Pick-up all 2WD & 4WD '72 thru '82
Malibu - see GM (38026)
24055 Monte Carlo all models '70 thru '88
Monte Carlo '95 thru '01 - see LUMINA
24059 Nova all V8 models '69 thru '79
24060 Nova/Geo Prizm '85 thru '92
24064 Pick-ups '67 thru '87 - Chevrolet & GMC, all V8 & in-line 6 cyl, 2WD & 4WD '67 thru '87; Suburbans, Blazers & Jimmys '67 thru '91
24065 Pick-ups '88 thru '98 - Chevrolet & GMC, all full-size models '88 thru '98; C/K Classic '99 & '00; Blazer & Jimmy '92 thru '94; Suburban '92 thru '99; Tahoe & Yukon '95 thru '99
*24066 Pick-ups '99 thru '02 - Chevrolet & GMC Silverado & GMC Sierra '99 thru '02; Suburban/Tahoe/Yukon/Yukon XL '00 thru '02
24070 S-10 & GMC S-15 Pick-ups '82 thru '93
*24071 S-10, Gmc S-15 & Jimmy '94 thru '01
*24072 Chevrolet TrailBlazer & TrailBlazer EXT, GMC Envoy & Envoy XL, Oldsmobile Bravada '02 and '03
24075 Sprint '85 thru '88, Geo Metro '89 thru '01
24080 Vans - Chevrolet & GMC '68 thru '96

CHRYSLER
10310 Chrysler Engine Overhaul Manual
25015 Chrysler Cirrus, Dodge Stratus, Plymouth Breeze, '95 thru '98
25020 Full-size Front-Wheel Drive '88 thru '93
K-Cars - see DODGE Aries (30008)
Laser - see DODGE Daytona (30030)
25025 Chrysler LHS, Concorde & New Yorker, Dodge Intrepid, Eagle Vision, '93 thru '97
*25026 Chrysler LHS, Concorde, 300M, Dodge Intrepid '98 thru '03
25030 Chrysler/Plym. Mid-size all '82 thru '95
Rear-wheel Drive - see DODGE (30050)
*25035 PT Cruiser all models '01 thru '03
*25040 Chrysler Sebring/Dodge Avenger '95 thru '02

DATSUN
28005 200SX all models '80 thru '83
28007 B-210 all models '73 thru '78
28009 210 all models '78 thru '82
28012 240Z, 260Z & 280Z Coupe '70 thru '78
28014 280ZX Coupe & 2+2 '79 thru '83
300ZX - see NISSAN (72010)
28016 310 all models '78 thru '82
28018 510 & PL521 Pick-up '68 thru '73
28020 510 all models '78 thru '81
28022 620 Series Pick-up '73 thru '79
720 Series Pick-up - NISSAN (72030)
28025 810/Maxima all gas models, '77 thru '84

DODGE
400 & 600 - see CHRYSLER (25030)
30008 Aries & Plymouth Reliant '81 thru '89
30010 Caravan & Ply. Voyager '84 thru '95
*30011 Caravan & Ply. Voyager '96 thru '02
30012 Challenger/Plymouth Saporro '78 thru '83
Challenger '67-'76 - see DART (30025)
30016 Colt/Plymouth Champ '78 thru '87
30020 Dakota Pick-ups all models '87 thru '96
*30021 Durango '98 & '99, Dakota '97 thru '99
30025 Dart, Challenger/Plymouth Barracuda & Valiant 6 cyl models '67 thru '76
30030 Daytona & Chrysler Laser '84 thru '89
Intrepid - see Chrysler (25025, 25026)
*30034 Dodge & Plymouth Neon '95 thru '99
*30035 Omni & Plymouth Horizon '78 thru '90
30040 Pick-ups all full-size models '74 thru '93
*30041 Pick-ups all full-size models '94 thru '01
*30045 Ram 50/D50 Pick-ups & Raider and Plymouth Arrow Pick-ups '79 thru '93
30050 Dodge/Ply./Chrysler RWD '71 thru '89
30055 Shadow/Plymouth Sundance '87 thru '94
30060 Spirit & Plymouth Acclaim '89 thru '95
*30065 Vans - Dodge & Plymouth '71 thru '03

EAGLE
Talon - see MITSUBISHI (68030, 68031)
Vision - see CHRYSLER (25025)

FIAT
34010 124 Sport Coupe & Spider '68 thru '78
34025 X1/9 all models '74 thru '80

FORD
10355 Ford Automatic Transmission Overhaul
10320 Ford Engine Overhaul Manual
36004 Aerostar Mini-vans '86 thru '97
Aspire - see FORD Festiva (36030)
36006 Contour/Mercury Mystique '95 thru '00
36008 Courier Pick-up all models '72 thru '82
*36012 Crown Victoria & Mercury Grand Marquis '88 thru '00
36016 Escort/Mercury Lynx '81 thru '90
36020 Escort/Mercury Tracer '91 thru '00
Expedition - see FORD Pick-up (36059)
36022 Ford Escape & Mazda Tribute '01 thru '03
*36024 Explorer & Mazda Navajo '91 thru '01
36025 Ford Explorer & Mercury Mountaineer '02 and '03
36028 Fairmont & Mercury Zephyr '78 thru '83
36030 Festiva & Aspire '88 thru '97
36032 Fiesta all models '77 thru '80
*36034 Focus all models '00 and '01
36036 Ford & Mercury Full-size '75 thru '87
36044 Ford & Mercury Mid-size '75 thru '86
36048 Mustang V8 all models '64-1/2 thru '73
36049 Mustang II 4 cyl, V6 & V8 '74 thru '78
36050 Mustang & Mercury Capri '79 thru '86
*36051 Mustang all models '94 thru '03
36054 Pick-ups and Bronco '73 thru '79
36058 Pick-ups and Bronco '80 thru '96
*36059 Pick-ups, Expedition & Lincoln Navigator '97 thru '02
*36060 Super Duty Pick-ups, Excursion '97 thru '02
36062 Pinto & Mercury Bobcat '75 thru '80
36066 Probe all models '89 thru '92
36070 Ranger/Bronco II gas models '83 thru '92
*36071 Ford Ranger '93 thru '00 & Mazda Pick-ups '94 thru '00
36074 Taurus & Mercury Sable '86 thru '95
*36075 Taurus & Mercury Sable '96 thru '01
36078 Tempo & Mercury Topaz '84 thru '94
36082 Thunderbird/Mercury Cougar '83 thru '88
36086 Thunderbird/Mercury Cougar '89 thru '97
36090 Vans all V8 Econoline models '69 thru '91
*36094 Vans full size '92 thru '01
*36097 Windstar Mini-van '95 thru '03

GENERAL MOTORS
10360 GM Automatic Transmission Overhaul
38005 Buick Century, Chevrolet Celebrity, Olds Cutlass Ciera & Pontiac 6000 '82 thru '96
*38010 Buick Regal, Chevrolet Lumina, Oldsmobile Cutlass Supreme & Pontiac Grand Prix front wheel drive '88 thru '02
38015 Buick Skyhawk, Cadillac Cimarron, Chevrolet Cavalier, Oldsmobile Firenza Pontiac J-2000 & Sunbird '82 thru '94
*38016 Chevrolet Cavalier/Pontiac Sunfire '95 thru '04
38020 Buick Skylark, Chevrolet Citation, Olds Omega, Pontiac Phoenix '80 thru '85
38025 Buick Skylark & Somerset, Olds Achieva, Calais & Pontiac Grand Am '85 thru '98
*38026 Chevrolet Malibu, Olds Alero & Cutlass, Pontiac Grand Am '97 thru '00
38030 Cadillac Eldorado & Oldsmobile Toronado '71 thru '85, Seville '80 thru '85, Buick Riviera '79 thru '85
*38031 Cadillac Eldorado & Seville '86 thru '91, DeVille & Buick Riviera '86 thru '93, Fleetwood & Olds Toronado '86 thru '92
38032 DeVille '94 thru '02, Seville '92 thru '02
38035 Chevrolet Lumina APV, Oldsmobile Silhouette & Pontiac Trans Sport '90 thru '96
*38036 Chevrolet Venture, Olds Silhouette, Pontiac Trans Sport & Montana '97 thru '01
General Motors Full-size
Rear-wheel Drive - see BUICK (19025)

GEO
Metro - see CHEVROLET Sprint (24075)
Prizm - see CHEVROLET (24060) or TOYOTA (92036)
40030 Storm all models '90 thru '93
Tracker - see SUZUKI Samurai (90010)

GMC
Vans & Pick-ups - see CHEVROLET

HONDA
42010 Accord CVCC all models '76 thru '83
42011 Accord all models '84 thru '89
42012 Accord all models '90 thru '93
42013 Accord all models '94 thru '97
*42014 Accord all models '98 thru '02
42020 Civic 1200 all models '73 thru '79
42021 Civic 1300 & 1500 CVCC '80 thru '83
42022 Civic 1500 CVCC all models '75 thru '79
42023 Civic all models '84 thru '91
42024 Civic & del Sol '92 thru '95
*42025 Civic '96 thru '00, CR-V '97 thru '00, Acura Integra '94 thru '00
Passport - see ISUZU Rodeo (47017)
42026 Civic '01 thru '04, CR-V '02 thru '04
*42040 Prelude CVCC all models '79 thru '89

HYUNDAI
*43010 Elantra all models '96 thru '01
43015 Excel & Accent all models '86 thru '98

ISUZU
Hombre - see CHEVROLET S-10 (24071)
*47017 Rodeo '91 thru '02, Amigo '89 thru '02, Honda Passport '95 thru '02
47020 Trooper '84 thru '91, Pick-up '81 thru '93

JAGUAR
49010 XJ6 all 6 cyl models '68 thru '86
49011 XJ6 all models '88 thru '94
49015 XJ12 & XJS all 12 cyl models '72 thru '85

JEEP
50010 Cherokee, Comanche & Wagoneer Limited all models '84 thru '01
50020 CJ all models '49 thru '86
*50025 Grand Cherokee all models '93 thru '04
50029 Grand Wagoneer & Pick-up '72 thru '91
*50030 Wrangler all models '87 thru '00
50035 Liberty '02 thru '04

LEXUS
ES 300 - see TOYOTA Camry (92007)

LINCOLN
Navigator - see FORD Pick-up (36059)
*59010 Rear Wheel Drive all models '70 thru '01

MAZDA
61010 GLC (rear wheel drive) '77 thru '83
61011 GLC (front wheel drive) '81 thru '85
61015 323 & Protegé '90 thru '00
*61016 MX-5 Miata '90 thru '97
61020 MPV all models '89 thru '94
Navajo - see FORD Explorer (36024)
61030 Pick-ups '72 thru '93
Pick-ups '94 on - see Ford (36071)
61035 RX-7 all models '79 thru '85
61036 RX-7 all models '86 thru '91
61040 626 (rear wheel drive) '79 thru '82
61041 626 & MX-6 (front wheel drive) '83 thru '91
61042 626 '93 thru '01, & MX-6/Ford Probe '93 thru '97

MERCEDES-BENZ
63012 123 Series Diesel '76 thru '85
63015 190 Series 4-cyl gas models, '84 thru '88
63020 230, 250 & 280 6 cyl sohc '68 thru '72
63025 280 123 Series gas models '77 thru '81
63030 350 & 450 all models '71 thru '80

MERCURY
64200 Villager & Nissan Quest '93 thru '01
All other titles, see FORD listing.

MG
66010 MGB Roadster & GT Coupe '62 thru '80
66015 MG Midget & Austin Healey Sprite Roadster '58 thru '80

MITSUBISHI
68020 Cordia, Tredia, Galant, Precis & Mirage '83 thru '93
68030 Eclipse, Eagle Talon & Plymouth Laser '90 thru '94
*68031 Eclipse '95 thru '01, Eagle Talon '95 thru '98
68035 Mitsubishi Galant '94 thru '03
68040 Pick-up '83 thru '96, Montero '83 thru '93

NISSAN
72010 300ZX all models incl. Turbo '84 thru '89
72015 Altima all models '93 thru '04
72020 Maxima all models '85 thru '92
*72021 Maxima all models '93 thru '01
72030 Pick-ups '80 thru '97, Pathfinder '87 thru '95
*72031 Frontier Pick-up '98 thru '01, Xterra '00 & '01, Pathfinder '96 thru '01
72040 Pulsar all models '83 thru '86
72050 Sentra all models '82 thru '94
72051 Sentra & 200SX all models '95 thru '99
72060 Stanza all models '82 thru '90

OLDSMOBILE
*73015 Cutlass '74 thru '88
For other OLDSMOBILE titles, see BUICK, CHEVROLET or GM listings.

PLYMOUTH
For PLYMOUTH titles, see DODGE.

PONTIAC
79008 Fiero all models '84 thru '88
79018 Firebird V8 models except Turbo '70 thru '81
79019 Firebird all models '82 thru '92
79040 Mid-size Rear-wheel Drive '70 thru '87
For other PONTIAC titles, see BUICK, CHEVROLET or GM listings.

PORSCHE
80020 911 Coupe & Targa models '65 thru '89
80025 914 all 4 cyl models '69 thru '76
80030 924 all models incl. Turbo '76 thru '82
80035 944 all models incl. Turbo '83 thru '89

RENAULT
Alliance, Encore - see AMC (14020)

SAAB
*84010 900 including Turbo '79 thru '88

SATURN
*87010 Saturn all models '91 thru '02
87020 Saturn all L-series models '00 thu '04

SUBARU
89002 1100, 1300, 1400 & 1600 '71 thru '79
89003 1600 & 1800 2WD & 4WD '80 thru '94

SUZUKI
90010 Samurai/Sidekick/Geo Tracker '86 thru '01

TOYOTA
92005 Camry all models '83 thru '91
92006 Camry all models '92 thru '96
*92007 Camry/Avalon/Solara/Lexus ES 300 '97 thru '01
92015 Celica Rear Wheel Drive '71 thru '85
92020 Celica Front Wheel Drive '86 thru '99
92025 Celica Supra all models '79 thru '92
92030 Corolla all models '75 thru '79
92032 Corolla rear wheel drive models '80 thru '87
92035 Corolla front wheel drive models '84 thru '92
92036 Corolla & Geo Prizm '93 thru '02
92040 Corolla Tercel all models '80 thru '82
92045 Corona all models '74 thru '82
92050 Cressida all models '78 thru '82
92055 Land Cruiser FJ40/43/45/55 '68 thru '82
92056 Land Cruiser FJ60/62/80/FZJ80 '80 thru '96
92065 MR2 all models '85 thru '87
92070 Pick-up all models '69 thru '78
92075 Pick-up all models '79 thru '95
*92076 Tacoma '95 thru '00, 4Runner '96 thru '00, T100 '93 thru '98
*92078 Tundra '00 thru '02, Sequoia '01 thru '02
92080 Previa all models '91 thru '95
*92082 RAV4 all models '96 thru '02
92085 Tercel all models '87 thru '94

TRIUMPH
94007 Spitfire all models '62 thru '81
94010 TR7 all models '75 thru '81

VW
96008 Beetle & Karmann Ghia '54 thru '79
*96009 New Beetle '98 thru '00
96016 Rabbit, Jetta, Scirocco, & Pick-up gas models '74 thru '91 & Convertible '80 thru '92
96017 Golf, GTI & Jetta '93 thru '98, Cabrio '95 thru '98
*96018 Golf, GTI, Jetta & Cabrio '99 thru '02
96020 Rabbit, Jetta, Pick-up diesel '77 thru '84
96023 Passat '98 thru '01, Audi A4 '96 thru '01
96030 Transporter 1600 all models '68 thru '79
96035 Transporter 1700, 1800, 2000 '72 thru '79
96040 Type 3 1500 & 1600 '63 thru '73
96045 Vanagon air-cooled models '80 thru '83

VOLVO
97010 120, 130 Series & 1800 Sports '61 thru '73
97015 140 Series all models '66 thru '74
97020 240 Series all models '76 thru '93
97025 260 Series all models '75 thru '82
97040 740 & 760 Series all models '82 thru '88

TECHBOOK MANUALS
10205 Automotive Computer Codes
10210 Automotive Emissions Control Manual
10215 Fuel Injection Manual, 1978 thru 1985
10220 Fuel Injection Manual, 1986 thru 1999
10225 Holley Carburetor Manual
10230 Rochester Carburetor Manual
10240 Weber/Zenith/Stromberg/SU Carburetor
10305 Chevrolet Engine Overhaul Manual
10310 Chrysler Engine Overhaul Manual
10320 Ford Engine Overhaul Manual
10330 GM and Ford Diesel Engine Repair
10340 Small Engine Repair Manual
10345 Suspension, Steering & Driveline
10355 Ford Automatic Transmission Overhaul
10360 GM Automatic Transmission Overhaul
10405 Automotive Body Repair & Painting
10410 Automotive Brake Manual
10415 Automotive Detailing Manual
10420 Automotive Eelectrical Manual
10425 Automotive Heating & Air Conditioning
10430 Automotive Reference Dictionary
10435 Automotive Tools Manual
10440 Used Car Buying Guide
10445 Welding Manual
10450 ATV Basics

SPANISH MANUALS
98903 Reparación de Carrocería & Pintura
98904 Códigos Automotrices de la Computadora
98910 Frenos Automotriz
98915 Inyección de Combustible 1986 al 1999
99040 Chevrolet & GMC Camionetas '67 al '87
99041 Chevrolet & GMC Camionetas '88 al '98
99042 Chevrolet Camionetas Cerradas '68 al '95
99055 Dodge Caravan/Ply. Voyager '84 al '95
99075 Ford Camionetas y Bronco '80 al '94
99077 Ford Camionetas Cerradas '69 al '91
99088 Ford Modelos de Tamaño Mediano '75 al '86
99091 Ford Taurus & Mercury Sable '86 al '95
99095 GM Modelos de Tamaño Grande '70 al '88
99100 GM Modelos de Tamaño Mediano '70 al '88
99110 Nissan Camionetas '80 al '96, Pathfinder '87 al '95
99118 Nissan Sentra '82 al '94
99125 Toyota Camionetas y 4-Runner '79 al '95

Nearly 100 Haynes motorcycle manuals also available

2-05

Haynes North America, Inc., 861 Lawrence Drive, Newbury Park, CA 91320 • (805) 498-6703